Josette Baer

"Spirits that I've cited ... ?"

Vladimír Clementis (1902–1952)

The Political Biography
of a Czechoslovak Communist

Josette Baer

"Spirits that I've cited … ?"

VLADIMÍR CLEMENTIS (1902–1952)

The Political Biography
of a Czechoslovak Communist

ibidem-Verlag
Stuttgart

Bibliografische Information der Deutschen Nationalbibliothek
Die Deutsche Nationalbibliothek verzeichnet diese Publikation in der
Deutschen Nationalbibliografie; detaillierte bibliografische Daten sind im
Internet über http://dnb.d-nb.de abrufbar.

Bibliographic information published by the Deutsche Nationalbibliothek
Die Deutsche Nationalbibliothek lists this publication in the Deutsche Nationalbibliografie;
detailed bibliographic data are available in the Internet at http://dnb.d-nb.de.

Cover picture: Vladimir Clementis in 1947, SNK, Martin, Slovakia.
Reprint with kind permission.

∞
Gedruckt auf alterungsbeständigem, säurefreien Papier
Printed on acid-free paper

ISBN-13: 978-3-8382-0746-9

© *ibidem*-Verlag
Stuttgart 2017

Alle Rechte vorbehalten

Das Werk einschließlich aller seiner Teile ist urheberrechtlich geschützt. Jede Verwertung außerhalb der engen Grenzen des Urheberrechtsgesetzes ist ohne Zustimmung des Verlages unzulässig und strafbar. Dies gilt insbesondere für Vervielfältigungen, Übersetzungen, Mikroverfilmungen und elektronische Speicherformen sowie die Einspeicherung und Verarbeitung in elektronischen Systemen.

All rights reserved. No part of this publication may be reproduced, stored in or introduced into a retrieval system, or transmitted, in any form, or by any means (electronic, mechanical, photocopying, recording or otherwise) without the prior written permission of the publisher. Any person who does any unauthorized act in relation to this publication may be liable to criminal prosecution and civil claims for damages.

Printed in the EU

This study is dedicated to my former teachers Carsten Goehrke, Herrmann Lübbe and Georg Kohler.

I am immensely grateful to my Slovak and Czech friends and colleagues who taught me, from different political viewpoints, about Czechoslovakia's Communist regime and how the rule of the proletariat affected their daily life. They are still teaching me.

Table of Contents

Abbreviations VII

Acknowledgements XI

The Drama of Vladimír Clementis. The Tragic Life of
a Communist XV

X. Introduction 1
   X. 1 Vladimír Clementis – victim of Stalinism or
         gravedigger of democracy? 1
   X. 2 Analytical framework and conceptual matrix 12
   X. 3 Method, key issues, research interest 14
         X. 3. 1 Method: contextual biography 14
         X. 3. 2 Key issues 16
               X. 3. 2. 1 Czechoslovakism and the Czechoslovak Nation. 16
               X. 3. 2. 2 Antisemitism 29
         X. 3. 3 Research questions 34

I. Childhood, Education and Pre-War Political Activities
(1902–1939) 37
   I. 1. Childhood in Tisovec 38
   I. 2. DAV and the Davists 46
         I. 2. 1 The Themes of DAV – Applying
               Marxism-Leninism to Slovakia 51
               I. 2. 1. 1 The Question of the Czechoslovak Nation (1924) 53
               I. 2. 1. 2 Agrarian Thought as New 'Ideology' (1924) 59
               I. 2. 1. 3 The Electoral Defeat of the Communists (1929) .. 66
               I. 2. 1. 4 The Trips to the Soviet Union (1929, 1930) 69
               I. 2. 1. 5 The Anti-Soviet Press Campaign (1935) 80
   I. 3 Black Whitsuntide in Košuty (1931) 84
   I. 4 Member of Parliament (1935–1938) 94
         I. 4. 1 On National Security (1936) 96
         I. 4. 2 Lex Sidor – on Slovak Antisemitism (1937) 106
         I. 4. 3 A Farewell to President Masaryk (1937) 111

| | | I. 4. 4 | On Slovak Autonomy (1938) .... 122 |
| | | I. 4. 5 | Munich 1938 – The End of the Republic .... 126 |

II. In Exile (1939–1945) **133**
    II. 1 From France to Great Britain (1939–1940) 133
    II. 2 In Great Britain... 137
        II. 2. 1 Lída's Living Conditions 140
        II. 2. 2 A Political Decision 145
    II. 3 The BBC Broadcasts (1941–1945)................................... 150
        II. 3. 1 Slovakia's Declaration of War on America (1941) ... 156
        II. 3. 2 At the Grave of Vančura (1942) 159
        II. 3. 3 Hitler, Hlinka – One Line! (1942) 162
        II. 3. 4 The Expulsion of the Czechs from the
                  Slovak State (1943) 166
        II. 3. 5 The Slovak Workers in Germany (1943–1944) 169
        II. 3. 6 To the Slovak Women (1944) 175
        II. 3. 7 The Attempt on Hitler's Life (1944)..........................179
        II. 3. 8 The Slovak National Uprising (1944) 181
        II. 3. 9 About the Future (1945) 183
        II. 3. 10 Banská Bystrica – Liberated! (1945) 186

III. The Ministry of Foreign Affairs (1945–1950)...............**205**
    III. 1 Assistant Secretary of State (1945–1948)...................... 207
        III. 1. 1 The Communist Coup d'Etat (25 February 1948).....207
        III. 1. 2 The Yugoslav-Soviet Split (29 June 1948)................211
        III. 1. 3 Czechoslovakia's International Relations (1945)....215
        III. 1. 4 On Money (1946)..221
        III. 1. 5 Czechoslovakia's New Foreign Policy (1947) 228
        III. 1. 6 On Germany and the Marshall Plan (1947) 236
        III. 1. 7 The Slovak-Hungarian Transfer of Population
                   (1945–1949)..241
    III. 2 Minister of Foreign Affairs (1948–1950)...................... 250
        III. 2. 1 The Mysterious Death of Jan Masaryk (1948) 250
        III. 2. 2 Operation Balak (1948)...261
        III. 2. 3 The UN Summit in New York (1949) 270

III. 3　The End (1950–1952) 279
　　　　III. 3. 1　Arrest and Interrogation (1951–1952) 282
　　　　III. 3. 2　Show Trial and Execution (1952) 296
　　　　III. 3. 3　Rehabilitation (1963–1968) 302

Conclusion – and a few questions **309**

Oral History Interview with Mr Antonín Liehm (∗1924) ... **325**

Appendix **327**
　　Clementis in Data 327
　　Chronology 329
　　Bibliography 345
　　Index 375

Abbreviations

Archives and libraries

ABS USTRČR	Archiv Bezpečnostných Sílů – Ústav pro Studium totalitních režimů České Republiky – Archives of the State Security Services at the Institute for the Study of Totalitarian Regimes of the Czech Republic, Prague.
AMZV ČR	Archiv Ministerstva Zahraničnich Věcí České Republiky – Archive of the Ministry of Foreign Affairs of the Czech Republic, Prague.
HÚ SAV	Historický Ústav Slovenskej Akadamie Vied – Institute of History at the Slovak Academy of Sciences
SNA	Slovenský Národný Archív, Bratislava – The Slovak National Archives, Bratislava, Slovak Republic.
SNK	Slovenská Národná Knižnica, Martin – The Slovak National Library, Martin, Slovak Republic.
OF VC	Osobní Fond Vladimír Clementis – Personal Fond Vladimír Clementis
USD AV ČR	Ustav pro Soudobé Dějiny Akademie Věd České Republiky – Institute for Contemporary History at the Academy of Sciences of the Czech Republic

Political parties, associations and organizations

COMECON	Council for Mutual Economic Assistance; see RVHP
CP	Communist Party
CPI	Communist Party of Israel
ČSSD	Česká Strana Sociálně Demokratická – Czech Social Democratic Party

ČT	Česká Televize – Czech National TV
DS	Demokratická Strana – Slovak Democratic Party
HG	Hlinkova garda – Hlinka Guards
HSĽS	Hlinkova Slovenská Ľudová Strana – Hlinka's Slovak People's Party
IDF	Israel Defence Forces
IMRO	Inner Macedonian Revolutionary Organization
KPSS	Kommunističeskaia Partiia Sovetskogo Soiuza – Communist Party of the Soviet Union
KSČ	Kommunistická Strana Československa – Czechoslovak Communist Party
KSS	Kommunistická Strana Slovenska – Slovak Communist Party
MP	Member of Parliament
MZV	Ministerstvo Zahraničních Věcí – Czechoslovak Ministry of Foreign Affairs
NAM	Non-Aligned Movement
NATO	North Atlantic Treaty Organisation
NF	Národní Fronta – National Front
NKVD	Narodnii Kommissariat Vnutrënnikh Del – The People's Commissariat for Internal Affairs
OSS	Office of Strategic Services, USA
RVHP	Rada vzájomnej hospodárskej pomoci – Council for Mutual Economic Assistance
SPS	Slovenský Poslanecký Klub – Slovak Parliamentarians Club
SĽS	Slovenská Ľudová Strana – Slovak People's Party
SNP	Slovenské Národnie Povstanie – the Slovak National Uprising against Nazi Germany on 29 August 1944

SNR	Slovenská Národná Ráda – Slovak National Council
SNS	Slovenská Národná Strana – Slovak National Party
SSSR	Soiuz Sovietskich Socialističeskych Respublik – Union of the Soviet Socialist Republics
StB	Státní Bezpečnost – Czechoslovak State Security Service
STV	Slovenská Televízia – Slovak National TV
UNRRA	United Nations Relief and Rehabilitation Administration
ÚV KSČ	Ústředný výbor Kommunistická Strana Československa – Central Committee of the Czechoslovak Communist Party
ÚV KSS	Ústředný výbor Kommunistická Strana Slovenska – Central Committee of the Slovak Communist Party
WJC	World Jewish Congress

Acknowledgements

Writing the first political biography of Vladimír Clementis in English was a journey to the past, to my student years at the University of Zurich. In the early 1990s, I attended a seminar on East European History, focussing on the show trials in the Soviet satellite states. Carsten Goehrke was our professor, an excellent teacher.

We students wondered why stout Communists in Hungary, Czechoslovakia, Romania, Bulgaria and Poland, who had fought in the Spanish Civil War and survived Nazi concentration camps, would admit to crimes that, given their dedication to Marxism-Leninism, they could not possibly have committed. In the course of the seminar we realized that we too would have confessed, that everybody would confess if subject to that particular kind of physical and psychological torture.

Systematic deprivation of sleep, beatings, cold prison cells, the loss of one's high position, the sorrows about one's family, endless interrogations and, above all, the appeal to Party discipline. These methods destroyed the resilience and resistance of the fiercest believers in Marxism-Leninism, all of them in top Party and government positions at the time of arrest.

We students further learnt that the blueprints of the show trials in the satellite states had been drawn up in Moscow in the 1930s. The show trials of Grigorii I. Sinoviev (1883–1936), Lev B. Kamenev (1883–1936) and Nikolai I. Bukharin (1888–1938) enjoyed a brutal renaissance in Central and Eastern Europe, starting with the trial of László Rajk in Budapest in the autumn of 1949. In view of the emerging Cold War, the Soviet Union needed a disciplined bloc to be prepared for the fight against Western Capitalist

Imperialism. The mastermind, whose shadow loomed over Prague in 1952, was Generalissimus Stalin. The Czechoslovak show trial focussed on the Czech Rudolf Slánský, the former General Secretary of the Czechoslovak Communist Party.

I was curious about the Slovak Communists, in particular, Vladimír Clementis, Foreign Minister and member of the Central Committee. In this volume, I tried to convey to the reader how the political history of Central Europe affected the life of a Slovak Communist, intellectual and politician. I tried to probe into Clementis' thought and activities with a dispassionate and rational approach. The history of Czechoslovakia in the crucial years from 1945 to 1948 can teach us a lot about *Realpolitik*, political strategy in domestic and foreign affairs, psychology and lastly, the range of choices a Communist politician and diplomat had at his disposal.

Almost thirty years after the fall of Communism in Europe in 1989, there are still blank spots in the history of Slovak Communism. The Czechoslovak show trial of 1952 has been largely researched, but the Western reader is much more familiar with the fates of the Czech Communists. I hope that this biography will be helpful, especially for the younger generation that did not witness the Cold War, in understanding the Slovak part of Czechoslovak Communism with its distinct goals and plans, emblematically embodied in the fate of Clementis. Cicero was perfectly right in saying that history is *magistra vitae*, the grand teacher of mankind. Where else could we learn about politics than from history?

As a scholar specializing in Central European intellectual history, I want to understand how people thought in their particular historical context and why they acted the way they did. What motivated Clementis to join the Czechoslovak Communist Party as a law student at the prestigious Charles University in Prague, the capital of the only democracy in Central Europe in the interwar period? Why did he return to the Party after having broadcasted for the Beneš exile government in London during WWII? These are but two of the questions that have puzzled me over the last three years while writing this book.

My thanks: The Stiftung zur Förderung der wissenschaftlichen Forschung at the University of Zurich UZH granted me a generous stipend, which allowed me to do research in the archives. I am greatly indebted to my colleagues and friends for their interest in my research and willingness to discuss specific issues with me. In alphabetical order: Jozef Banáš, Juraj Benko, Valerián Bystrický (†), Zdenka Garnotová, Frank Grüner, Ivan Kamenec, Kristina Larischová, Hermann Lübbe, Adis Merdzanovic, Slavomír Michálek, Daniel E. Miller, Marie Neudorflová, Jan Pešek, Francis Raska, Dušan Šegeš, Nikola Todorović, Valentina Welser, and my friend XY, whose wish for anonymity I respect.

I thank the following persons for their professional, friendly, swift and uncomplicated assistance: Ľudmila Šimková and the ladies at the Slovak National Library (SNK) in Martin; Erika Javošová at the Slovak National Archives (SNA) in Bratislava; Markéta Kuncová and Michal Majak at the Archives of the Czech Foreign Ministry (AMZV) in Prague; Jitka Bílková, Veronika Chroma, Tereza Douchová, Zuzana Svobodová and Petr Zeman at the Archives of the State Security Forces at the Czech Institute for the Study of Totalitarian Regimes (ABS ÚSTRČR) in Prague and Lisa Brun at the Institute of Philosophy at UZH.

The ladies at the housing office of the Slovak Academy of Sciences have made my annual research stays since 2008 such a joyful and uncomplicated matter: Maria Vallová, Božena and Ľubica Konečná, thank you. Valerie Lange at ibidem publishers is an exceptionally patient, effective and supportive editor. Since the autumn of 2013, ibidem has a cooperation agreement with Columbia University Press. I thank Peter Thomas Hill for proofreading my manuscript and teaching me how to express myself in an elegant and scholarly English.

This study could not have been written without Vlasta Jaksicsová's expertise. Vlasta was my supervisor for three years. She taught me how to look at Slovak history from the perspective of leftist intellectuals and artists. Born at the turn of the 20th century, they had a particular mindset: they had clear ideas, a holistic approach to the organization of social life. Although I focus on Clementis' political thought, Vlasta's advice was invaluable; thanks to her, I was able to understand Clementis' mindset within the context of the leftist intellectuals in the first half of the 20th century.

Needless to say, any errors and shortcomings in this volume are my own.

Josette Baer
Zurich, Bratislava and Prague, March 2017

The Drama of Vladimír Clementis
The Tragic Life of a Communist

"We are all more like vast subterranean caverns, uncharted even by ourselves, than we are like holes dug straight into the ground. The urge to insist that the complex is just a disguise for the simple was one of the plagues of the twentieth century."[1]

Timothy Snyder, 2010

"An emigrant without a home, yet everywhere at home, a cynical cosmopolitan with a secret longing, a perennial Jew by the waters of Babylon ..."[2]

When, at the beginning of WWII, Laco Novomeský wrote these sad words about Clementis' brutal fate, he had no idea (or did he just have an inkling?) what tragic and bizarre end the lives of two communist intellectuals would meet after the war. Intellectuals who blindly believed (indeed, belief has to be blind) in a better world that would also be more just, by dint of critical thinking, sacrificed more than their personal freedom.

The sacrifice of Vladimír Clementis was a final one, the ultimate sacrifice. With regard to his biography and tragic end, known and documented by historiography, his sacrifice was for nothing, bereft of sense.

---

[1] *Thinking the Twentieth Century. Tony Judt with Timothy Snyder* (New York: Penguin, 2013), xiii. The Czech edition: *Intelektuál ve dvacátém století. Rozhovor Timothyho Snydera s Tonym Judtom* (Praha: Prostor 2013), 17.

[2] Ladislav Novomeský, "Aký si (How you are)", from the collection *Svätý za dedinou* (*Patron Saints for the Country*) (1939) (Bratislava: Literárne informačné centrum, 2005). Novomeský dedicated the poem to his friend Clementis; the collection was a hommage to the past of the 1930s.

Clementis' life that was so tightly connected with the trajectories of the development of Slovak society and the politics of the first half of the 20th century was neither exceptional nor original; it was the common life of a Slovak and Czechoslovak intellectual, trying to catch up with the life of Western intellectuals.

***

Was it 'only' duty born of fanatical conviction, which an engaging and disciplined communist 'had' to exercise in the times of European and national crisis? Did he have to fight not only Fascism after Hitler's attack on the Soviet Union (!), but also follow 'the party's instructions' (which he, from time to time, allowed himself to criticize) that demanded the active participation in the revolutionary change of the world?

Or was it just the task of a communist intellectual, cast in the eschatological and visionary belief in the historical inevitability of the global victory of the dictatorship of the proletariat? That one single 'rational event in history', according to Marx, that 'pragmatic and successful' event that Lenin's communist party of Soviet Russia had been the first to realize, followed by Stalin in the Soviet Union?

Or was it the duty of a myopic politician, who, after his experience of the war and a brief 'aberration', acted, first, as secretary of state under Jan Masaryk and, after the communist *coup d'état* of February 1948, as Foreign Minister, supporting the establishment of communism in Czechoslovakia? Was he, after the victorious revolution, one of the Jacobin victims of the 'war Diadochi' and the powerful, intent on 'settling old bills'?

Was he a perpetrator or a victim – or, according to Hannah Arendt, both? Was Clementis an intellectual or rather an ambitious man, eager to distinguish himself in politics at all costs?

Even if we have the impression that a part of the answer is already encoded in the questions, we shall find no satisfactory explanation, only a general one. All the more so, as we are, in Clementis' case, confronted with a blend of biography and history. Nevertheless, I am trying to find answers, risking overgeneralization. Naturally, I am also aware that if a historian wants to understand and carefully and consistently interpret a distinct historical event, he or she has to ignore the framework of a single perspective and accept the validity of several. That is, to explain the phenomenon within the historical context and scrutinize the key factors. Yet, a historical essay, which this text aspires to be, has the advantage that it neither can nor has to stick to the scientific principles mentioned.

It seems to me that Vladimír Clementis (1902–1952), 'a modern man of today' who breathed in 'the air of the new times' with a vengeance, who, after WWI, got involved with the limits and stagnations of Slovak society, was no typical intellectual. There is no doubt that he fervently contributed to Slovak culture as an organizer and spokesman of the Davists, publishing uncountable texts and articles about literature and history in DAV, the journal of the Slovak leftist avantgarde. But he lacked the independent artistic-creative character trait that was so typical of the Slovak (and Czech) intellectuals of those times, most of them writers or poets. First and foremost, Clementis loved and promoted the arts, but he did not excel in any artistic activities. Yet, he did acknowledge his shortcomings (with a certain regret), not only in his *Unfinished History*. Because of his dominant personality, his psychological and professional skills, Clementis was much more of a 'homo politicus' than an artist.

***

To understand the origins of Clementis' opinions and ideas, concepts and thoughts that usually originate in one's youth, we ought to go back in history, not only to the historical events in Russia on the eve of WWI that became a kind of 'certificate of baptism' of the European leftist intellectuals. This was the generation born in 1900 to 1905: Jean-Paul Sartre, Arthur Koestler, George Orwell, Raymond Aron, Vítězslav Nezval, Jaroslav Seifert, Karel Teige, Ladislav Novomeský and others.

In intellectual terms, this young generation was clearly the most influential group in the 20th century. By inheriting and interpreting modernism, it tore itself away from religion and tried with great personal enthusiasm to think about the world and society as a complex of secular problems. The leftist avant-garde adopted Nietzsche's 'God is dead', and the spiritual vacuum as its consequence replaced the Kantian ethical imperative one had hitherto had to obey in all decisions of a moral nature. Yet, the so-called socialist ethics that this generation tried to extract from Marx's analysis of capitalism was both a relic and a replacement of religious authority, which Lenin, Marx's successor, very quickly understood, presenting himself as a genius of Marxist dialectics.[3]

As a secular religion, Marxism could explain everything: not only was it political narrative, economic analysis and social critique, it was also a fundamental 'theory of the universe'. And Lenin, the Bolshevik, the political strategist and master tactician, demonstrated his 'genius' with blending the secular religion of the progressive West with the backward East's radicalism. To be a revolutionary Marxist meant that it was absolutely necessary to decide about the fate of others in the name of their own future. Clementis' generation was fascinated (enchanted) by the revolution. The intellectuals thought of it as a distinct secret, a particular meaning, which they could hold on to, and so they kept justifying all sacrifices, mainly the sacrifices of others. In the spirit of Lenin's

---

[3] Jaksicsová, "Intelektuál ve ...", 97.

ethically doubtful apologetics of "*petty lies, frauds, betrayals or false pretences*", these sacrifices were morally legitimate in view of the honest goals of the Socialist future.[4]

That generation felt the attraction of Leninism already in the first years after the revolution; Leninism reached the peak of its attraction when Hitler assumed power, and the currents of history dragged and forced that generation willy-nilly to face the tragic issues of their times. If one did not make a personal choice of one's party comrades, one's co-travellers through time, one was not able to choose at all. And many of them, in particular Clementis, had chosen their comrades already in their early youth, although some who survived the human consequences of the theory changed their beliefs at a later point in time (André Gide or Arthur Koestler, but also the younger Albert Camus).

Clementis, however, did not question his beliefs. To tell the truth, he could not, because he fatally missed out on the three opportunities offered to him by life's circumstances. First, at the end of the 1930s, he closed his eyes, ignoring the consequences of Stalin's regime of terror – he neither wanted to nor could believe the news, since he was afraid (like so many of his comrades) of losing faith. Most probably, he dismissed his doubts (he talked about them with Ehrenburg) with the pseudo-powerful argumentation of the revolutionary: "The situation is difficult, we have to take serious decisions, we cannot renounce on violence, this is a revolution, after all" and "if you work in the forest, wood chips will fly". The second opportunity presented itself at the beginning of WWII: certainly, Clementis openly criticized Hitler's pact with Stalin and the latter's aggressive foreign policy against unarmed Finland, but he did not draw the obvious conclusions – clearly, he

---

[4] Jaksicsová, "Intelektuál ve ...", 106.

could not bear the sad life of a refugee and the feeling of being excluded from the party that was like a family to him.

There is no doubt that one crucial principle had its validity also for Clementis: to be a communist in the 20th century meant to believe that there was no other purposeful way of life. He missed also the third opportunity, which was no longer about waking up and seeing the reality, but the last chance to save his life. A few short days before the beginning of his fall, while he was attending a session of the UNO in the USA, he refused to believe a trustworthy source warning him that the comrades at home were preparing a trap for him. Much like in a classic Slovak fairy tale, fate did not bestow a fourth opportunity on him.

He failed as a politician, since he obviously could not adapt himself to Marx's winged words, inspired by Machiavelli that "in politics, it is possible to connive even with the devil to reach a certain goal, but you should make sure that it is you who deceives the devil, not the other way round".[5] He failed also as an intellectual, because he forgot that in life, unlike politics, one's personal truth has no influence on an unstable society. "To insist on more courageous and less transient principles ... to give preference to doubt, to the relativism of tolerance, to scepticism ... but with well-meaning resignation and the understanding that one cannot steer the political reality like a politician usually can ..."[6]

***

The party the 23-year-old doctor of law joined in 1925 certainly stressed its adherence to Czechoslovakia with its name, Czechoslovak communist party,[7] but it was the Communist International

---

[5] Karel Kosík, "Iluse a realismus", *Listy*, no. 1, 7 November 1968, quoted after Milan Jungmann, *Literárky můj osud. Kritické návraty ke kultuře padesátých a šedesátých let s akuálními reflexemi* (Praha: Atlantis, 1999), 300.

[6] "Úvodník", *Listy*, no. 15, 17 April 1969, 312-313.

[7] The KSČ emerged in 1921 in the traditional way by splitting from the Social Democrats. Both parties enjoyed legal recognition and participated in the

that directed it according to the spirit of Lenin's words about "the necessity of the revolutionary struggle for socialism". The goal of the International was to impose on their European political allies the principles and methods of the Russian Bolsheviks, the victorious comrades of the 1917 revolution. The European comrades should be reliable and trustworthy, defending "the interests of the first state of workers and peasants".

In the spirit of their traditional conspirational attitude, the Soviet comrades prepared an overthrow in the Czechoslovak communist party; in 1929, they established a new leadership under Klement Gottwald, a man who lacked in education as much as in decent behaviour. Gottwald was hardly capable of pronouncing properly a word with four syllables (in phonetic Czech: *demogratsie*; in phonetical English: dimograsi). The new leadership adopted 'democratic centralism' as the strict Bolshevik principle of party work and thought like a cult, which alone knows what is right; its task was to convince the members of its principles or then, destroy them, because, from the viewpoint of the Russian Bolsheviks, this was the only way to achieve absolute political power. Twenty years later, Gottwald and his followers (Jan Šverma, Rudolf Slánský, Václav Kopecký, and others) would assume absolute power.

The conservative group of the old communist writers protested against the new leadership with the open letter of 'seven' writers, but together with 'other communist artists of the younger generation' the two Slovaks Clementis and Novomeský, already famous because of their activities for DAV, condemned the protest as a 'grave mistake'. I think that this event, which was unique in the history of the communist movement, rendered problematic

---

Czechoslovak parliamentary life of the First Republic. In the tradition of the European Socialists, Bohumír Šmeral, the chairman of the Czech communists, believed that Socialism would win by parliamentary means.

not only the ideological development of Czechoslovak communism, but also its historical assessment. Yet, in those years – and under the particular conditions pertaining in Czechoslovakia – the odd union of the Slovak Davists with the Czech non-conformist avant-garde (Teige, Nezval) and the Stalinist party leadership had its distinct logic. Apart from their age, these factions shared not only an unconditional admiration for the Soviet Union, a country "where tomorrow means already yesterday"; they also shared the view that political radicalism had to decide about the reality of society.

The European intellectual elite, hence also the Slovak and Czech avant-garde, was in awe of the young Soviet artists' commitment to the revolution (Isaak Bábeľ, Vladimír Maiakovskii, Boris Pasternak, Sergei Eizenštein, Viacheslav Maierchold, Vladimír Tatlin and others); but they were not aware that the freedom of art was already gravely restricted. In the European artistic and intellectual circles of the mid-1930s, particularly in the French (Breton and the surrealists) tightly connected with Czech culture, the illusion still prevailed that the interaction of artistic freedom and political power was a distinct possibility. The rift between the party and the revolutionary intellectuals became visible only at the end of the 1930s as a consequence of the Moscow show trials and Stalin's international diplomacy; this rift made the position of the European communist intellectuals in their anti-Fascist struggle more difficult, because it unsettled their unconditional belief in their 'second home country'.

***

Leaving aside for a moment the perspective of the Czechoslovak state and the rather grave and fundamental 'problems' of the leftist avant-garde artists compelled to express the tone and direction of the modern national (Czech-dominated) culture, we find that the starting point of the Slovak communist intellectual (artist and functionary alike) was a particular one in the years of the First Republic. To the Slovak intellectual, the existential theme of political, societal and cultural activities, add to this also his personal positions, was the Slovak question, an issue that would soon turn into the fatal accusation of 'Slovak bourgeois nationalism'. In these 'accelerating' times Slovakia, in search of her modern national and political face, was condemned to 'all-national' cooperation, especially in the cultural sphere, which did not reflect the actual political representation of Slovaks and Czechs. The moral and political goal of the union of both nations was a fundamental matter. The whole of Czechoslovak society and the entire spectrum of political parties were aware of it, the conservative right as much as the liberal centre and the left. Against the deepening differences in thinking about that cooperation, there was one principal opinion that united all national and political factions: any solution of the economic, political and cultural problems was existentially connected with the solution of the Slovak national question. And the Davists led by Clementis who had just left the first brief aberrations of sectarian *proletkult* thinking behind them, began to think against the canon of communist internationalism; they very well understood the challenging issue of Slovak equality within the common state.

In spite of the fact that Slovak historiography has sufficiently analysed the Davists' significance for Slovak society, I would, nevertheless, like to draw the reader's attention to the group's quite successful attempts at integration into Slovak public life, especially in the areas of politics, society and culture. After the first sectarian episodes, the Davists (certainly with the political consent of the party leadership) destroyed the senseless party principle that demanded of its adherents to focus exclusively on their own thought; they opened the journal DAV also to other ideas, thoughts that sometimes went against the official party line. Clearly, the Davists were not afraid of open and sharp polemics.

They understood very well that the journal was a platform, where they could present their opinions, influence not only their followers, but also convince their ideological adversaries of their arguments, and first and foremost, win the young generation of educated Slovaks.

They thus largely contributed to the entire spectre of Slovak cultural journals, among them the eminent revue *Kultúra*, the voice of the association of Holy Adalbert (*spolok Svätého Vojtěcha*). Against all odds, these passionate members of the leftist avant-garde were very successful in becoming a part of the consciousness of Slovak society. They were very active: they chaired student associations and played a significant role in organizing and conducting manifestations of an all-national character, for example the Convention of Slovak Youth in 1932 or the first Congress of Slovak Writers in 1936 (Clementis, Tido Jozef Gašpar and Milo Urban wrote the draft of the writers' resolution). Their almost fanatical ethos gained them not only the sympathy of their generation and younger followers (for example, the 'R–10' group, the surrealists), who (as became very quickly evident) followed in their wake; they could also arouse the admiration of their intellectual adversaries. Although the Christian nationalists Gašpar and Urban refused to become what Clementis referred to as 'a modern man of today', both stated approvingly that nobody in the Slovak cultural sphere had such clear ideas about the rightfulness of their programme as the leftist intellectual minority: "*Whoever was searching for justice, disgusted with the hypocrites, egotists and moneychangers ... could not help but admire and support them*", even if "*one, owing to inner personal barriers, could not join them in their path*".[8] The radical leftists had no hope of convincing the

---

[8] Milo Urban, *Kade-tade po Halinde. Neveselé spomienky na veselé roky* (Bratislava: Slovenský spisovateľ, 1992), 261. Milo Urban would become a principal representative of the clerical-fascist Slovak state in 1939. His mentioning

wider conservative Slovak society that only the socialist revolution and the dictatorship of the party could be a remedy of all problems. But they achieved a firm authority and an influence that could not be neglected, especially in the sphere of art and the organisation of cultural events. Particularly in the latter, they enjoyed the highest autonomy, because they were able to leave their own political dogma behind.

In the inter-war years, it seemed that the KSČ politically accepted the cultural activities of the Davists, who co-operated with the representatives of the right and the Catholic and nationalist cultural circles tightly or loosely connected to the Hlinka party. Yet, this radically changed after the war. Naturally, the events during the war contributed to that change, especially the different positions about the anti-Fascist resistance, which divided the home camp and the exile, including the communists in exile. After the war, the KSČ turned from an oppositional party into a state-building party; in view of its ambitions to centralize and embark on a struggle for power, the issue of Slovak autonomy became a burden, since the Slovak communists who had fought for it in the national uprising of 1944 refused to give it up. On the way towards a successful installation of its monopoly of power, the Prague party centre thus did not hesitate to sacrifice the Slovak communists.

***

The history of mankind is full of senseless human sacrifices and victims; why should the recent 20th century, a century with two world wars, violence and genocide, be different? The Stalinist show trials of the 1950s were a phenomenon hitherto unknown in European history and modern Slovak history alike. Because of

---

of 'moneychangers' was not only an antisemitic remark, but also a critique of the representatives of big business, to whom money was everything and culture a negligible area.

the theatrical Asiatic perfidity that demonstrated the burial of law and human courage, psychiatrists are more capable of analysing the show trials as a morbid legacy of communism than historians. Fifty years of lawlessness, political trials and organised violence in the communist part of Europe, leniently referred to as the era of 'personality cult' were, however, only a kind of a 'déjà vu' of what had happened in the Soviet Union in the 1930s, when Stalinism established itself as a system of power.

The 1930s was a point of reference, the neuralgic point and magic circle alike, around which the majority of the leftist intellectuals of those times moved, incapable of tearing down that fatal web. And the majority of them, starting with the French communists (and the non-communists) and ending with our home grown epigones, did not even come to their senses when our own party members, especially Clementis, stood in the dock. Had they learned nothing? Had they not read Gide's *Return from the USSR* and *Afterthoughts on my Return from the USSR* (1937)? After all, newspapers and journals of the entire political spectrum commented about Gide's *Return* (1936). What did they think of the words of František X. Šalda, a respected humanist and intellectual authority? Šalda had written that "*the trial turned the stomach of the more decent Europe*", while "*in the Czech lands* (and also in Slovakia – VJ) *one remained silent, because it is opportune to keep quiet about Russian matters and because we are a country of oppressed dwarfs; nobody wants to get his fingers burnt*".[9] No Slovak leftist intellectual joined in to support Teige's revolt against Stalin.

Yet, the thought that Clementis stopped the publication of DAV in 1937 so that he would not have to react to the Stalinist purges, is a very likely explanation. The question, however, is: how would he have reacted – would he have toed the party line or

---

[9] František Xaver Šalda, "Gidovo zklamání ze Sovětskeho Ruska", *Zápisník IX* (1936-1937): 109-120.

stood up against the party, demonstrating that he was a learned man, a man of culture? Again, we can find an answer only from a general perspective.

For those who believed in the country that was realizing the utopia, the Soviet events had no influence on what they saw with their own eyes or how they immediately experienced the reality of a life under Bolshevism. Those who went there with burning belief, Clementis among them, usually returned in the same state of mind; only André Gide was a famous and remarkable exception. Clementis, the future Slovak 'advocate of the poor', lover of the arts and social life, missed in Moscow, just so, the coffee houses: *"To a Central European, it is a somewhat strange feeling ploughing through the city all day and not being able to leave one's tracks to jump to the next coffee house for a break."*[10] True, this dedicated disciple of communism did not look for an assessment of the current reality, but for the future successes of communism as the only criterion of judgement.

Moreover, in terms of the show trials of 1936, there was no historical precedent, no example from history that would have prompted understanding of the significance of these events and the deeper sense of Stalin's enterprise. To any contemporary person living in a European liberal democracy (with the exception of the French intellectuals who conceived of them as terror regime of Robespierrian proportions), it was simply inconceivable that people would confess to terrible crimes if the accusations did not bear some truth.[11] At the end of the 1930s, the communist intellectual (and the decent non-communist intellectual alike) had a higher purpose to keep quiet – the logics of anti-Fascism: any open

---

[10] Vladimír Clementis, "V centre päťročnice", in *Vzduch našich čias. Články, state, prejavy, polemiky 1922-1934, vol. I* (Bratislava: Vydavateľstvo politickej literatúry, 1967), 179.

[11] Jaksicsová, "Intelektuál ve ...", 189, 199, 201.

criticism of Stalinism would have weakened the only faction that fought against Fascism. That was the reason why it was so hard for Clementis to criticise Stalin.

With the historic and political events of 1938 inundating Europe, the Moscow show trials ceased to be the focus of international attention. During the following years of the terrible war, when Europeans fought for the survival of their civilisation, the 'dust' of benign forgetting began to cover their historical memory. In 1945, immediately after the end of the war, there was neither purpose nor political will to remember, to go back to the Moscow trials of the 1930s. Yet, only three (!) years after the war, the 'spirit' of the trials came alive in Czechoslovakia, in the historic reality after the Communist coup d'état of 25 February 1948.

***

One cannot understand this shameful 'episode' of recent history by simply tearing it away from its historical trajectory and studying it in isolation. It can only be understood in the context of the war and immediate post-war Europe, as the British historian Keith Lowe so superbly showed in his myth-destroying volume *Savage Continent*, a shocking portrait of chaos, lawlessness and terror. The famous Czech writer Ivan Klíma: "*War destroys everything, not only human lives, not only houses, churches and factories, but also something delicate that can live only in times of peace: we may call it law, culture or just the ability to uphold the respect for human life.*"[12]

Yet, as fervently as the post-war wave of violence countered the previous wave of violence, there was nothing left to counter after the February *coup d'état*. Or, was there, just about? As well as victors, every revolution also has its losers and, even if

---

[12] Ivan Klíma, *Moje šílené století I* (Praha: Academia 2009), 345.

the latter are in the majority, they have to be punished with violence, silenced with fear. Therefore, the unsuccessful got even with the successful; the uneducated and half-educated with the educated and the cowards with the courageous. And finally, every revolution offers the masses material and spiritual opportunities to act: it demands the humiliation of all who have put themselves above it. It claims that the revolutionaries act in the service of some higher historical justice, in the name of progress, for the good of all *"and the people, that undefined but artifically projected entity"*.[13]

***

In modern times, too many educated people served a fanatical idea opposed to everything mankind had so far achieved; these persons betrayed everything that bound them to their knowledge and profession. The mass failure of the intellectuals (especially those, who did not directly participate in the execution of totalitarian power, but spoke out in favour of it or tolerated it) is a simple historical fact many researchers have been occupied with for decades. There is no doubt that one requires significant moral strength to resist the pressure of a totalitarian regime. The failure of many intellectuals in the countries controlled by the communists cannot be excused, but one can at least explain it. However, the thought of intellectuals who, over mass graves, lost themselves in revolutionary ideologies while enjoying the liberty of their democratic countries, completely defies understanding. This mindset is absurdity in perfection. Lenin might have thought exactly of this kind of intellectual when he spoke of "useful idiots".

When Jean-Paul Sartre visited Czechoslovakia in 1963 with his partner Simone de Beauvoir, he declared in a discussion with Czech and Slovak intellectuals who considered him an icon

---

[13] Klíma, 130.

of philosophy and literature that "*to him, the perfect humanist was the hero, who, in spite of all the terrible experiences, remained a socialist*".[14] Sartre stressed that he spoke of those who had survived the Stalinist prisons and were still communists. Soon after, the writer was awarded the Nobel Prize (which he refused); a further statement of his is worthy of remembering: "*The only really great novel that can be written in this century is a novel about the socialist experience.*"[15] And the great writer justified his big illusion in front of a public that was surviving that 'experience' first-hand and regarded contemporary socialism as a pointless error of history: "*Socialism, whether it has a future or not, is moulding the mind of our entire epoch, it might be hell, but hell too can be a subject for literature – disappointed hopes, the deaths of comrades – is this not the most modern perfection of tragedy?*" By no means few of the shocked listeners might have thought exactly the same as the writer Ivan Klíma: "*Hell is a great subject, as long as one doesn't have to live in it.*"[16]

***

The 20th century was the era of the intellectuals with all the concomitant betrayals, resignations and compromises. The story of the European leftist intellectual, the first and also the last educated man in modern history organized in a group, came, after a brief revival at the end of the 1960s, to an end. He was simply no longer needed nor taken seriously, because, after the experience with communism in practice, the world no longer believed in any kind of paradise on earth; that is why the search for a solution by universally valid ideologies ceased to exist. The last generation of the radical communists of the 1960s disbanded. Even if some individuals turned for a brief time to Maoism or Fidel Castro, the

---

[14] Klíma, 448.
[15] "Sartre a de Beauvoir v Bratislave", *Kritika & Kontext VII*, no 1 (2002): 17.
[16] Klíma, 448, 449.

major part of the Western European leftist intellectuals either joined the right or shut themselves away in postmodern discourses (individual or group rights, the horrors of globlization etc.) And, until the very end in 1989, the East European intellectual (especially the Czech and Slovak) looked with disgust at the twenty-year regime of socialism in practice that was realizing the communist ideals. In terms of political culture, Marxism became a marginal phenomenon; in the 1970s, it retired to the universities and academies, where it slowly withered away.

Bratislava, January 2017
Vlasta Jaksicsová

X. Introduction

X. 1 Vladimír Clementis – victim of Stalinism or gravedigger of democracy?¹

> "I entered the Minister's office with Vavro Hajdu. Clementis had not heard us knock and was standing by the window, cautiously raising the curtain and looking out into the street. He was nervous and worried. He told us that an additional group of men from the Security Services had been added to his bodyguard that morning. [...] I saw Clementis several times since he continued to live in the Ministry apartment, while his new flat was being decorated by the Ministry of the Interior. I had become particularly sensitive to the police methods in use so I concluded that security agents were installing microphones in his apartment to increase surveillance. When I saw him for the last time we merely hinted at it; he had the same suspicions as I."²

Artur London (1915–1986), born into a Jewish Communist worker's family from Ostrava in Moravia, remembered how the 1952 show trial of the former General Secretary of the KSČ Rudolf

---

1 All translations into English are by me, if not otherwise referred to.
2 Artur London, *On Trial* (London: Macdonald, 1970), 40, 42. The Slovak Vavro Hajdu (1914–1977) was London's best friend and worked with him at the Foreign Ministry under Clementis. In 1970, Simone Signoret and her husband Yves Montand starred as Lise and Artur London in the movie *L'aveu* (*The Confession*), based on London's memoirs. The movie shows how the Czechoslovak authorities, instructed by Soviet NKVD officers, prepared the victims for the show trials by depriving them of sleep, subjecting them to beatings and exhausting discussions about the principles of Marxism-Leninism and the duties of a party member. Costa Gavras' *L'aveu* on http://www.imdb.com/title/tt0065439/; accessed 3 July 2015. For an account of what the wives of the accused had to undergo see the memoirs of Heda Margolius Kovály, *Under a Cruel Star. A Life in Prague 1941–1968* (London: Granta, 2012), and Jo Langer, *Convictions. My Life with a Good Communist* (London: Granta, 2011). See also the excellent Czechoslovak film *Ucho* (*The Ear*) by Karel Kachyna from 1970, on http://www.imdb.com/title/tt0066498/; accessed 16 May 2016. I thank my friend XY for recommending this film that portrays the regime's invasion of the private lives of top Czechoslovak government officials in the 1950s, causing unbearable psychological distress.

Slánský (1901–1952) and fellow accused was being prepared in 1950. London had been the Deputy Minister of foreign affairs, Vladimír Clementis his boss. Of the fourteen high-ranking Party members accused, only London, Vavro Hajdu and Evžen (Eugen) Löbl (1907–1987) survived – they received life sentences. London was released from prison on 2 February 1956 and officially rehabilitated by Prime Minister Viliam Široký (1902–1971) on 14 April 1956.

Clementis, Slánský and nine other Party members[3] were sentenced to death for their betrayal of Communist Czechoslovakia, charged with Titoism, Zionism, conspiracy, sabotage and espionage on the payroll of Western Capitalist Imperialism. The eleven sentenced were hanged on 3 December 1952, one after the other, starting at three o'clock in the morning. Clementis died at five o'clock. Who was Vladimír Clementis? I think that there are three ways to address this question.

First, from a democratic viewpoint that opposes totalitarian rule, in particular the Nazi regime and the Marxist-Leninist regimes in Central Europe in the 20th century, one could describe Clementis as a *champagne communist*: he had a doctorate in law from the prestigious Charles University in Prague, loved good food, the arts, literature and enjoyed wearing expensive suits, sporting elegant pipes. He had joined the Party as a privileged student of law in Prague in 1925, despising the liberal atmosphere of the First Republic. He had had only contempt for the democratic

---

[3] The other nine sentenced to death and executed were Otto Fischl (1902–1952), Jozef Frank (1909–1952), Ludvík Frejka (1904–1952), Bedřich Geminder (1901–1952), Rudolf Margolius (1913–1952), Bedřich Reicin (1911–1952), André Simone (Otto Katz) (1895–1952), Otto Šling (1912–1952) and Karel Švab (1904–1952).

values of the state Tomáš G. Masaryk (1850–1937)[4] had established on 28 October 1918 after four tireless years of lobbying in France, Great Britain and the USA.

Clementis represented the KSČ's interests in the Czechoslovak parliament, enjoying the democratic liberties bestowed on the members of parliament (MPs) by the very political system he wanted to abolish. After the Munich Agreement of 1938, he and his wife Lída left Bratislava for Prague. The Germans forced Slovak President Jozef Tiso (1887–1947) to declare Slovakia's sovereignty in March 1939, and occupied the Czech lands, establishing the *Reichsprotektorat Böhmen und Mähren*. Clementis fled to Paris and thence to London, where he worked for the exile government of President Edvard Beneš (1884–1948).[5] Resistance fighters of

---

[4] A selection of studies about Masaryk in chronological order: Otakar Funda, *Thomas Garrigue Masaryk. Sein philosophisches, religiöses und politisches Denken* (Bern: Peter Lang, 1978); Roland J. Hoffmann, *Thomas G. Masaryk und die tschechische Frage* (München: Oldenbourg, 1988); Jozef Novák, ed., *On Masaryk. Texts in English and German* (Amsterdam: Rodopi, 1988); Stanley B. Winters, ed., *T. G. Masaryk (1850–1937). Thinker and Politician* (Basingstoke: MacMillan, SSEES, University of London, 1989); Robert B. Pynsent, ed., *T. G. Masaryk (1850–1937). Thinker and Critic* (Basingstoke: MacMillan, SSEES, University of London, 1989, 1990); Harry Hanák, ed., *T. G. Masaryk (1850–1937). Statesman and Cultural Force* (Basingstoke: MacMillan, SSEES, University of London, 1990); Jaroslav Opat, *Filozof a politik T. G. Masaryk, 1882–1893* (Praha: Melantrich, 1990); *Masaryk a myšlenka evropské jednoty* (Praha: Filosofická Fakulta Univerzity Karlovy FFUK, 1992); Zwi Batscha, *Eine Philosophie der Demokratie. Thomas G. Masaryks Begründung einer neuzeitlichen Demokratie* (Frankfurt a. Main: Suhrkamp, 1994); Dalibor Truhlar, *Thomas G. Masaryk. Philosophie der Demokratie* (Frankfurt a. Main: Peter Lang, 1994); my *Politik als praktizierte Sittlichkeit. Zum Demokratiebegriff von Thomas G. Masaryk und Václav Havel* (Sinzheim: Pro Universitate, 1998) and Radan Hain, *Staatstheorie und Staatsrecht in T. G. Masaryks Ideenwelt* (Zürich: Schulthess, 1999). See also the Masaryk Institute and the Archive of the Academy of Sciences of the Czech Republic in Prague on http://www.mua.cas.cz/index.php/en/; accessed 22 June 2014.
[5] US President Franklin D. Roosevelt (1882–1945) recognized the Czechoslovak exile government on 30 July 1941. Roosevelt's letter in the latest critical

many nationalities, the majority of them Slovaks, lost their lives in the Slovak National Uprising (*Slovenské Národní Povstanie*, SNP) of 1944,[6] fighting the Germans and the troops of the clerical-fascist Tiso regime, while the Czechs were suffering under brutal Nazi rule in the protectorate.[7]

Clementis, however, had a cushy job in safe London, broadcasting with the BBC for the exile government. Appointed assistant secretary of state (deputy foreign minister) in 1945 and foreign minister after the mysterious death of Jan Masaryk (1886–1948) on 10 March 1948, he faithfully served the KSČ, led by Klement Gottwald (1896–1953). In the mindset of a vengeful democrat, Clementis eventually got what he deserved, much like the sorcerer's apprentice in Goethe's famous poem: *Spirits that I've*

---

    edition of Beneš's memoirs: Edvard Beneš, *Paměti. vol III Dokumenty* (Praha: Academia, 2008), 435-436. Great Britain recognized the exile government on 21 July 1940 and on 29 September 1942, Charles de Gaulle (1890–1970), speaking for the French exile government, declared the Munich Agreement of 1938 as null and void.

[6] A selection of studies in chronological order: Alice Dubova, "War experiences with Slovakian partisans (1958)", Yad Vashem Archives, Israel, Wiener Library Collection, record group 0.2, file no. 668, 14 pages; Terézia Kováčiková, "Ženy v národnooslobodzovacom zápase (1939–1945)", in *Zborník múzea Slovenského Národného povstania 7* (Martin, Múzeum SNP v Banskej Bystrici: Osveta, 1982), 5-24; Jozef Jablonický, *Z ilegality do povstania. Kapitoly z občianskeho odboja* (Banská Bystrica: Muzeum SNP, 2009 (2)); Miroslav Pekník, ed., *Slovenské národné povstanie 1944. Súčať europskej antifašistickej rezistencie v rokoch druhej svetovej vojny* (Bratislava: Veda, 2009) and Rudolf M. Viest, *General Viest's notebooks. Call to arms came in 1938* (Brainigsville, PA: JMV, 2009).

[7] An informative account of the Czech resistance in the protectorate is Radomír Luža with Cristina Vella, *The Hitler Kiss. A Memoir of the Czech Resistance* (Baton Rouge: Louisiana State University Press, 2002). An excellent illustrated volume about how Nazi rule changed the look of all fifteen Prague districts in the protectorate is Jiří Padevět, *Průvodce protektorátní Prahou. Místa – události – lidé* (Praha: Academia, Archiv hlavního města Prahy, 2014)

cited / My commands ignore.⁸ His fate was poetic justice *par excellence* and bitter proof of how the Communists thanked their members: the Party he had been so eager to serve not only stripped him of his political power and ruined his reputation in the show trial, but sentenced him to death, and the fact that he was utterly innocent was but the perfect icing on the cake – *Schadenfreude*.

A second interpretation is based on a principal understanding of the idealistic appeal and political attraction Marxism-Leninism⁹ had had for intellectuals in the first half of the 20th century. Like so many intellectuals all over the world, Clementis sincerely believed that Socialism would change the world and humanity for the better, bestowing justice on the oppressed workers. His criticism of the Molotov-Ribbentrop Pact of 1939 resulted in his expulsion from the Party while in exile. During the war, Communists from a proper proletarian background, that is, the working class, such as Alexander Dubček (1921–1992), who would be elected general secretary of the KSČ in January 1968,¹⁰

---

8 "Die ich rief, die Geister, werd ich nun nicht los"; the English translation is by Edwin Zeydel from 1955 on germanstories.vcu.edu/goethe/zauber_dual.html; accessed 22 June 2014.

9 I shall be using the concept "Marxism-Leninism" as the official ideology of the Soviet Union after Lenin's death in 1924 and the satellite states after the building of the Soviet bloc in the aftermath of WWII.

10 A selection in chronological order: Gordon H. Skilling, *Czechoslovakia's Interrupted Revolution* (Princeton, NJ: Princeton University Press, 1976); *Sedm pražských dnů. 21.–27. srpen 1968. Dokumentace* (Praha: Academia, 1990); Alexander Dubček, *Leben für die Freiheit* (München: Bertelsmann, 1993); *Hope Dies Last. The Autobiography of Alexander Dubcek* (London: HarperCollins, 1993); Jan Pauer, *Prag 1968. Der Einmarsch des Warschauer Paktes. Hintergründe – Planung – Durchführung* (Bremen: Edition Temmen, 1995); Kieran Williams, *The Prague Spring and its Aftermath. Czechoslovak Politics 1968–1970* (Cambridge: Cambridge University Press, 1997); with a focus on Slovakia see the excellent Valerián Bystrický a kol., *Rok 1968 na Slovensku a v Československu* (Bratislava: HÚ SAV, 2008).

and non-Communists alike were fighting the Germans in the Eastern Slovak Tatra mountains, while Clementis was contributing to the war effort with his radio broadcasts from London, instilling hope and strengthening morale at home.

In 1945, the KSČ rehabilitated him, restoring his membership because of his talent for strategic thinking, brilliant rhetoric and unremitting loyalty to Marxism-Leninism. He was the only Slovak fluent in the languages of the Allies: he spoke French, English, German, Hungarian and Russian. The comrades in the Slovak National Council (SNR) suggested appointing him assistant secretary of state, because he had worked with the Beneš government in exile and had always spoken out for an equal standing of the Slovaks with the Czechs in the post-war Republic.

By 25 February 1948, the KSČ was in control of the country, referred to as the "victorious February" (*vítězní únor*).[11] Clementis' political career blossomed. In 1952, he was one of those accused of high treason in the Stalinist show trial of Slánský et al. and executed. But four years later, the political tides turned again: in his secret speech to the 20th Congress of the Soviet Communist Party on 25 February 1956, General Secretary Nikita S. Chruščev (1894–1971) revealed Stalin's crimes, which prompted the *thaw*,

---

[11] Selected and recommended studies in chronological order: Karel Kaplan, *The Short March. The Communist Takeover in Czechoslovakia 1945–1948* (London: Hurst & Co, 1987); *1948. Únor 1948 v Československu: Nástup komunistické totality a proměny společnosti* (Praha: Ústav pro soudobé dějiny AV ČR, v.v.i., 2011); "Na cestě k moci a ovládnutí státu", in *Český a slovenský komunismus (1921–2011)* (Praha: Ústav pro studium totalitních režimů, 2012), 70-116. For an analysis of the political persecutions after 1948 in Slovakia see the superb Jan Pešek, "Najbrutálnejšie obdobie komunistického režimu (1948–1953)", in *Štátna moc a spoločnosť na Slovensku 1945 – 1948 – 1989* (Bratislava: HÚ SAV a Prodama, 2013), 193-311. For an analysis of media reports about the 'victorious 25 February 1948' see Stanislav Holubec, "Léta 1948–1949", in *Ještě nejsme za vodou. Obrazy druhých a historická paměť v období postkomunistické transformace* (Praha: Scriptorium, 2015), 124-136. I thank Francis Raska for recommending Holubec's study to me.

the short-term liberalization in domestic affairs of the bloc states and Soviet relations with the principal class enemy USA. In Marxist-Leninist terms, the Stalin cult and the crimes and purges committed under the reign of the *velikii vožd* (the Great Leader Stalin) had been a subjective aberration, a mistaken interpretation of the legacy of Marx and Lenin. In its perennial wisdom, the KSČ understood the objective signs of the times, the need for social, political and economic reforms. Because of General Secretary Antonín Novotný's (1904–1975) ideological intransingence, Czechoslovakia did not de-stalinize until the early 1960s. Novotný ruled the country with an iron fist. The KSČ embarked on a reform course only in January 1968, when even the loyal StB had had enough of Novotný, who was driving a wedge between the Slovaks and the Czechs, endangering the unity of the state and the people. The CC voted Novotný out and appointed Dubček head of state and party.

Had the show trial of 1952 not happened and Clementis not been executed, he might have been elected Deputy General Secretary to Slánský after Gottwald's death in 1953 and steered the country onto a reform course. He might have, and this is, of course, speculation, established a Czecho-Slovak federation with the support of reform-minded Slovak and Czech comrades. With Clementis as a powerful Slovak voice in the CC KSČ, the much-needed economic and political reforms might have begun already in 1953, after Stalin and Gottwald's deaths. The Prague Spring thus might not have happened with the vehemence it did under Dubček – and spared the country the invasion of Warsaw Pact troops on 21 August 1968 and the Soviet occupation that would end in 1990.

A third viewpoint is a combination of the first and second. I am an ardent defender of modern liberal democracy and Capitalist market economy, but I also understand why Marxism-Leninism was so attractive a choice in the first half of the 20th century, not only to intellectuals and academically trained professionals, but also to the agricultural workers in Slovakia. I shall attempt to present a *fair and balanced interpretation* of Clementis' political thought, rendered vibrant in his articles, speeches for the BBC in exile and the unfinished memoirs his wife Lída (*1910–??) published in 1964, after the accused of the show trial were rehabilitated in 1963.[12] The source material I found in the archives in Bratislava, Martin and Prague is available to the English reader for the first time.

I want to find out who Clementis was as a person and understand his reasoning, ideas and political motivation on the background of the historical context. My aim is to present a comprehensive portrait of a politician, diplomat and thinker, who was of crucial importance for his country's politics before, during and after WWII. Clementis has been undeservedly forgotten by European history; the intention of this volume is thus to bring him back to the European historical memory – and with him, an insight into Slovak politics in the 20th century.

Communism in Czechoslovakia collapsed in November 1989 with the Velvet Revolution; the Cold War ceased to exist in 1991 with the dissolution of the Warsaw Pact. On 1 January 1993, Slovakia became a sovereign state, in spite of the fact that the dissolution, also referred to as Velvet Divorce, was a violation of the Czechoslovak Federal Constitution.[13] The Velvet Divorce ended

---

[12] Vladimír Clementis, *Nedokončená kronika* (Bratislava: Slovenské vydavateľstvo krásnej literatúry, 1964). Lída Clementisová was born in Bratislava in 1910; the exact date of her death is unknown.

[13] After long negotiations, Czech Prime Minister Václav Klaus (*1941) and Slovak Premier Vladimír Mečiar (*1942) could find no common course of economic privatization; they agreed in the summer of 1992 to divide the state, popularly referred to as the Velvet Divorce (*Sametový rozchod*), an analogy to the Velvet Revolution (*Sametová revolúcia*) of 1989, stressing the non-violent character of the revolution and the negotiations. The agreement was a violation of the Czechoslovak Federal Constitution, since only a plebiscite

the Czechoslovak Federation (ČSFR), and the Czech and Slovak Republics became sovereign states.[14] The Slovak Republic joined NATO and the EU in 2004. Twenty-five years after the collapse of Communism in Europe, it is high time for a critical biography of Clementis, who was a loyal Party member, a talented lawyer and gifted intellectual. Whether one agrees with his unremitting belief in Marxism-Leninism or not, there is no doubt that Clementis was a crucially important politician for the Slovaks.

Why is this study the first biography of Clementis in English? I think there are two reasons: first, he was a Communist, dedicated to the ideals of Marxism-Leninism, the West's principal theoretical adversary during the Cold War. The Marxist-Leninist system in Europe, save for Belarus that is being governed by what one could call a neo-Soviet regime, is *de facto* and *de jure* a thing of the past. Second, international academe is still largely ignoring Slovak

---

could have rendered such a decision legitimate. See Karel Vodička, "Wie der Koalitionsbeschluss zur Auflösung der ČSFR zustande kam", in *Osteuropa 45*, no. 2 (1994): 175-186, 182. In a survey in 1990, 9.6% of Slovaks and 5.3% of Czechs were in favour of separation; in 1991, 11% of Slovaks and 6% of Czechs supported the dissolution of the federation. The separation prompted President Václav Havel (1936–2011) to resign in protest; Vodička, 181. Because of the different structures of the Slovak and Czech economies, the transformation hit the Slovaks much harder than the Czechs: the unemployment rate in the first half of 1992 was 2.7% in the Czech part and 11.3% in the Slovak part; Jiří Kosta, "Systemwandel in der Tschechoslowakei. Ökonomische und politische Aspekte", in *Osteuropa 41*, no. 9 (1990): 802-818, 993. The most detailed analysis of the political and economic aspects of the separation is Jan Rychlík, *Rozdělení Česko-Slovenska, 1989–1992* (Praha: Vyšehrad, 2012).

[14] The best reference book in English is Mikuláš Teich, Dušan Kováč and Martin D. Brown, eds., *Slovakia in History* (Cambridge: Cambridge University Press, 2011). See also the encyclopaedia of Slovak history by Vojtech Dangl, Valerián Bystrický a kol., *Chronológia Dejín Slovenska a Slovákov. Od najstarších čias po súčasnosť. Dejiny v dátumoch, dátumy v dejinách, vol I a II* (Bratislava: Veda, 2014).

history and historiography, mainly because regrettably few excellent Slovak historical studies are available in a world language such as English, French or German. Therefore, a biography that scrutinizes the political circumstances and conditions Clementis faced and acted upon should also be understood as a contribution to the history of Central European political thought in the first half of the 20th century.

The scientific literature about Clementis in Slovak is modest, in Czech non-existent. The principal study in English[15] about the show trial of 1952 focuses on the former General Secretary Slánský, mentioning Clementis briefly in connection with the charges brought against Gustáv Husák (1913–1991) and Laco Novomeský (1904–1976), the most prominent Party members accused of 'Slovak bourgeois nationalism'.[16]

There are only four Slovak studies analysing Clementis' political thought and activities: Holotíková and Plevza[17] published their superb biography in the liberal atmosphere of the Prague

---

[15] Karel Kaplan, *Report on the Murder of the General Secretary* (Columbus: Ohio State University Press, 1990), 60-73.

[16] The first scholarly biography of Husák is Slavomír Michálek, Miroslav Londák a kol., *Gustáv Husák. Moc politiky. Politik moci* (Bratislava: Veda, 2013). For a review see my "A Man Motivated by Power", *New Eastern Europe 4*, no. 5 (2014): 156-160. See also my attempt at a psychological profile of Husák in "Vertrauen ist nichts, Macht ist alles. Gustáv Husák (1913–1991) und die tschechoslowakische Normalisierung. Versuch eines politischen Psychogramms", in *Vertrauen* (Basel: Schwabe, 2015), 161-179. Excellent analysis of the trial of the 'Slovak bourgeois nationalists' and its connection with the Slánský trial is Jan Pešek, "Nepriateľ so straníckou legitimáciou. Proces s tzv. Slovenskými buržoáznymi nacionalistami", in *Storočie procesov. Súdy, politika a spoločnosť v moderných dejinách Slovenska* (Bratislava: Veda, 2013), 210-226.

[17] Zdenka Holotíková a Viliam Plevza, *Vladimír Clementis* (Bratislava: Vydavateľstvo politickej literatúry v edícii Postavy slovenskej politiky, 1968); in the years of the so-called *normalization* (*normalizácia*), the neo-Stalinist *status quo ante* 1968, the publishing house *Pravda* published a second censured edition in Bratislava in 1972. I shall be referring to the uncensored edition of 1968. I thank Slavomír Michálek for providing me with a copy of the 1968 version.

Spring in 1968. Drug's study is an informative compilation of Clementis' journalism.[18] Čierny scrutinizes Clementis' diplomatic efforts and political positions at the Czechoslovak Foreign Ministry after 1945.[19] To honour the acting Assistant Secretary of State (Deputy Foreign Minister), the Czechoslovak publisher *Obroda* issued a collection of Clementis' London broadcasts in 1947.[20] In 1967, Holotíková published a collection of his articles, speeches and interpellations in parliament, covering the years 1922 to 1938 in two volumes.[21] An anthology summarizes the contributions to the scientific conference about Clementis that took place in May 2002, organized jointly by the Foreign Ministry of the Slovak Republic and the Slovak Institute for International Studies in May 2002.[22] In 2012, a conference remembered Clementis as a patriot and European;[23] a compilation of his memoirs and letters was published in 1998.[24] A brief summary of Clementis' life appeared in 2002.[25]

---

[18] Štefan Drug, *Vladimír Clementis. Život a dielo v dokumentoch* (Martin: Osveta, 1993).
[19] Ján Čierny, *Vladimír Clementis. Diplomat* (Bratislava: Literárne informačné centrum, 1999).
[20] Dr. Vladimír Clementis, *Odkazy z Londýna* (Bratislava: Nakladateľstvo Obroda, 1947).
[21] Vladimír Clementis, *Vzduch našich čias. Články. State, prejavy, polemiky 1922–1934, vol. I, 1934–1938, vol. II* (Bratislava: Vydavateľstvo politickej literatúry, 1967).
[22] *Vladimír Clementis. 1902–1952. Zborník príspevkov z konferencie 28. 5. 2002 v Bratislave* (Bratislava: Ministerstvo zahraníčných vecí Slovenskej republiky, Slovenský inštitút medzinárodných štúdií, 2002).
[23] Peter Juza, ed., *Vlastenec a Európan Vladimír Clementis. Zborník príspevok zo spomienkovej konferencie 20. 9. 2012 v Bratislave* (Bratislava: Institút ASA, 2012).
[24] *Vladimír Clementis o sebe a o Slovensku* (Topoľčany: Edícia osobnosti ľavice, primoprint, 1998), 3-44.
[25] Viliam Bernáth, *Spomienky na Vladimíra Clementisa* (Bratislava: T.R.I. MEDIUM v spolupráci s vydavateľstvom Spolku slovenských spisovateľov v edícii *SocietaS*, 2002).

X. 2 Analytical framework and conceptual matrix

The biography of a politician who had held executive functions in Party and state should include various aspects: negotiations and decision-making in his functions as MP, assistant secretary of state, foreign minister and member of the CC of the KSČ; relations to domestic politicians, parties and interest groups; foreign policy strategy; analysis of the international situation; personal allegiances, political friends and adversaries; relations to Czech and Slovak exile communities abroad; relations to the country's ethnic and political minorities; strategies on economic, education and social policy, to name but the most common ones. This biography cannot cover all these aspects.

I shall focus on two principal aspects of Clementis' thought and activities: first, an analysis of his *ideas about domestic politics,* in particular Slovakia's status in the common state. Second, an analysis of his ideas about *Czechoslovakia's foreign policy in the post-war years*, in particular, Communist Czechoslovakia's position and role as a member of the Soviet bloc in Europe and thus the country's relations with the West.

This biography consists of three chapters: chapter I introduces the reader to Clementis' childhood, upbringing, and early political activities, especially his journalism for *DAV*. In chapter II, I present his political activities in exile in France and Great Britain during WWII. Chapter III is dedicated to his last years, when his political career reached its peak. In chapter III, I present his arrest, interrogation, the show trial and, lastly, his rehabilitation in the early 1960s. In the conclusion, I shall try to answer my research questions, see below.

Analytical framework

My analysis of Clementis' political ideas and decisions unfolds in selected areas of Czechoslovak domestic politics in the years of the First Republic (1918–1938) and Czechoslovakia's foreign policy from 1945 until his fall from grace in 1950. To assume that political thought or political ideas *per se* prompt immediate political decision-making would be overly idealistic. From 1948 on, several factors determined Czechoslovakia's domestic and international affairs; these factors were crucially different from the country's affairs in the three brief years of the guided democracy of the National Front (*Národná fronta*) from 1945 to 1948. The establishment of the Stalinist system on 25 February 1948 came along with the rebuilding and centralization of governmental and state institutions according to the Soviet model.

Conceptual matrix

The aim of the following questions is to guide the reader through the analysis; they represent a conceptual matrix that is divided into two parts, the first one focussing on *Clementis' political thought* and, the second one, on his *political goals*. The conceptual matrix serves as a guideline for the reader to orientate himself.

Political thought, key concepts: national identity, political identity, Czechoslovakism, Realism, Socialism, Constitutionalism. What political arguments did Clementis use to legitimate his political goals? Which thinkers or philosophers inspired him? If he referred to Western thinkers, how did he apply their ideas to the social and economic conditions in Slovakia? Did he develop his own ideas about politics? How did he conceive of the Slovak autonomy movement led by Andrej Hlinka and the Slovak People's Party? Why was Liberalism not a political option for Slovakia? How did he reconcile his belief in Socialism with working for the centre-right exile government, the class enemy? Why, in 1945, did he join the KSČ that had expelled him for failure to toe the party line in 1939?

Political goals, key concepts: rule of law state, minority rights, foreign policy, Slovakia's status within Czechoslovakia, relations with the Soviet Union, Great Britain, France and the USA. What political goals, long-term and short-term, did Clementis pursue? What was the constitutional status of Slovakia that he projected as an MP in the First Republic and after WWII?

X. 3 Method, key issues, research interest

X. 3. 1 Method: contextual biography

This study has an interdisciplinary focus: it presents an analysis of political ideas on the background of established historical facts. My aim is to contribute to the research on the history of Central European thought. The combination of political theory analysis with contextual biography[26] is particularly suitable for Clementis' biography since it is based on a specific approach to biographical and historical writing. The *contextual biography method* offers us a deeper insight into the historical context, presupposing that a person's activities, thoughts and personal impressions cannot be separated from the historical circumstances he or she was subject to. The British historian Sir Ian Kershaw, an FBA (Fellow of the British Academy), on the method and its relevance:

> "Any attempt to incorporate such themes [technology, demography, prosperity, democratization, ecology, political violence, add. JB] in a history of twentieth-century Europe *would not by-pass the role of key individuals* who helped to shape the epoch. [...] *They are neither their prime cause nor their inevitable consequence.* New biographical approaches, which recognize this are desirable, even necessary. Their value will be, however, *in using biography as a prism on wider issues of*

---

[26] Simone Lässig, "Introduction: Biography in Modern History – Modern Historiography in Biography", in *Biography between structure and agency. Central European lives in international historiography* (New York: Berghahn, 2008), 1-26.

historical understanding and not in a narrow focus on private life and personality."[27]

The method of contextual biography and the analysis of political thought as a *dimension* of biographical writing present an interdisciplinary approach that affords a unique insight into Slovakia and Czechoslovakia's political environment: Clementis' descriptions and personal views render vibrant the historical context in which he thought and acted. His ideas and thoughts open up a *prism* on the intellectual atmosphere in the first half of the 20th century in Czechoslovakia. Clementis adhered to the Leninist principle that a Communist is allowed to think on his own, that the Party, within the confines of the theory and practice of the revolutionary road to Socialism, is tolerant of its members' differing views and opinions.

Note that I shall present no summary of the ideology that had captivated so many minds at the turn of the 20th century; Marxism-Leninism has been subject to countless historical, philosophical and sociological studies. Marx, Engels, Lenin and Stalin's works can be found in libraries and on the Internet. For those willing to delve into the depths of Marxist-Leninist theory, I recommend Sir Isaiah Berlin's (1909–1997) biography of Marx,[28] the texts of Ernest Mandel,[29] Neil Harding's analysis of Leninism[30] and Leszek Kołakowski's superb study of Marxist thought.[31] Excellent historical information is offered by Edvard Radzinsky's biography of Stalin,[32] William Taubman's biography of Chruščev,[33] *The Black*

---

[27] Ian Kershaw, "Biography and the Historian", in *Biography between* ..., 27-39; 34, 38, italics by me.
[28] Isaiah Berlin, *Karl Marx* (Princeton, NJ: Princeton University Press, 2013, (5)).
[29] Ernest Mandel's texts on http://www.ernestmandel.org; accessed 23 May 2016.
[30] Neil Harding, *Leninism* (London: MacMillan, 1996).
[31] Leszek Kołakowski, *Main Currents of Marxism* (New York, London: Norton, 2005).
[32] Edvard Radzinsky, *Stalin* (New York, Toronto: Anchor books, 1996).
[33] William Taubman, *Khrushchev. The Man and His Era* (New York, London: Norton & Co., 2004).

Book of Communism[34] and Tony Judt and Timothy Snyder's debate about intellectuals in the 20th century.[35] The series of the Cold War International History Project (CWIHP papers),[36] published at the Woodrow Wilson Centre in Washington D.C., USA, offers outstanding research about the Soviet bloc, China and international politics during the Cold War.

X. 3. 2 Key issues

X. 3. 2. 1 Czechoslovakism and the Czechoslovak Nation

Prior to the foundation of the First Czechoslovak Republic in 1918, Czech intellectuals in the Austrian and Slovak intellectuals in the Hungarian part of the Habsburg monarchy engaged in debates about their kinship, focussing on their close cultural and linguistic features.[37] For the purpose of a clear understanding of the different Slovak and Czech perceptions of the state in the interwar years, I shall briefly elaborate on Czechoslovakism as the principal political programme and philosophical basis of the state.

Czechoslovakism is a historical concept with two interpretations: first, it is the theoretical basis, the idea that Czechs and Slovaks form one nation, and second, it is the political programme of the state of the Czechs and Slovaks.[38]

---

[34] Stéphane Courtois et al., *The Black Book of Communism. Crimes. Terror. Repression* (Cambridge, MA, London: Harvard University Press, 1999).

[35] Tony Judt with Timothy Snyder, *Thinking The Twentieth Century* (New York: Penguin, 2012).

[36] Cold War International History Project at the Woodrow Wilson Centre on https://www.wilsoncenter.org/program/cold-war-international-history-project; accessed 23 May 2016.

[37] For a detailed chronology of the beginnings of political Czechoslovakism see Jan Rychlík, *Češi a Slováci ve 20. století. Česko-slovenské vztahy 1914–1945* (Bratislava, Praha: AEP, Ústav T. G. Masaryka, 1997), 23-39, referred to as *Češi a Slováci I*. Jan Rychlík, *Češi a Slováci ve 20. století. Česko-slovenské vztahy 1945–1992* (Bratislava, Praga: AEP, ÚTGM, 1998), referred to as *Češi a Slováci II*.

[38] Dušan Kováč, *Slováci. Češi. Dejiny* (Bratislava: AEP, 1997), 118-119.

At the end of WWI, on 28 October 1918, Czechoslovakia came into being as a new state in Central Europe that had formerly been ruled by the Habsburg monarchy – thanks to the efforts of the *exile troika* of Masaryk, Beneš and Milan Rastislav Štefánik (1880–1919).³⁹ In a pragmatic step, Masaryk had reformulated his Czech nation-building theory into his Czechoslovak state-building theory to convince the Allies in WWI that, on the grounds of natural law,⁴⁰ the *Czechoslovak nation* deserved sovereignty as much as Poland, whose reconstruction and sovereignty was a stipulation of US President Woodrow Wilson's famous plan of 14 points. Masaryk conceived of the Slovaks as kin of the Czechs who spoke an Eastern Czech dialect, which was clearly not the case, as Slovak had been established as a written language since 1843,⁴¹ but it

---

39 The best biography of Milan Rastislav Štefánik known to me is Peter Macho, *Milan Rastislav Štefánik. V hlavach a v srdciach* (Bratislava: HÚ SAV a Prodama, 2011). For an analysis of Štefánik's activities in France see Fréderic Guelton, Emanuelle Braud a Michal Kšiňan, *Milan Rastislav Štefánik v archívnich dokumentov Historickej služby francúzskeho ministerstva obrany* (Paris, Bratislava: service historique de la Défense, Vojkenský historický ústav, Ministerstvo obrany SR, 2008, 2009).
40 About natural law and positive law prior to the foundation of Czechoslovakia see my study "The Genesis of Czechoslovakism. An Interdisciplinary Inquiry into the Influence of Rousseau's Réligion Civile", in *East European Faces of Law and Society: Values and Practices* (Leiden: Brill Nijhoff, 2014), 307-345.
41 The Slovak patriots Ľudovít Štúr (1815–1856)), Michal Miloslav Hodža (1811–1870) and Jozef Miloslav Hurban (1817–1888) coined the Slovak written language in 1843, based on the central Slovak dialect, which was a political decision. Masaryk wrote in the first volume of his study of Russian philosophy and thought in 1913: "The Slovaks lack a language of their own, and the political conditions [they are subject to in the Hungarian kingdom, add. JB] led to the fact that the Slovak dialect vanished as a literary language"; T. G. Masaryk, "Slavjanofilství. Mesianismus právoslavné teokracie. Slavjanofilství a Panslavismus", in *Rusko a Evropa. Studie o důchovních proudech v Rusku, vol. I* (Praha: Ústav T. G. Masaryka, 1995), 181-246; 225. This was a pragmatic, clever, and, in terms of political strategy, very astute spin. Masaryk was familiar with the situation in Slovakia, since he was in constant contact with the Hlasists. One has to understand this quote not only with regard to his independence plans, but also in the context of his self-defence: he was fighting his Slovak enemies, the conservative Martinists led by Svetozár Hurban Vajanský, who were attacking him and his associates for their modern views. In the late 1890s, Masaryk and Vajanský's families befriended each other, since the Masaryks used to spend

was not internationally recognized. For reasons of political pragmatism, Masaryk conveniently ignored the efforts of the Slovak patriots in the early 19th century for their language. By declaring the Czechs and Slovaks one nation, he was able to convince the Czech and Slovak exile communities in the USA of his plan of founding the Czechoslovak nation state; they supported him by signing the Pittsburgh Agreement on 31 May 1918. Masaryk thus created a historically incorrect yet politically successful portrait of the Czechs and Slovaks as one nation, thereby liberating two nations from the Habsburg monarchy, the Czechs from Austrian and the Slovaks from Hungarian rule. In 1905 he had written:

> "Just think how we consider Bohemia, Moravia, Silesia and, finally, Slovakia as separate units! Two million Czechs [*dva miliony Čechů*] live in the Hungarian kingdom! [...] We won't give up *a third of our nation*."[42]

In the decade before the war, Masaryk had pragmatically blended the historic rights of the lands of the Bohemian Crown with the natural law justification for the Czechoslovak nation.[43] With natural law, he justified to the WWI Allies the Czechoslovak nation's right to a sovereign nation state; with the historic rights of the Bohemian Crown, he legitimated the sovereignty of the Czechoslovak nation

---

their summer holidays in Slovakia. About the end of their friendship see my "Thomas G. Masaryk and Svetozár Hurban Vajanský. A Czecho-Slovak friendship?", *KOSMAS. Czechoslovak and Central European Journal 26*, no. 2 (2013): 50-62. On Masaryk's role in the foundation of the Slovak *Hlas* movement I recommend Zdeněk Urban, "K Masarykovu vztahu ke Slovensku před první světovou válkou", in *Masaryk a Slovensko (soubor statí)* (Praha: Masarykova společnost a Ústav T. G. Masaryka, 1992), 68-89; Dušan Kováč, *Slováci. Češi. Dějiny*, 59-63, and Tomas D. Marzík, "The Slovakophile Relationship of T. G. Masaryk and Karel Kálal prior to 1914", in *T. G. Masaryk (1850–1937), Thinker and Politician (London: SSEES, 1989)*, 191-209. Masaryk's political advice was crucial to the Slovak student association *Detvan*, as its members lacked a political perspective for Slovakia. At the turn of the 20th century, the Slovak students in Prague could gather freely for political and cultural discussions in their mother tongue.

42 Tomáš G. Masaryk, "Proststředky národa malého", in *Ideály humanitní* (Praha: Melantrich, 1991), 85-88; 87; italics by me.
43 Anton Štefánek, *Masaryk a Slovensko* (Praha: Náklad spisovatelový, 1931), 34.

over the territory of the Czech lands with a large German minority and Slovakia with a large Hungarian minority. Masaryk shared the view of the Czech intellectual and journalist Karel Havlíček (1821–1856)[44], who had pursued the argument that the codification of the Slovak language in 1843 had been a breach of faith, similar to the breaking of a contract, which is referred to in the literature as *odtrhati se* (to tear oneself away, to leave the union, or, to cut the umbilical cord). Such a contract, however, had never existed:

> "In the historical literature, in particular the Czech literature, the concepts of 'linguistic separation' [*jazykovej odluke*] or 'farewell' [*rozluke*] have been in use for years. These concepts, however, are incorrect. The concepts of 'separation' and 'farewell' implicate a former union [*jednota*] that did not exist. Not even the Slovaks were at one with themselves. And only a part of the Slovaks used Czech as their written language."[45]

From Masaryk's point of view, the Czechoslovak state had a threefold legitimacy: first, the state was legitimate in ethical terms, since the people would be sovereign in a democracy and rule-of-law state that embodied the values of liberty, equality and fraternity. An important factor was Masaryk's personal life; he was married to the American Protestant Charlotte Garrigue (1850–1923).[46] Thanks to his wife, Masaryk had an insight into how US democracy worked – and why Austrian Imperial rule did not and should not.

Second, Czechoslovakia would be legitimate in terms of public international law, since the victorious Allies would dictate

---

[44] A selection of studies on Havlíček: Barbara K. Reinfeld, *Karel Havlíček (1821–1856). A National Liberation Leader of the Czech Renascence* (New York, NY, Boulder, CO: Columbia University Press, 1982); Ilona Bažantová, "Zapomenutý ekonom Karel Havlíček Borovský", *Politická Ekonomie 5*, no. 2 (1999): 621-629; Marie L. Neudorflová, "Karel Havlíček, T. G. Masaryk a demokracie", in *Spisovatelé, společnost a noviny v promínách doby* (Praha: Literární Archiv Národného Písemnictví, 2006), 11-28.

[45] Kováč, *Slováci. Češi. Dejiny*, 36-37; emphasis by me.

[46] For a portrait of Masaryk's wife Charlotte and their eldest daughter Alice see my *Seven Czech Women. Portraits of Courage, Humanism and Enlightenment* (Stuttgart, New York: ibidem, Columbia University Press, 2015), 35-85.

the terms and conditions of the peace negotiations in St. Germain and, of crucial importance since Hungary was involved, at Trianon. The Allies should reward the Czechoslovaks for their military support; the *legia*, an army of a state that was not yet internationally recognized, had been fighting at the Allies' side on all fronts and also against the Bolshevik government in Russia.

Third, the state would be legitimate because of the consent of the Czech and Slovak émigré communities in the USA who had emigrated from Austria-Hungary exactly because of the political system of Feudalism and Aristocratism. The distinguished Czech historian Jan Rychlík about Czechoslovakism:

> "To pretend that the Czechs and Slovaks were one nation was generally accepted. While many Czechs truly believed that Czechs and Slovaks formed one nation, the Slovaks considered the Czechoslovak nation as a strategic construct that should be given up once the goal [the international recognition of the Czechoslovak Republic, add. JB] had been achieved. From a Czech perspective, the idea of one nation should form the basis of the state. [...] Yet in that phase of development one should not understand the concept of Czechoslovakism in a negative fashion, since, without it, there would have been no Czechoslovakia at all."[47]

The distinguished Slovak historian Dušan Kováč about the building of the state:

> "Czech politicians often said that the Slovaks would get everything they wished for. The majority of the Slovaks accepted the idea that, in the first phase, in the interest of international recognition and a smooth separation from the Hungarian administration, the centralist model of the state would be the best solution. All forces concentrated on achieving that basic goal – a plan that not too long ago had been referred to as the crazy ideas of an ageing Prague professor."[48]

---

[47] Jan Rychlík, *Češi a Slováci I*, 54-55.
[48] Kováč, *Slováci. Česi. Dejiny*, 66-67. Quoting "the crazy ideas of an ageing Prague professor", Kováč refers to the Czech journalist Ferdinand Peroutka (1895–1978), a close confidant of Masaryk's who published, in 1927, a book about the foundation of the state. Peroutka criticized the Prague politicians who, during WWI, conceived of Masaryk as a "dangerous nut", since he planned to break up Austria-Hungary; Ferdinand Peroutka, "O účasti na revoluci" (1924), in *Kdo nás osvobodil?* (Praha: Náklad Svazu národního osvobození, Tisk 'Pokrok', 1927), 5-25.

Was the foundation of Czechoslovakia on 28 October 1918 legitimate in democratic terms? Yes, for three reasons: first, the independent wish to form a state with the Czechs expressed by the Slovak National Council (SNR) on 30 October 1918;[49] second, the negotiations with Czech politicians in Geneva in October 1918;[50] and

---

[49] The Martin Declaration signed on 30 October 1918 was the Slovak National Council's (SNR) independent expression of the desire to leave the Hungarian kingdom and form a common state with the Czechs, while the Prague Declaration of 28 October included Slovakia as a part of the common state. Because of war censorship, the signatories in Martin did not know about the events in Prague when they agreed on the contents and formulation of the declaration. Milan Hodža (1878–1944) informed them when he reached Martin during the evening of 30 October. Vavro Šrobár signed the Prague Declaration as representative of the SNR in Prague; Márian Hronský a Miroslav Pekník, *Martinská deklarácia. Cesta slovenskej politiky k vzniku Česko-Slovenska* (Bratislava: Veda, 2008), 264. See also Jörg K. Hoensch, *Geschichte der Tschechoslowakei* (Stuttgart, Berlin, Köln: Kohlhammer, 1992 (3)), 39, and Jan B. Kozák, *T. G. Masaryk a vznik Washingtonské deklarace v říjnu 1918* (Praha: Melantrich, 1968), 27. Hoensch and Kozák consider the Slovak radicals' claims for autonomy in the 1920s and 1930s as unsubstantial; their questioning of the legitimacy of the Pittsburgh Agreement and the Prague Declaration had no legal grounds, as no government of the nations at war had officially recognized the SNR. The council emerged as a result of a pragmatic *ad hoc* decision of the patriots convening in Martin to validate their subsequent declaration. The foundation of the SNR and the Martin declaration should be understood as an immediate reaction to Austro-Hungarian foreign minister Gyula Andrassy's (1823–1890) receipt of President Wilson's (1856–1924) note on the conditions for signing a peace agreement on 27 October 1918. Hronský and Pekník stress that the Martin Declaration did not create a "new nation, but a new state", 281.

[50] In mid-October, Beneš met with delegates from the Czech National Council in Geneva: they agreed on the political system of a Republic and the composition of the first provisional government with Masaryk as president. Karel Kramář (1860–1937) was the first Prime Minister, Beneš kept the Ministry of Foreign Affairs, Antonín Švehla (1873–1933) led the Ministry of Internal Affairs, Alois Rašín (1867–1923) the Ministry of Finance and František Soukup (1871–1940) the Ministry of Justice. Václav Klofáč (1868–1942) was the Minister of Defence and Štefánik the Minister of War. On 28 October, the Revolutionary National Assembly (*Revoluční Národní Shromáždění*) declared the independence of the sovereign Czechoslovak Republic in Prague; the first Czechoslovak government was established the same day.

third, the consent of the émigré communities of Czechs and Slovaks in the USA who had signed the Pittsburgh Agreement.

The *zeitgeist* was friendly to democracy and the nation state, but without the lobbying of the exile *troika* in France, Great Britain and the USA, the Allies would not have recognized Czechoslovakia at the peace conferences in Versailles and Trianon. A crucially important factor was the *legia*, the Czechoslovak army that Slovak and Czech soldiers who had deserted from the Austro-Hungarian army had formed during the war. The *legia* had proved the Czechs and Slovaks' wish for independence in a common state, fighting at the side of the Allies. The Allies perceived the *legia* as the army of a future state, a state in the making. A third reason for the Allies' recognition of Czechoslovakia's new territorial borders was the *fait accompli* in Slovakia: Czechoslovak troops had secured the state's borders at the Danube by November 1918. Masaryk's associates in Slovakia immediately began to replace the Hungarian administration in early November, and by the summer of 1920, when the Trianon peace negotiations with Hungary started, Czechoslovak rule was firmly established in Slovakia.

Thanks to Masaryk's conception of the Czechoslovak state and the continuous efforts of Štefánik, Beneš and Vavro Šrobár (1867–1950)[51] in Slovakia, the Republic came into being. According to Masaryk's thinking, the last phase of the historical democratization process had begun with the foundation of the sovereign state. From now on, there was only one goal the Czechoslovaks had to concentrate on: to secure the state and its institutions through the citizens' continuous improvement of the social, economic and political conditions – their lives in a democracy and sovereign state.

---

[51] Josette Baer, *A Life Dedicated to the Republic. Vavro Šrobár's Slovak Czechoslovakism* (Stuttgart, New York: ibidem, Columbia University Press, 2014).

Masaryk achieved what no philosopher before him had achieved – he had created a state, his Platonic dream of the *polis*, yet without Plato's authoritarian order. The professor had created a state with the people as the sovereign, fulfilling Rousseau's dream of democracy. He was the *spiritus rector* of Czechoslovak sovereignty, following his admired Plato's imperative that philosophers should be kings, *viz.*, in the 20th century, presidents and moral leaders.

The First Republic's inherent problem that Hitler would use to carve up Czechoslovakia was Masaryk's *constitutional construct of the Czechoslovak nation*, a concept Czechs and Slovaks were divided about. The Czechs conceived of the state as a unitarist one,[52] a realisation of the Czech programme of independence, with Slovakia as a territorial attachment and enlargement. The Slovaks, on the other hand, rejected the idea of the political nation, because they had only the worst memories of the concept of a 'political nation': the Magyar interpretation of a united Hungarian political nation had resulted in the policy of assimilation of non-Magyar citizens.[53] Masaryk, however, did not see the Slovak viewpoint as a problem:

> "Masaryk's personal origins made it difficult for him to understand an issue that was no problem to him. [...] He felt a Czechoslovak in the truest sense of the word, that is, as Czech and Slovak in one person."[54]

At the turn of the 20th century, intellectuals of the two nations began to promote *cultural Czechoslovakism*, the idea of kinship that originated in the closeness of their languages. In 1908, the annual meeting of the association *Československá jednota* (Czechoslovak

---

[52] Kováč, *Slováci. Češi. Dejiny*, 122.
[53] Kováč, *Slováci. Češi. Dejiny*, 123.
[54] Hain, 225. Masaryk's father was a Slovak coachman, his mother a Moravian cook who spoke German; Masaryk grew up in the Eastern Moravian Hodonín, a village close to the Slovak border.

union) in the Moravian spa town of Luhačovice⁵⁵ became a tradition of Czechoslovakism and its adherents; the meetings improved relations, since the members not only discussed themes of cultural exchange and education, but also economic and political issues.

In a survey the Slovak journal *Prúdy* (*Currents*), edited by former Hlasists,⁵⁶ undertook in 1914, 39 Czech and 37 Slovak intellectuals addressed issues of political unity in terms of agriculture, politics, economy and culture; because of the war, the survey's results were published only in 1919. But they illustrated that progressive Czech and Slovak intellectuals truly believed in the

---

[55] Rychlík, *Češi a Slováci I*, 38.
[56] The Hlasists derived their name from the journal *Hlas* (*The Voice*) that they published from 1898 to 1904; they were inspired by the progressive and modern political thought of Masaryk. Masaryk's Realism was his method of thinking about politics and society; his approach was based on the empiricism and positivism applied in the natural sciences. Vajanský, on the other hand, was preaching passivity, endurance, instilling fantasies of liberation by the Russian Tsar. In general, the Catholic faction was preaching very much the same – save for the hope of liberation by Russia, since they were loyal to the Vatican. Both camps, the Lutherans and the Catholics alike, were neither capable of nor willing to offer the citizens a feasible political programme that would fight the assimilation and the concomitant discrimination of the Slovak patriots. True, the Hlasists were a tiny group, struggling to survive, but after the *prevrat*, they were representing the young Republic and its democracy in Slovakia, forming the new political elite and governing Slovakia according to the democratic principles of Czechoslovak state theory. Two former Hlasists crucially determined Czechoslovak history: the astronomer and general of the French Army Štefaník and the physician Šrobár. An attempt in the 1930s to renew the Hlasist movement with the journal *Nový hlas* (*New Voice*) failed, owing to major changes in the Slovak political landscape; Ivan Kamenec, "Novohlasistická skupina a Robotnická academia na Slovensku v rokoch 1933–1937", in *Slovensko v labyrinte moderných európskych dejín. Pocta historikov Milanovi Zemkovi* (Bratislava: HÚ SAV, 2014), 211-222.

existence of a Czechoslovak nation.[57] Yet, prior to WWI, the majority of the Czech politicians considered the monarchy as a fact and could not imagine the Czech lands outside of Austria, let alone the end of the monarchy.

The activities of cultural Czechoslovakism formed the ideological basis of *political Czechoslovakism*, the programme of and demand for a common independent state. For both nations, Czechoslovakia was a perfect political solution. The Slovaks would benefit from the political experience and economic support of the Czechs. The Czechs on their own, that is, without the argument of the Czechoslovak nation and her right to sovereignty over her territory, could not have convinced the Allies to recognize the new state, which prompted the dissolution of the Habsburg Monarchy. The plan of a Czechoslovak state, carved out of the Habsburg Empire, attacked the core of the Austro-Hungarian Empire: the regime of Dualism that had been in power since 1867.

Slovak and Czech politicians supported Czechoslovakism as the state's ethical legitimation. Some had a Czechoslovak political identity, considering themselves members of the Czech or Slovak nation, respectively. Others embodied a Czechoslovak national and political identity, thus believing that Czechs and Slovaks formed one nation. National and political identities were also formed along confessional lines. In general, it can be said that Czech Protestants, Catholics and Jews welcomed the common state. Slovak Lutherans and Jews were generally supportive of the common state, as it meant liberation and democratization, while,

---

[57] *Prúdy V*, no. 9-10 (1919): 399-567. *Prúdy* can be seen as a re-edition or follow up journal of *Hlas*: it offered the readers a secular political perspective, a focus on scientific methods in politics and the promotion of the political union and kinship of Czechs and Slovaks. For a superb summary of the history and significance of *Prúdy* see Milan Zemko, "Prúdisti v čase, ktorý trhol oponou", in *Kapitoly z histórie stredoeurópskeho priestoru v 19. a 20. Storočí. Pocta k 70-ročnému jubileu Dušana Kováča* (Bratislava: HÚ SAV, 2012), 269-280.

on the other hand, Slovak Catholics conceived of the ruling Czech liberalism as atheistic. They perceived the Czech leadership in the common state as centralistic, in the sense of discriminating against their religious beliefs and way of life.

Central planning from Prague was necessary because of the different economic conditions in the Czech lands and Slovakia. While the Czech lands had experienced an industrial boom in the 19th century, Slovakia's industrialization was protracted because of Hungary's socio-economic system. Industrialization in Slovakia began only in the 1920s. Czechoslovak institution-building began immediately after the Prague declaration of independence on 28 October 1918; it replaced the Austrian and Hungarian administrations with the institutions of a modern representative democracy that included minority rights.[58]

This process of coordination and centralization would provoke resistance from Slovak circles. The new administrative institutions, universities, hospitals and factories required trained personnel, which only the Czechs could provide, since the Magyar personnel refused to serve Czechoslovakia or left for Hungary after 1918. Some Slovaks, led by the Catholic priest Andrej Hlinka (1864–1938), who became a radical autonomist in the mid-1920s, felt overruled by the 'atheist and Hussite Czechs' in their own homeland.

---

[58] The Germans and the Hungarians formed the two largest minorities and the delegates of their parties enjoyed political participation and representation in the Czechoslovak parliament; for the legal aspects of minority rights in the Czechoslovak constitution I recommend Hain, 217-229. For a historiography of identity-formation see Jiří Kořalka, "Nationsbildung und nationale Identität der Deutschen, Österreicher, Tschechen und Slovaken um die Mitte des 19. Jahrhunderts", in *Ungleiche Nachbarn. Demokratische und nationale Emanzipation bei Deutschen, Tschechen und Slovaken (1815–1914)* (Essen: Klartext, 1993), 33-48.

From the text of the Pittsburgh agreement, American Slovaks and autonomists at home deduced an alleged promise by Masaryk to establish Slovak autonomy. Equating the sentences "Slovakia will have her own administration, her parliament and her courts" and "Slovak will be the administrative language in schools, in the administration and overall in public life" with a constitutionally granted autonomy, they protested against what they conceived of as "Czech centralism".[59]

Czechoslovakism as state-building theory ceased to exist with the Munich Agreement of 30 September 1938. Great Britain, Italy and France considered Czechoslovakia a pawn sacrifice to save the peace. In Czechoslovakia, the majority of the Sudeten Germans had been rallying against the Republic, supporting the *Sudetendeutsche Partei* led by Konrad Henlein (1898–1945). Czechoslovak politicians were trying to save what could be saved of the Republic, but the radicals of the HSĽS (Hlinka's Slovak People's Party) used Munich as a platform to push forward the issue of Slovak autonomy. Munich prompted the Žilina Agreement (*Žilinská dohoda*) in October 1938, which led to Slovakia's autonomy; the Vienna Arbitration (*Viedenská arbitráž*) in November 1938 consigned southern and eastern parts of Slovakia to Hungary and, on 15 March 1939, the Republic ceased to exist: Germany invaded the Czech lands and established the protectorate of Bohemia and Moravia. On 14 March, Slovakia had to proclaim independence; she was a pseudo-sovereign state at Hitler's beck and call.

The majority of the Slovaks accepted the declaration of Slovak autonomy on 6 October 1938. A prominent signatory of the Žilina Agreement was Jozef Tiso (1887–1947),[60] who had been an

---

[59] The text of the Pittsburgh agreement, document no. 14, in Jan Galandauer, *Vznik Československé Republiky 1918* (Praha: Svoboda, 1988), 299-300.

[60] The best biography of Tiso known to me is Ivan Kamenec, *Tragédia politika, kňaza a človeka. Dr. Jozef Tiso, 1887–1947* (Bratislava: Premedia, 2013).

MP for the HSĽS in the First Republic. The Czechoslovak government, betrayed by its former allies and in a state of disorientation because of the resignation of President Edvard Beneš and his government, accepted the Agreement. Czechoslovakia's status changed to a federation with a new official name for Slovakia, *Slovenska krajina*; the country's new official name was the hyphenated *Czecho-Slovakia*. The government in Prague was responsible for international affairs, defence, currency, the state budget and customs, public traffic and the post.[61]

The Žilina Agreement's rationale was that of *loyalty to the Republic in exchange for autonomy*. Slovak self-government would only strengthen the Republic. From the viewpoint of a Slovak citizen, the Žilina Agreement made sense: why would they want to support 'Prague centralism' if Prague did not acknowledge their demands for self-government within the common state? From a Czech perspective, 'Slovak autonomism' unnecessarily burdened the Republic at the time the state had lost the substantial territories of the Sudetenland to Germany. But in the municipal elections of May 1938, the HSĽS was no longer the strongest party:

> "1,452 communities held elections. Slovenska Jednota [an electoral association of Agrarians, Social Democrats, the Slovak National Party and other small parties, add. JB] received the majority of the votes with 43.93%, followed by HSĽS with 26.93% and KSČ with 7.4%. [...] The results of these elections were never published, but they confirm that the Slovak citizens were aware of the threat against the Republic and supported its preservation."[62]

---

[61] Kováč, *Dejiny Slovenska* (Praha: Nakladatelství Lidové Noviny, 2007 (2)), 210.

[62] Kováč, *Dejiny Slovenska*, 209. Slovenská Jednota won the majority because SNS left the autonomist bloc and joined the former centralist parties. In the parliamentary elections of 1935, the autonomist bloc of HSĽS and SNS had won 30.1% of the vote; the parties of the Rusinian and Polish minorities had supported them, because they also pursued autonomy. The ruling Agrarians had achieved 17.6% and their coalition partner, the Social Democrats 11.3%;

After WWII, the idea of Czechoslovakism became again the theoretical fundament of the common state, but now with a different interpretation: Czechoslovakia was formally declared as a *common state of two brother nations*, which meant that Czechoslovakism as the idea of the Czechoslovak nation *de jure* ceased to exist – yet not *de facto*. In practice, the old centralism was back with the NF, and the Slovaks' attempts to achieve self-government failed. The federation, planned in April 1968 as an expression of the political liberalism of the eight months of the Spring of Prague, would foresee a better representation of the Slovaks' interests in Prague. Yet, the law about the federation the Husák government adopted in 1969 was bereft of its true sense, since the KSČ did not federalize. In a single-Party system without clear rights for the Czechoslovak Communist Party KSČ and the Slovak Communist Party KSS, a federation that would have deserved the name, even in Marxist-Leninist theory, simply did not work. Marxism-Leninism and the very thought of a federation mutually exclude themselves in theoretical terms.

X. 3. 2. 2 Antisemitism

A few remarks on *antisemitism* are necessary to understand the 1952 show trial with its characteristic aspect of antisemitism. In the first decade of the 20th century, antisemitism was as virulent in Central as in Western Europe. In the 19th and 20th centuries, the Christian world adhered to the antisemitism promoted by the Christian churches of all confessions. Contemptuous and despicable remarks about the economically successful Jews were socially acceptable, reinforcing traditional Christian stereotypes. Even after WWII and the horrors of the Holocaust, the liberal USA had quotas that restricted Jewish students' access to universities.

Alena Bartlová, "Posledné parlamentné voľby v máj 1935", in *V medzivojnovom Československu 1918–1939* (Bratislava: Veda, 2012), 439-440; 439.

In the Austro-Hungarian Empire, Jewish citizens had to speak German and Hungarian, the language of the ruling nations, to protect their sources of income. As an *entrepreneurial minority*, they were shopkeepers, worked in trade and owned inns and pubs since they were not allowed to own land; business demanded that they comply with the administration, which implied the maintenance of smooth relations with the authorities. The Jewish term "assimilation" signified a current of thought that projected political equality with the gentiles; modernization, that is, the rejection of religious and social conservatism, was an important factor of Jewish assimilation, the melding into the gentiles' society and adoption of their cultural and social values. Assimilated Jews in the empire became nationalized in the sense that they showed a strong commitment to the local languages and cultures and engaged in civic and political life of the ruling nations, the Austrians and Hungarians. Prior to the foundation of Czechoslovakia, the alternative to assimilation to Vienna and Budapest was Zionism, hence emigration to Palestine.[63]

---

[63] For a detailed analysis of Jewish assimilation, I refer to Hannah Arendt, "Antisemitism", in *The Origins of Totalitarianism* (San Diego, New York, London: Harcourt Brace & Company, 1973), 1-302; for a historiography of persecuted entrepreneurial minorities see Daniel Chirot and Anthony Reid, eds., *Essential Outsiders. Chinese and Jews in the Modern Transformation of Southeast Asia and Central Europe* (Seattle: University of Washington Press, 1997); Wolfdieter Bihl, "Die Juden", in *Die Habsburgermonarchie 1848–1918, Die Völker des Reiches, vol III/2,* (Wien: Österreichische Akademie der Wissenschaften, 1980), 880-948; Steven Beller, "'Pride and Prejudice' or 'Sense and Sensibility'? How reasonable was Anti-Semitism in Vienna, 1880-1939?", in *Essential Outsiders*, 99-124; Petra Rybářová (†), *Antisemitizmus v Uhorsku v 80. rokov 19. storočia* (Bratislava: Pro Historia, 2010). On antisemitism in Czech literature see Alexej Mikulášek, *Antisemitismus v česke literatuře 19. a 20. stoleti. Teoreticka a historicka studie* (Praha: Votobia, 2000). On antisemitism in Central Europe after 1989, I recommend Hana Bilková and Jan Hančil, eds., *Antisemitismus v posttotalitni Evrope. Sbornik z Mezinarodního seminare o antisemitismus v posttotalitni Evrope* (Praha: Nakladátelství Franze Kafky, 1993). The following studies offer excellent analysis of the history of the Jews

I use the concepts *antisemitic* and *antisemitism* without hyphen, following Shmuel Almog: the concept of *antisemitism* by Wilhelm Marr (1819–1904) has, ever since its coinage, been used to describe and provoke the systematic rejection and hatred of the Jewish people. Antisemitism as a term was never used to incite racist hatred against people that belong to the group of Semitic languages, such as Arabic, Aramaic, Amhari and some North-African dialects. The hyphen thus blurs the linguistic definition of Semitic languages with the nationalist definition of the Jewish people, serving as an argument to weaken the concept by expanding its alleged target group to people that speak a Semitic language.[64]

On the basis of Steven Beller's definition and under special consideration of the political and economic situation in 20th century Czechoslovakia I define antisemitism as

> "A political movement of 19th century monderdity, yet no clearly defined ideology, let alone a political programme, which originated in Central Europe in the late 19th century and was based upon the religiocentric anti-Judaism of the Christian Church of both Catholic and Protestant confessions and enforced by the increasing nationalistic pressure of Magyarization. It achieved its evil apogee in the Holocaust."[65]

---

in Slovakia in the 20th century: Ivan Kamenec, *Po stopách tragédie* (Praha: Archa, 1991); Peter Salner, "Die Juden in der bürgerlichen Gesellschaft der Slowakei", in *Bürgertum und bürgerliche Gesellschaft in der Slowakei 1900–1989* (Bratislava: AEP, 1997), 153-163; Ivan Kamenec a Eduard Nižňanský, eds., *Holokaust na Slovensku: Prezident, vláda, snem SR a štátni rada o židovskej otázke* (Zvolen: Klemo; Bratislava: nadacia Milana Šimečka, židovská náboženská obec, 2003).

[64] Shmuel Almog, "What's in a hyphen?" on http://sicsa.huji.ac.il/hyphen.html; accessed 1 July 2012.

[65] "Antisemitism is a hatred of Jews that has stretched across millennia and across continents; or it is a relatively modern political movement and ideology that arose in Central Europe in the late 19th century and achieved its evil apogee in the Holocaust; or it is the irrational, psychologically pathological version of an ethnocentric and religiocentric anti-Judaism that originated in Christianity's conflict with its Jewish roots – and achieved its evil apogee in

In Slovakia, the HSĽS was the main party that promoted non-racist antisemitism in the years of the First Republic. The distinguished Slovak historian Eduard Nižňanský defines Slovak antisemitism as a psychological and political phenomenon:

> "First, the autochthone Christian level: 'The Jews killed Jesus Christ'. Second, the economic level: 'The Jews exploited the Slovaks'. Third, the national level: 'Jews are not Slovaks'. Fourth, the political level: 'The Jews are leftists or oriented towards liberalism'."[66]

The Slovak state had not emerged as result of a national emancipatory movement, but as a by-product of Hitler's aggression, facilitated by the rule of clerical Fascism. The 'Jews-Bolsheviks' and the atheist Czechs were perceived as the enemies of the Slovaks, who, so the propaganda of the *Ľudáci* claimed, had finally achieved their independence in a state of their own – after a thousand years of oppression.

Because of the fact that many Jews had joined the Communist Party that had promised the end of discrimination and equality of citizens, Party members, unaware of Stalin's antisemitism, embarked on a campaign that was presented as the state's defence against the alleged dangers of Zionism. Neither Stalin nor his dutiful NKVD commissars, busy with organizing the Czechoslovak show trial of 1952, were bothered with the philosophical contradiction they created with their trial scripts. They were realists, focussing on the pragmatic elimination of the Titoist and Zionist enemies, who, in the service of Western Imperialism, were

---

the Holocaust; or it is a combination of all of these;" Steven Beller, *Antisemitism. A Very Short Introduction* (Oxford, New York: Oxford University Press, 2007), 1.

[66] Eduard Nižňanský, "Deportácie v roku 1942", in *Nacismus, Holokaust, Slovenský Štát* (Bratislava: Kalligramm, 2010), 104-181, 105.

allegedly intent on undermining the People's Democracies in Central and Eastern Europe – and with that, their fight against Western Capitalist Imperialism.

A Czech or Slovak Jewish member of the Communist Party could not be a Zionist at the same time, since this posed an intrinsic and inextricable theoretical contradiction. Zionism[67] demanded, first and foremost, loyalty and allegiance to the building of the State of Israel Theodor Herzl (1860–1904) had projected at the Zionist Congress in Basel in 1897.[68] Thus, to be a Zionist meant to pledge allegiance to a bourgeois concept – the Jewish nation – Nationalism. A Jew born in Czechoslovakia would never be a reliable Party member.

In the framework of the Jewish settlement in Palestine, one was allowed to join or found any political party. In the Communist states, the allegiance of a Jewish Party member was questioned – simply because of the fact that he or she was a Jew. The projected trial of the Jewish doctors in the Soviet Union did not happen because of Stalin's death on 5 March 1953, but it presented the antisemitic blueprint of the message that Jews could not be trusted. The trial of Slánský and co-accused thus conveyed a particular nasty antisemitic trait:

> "Interrogations [...] shifted to what politically was the most important area – Zionism, which would provide the show trial with its basic ideological underpinning of anti-Semitism. Anti-Semitic outbursts were far more frequent in State Security since the arrival of Soviet advisors, and in the rest of society since Slánský's arrest."[69]

---

[67] For a superb account of the principal role leftist Russian and Polish Jews played as the pioneers of the foundation of Israel see Isaiah Berlin, "The Origins of Israel", in *The Power of Ideas* (Princeton, NJ, Oxford: Princeton University Press, Oxford University Press, 2002), 143-161.

[68] Theodor Herzl on http://www.jewishvirtuallibrary.org/jsource/biography/Herzl.html; accessed 23 April 2016.

[69] Kaplan, *The murder of ...*, 187-188.

X. 3. 3 Research questions

The research questions of this study focus on two main areas:

1. Democracy: Clementis grew up in a Protestant environment and completed his studies in democratic Czechoslovakia. Why did he return to the Party after five years of working with and for the London exile government? Was Party membership to him a stepping-stone to political power? Was he ambitious, arrogant, or naïve?

2. Constitutional status of Slovakia within Czechoslovakia: what constitutional arrangement did Clementis pursue for Slovakia?

"It is said that No. 1 has Machiavelli's *Prince* lying permanently by his bedside. So he should: since then, nothing really important has been said about the rules of political ethics. We were the first to replace the nineteenth century's liberal ethics of 'fair play' by the revolutionary ethics of the twentieth century. In that also we were right, a revolution conducted according to the rules of cricket is an absurdity. [...] Politics can be relatively fair in the breathing spaces of history; at its critical turning points there is no other rule possible than the old one, that the end justifies the means."[1]

"Major Ozunov to Khristo Stoianov:

Fair play, he called it. Not such a simple notion, perhaps, when you probe to find its heart. A kind of code, which each gentleman must honour individually in order for all to benefit. In time I came to understand that it was a good system for those who had more than they needed, for those who could afford to give something away. But I also realized that I had never known anybody like that. Nobody I ever knew could say "Here, you take it, I do not deserve it. I do not need it so badly that I will cheat and lie to get it." Perhaps some day we may indulge ourselves in that fashion, we may have so much that we can afford to give some of it away, but not now."[2]

---

[1] Arthur Köstler, *Darkness at Noon* (London: Vintage, 2005), 81. Köstler's novel is a fictitious account of the Moscow show trials of the 1930s, which he observed as a young Party member from Europe. The Moscow trials served as a blueprint for the show trials that purged the Communist Parties in the Soviet bloc, starting with the trial of László Rajk in Hungary in 1949. No 1, the fictitious Chairman of the Party, is Stalin. The rules of cricket are a synonym and metaphor for fair play in Britain. Due to the absence of a written constitution as such, the rules of cricket are to this day referred to humorously as the nearest thing Britain has to one. For a superb and insightful account of the mindsets of Communist intellectuals born at the turn of the 20th century see Vlasta Jaksicsová, "Komunistický intelektuál – víťaz a porazený hodnotového sporu v 'medzičase' pred komunistickou diktatúrou", *Historický časopis LXII*, no. 1 (2014): 61-89.

[2] Alan Furst, *Night Soldiers* (London: Weidenfeld & Nicolson ebook, 2011), loc. 813, Kindle edition.

I. Childhood, Education and Pre-War Political Activities (1902–1939)

European intellectuals born at the turn of the 20th century who had witnessed WWI and its fatal socio-economic consequences were besotted with Socialism in its Marxist-Leninist form. They considered it the only answer to the main problem of the times: Capitalism with its concomitant social and economic neglect of the weak and poor. The Capitalist Empires had operated in an authoritarian fashion, dictated by the ruling aristocracy and bourgeoisie. They had sacrificed the masses as pawns in a global play for power and wealth. In the leftist intellectuals' minds, Marxism-Leninism offered the only political programme and system that could, by the sheer force of its egalitarianism, revolutionary fervour and international appeal, not only establish real justice and true liberty; it was also the only guarantee of peace in the future. And this peace would not be the peace of those who lived in castles, manor houses and palaces, but the peace of the powerless masses, the workers, labourers, chambermaids, servants and peasants. A world ruled by Socialism, by the proletariat and the Party as its avant-garde, would guarantee true fraternity and real liberty. The conditions that had catapulted the world into WWI would cease to exist, since the old class system would be liquidated.

The rise of National-Socialism in Germany and Fascism in Italy and Spain in the 1930s prompted intellectuals to react; one could see what fate awaited critical citizens in a Fascist state and, particularly, in Germany ruled by Hitler's NSDAP. Everybody who considered Fascism and National Socialism a threat to mankind took the side of the anti-Fascist opposition. Prior to December 1941, when the USA with her military might entered the war after the Japanese attack on Pearl Harbour, a European citizen thought that he had only two alternatives: either support Fascism and National Socialism, or Communism, a global movement led by the Soviet Union. The anti-Fascists' litmus test was the Spanish Civil War (1936–1939); it was a good Republican cause, worth sacrificing one's life for. Ernest Hemingway's *For Whom The Bell Tolls* (1940) and George Orwell's *Homage to Catalonia* (1938) are classics of world literature.

The Spanish Civil War affected Clementis insofar as it demonstrated to him that he had made the right decision, taken the right side; in 1936, he was practising law in Bratislava and was an MP for the KSČ in the Czechoslovak parliament in Prague. A Party member since January 1925, he was a respected politician and intellectual, trained in the details of Marxist-Leninist theory; he was a *virtuoso* playing the piano of his credo. He spoke English, German, French, Hungarian and Russian fluently. Marxism-Leninism, not US democracy as the political role model of Masaryk's Czechoslovakia, would win this secular – and in Marx and Lenin's thought – global battle of ideas.

In this chapter, I present a summary of Clementis' upbringing, education and early political activities.

I. 1 Childhood in Tisovec

Vladimír was born on 20 September 1902 into a family of the Lutheran confession in Tisovec in Central Slovakia. His father Ľudovít was a teacher; his mother Mária Adela Vraná was Ľudovít's second wife. They had five children: Miroslav, Vladimír, Božena, Viera, who died as a baby, and Oľga. In his memoirs *Nedokončená kronika* (*Unfinished History*), written in a POW Camp in Britain in

1940,¹ Clementis described his happy childhood in the idyllic countryside of Central Slovakia. His family was comfortably off; they did not live in luxury, but Vlado and his older brother Miro enjoyed a high school (*gymnasium*) education.

As a teenager, Vlado was interested in the origins of his father's family, but the family tree was lost. He had studied Latin and was thus able to figure out the origins of his family's name:

> "Although I cannot prove it with documents or historical research, I assume that our family came to its name much like other Slovak families who were lower gentry and Protestants. Their Latin or Greek names such as Qutidian, Sutoris, Ormis, Braxatoris, etc. originated in the epoch of Humanism in Slovakia. The Slovak names had taken on a Latin form, at least the suffixes, because the administrative language in Hungary had been Latin. Our family name features the genitive case, which is comparable in linguistic terms to the Slavic patronymic: Clement-is filius."²

---

[1] Vladimír Clementis, *Nedokončená kronika* (Bratislava: Slovenské vydavateľstvo krásnej literatúry, 1964). Clementis deeply disliked references to himself in his speeches, essays and articles. Therefore, I translated the term *kronika* with *History*, not *Memoirs* – although the text qualifies as autobiography. He described his childhood and youth only for Lída, with no intention to have it published. She published the text with the help of Laco Novomeský to honour her late husband's memory; in 1963, the *predjarie*, the liberalization in culture and politics that would peak in the Prague Spring in 1968, began with the rehabilitation of the victims of the show trial of 1952. A superb account of those years is Miroslav Londák, Stanislav Sikora a Elena Londáková, *Predjarie. Politický, ekonomický a kultúrny vývoj na Slovensku v rokoch 1960–1967* (Bratislava: Veda, 2002).

[2] Clementis, *Nedokončená kronika,* 18. The epoch of Humanism in the Hungarian kingdom was the reign of Matthias Corvinus (1443–1490), a great patron of the arts and the new thinking of the Italian Renaissance that had reached Hungary in the early 15th century. The Academia Istropolitana in Pozsony, today Bratislava, and the Bibliotheca Corviniana in Buda, today Budapest, were cultural institutions founded in the epoch of Hungary's Renaissance; Peter F. Sugar, Péter Hanák and Tibor Frank, eds., *A History of Hungary* (Bloomington: Indiana University Press, 1994), 74-75.

Vlado felt a deep admiration, a loyal and loving reverence for his father: Ľudovít was tender, but not weak; he was patient without being hesitant, promoting ethical values without moralizing. He was psychologically balanced and opinionated at the same time and did not hesitate to commit himself to a cause he deemed worthy of his engagement. The parents never punished the children with physical violence, and the children addressed the parents with the polite form *Vy* (*You, Vous, Sie*), a source of respect and order in the family.³ The mother was quiet and loving; the upbringing of her children her only care.

Vlado's father was a *narodovec*, a pioneer of the Slovak national awakening, who had considerable intellectual influence on his sons. From the 1840s on, Evangelicals and Catholics alike were defending their language and cultural rights, which the Magyar assimilation was violating; the Magyarization of the non-Magyar citizens in Hungary would peak with the language law of 1868.⁴ Turčiansky Sv. Martin (today Martin) in Central Slovakia had hosted the first meeting of Slovak patriots, who had issued the *Memorandum of the Slovak Nation* in 1861. Martin was the centre of the conservative faction of the national movement until Slovakia became a part of Czechoslovakia in 1918. To be a *narodovec* meant to speak, write and read Slovak: acts of national self-defence.

According to Clementis' memoirs, the citizens of Tisovec experienced a relatively mild assimilation, most probably because Hungarians, Slovaks and Jews had been living peacefully side-by-

---

3   Clementis, *Nedokončená kronika*, 21.
4   For an account of the assimilation and how it affected the main political currents of the Slovak national movement see my *Revolution, Modus Vivendi or Sovereignty? The Political Thought of the Slovak National Movement from 1861 to 1914* (Stuttgart: ibidem, 2010).

side for decades. Before the *prevrat* of 1918, Tisovec had three primary schools; an evangelical, a catholic and a state school. Only the evangelical school operated in Slovak. Clementis remembered:

> "In the second class, we started to learn Hungarian. The teachers did not take it too seriously. We children picked up a few Hungarian words easily, which we had to perform once or twice a year for the Hungarian school inspector. These visits were not pleasant for the teachers. [...] Slabej, our teacher, called me up, and as soon as I had fluently replied, the inspector expressed his discontent, probably about my 'Slovak' pronunciation. Then he began calling up the pupils himself – the disaster was ready. His random tests in other classes were equally successful. [...] I remember that the conference of our three teachers with the inspector took place in our little school building. All of them received a fine, I think, up to the sum of one hundred gold coins. And, considering their salary, this was no triviality."[5]

The Slovaks formed the majority in Tisovec. The Hungarian state school led to fights between the pupils, since only Hungarian children, Jewish children and those Slovak children whose parents were dependent on the state went to the state school. Although they differed in language, confession and employment, the citizens were tolerant. The people of Tisovec were farmers, of the evangelical confession and had been settling there for centuries. The people of Hámor, an administrative part of Tisovec, were mainly workers and Catholics.[6]

The Slovaks met in the building of the *spolok*, their cultural association that had a library with Slovak and Czech newspapers; those who liked to play chess or *Tarock* used to meet at the *biliardárňa*. The local firemen's association was a traditional institution that would later become the *Sokol*, the national Czechoslovak sports association. The Hungarians had their *kazsinó* and met also

---

[5] Clementis, *Nedokončená kronika*, 91.
[6] Clementis, *Nedokončená kronika*, 99.

at the *Gentlemen's room* at the factory pub in Hámor.[7] A few citizens were opportunists who were frequenting the *spolok*, but also made sure to maintain good relations with the local representatives of the government. There was no national chauvinism in Tisovec, as Clementis remembered. Citizens had also very friendly relations with the local Jews, especially the older ones. Antisemitism was unknown and, unlike in other villages in Slovakia, no Jews were robbed in the days of the *prevrat* in 1918.[8]

The tolerant atmosphere in the village – one could describe it with the motto 'Live and let live' – but also the lack of political education created an apolitical attitude among the people. In the citizens' minds, politics were made from above, in Budapest; in Tisovec, one lived as one had for decades, in good neighbourly relations. Clementis mentioned politics only briefly, and only the party he was interested in:

> "The failure, opportunism and lack of political education of the Hungarian Social Democratic Party, which was not even capable of properly applying the national question to the Hungarian context, resulted in the fact that the Socialist movement could not win over the very thin stratum of the Slovak workers. The so-called Slovak Social Democrats, who were recruiting members mainly from Czech small towns, […] were not a whit better. […] And that is why the workers from Hámor were left to fend for themselves; as they lived in the countryside and not in a proletarian environment, their political horizon was rather limited. Some demonstrated their incorrect understanding of internationalism with caving in to the Magyarization, denying their Slovak national identity."[9]

Besides his father, grandfather Václav Vraný, the father of Vlado's mother, had a decisive influence on the boy's intellectual

---

[7] Clementis, *Nedokončená kronika*, 102, 109.
[8] Clementis, *Nedokončená kronika*, 110.
[9] Clementis, *Nedokončená kronika*, 101. For a summary of the difficulties the Slovak Social Democratic Party had to deal with see my "Ein Catch-22? Die slowakischen Sozialdemokraten zwischen nationaler Identität und internationaler Arbeitersolidarität (1905–1918)", in *Arbeit. Philosophische, juristische und kulturwissenschaftliche Studien* (Basel: Schwabe, 2014), 193-206.

development. Grandfather Vraný was born in a village close to Kolín in Central Bohemia and had moved in the second half of the 19th century to Veľká Revúca in Slovakia to study at the evangelical *lyceum* (high school).[10] He had received his first employment as a teacher in the North Eastern county of Spíš (Szepes county, *Zips*), where the majority of the population was German.

With their mother, the Clementis children often visited the grandparents and their half-brother Dušan in Bystrica and, later, in Mikuláš, Martin and Tisovec. There was a mysterious taboo ruling in the Vraný family, concerning a person, whose name was never mentioned, as Clementis remembered. Later he found out that the *persona non grata* was Milo, his mother's brother, who lived in Budapest and was a notary public. Milo had turned into a Magyar Hungarian, had caved in to the pressure of the assimilation; grandfather Vraný never mentioned Milo. He ceased to exist for his father because he had betrayed his Slovak national identity for professional advancement.[11]

Before he enrolled at the high school in Uhorská Skalica, Vlado had admired from afar Svetozár Hurban Vajanský.[12] The famous poet lived in Martin, where grandfather Vraný had found

---

[10] Clementis, *Nedokončená kronika*, 35.
[11] Clementis, *Nedokončená kronika*, 35.
[12] Behind the tiniest attempts at modernization, Vajanský immediately suspected Socialist, hence godless, thought. For politics and pragmatism he had only contempt. Slovak literature and poetry, art was everything – and it was he and his associates who determined what art was. Vajanský in 1897: "The spark of spiritual life is glimmering in us. [...] We are no political party, we are the nation, pars pro toto, like the head that guides the body", Svetozár Hurban Vajanský, *Nálady a výhľady* (Turčiansky Sv. Martin: Kníhtlačiarsko-účastinarský spolok, 1897), 12. See my "Svetozár Hurban Vajanský (1847–1916). Messianism, Panslavism and the superiority of art", in *Revolution. Modus Vivendi or Sovereignty?*, 151-177. It was not below his dignity to deliberately plagiarize, at least once: he condemned Nietzsche in a lengthy article, but shamelessly copied Nietzsche's philosophical method of inquiry to warn

employment as custodian of the National Museum after he had lost his teaching position because of his anti-Magyar activities, a consequence of the *Lex Apponyi* of 1907.[13] Vlado had read Vajanský's poems and novels, considering him in his youthful patriotism as "the patriarch of all things mystic, mysterious and forbidden, but also uplifting, ideas, views and emotions born from the soul of the oppressed nation".[14] In 1914, Vlado and Miro had spotted Vajanský in Vrútky while waiting for the train to Skalica, but they did not dare to address him.

Clementis had unforgettable memories about grandfather Vraný; the following account illustrates the self-critical view of the middle-aged lawyer who recalled his youthful fervour:

> "Grandfather was a Masarykian, he was in touch with Masaryk's followers in Slovakia and, because of his low tolerance, bore fierce grudges against the representatives of the 'Martin' ideology. [...] It was my *Sturm und Drang* period, my militant and intolerant years. Completely unaware, I got into conflict with him. [...] I returned from Dresden, where I had studied for a few months, it was 1923. From Dresden, I had sent an

---

Slovak youth; Josette Baer, "Twilight of the Idols in Slovakia – or using Nietzsche's hammer to strengthen the nation", in *Kapitoly z histórie ...* 64-85.

13 The Education Act or *Lex Apponyi*, named after the Minister of Religion and Education Count Albert Apponyi de Nagyappony (1864–1933) extended Magyarization to the primary schools in the Hungarian system of education. The new directives pushed along the process of assimilation with "concomitant suppression of the nationalities [the non-Magyar citizens of the kingdom, add. JB]" by putting into effect Magyar as language of instruction at the lowest level of schooling; Robert A. Kann, *A History of the Habsburg Empire 1526–1918* (Berkeley: University of California Press, 1974), 457. The new laws bound the teachers to instil in the pupils a "patriotic spirit". All non-Magyar children should be fluent in Hungarian in speech and writing at the end of the fourth class; thorough checks on the teachers by school inspectors ensured that the laws were followed; as a result, illiteracy among the children rose; Kováč, *Dejiny Slovenska*, 156. For statistics of the assimilation see Roman Holec, "Úvahy k fenoménu maďarizácie pred rokom 1918", in *Kľúčové problémy moderných slovenských dejín 1848–1992* (Bratislava: Veda, 2012), 80-135.

14 Clementis, *Nedokončená kronika*, 33.

article to *Mladé Slovensko*, I think it was 'Chapters about us' – about our generation's problems. *Mladé Slovensko* published a series on this topic. Štefan Janšák reacted in *Prúdy* with a rather ill-mannered criticism of several articles. He liked only my article. He dedicated to me a lengthy text with well-meant teachings, which I, with thanks, rejected in *Mladé Slovensko* (*'Briefly about Janšák's article'*), substantiating my rather superficial statements about 'work and capital'. Grandfather read only *Prúdy*, thus knew only Janšák's point of view. Our opinions clashed; he quoted Janšák to me as an authority. 'You see, Janšák too told you that you are wrong and are not thinking problems through.' [...] Grandfather and I separated, he in a very cold manner. [...] I was sorry [...] – but I couldn't help myself. [...] I was so convinced that I had the right to defend what I thought was the truth, my truth, that I had the duty to speak the truth in all circumstances [...] that I kept repeating to myself Luther's saying 'Here I stand, I cannot do otherwise'."[15]

From the autumn of 1912 to 1921, Vlado studied at a traditional school that had a significant meaning for the national movement; the Evangelical *lyceum* in Skalica had been attended by famous Slovak patriots such as the poet Ján Hollý (1785–1849), the historian František Sasinek (1830–1914) and the Hlasist Pavol Blaho (1867–1927). Vlado did well in his first year: in twelve subjects he received three grade 1s, the highest grade, and for the other subjects the second-best grade 2.[16] In the school year of 1915/1916 he received, for the first time, a 3 – for Hungarian.

The years at Skalica high school deepened the teenager's sense of his Slovak identity: the professors were teaching the students according to the rules of the assimilation, trying to press them into 'confessing' that they were members of the *natio hungarica*.[17] But soon, in the school year of 1917/1918, the assimilation ceased to be an important issue; the teachers were concerned

---

[15] Clementis, *Nedokončená kronika*, 38-39. Janšák was a former Hlasist; about the journals *Hlas* and *Prúdy* see chapter X. 3. 2. 1.
[16] Holotíková a Plevza, 7.
[17] Holotíková a Plevza, 8-9.

for their future, threatened by the loss of the war and the impending regime change. After the *prevrat* in 1918, the high school changed its name: it was now called the Masaryk High School for Sciences (*reálne gymnasium*). The Hungarian teachers and administrators left, and Czechs now filled the positions, eager to establish Czechoslovak rule in Slovakia.

Since his childhood, Vlado was familiar with Czech literature and culture; he read and spoke Czech. He had never been religious; he welcomed the regime change and the new national and political spirit. A new friend was Jan Doležal from the Czech lands; Jan was the first Marxist the Slovak boys at Skalica high school met, and the intelligent and educated young Czech made a considerable impression on them.[18] Vlado learnt from Jan's Czech books about Marxist theory; it was the beginning of a life-long dedication.

In the spring of 1921, Vlado graduated with honours. It was clear to his family, the director of the school, the chairman of the exam commission and his teachers that his education was not yet finished: the mind of young Clementis was prepared – he was ready for university. The young Slovak arrived in the Czechoslovak capital in October 1921.

I. 2. DAV and the Davists

Vladimír was not alone in Prague. For a few months, he stayed at a student dormitory; then he moved in with his elder brother Miro, who was renting an apartment. The Clementis boys attended regularly the meetings of the Slovak Academic Association *Detvan* (*Slovenský akademický spolok Detvan*), which was a family tradition, as their half-brother Dušan had also been active in the

---

[18] Holotíková a Plevza, 10.

student circle. Vladimír was working very hard: he was studying law, took extra-curricular lessons in Practical Philosophy and brought his English to perfection. In the spring of 1923, he went to Dresden for a couple of months to improve his knowledge of German.[19]

Some of his friends and associates described him as self-contained, tight-lipped, a young man who did not look for friendship, but once he got to know somebody and approved of him, he was a loyal friend. His primary occupation was his studies, but it would be wrong to label him as secretive or withdrawn. He was ambitious, focussed and had a simple goal: to study. At that time, *Detvan* counted some two hundred members; the circle soon lost its attraction for him, because he was interested in subjects the majority of the members were not: a new kind of enquiry, a leftist view of politics and culture.

Detvan was a cultural association, Slovak literature its main focus. In Vladimír's eyes, *Detvan's* traditional theme of Slovak national identity was outdated. Back in 1882, Slovak students had founded the cultural and national association; that generation had been born in the second half of the 19th century and experienced the harshness of the assimilation.[20] In Prague, they could study in a language they understood, as, unlike in Upper Hungary,

---

[19] Holotíková a Plevza, 11. Vladimír attended the lectures of the famous philosopher Emanuel Rádl (1873–1942), who was a teacher of Jan Patočka (1907–1977), the future founder of the Czechoslovak dissident group *Charter 77*. See Shimona Löwenstein, *Emanuel Rádl. Philosoph und Moralist 1873–1942* (Frankfurt am Main: Peter Lang, 1995). Patočka was a student of Edmund Husserl (1859–1938) and Martin Heidegger (1889–1976); his asubjective phenomenology is his most important contribution to philosophy: *Die Bewegung der menschlichen Existenz* (Stuttgart: Klett Cotta, 1990). The Vienna Institut für die Wissenschaft vom Menschen published Patočka's studies in five volumes from 1984 to 1992.

[20] For a history of the circle see *Detvan. 50 rokov v Prahe. Rozpomienky, štúdie, úvahy* (Praha, Turčiansky Sv. Martin: Matica Slovenska, 1932).

the Austrian and Czech authorities in Prague could not be bothered with the language issue. The atmosphere in Prague had been a much more liberal one than at home. To that older generation, *Detvan* had been like home in a friendly environment; they had read Slovak books and poems and discussed how to improve the fate of their oppressed nation.

To Vladimír's generation and, in particular, the progressive and leftist students, *Detvan* was no basis for their ideas, efforts and plans. Slovak identity was no longer a political issue they had to fight for like the generation of the Hlasists Janšak, Blaho and Šrobár. They knew that they were Slovaks; some of them considered themselves Czechoslovaks. Times had changed; they were living in a new world, in a new state. Theirs was thus the task of addressing actual problems and current issues. Idle discussions or reminiscences about Slovak poems of the 19th century would get them nowhere.

In the spring of 1922, Vladimír and his friends Daniel Okalí and Andrej Siracký founded the Free Association of Slovak Socialist Students (*volné združenie študentov-socialistov zo Slovenska*); they were reading *The Communist Manifesto* and Lenin's *State and Revolution* and meeting on a weekly basis to discuss contemporary cultural, philosophical and political themes.[21]

The liberty of the First Republic, the free press and the right to express one's opinion was visible in the debates and polemics the students were engaging in; when Jan Poničan was appointed editor of *Detvan's* journal *Mladé Slovensko*, Vladimír published an article that led to Janšak's criticism, the criticism that would result in the rift with grandfather Vraný and prompt the foundation of DAV. In his first article "Chapters about us" (*Kapitoly*

---

[21] Holotíková a Plevza, 15.

o nás), the twenty-one year old student described the intellectual state of mind of the Slovak students.

At the beginning of his article, Vladimír quoted the famous Slovak artist Bohdan Pavlů (1883–1938), a writer and associate of *Prúdy*, known under his pen name Paľo. Paľo stated that Slovak youth lacked radicalism and courage. Others thought that the younger generation was too conservative and intellectually sterile.[22] Vladimír accused the students of provincialism, including himself and his associates. Apparently, his generation was less progressive than the previous one. Was that true?

> "To me, progressiveness means to follow one's truths, the new truths, no compromises whatsoever. The truth is continuously developing, and we are its measuring stick, as individuals as much as a whole. However, every assessment is always a subjective one. The young generation doesn't have abstract and truths at its disposal, truths that seem to be serving the current state of mind. They have only those truths they have experienced and felt themselves. This subjective, hence engaging, understanding of the truth is raising our awareness for social issues today's world is occupied with, calling for solutions. He who doesn't see these problems, who refuses to attempt to find appropriate solutions, is not a progressive. We can see these new problems in every area of contemporary culture. And new problems require new methods."[23]

It was certainly easy, so Vladimír stressed, to divide the students into clericals and the progressives of the Free Association; yet, the latter were at least trying to operate from the widest possible intellectual angle. Considering the brief time of the Free Association's existence, its members could be proud of their achievements for organizational and social work. He did not elaborate in detail.

---

[22] Clementis, "Kapitoly o nás", *Mladé Slovensko V*, no. 3 (1923): 66-69, in *Vzduch našich čias. Články, state, prejavy, polemiky 1922–1934, vol. I* (Bratislava: Vydavateľstvo politickej literatúry, 1967), 44-48; 45.
[23] Clementis, "Kapitoly o nás", 45.

True, the Czechoslovak state had successfully resolved the national question for Czechs and Slovaks; on the other hand, it had created a range of new problems. Socialists and Agrarians of the generation that had founded the state were still concentrating on merging the two nations, trying to make the state stronger by strengthening the Czechoslovak nation's unity.[24] The young members of the Free Association acknowledged these efforts, but to them, the Czechoslovak nation as a concept of state and culture was a given fact, a reality, thus neither a goal nor an intellectual basis. To progress meant to go ahead, moving from world to world. Tradition was an operational basis for the weak; without that backbone they would fall. The past had no answers to the current social problems:

> "Why keep looking to the past? That which is positive and lasting in the work of the previous generations is a starting point for the young, the thesis from which they are building the anti-thesis, […]. The war and its consequences have brought new problems, placing them at the centre of different interests. Not even the older ones have solutions. Therefore, facing these new problems, we are almost on an equal footing with them."[25]

Mentioning the Hegelian dialectic of thesis and anti-thesis and the concept of subjectivity, Vladimír applied Marxist theory to his explanations of the current state of the Slovak student body. He did not offer a solution, which, according to Hegelian and Marxist dialectics, would have required defining a synthesis from thesis and anti-thesis; he just defended the activities and views of the Free Association's members. His language was clear, precise and elegant, with a modest but convincing amount of rhetoric, his analysis sophisticated. He finished his text with a wake-up call: if the

---

[24] Clementis, "Kapitoly o nás", 47.
[25] Clementis, "Kapitoly o nás", 48.

Slovak students were incapable of understanding the global currents of thoughts and ideas, they would deserve to turn into what Pavlů had suggested: they would end as the nation's memory, which meant that the younger generation would forever abstain from contributing to the nation's political and social development – they would finish as the Slovak intellectuals' graveyard, forgotten forever. The young ones had to push forward for the good of all, no longer in terms of Slovak national identity, but now in terms of social justice.

The rift between the leftist-progressive faction and the traditional members of *Detvan* was too deep, their views too different to find a common basis for further co-operation. The progressives left in the summer of 1923 and started to prepare the foundation of a new journal: DAV, the journal of the young leftists.[26]

I. 2. 1   The Themes of DAV – Applying Marxism-Leninism to Slovakia

Passivity, to rest on the laurels of the previous generations, was neither a viable perspective nor a practical method to face the current social issues. Vladimír put into practice what he had preached: from 1924 to 1935,[27] he would head the journal as editor-in-chief, positioning it successfully in the landscape of leftist journals and revues in Slovakia. He would publish uncountable

---

[26] DAV was a composite of the founders' Christian names: *D*aniel Okalí, *A*ndrej Siracký and *V*lado Clementis; Drug, 72. The Slovak and Czech word "dav" has a negative connotation, referring to masses, a larger unorganized group of people. The closest word in English is "mob". The title has thus a double spin, hinting not only at the first names of its founders but reflecting also the journal's political orientation – the radical left that cared for the proletarian masses neglected by the Capitalist government.

[27] Laco Novomeský took over the journal's editorship in 1935, when Clementis was elected MP for the KSČ.

texts on politics, culture and literature, promoting the Marxist-Leninist view on themes such as the economic system, Prague's centralism in Slovak politics, Soviet films and novels. He also analysed the ideas and programmes of the centre-right Czech and Slovak parties and, from the mid-1930s on, he paid special attention to Hlinka's Slovak People's Party (HSĽS). Until 1937, when DAV stopped publication for good, Vladimír published not one article critical of the Soviet Union – on the contrary: he consistently portrayed the Soviet Union as a workers' paradise and role model for Czechoslovak Communism alike. Already DAV's first issue demonstrated the editors' dedication – they were toeing the Party line, slavishly following the Soviet Communist Party:

> "LENINISM is Marxism in the epoch of Imperialism and the proletarian revolution. Leninism is the theory and tactics of the all-encompassing proletarian revolution, the theory and tactics of the distinct dictatorship of the proletariat. Stalin."[28]

At the end of 1924, DAV came into being with the financial support of Klement Gottwald, member of the KSČ since its foundation in 1921 and chief organizer of the Communist press in Slovakia.[29] The journal's main target was the Slovak and Czech youth. Edo Urx (1903–1942), Vladimír, Andrej Sirácky and Daniel Okáli were the first editors; they were in their last years at university. At the beginning of December 1924, the four editors and colleagues from the Free Association gathered in front of the Straka Academy (*Straková akademie*) on Malá Strana in Prague and sold the first issue.[30] Couriers brought the journal to Bratislava, from where it was distributed to Žilina, Ružomberok and Vrútky. The leftist newspapers and journals *Pravda chudoby* (*The Truth of Poverty*), *Spartakus* (*Spartacus*), *Proletárka* (*The Proletarian Woman*), *Rudé*

---

[28] *DAV I*, no. 1 (1924): 49.
[29] Holotiková a Plevza, 29.
[30] Holotiková a Plevza, 30.

právo (*Red Right*) and *Avantgarda* (*Avant-Garde*) warmly welcomed DAV as a new member of the leftist Slovak press.[31]

In the following subchapters, I present articles Vladimír published in DAV from 1924 to 1935. The themes I selected from his approximately one hundred and fifty articles demonstrate not only his belief in Marxism-Leninism and his application of theory to practice, but also how closely he followed Slovak politics. The selected themes do not come even close to conveying Vladimír's journalistic efforts and the wide range of topics he covered, but they offer an insight into his writing and thinking, his talent for rhetoric, analysis and interpretation.

In spite of his young age, his enthusiastic, clever and well-written texts made him an authority among the Slovak youth whom the KSČ coveted to fill its ranks; party membership was thus a logical result of Vladimír's journalistic efforts. On the recommendation of Edo Urx, the Party made him a member in January 1925.

I. 2. 1. 1 The Question of the Czechoslovak Nation (1924)

"The theses about nationality the fifth congress of the Comintern issued stirred up the entire Czechoslovak public."[32] Vladimír's talent for explaining complex matters with simple but precise words and portraying the Communist view as the viewpoint of the future political elite is visible in his first text for DAV.

Comparing his writing for DAV with the text "Chapters about us" mentioned above, I had the impression that he was more courageous and dedicated; the flux of his diction sounded more decided. He still sounded modest, but seemed more self-assured, probably because the themes he was now addressing interested

---

[31] Holotiková a Plevza, 34.
[32] Clementis, "K národnostnej otázke", *DAV I*, no. 1 (1924): 2-4.

him much more than the rather general topic of the future of Slovakia's youth. Vladimír was always thinking one step ahead; he was anticipating the future, a great talent of his.

With his Party membership pending, the 22-year-old student of law had not only found his intellectual home, but was also shaping an intellectual nest for himself and his friends with every text he published in DAV. He wanted to participate and have a say in the building of the future, a new dawn for mankind. He went to great lengths to substantiate his arguments with careful research, demonstrating the academic training of Charles University.

Prior to the Comintern's fifth congress, so Vladimír wrote, the ideas about nationality had been based on the principle of the nations' right to self-determination, secession included. Although the Slovaks believed that they had achieved national independence thanks to the right to self-determination they were mistaken. Times had changed: the idealists had turned to *Realpolitik*, and the right to self-determination was a forgotten matter, accumulating dust much like an old piano in a flat, forgotten by its owners:

> "Today, our urban bourgeoisie [*mešťiactvo*] has simply lost the courage to show its colours. It is aware of the many objections to that principle. [...] But, the bourgeoisie doesn't feel the need for a serious revision of the right to self-determination, which would, if put into practise properly, result only in a stronger co-operation of Czechoslovakia's nationalities. [...] God, isn't it so much nicer not to rack ones brains about these issues, bury one's head in the sand and carry on one's back a shield promoting the saying: The Truth Shall Prevail [*pravda víťazí*]."[33]

Right at the beginning, Vladimír made his intellectual position clear: he criticized the Czechoslovak politicians who adhered to Jan Hus' famous words about the truth that President Masaryk had made the motto of the Republic. Czechoslovakia was no exception in terms of the problematic right to self-determination,

---

[33] Clementis, "K národnostnej otázke", 2.

yet the Czechoslovak centre-right politicians, as Vladimír stressed, kept refusing to address that difficult issue. After some rather polemical, yet logically consistent paragraphs about the problems of defining what the concept of 'nation' meant, and how differently the social classes interpreted it, he listed the interpretations of Czech Communists, among them the famous Zdeněk Nejedlý.[34] The Czech Communists' view, as Vladimír wrote, could be summarized as follows: the economic and political regime of the Czech bourgeoisie in Slovakia was directly connected with the emerging of the nationalist movement; the chauvinist-reactionary Slovak People's Party was a lively result of the Czech bourgeois regime.[35]

Thus, what point of view should a Communist defend? Vladimír advocated the promotion of a clear Communist standpoint. Any effort that would support the bourgeoisie, any co-operation with the Czech or Slovak bourgeoisie was a mistake:

> "We must smash [*podlomit*] the Czech bourgeoisie's power by taking away its platform [*platformu*], the basis of its imperialism [*imperializmu*]: 'the capitalists created for themselves a legend, a very young legend indeed, which dates from the year 1917, the legend of the unity of the Czechoslovak nation'."[36]

In historical terms, Vladimír was not wrong, since a Czechoslovak nation *de facto* had never existed; what he called 'legend' was the essential element of political Czechoslovakism. One might hold this critical view against him, arguing that he directly benefitted

---

[34] Zdeněk Nejedlý (1878–1962) was an adherent of Masaryk's Progressive Party at the turn of the 20th century. In his Moscow exile in 1939, the KSČ made him a member; his membership was *ex post facto* dated on 1929. Nejedlý was professor of musicology at Charles University, a member of the politburo and held several ministries; see Jiří Křešťan, *Zdeněk Nejedlý. Politik a vědec v osamění* (Praha: Paseka, 2012).
[35] Clementis, "K národnostnej otázke", 3.
[36] Clementis, "K národnostnej otázke", 3.

from that 'legend', since the Republic had made it possible for him not only to study law at Charles University, but granted also the political liberty and tolerance that had made possible the foundation of DAV. On the other hand, Slovak students had studied and graduated in Prague since the 1880s, when the Czech lands were a part of Austria. Regarding access to higher education, Vladimír could have enrolled at Charles University even if the Republic had not been founded. He certainly did not hate the Czechs, since he had Czechs in the family, but he was fighting the Czech bourgeois government.

Very visible in his text was his use of a distinct style of language for which George Orwell would coin the term "newspeak" in his famous novel *1984*.[37] The Leninist revolutionary and military newspeak made a clear distinction between friend and foe, left no room for a differentiated view of economics, social issues and culture and inculcated into the minds of the faithful how to deal with the enemy by repeated usage of distinct concepts: 'smashing the bourgeoisie', which, owing to its embodiment of 'capitalist Imperialism', had defined the concept of 'nation' according to its aims and goals.

Vladimír did not attend the fifth world congress of the Comintern in June and July in Moscow in 1924[38] since he was in Prague, studying and preparing the foundation of DAV, but I deem it safe to assume that he had read the congress minutes and final bulletin to prepare this text, a Philippic promoting Slovak Communism. His language reflected his sincere dedication to the cause, and also, his rejection of any other political opinion.

---

[37] George Orwell, *Ninety-Eighty-Four, Appendix, The Principles of Newspeak*, on http://orwell.ru/library/novels/1984/english/en_app; accessed 10 March 2016.

[38] The meetings of the Comintern on http://www.marxisthistory.org/subject/usa/eam/comintern.html; accessed 10 March 2016.

I had the impression that he had spent many hours over this text, eager to prove his knowledge of the ideology. I think it possible that Vladimír, not yet a Party member, wanted to impress Gottwald with his intellectual acumen, proving to the elder Czech comrade that the young Slovak editor of DAV was reliable in ideological terms. But there was also a new star on the rise in the Soviet Union, and Vladimír, up to date with what was happening in the Soviet Communist Party, presented his definition of 'nation':

> "According to Stalin, a nation is defined by a.) Common territory; b.) A shared or similar economic system; c.) Economic interdependence; d.) Psychological closeness; e.) Common culture; f.) Common language. If one of these factors is missing, a nation's unity ceases to exist."[39]

Although the first three of Stalin's conditions were fulfilled in Czechoslovakia, the last two were ambiguous; one could find arguments that were supportive of a common culture and language, but also arguments that spoke against the unity of culture and language. Vladimír came to the conclusion that the Slovaks had never been, were not and probably would never be an independent nation, but the future might bring about conditions that could result in the formation of the Czechoslovak nation.[40]

The Slovak bourgeoisie, led by the Ľudáci, was promoting Slovak nationalism by suggesting to the people that they were fighting for the Slovak way of life, for Church schools, Christian crosses in state schools and the strict employment of Slovaks in state institutions. The Communists, so Vladimír wrote, could not co-operate with the People's Party, since the slogan "Away with the Czech bourgeoisie [preč s českou buržuásiou]" was only a smokescreen behind which the Slovak bourgeoisie was hiding while gaining in strength.[41] The Communists should not fight on

---

[39] Clementis, "K národnostnej otázke", 3.
[40] Clementis, "K národnostnej otázke", 3.
[41] Clementis, "K národnostnej otázke", 4.

two fronts, against the Czech and the Slovak bourgeoisie – they should concentrate their efforts on the class struggle. He warned of *Ľudáci*-nationalism:

> "Slovakia doesn't have large industrial centres with a worker's class conscious of its rights and goals. And that's why it is twice as dangerous to support the slogan 'Away with the Czechs', adding fuel to the fire of current anti-Czech resentment. [...] Only one party can gain from this slogan: the party, which has all the favourable conditions and the traditional backing of the voters at its disposal. Wouldn't it be more effective and tactical to use the anti-Czech mood in Slovakia exclusively for the class struggle [*čisto triedne*]?"[42]

Theirs would be the task of pursuing the destruction of the Slovak bourgeois regime without joining in the anti-Czech mood the *Ľudáci* were promoting. This way, they could prevent the emerging of illusions in the people's minds about an improvement of the current situation. At the same time, by resolutely rejecting support of the Slovak nationalists-populists, the Communists would expose them as the most faithful ally of the Czech bourgeoisie the adherents of the People's Party seemed to hate so much. The industrial and agricultural workers would understand and see with their own eyes that the KSČ was the only party that was truly interested in improving their lives.

In strategical terms, Vladimír's suggestion was well informed, insightful and, above all, consistent with the Marxist-Leninist view of national identity. The anti-Czech mood in Slovakia was not an issue the Communists should concern themselves with. Besides the fact that the Slovak Communists needed the financial and organizational skills of their Czech comrades, national chauvinism or radical nationalism was a bourgeois idea. A Communist believed in internationalism: the proletariat defined itself only through its class identity. From a Communist viewpoint,

---

[42] Clementis, "K národnostnej otázke", 4.

there were no boundaries dividing the workers; the workers of the world, a class on its own, should unite since they had one common interest and one common goal – to shed the chains of Capitalism as the workers' yoke and burden. The bourgeois concepts of nations, nationalities and nationalism had always been to the exclusive benefit of the wealthy and the bourgeois middle class who were exploiting the workers.

Thus, the principal interest of the workers' movement was the class struggle, pursuing the global rule of the proletariat. Once the workers were in power, the class system would be liquidated; then, they would establish a paradise on Earth for mankind, a truly humanist world that would be free from political oppression, poverty and misery. According to Lenin, the masses had their fate in their own hands. There was no God, Lenin had thought, following Nietzsche and Marx in their atheism. There was no life after death; the Party that had killed the Russian Tsar Nikolai II and his family, had proven with this act that the old order was not only finished, but that God had not taken revenge – since he simply did not exist. Metaphysics was a bourgeois idea: a true Communist 'knew' that there was no God and no life after death. Led by the Party as the avant-garde, the Soviet proletariat had achieved real power on Earth, demonstrating the rightfulness of Marxism-Leninism.

Vladimír continued to prove his excellent knowledge of his credo with a salient criticism of the Agrarian Party and its political thought.

I. 2. 1. 2 Agrarian Thought as New 'Ideology' (1924)

Roughly one year before the parliamentary elections of November 1925, Vladimír published the article "Agrarian Thought as New

'Ideology'"[43] in DAV's first issue; he attacked the Agrarian movement, which he expected to be a strong competitor against the Communists and the Slovak People's Party in the forthcoming elections.

Milan Hodža had founded the Agrarian Party in August 1919 with the support of Vavro Šrobár, Prague's governor of Slovakia.[44] Hodža wanted to build a movement that would represent the interests of the Slovak peasants and, at the same time, create for the Slovak voters a political alternative to the strong People's Party led by Hlinka. The Slovak Club in Prague had been pursuing land reform to change the property situation in Slovakia, since Magyar aristocrats and the Catholic Church owned most of the land.

The government headed by Karel Kramář had supported the land reform, because in those early days of the Republic, the Czech politicians did not have a comprehensive overview of the economic situation and the state institutions of the Hungarian kingdom that were still operative in Slovakia. As analogy to Masaryk's socio-psychological and economic policies of *de-Austrianization* in the Czech lands, the land reform of 1919 and 1920 could be called *de-Magyarization* of Slovakia; its intention was to replace the power of the Hungarian aristocracy and the royal institutions

---

[43] Clementis, "Agrarizmus ako nova 'ideológia'", *DAV I* (1924): 34-39, in *Vzduch našich čias I*, 61-71. His emphasis on the concept 'ideology' in inverted commas demonstrated Vladimír's contempt for Agrarian thought – only Marxism-Leninism was an ideology that deserved the name. The Marxists connoted the concept 'ideology' in positive terms; it was, literally, a scientific approach to political ideas. For a history of the concept of 'ideology' see Karl Mannheim, *Ideology and Utopia. An Introduction to the Sociology of Knowledge* (San Diego, New York, London: Harvest Harcourt, 1936).

[44] Natália Krajčovičová, "The Programme and Objectives of Slovak Agrarianism in the Works of Milan Hodža", in *Milan Hodža. Statesman and Politician* (Bratislava: Veda, 2007), 229-243, 234.

with Czechoslovak industrialization and democratic-republican institutions.

In the early 1920s, the Agrarian Party was disintegrating, having to fight not only the People's Party but also the new Slovak Homeland Party of Small Farmers (*Slovenská domovina, strana maloroľnickeho ľudu*) that had emerged from the trade union known as Slovak Homeland. To strengthen their Slovak colleagues, the Czech Agrarians intervened; on 29 June 1922, both factions merged to form the Czechoslovak Agrarian Party, officially called The Republican Agrarian and Small Farmers Party (*Republikanská strana zemedelského a maloroľnickeho ľudu*). The party was organized centrally from Prague, but Hodža managed to establish an executive committee for the Slovak members, who enjoyed a certain degree of autonomy.[45]

Why did Vladimír, a few months short of membership of the KSČ, attack the Agrarian Party, criticizing its goals and political programme with ice-cold logic and mocking contempt? To him, the main reason was that the Agrarian Party did not have an elaborate and consistent theory that sufficiently justified and explained its activities and goals. Owing to its theoretical misgivings, Agrarian thought could never pose a serious threat to Marxism-Leninism. The political reality, however, was quite different: the People's Party – since 1925 it called itself Hlinka's Slovak People's Party (HSĽS) – would win the parliamentary elections of November 1925,[46] and the Agrarians would beat the Communists in the district and municipal elections in December 1928. Vladimír's love of theory, talent for rhetoric and intellectual enthusiasm

---

[45] Krajčovičová, 235.
[46] The results of the parliamentary elections of 1925 in Slovakia: HSĽS 34,31%; Agrarians 17,4% and KSČ 13,9%; *Chronológia Dejín Slovenska a Slovákov II*, 1202.

spoke for themselves; his description of the agrarian nature of the Slovak economic system was correct:

> "It is an indisputable fact that the agrarian question is one of the fundamental problems of Slovakia. According to the statistics of 1921, almost 59% of our people live from working the soil (agriculture, forestry). [...] The realization of the land reform, the poor conditions of the peasants, tariffs on agricultural products, the increasing indebtedness of the smallholders and many more economic and political problems call for the attention of everybody who concerns themselves, from whatever perspective, with the current situation of Slovakia."[47]

This was the materialistic and pragmatic side of the Agrarian question; he did not mention the benefits of the land reform that had been a first step towards economic democratization by providing the former agrarian workers with small plots of land, thereby liberating them from working for the land-owning aristocracy. Referring to Milan Hodža's speech of 7 September 1924, Vladimír analysed, or rather, tore to pieces the political thought of the Agrarian Party.

Recently, he stressed, eclecticism had become a typical feature of bourgeois sociology: this eclecticism was nice, convenient and also indisputable since it acknowledged dilettantism. Certainly, it was no easy task to build systems or ideologies. An ideology could be created in two ways: first, lay down a theoretical foundation, then think it through to find the inherent contradictions and explain how eclecticism took its revenge by creeping into the theory. Second, analyse in an objective fashion the principles of Agrarianism and check them against the conceptual possibilities of that way of thinking. Clearly, the first method sufficed. Vladimír did not give Agrarian thought an ounce of credit – owing to its bourgeois origins, it was simply not worth the trouble of a

---

[47] Clementis, "Agrarizmus ...", 61.

serious application of Marxist-Leninist analysis, a method of enquiry superior and supreme to him.

Vladimír quoted Hodža's main statements, summarizing the principles of Agrarian thought: all economic, societal and political life was based on the soil (*pôda*); the relationship of man with the soil was the principal moving force of mankind's efforts to create an undisturbed economic progress.[48] That fundamental statement was the point of origin of mankind's main concepts: fatherland; nation; state and societal order. These concepts then formed the conditions for culture, art, industry and exchange of goods, in brief, civilization.

This definition was quite confusing, Vladimír wrote, warming up. Allegedly, the soil was the basis of every material value, the foundation of Agrarian thought. What did the principle of 'the relationship of man to the soil' exactly mean? He was tempted to replace the concept of 'ideology' with "ideological superstructure [*ideologická nadstavba*]".[49] If one wanted to find an answer to the confusing statement that the soil was the origin of everything, one faced only contradictions:

> "Oh that soil! What is it not the mother of! [...] 'from the firm unity of the nation with the soil springs the nation's self-determination'. At the end of the day, perhaps also the integrity of our Republic? Can one really have a polemical debate about this with a solemn face? In that entire ideology you won't find a trace of logic and systematic reasoning [...] and one more thing: the ideology's elements, if we want to call them like that, are but pure bourgeois elements, characteristic for the Slavic way of life, for Slavdom and private property and all the other parts of that programme."[50]

---

[48] Clementis, "Agrarizmus ...", 62-63.
[49] Clementis, "Agrarizmus ...", 63.
[50] Clementis, "Agrarizmus ...", 64.

Those voicing the slogan that Agrarianism would unite the Slavic nations were in support of the corrupt politics of Capitalist Imperialism. The centre-right was reproaching the Communists that Marxism was primitive. What could one possibly say about 'Agrarian-historical materialism'?[51] One could only wonder, as Vladimír wrote, about the empty primitivism that was in denial of the most basic findings of sociology. How could one possibly deduce from the soil the entire organization of mankind and society? What were the origins of the development of society? Would the agrarian 'theoreticians' acknowledge that, for example, the sun was more important and fundamental to human life than the soil? Yet, nobody came up with an adjustment, no Agrarian had so far suggested having a look at mankind's relationship with the sun.

After some brief and polemical sideswipes against Anton Štefánek (1877–1964), a prominent associate of Hodža's, and the current Prime Minister Antonín Švehla (1873–1933),[52] Vladimír came to the conclusion that Agrarian thought was not an ideology that deserved the name:

> "At least in formal terms, Agrarianism wants to be an ideology. Its founders, however, did not have the courage to consider the consequences, to adopt an opinion based on the class system. [...] That is why we have in front of us a programme that is characterized by petit bourgeois eclecticism and theoretical naïveté [*dielo malomeštiackeho eklekticismu a teoretického naivizmu*]."[53]

Referring to Lenin and Eugen Varga (1879–1964), a Hungarian Marxist economist and Comintern functionary, Vladimír listed three fundamental features that characterized the class of the

---

51　Clementis, "Agrarizmus …", 66.
52　An excellent biography of Švehla and Agrarian politics is Daniel E. Miller, *Forging Political Compromise. Antonín Švehla and the Czechoslovak Republican Party 1918–1933* (Pittsburgh, PA: University of Pittsburgh Press, 1999).
53　Clementis, "Agrarizmus …", 69.

peasants in Slovakia. First, the rural-agrarian class was hostile towards the proletariat; it was composed of landowners, smallholders working their own piece of land, Capitalist rent seekers and large-scale farmers. Second, the rural-agrarian class consisted of different factions: the proletariat, the farmers of moderate wealth and the smallholders. If the proletariat assumed governmental power, the rural-agrarian class would be affected primarily by its politics. Economics would affect it only favourably, since the proletariat would do away with mortgages. It was therefore necessary that the agrarian-rural class and the workers' class became united. Third, the semi-proletarian strata and the agricultural workers were a part of the proletarian class living in the countryside.[54]

In his last paragraph, Vladimír referred to the Bulgarian Agrarian movement under Prime Minister Aleksandar Stamboliiskii (1879–1923), who was murdered on 9 June 1923 after a coup d'état of the right-wing military, supported by Italian Fascists and the IMRO (Inner Macedonian Revolutionary Organization). The Bulgarian Communists had remained passive. This example, as Vladimír stressed, demonstrated that the agrarian-rural class was not capable of controlling the complex and difficult organism of a modern state on its own:

> "To accomplish that, it is necessary to control the centres of technology and culture. Today, the bourgeoisie is in control of them; in the future, it will be the proletariat. Will the peasants join the bourgeoisie? Is it possible that they would really prefer not to join hands with the proletariat to achieve a great social ideal?"[55]

---

[54] Clementis, "Agrarizmus ...", 70.
[55] Clementis, "Agrarizmus ...", 71.

I. 2. 1. 3   The Electoral Defeat of the Communists (1929)

In his article "The Electoral Defeat of the Communists"[56] Clementis delivered an analysis of the district and municipal elections of 1928. Why did he use the pen name Vladimír Sopko?[57]

After graduation with a PhD in Law from Charles University on 22 December 1925, he had to absolve five years of internship as *koncipient*; from 1 February 1926, he was employed at the district court of Bratislava. The police had him registered as a member of the KSČ, which resulted in the loss of his first employment.[58] In the young Republic, it was a sensitive issue to be employed by the state and being a member of the Communist Party; Clementis was not the only Communist who was fired because of his political activities. Yet, because of the shortage of Slovak lawyers, he soon found a new position at the office of Dr Kuba, where he would complete his practical training that started on 1 June 1926 and ended on 22 January 1931. He used a pseudonym to protect his career. Also, his profession took up his entire energy and time; DAV was not published in 1927 and 1928.[59]

In the elections to the provincial assemblies of 2 December 1928, the KSČ won 190,595 votes; the Agrarians won 271,520 votes.[60] Clementis wrote that the KSČ had won a percentage of the votes they had gained in the parliamentary elections of 1925, although the intake of military personnel from three successive

---

[56] Clementis, "Volebná porážka komunistov", *DAV III*, no. 1 (1929): 6-7, in *Vzduch našich čias I*, 119-123.
[57] According to Evžen Klinger (1906–1981), Clementis began to use the pseudonym "Sopko" in *DAV*'s third year in 1929; Klinger used it in *DAV*'s fourth volume; *Vzduch našich čias I*, footnote 87, 454.
[58] Holotíková a Plevza, 45.
[59] Holotíková a Plevza, 45.
[60] *Vzduch našich čias I*, 454, footnote 88. Compared with its success in the parliamentary elections of 1925, HSĽS was less successful in the provincial elections because of the strong competition of the Agrarians and Communists.

years (*ročníky*) had been excluded from the vote, due to the amendment of the law about army personnel (*branny zákon*) that had been in effect since 8 April 1927. In its aim to "depoliticize" the army, the Czechoslovak parliament had extended military service from 14 to 18 months and excluded the soldiers, gendarmes and members of the state security service from the vote.[61] The Communists and Social Democrats protested since the amendment would weaken them in future elections; the KSČ had a certain influence and standing among young servicemen from the working class. Clementis quoted from the press releases of the Agrarians, Social Democrats and the People's Party, which were complaining about the Communists' success:

> "'The fight against Bolshevism has to be organized in a completely different manner. We have not been holding back our view that this fight must be the principal task of the *Ľudáci* and the Social Democrats. [...] They are responsible for the success of Bolshevism, not only now in our public sphere, but they will have to shoulder this responsibility also in the future. Neither in the past nor in the recent elections have they understood the true sense of their mission.'"[62]

The Social Democrat Ivan Dérer (1884–1973), as Clementis stressed in a mocking tone, did not even have the courage to admit that the reason why so many voted for the KSČ was the people's disappointment with the centre-right parties in the Prague parliament. Also, Dérer had delivered an embarrassing explanation: only illiterates living in the countryside, that is, the uneducated, had voted for the Communists. His lame statement reminded one of Gábor Ugron from the HSĽS who had cried out "with cowards and corrupt intellectuals one cannot carry the banner of independence to victory".[63] While the "state-building bands and gangs

---

[61] *Chronológia Dejín Slovenska a Slovákov II*, 602.
[62] From the anonymous article "Boj proti Bolševizmu", *Národný denník*, 6 December 1928, quoted from *Vzduch našich čias I*, 454, footnote 90.
[63] Clementis, "Volebná porážka ...", 121.

(*štatotvorné súručenstvo*)" were troubled by the success of the KSČ, the Communists were openly writing about defeat:

> "In view of their activities responding to the current conditions, the Communists should have won many more votes. [...] we have the strongest doubts that the reasons, which resulted in the 191,000 votes for the Slovak Communists, changed so drastically that the government coalition would benefit. [...] Neither the reform of the electoral law the selfish government and the patriotic-oppositional politics of the state-building parties issued, nor other 'possibilities' the gentlemen Hlinka, Dérer, Hodža or Ivanka have at their disposal can make this problem go away. [...] Until 15 November 1925, Slovakia could have been the reservoir of the forces of the reaction [*rezervou reakcie*]. [...] But given the mass character of her social composition, Slovakia is not reactionary – and never shall be."[64]

Since the parliamentary elections of 1925, the Communists had been a serious concern to the Prague government and the centre-right parties alike. In Clementis' way of thinking, Communism had a future in Slovakia – in spite of the fact that the Communists had lost the elections of 1925 and 1928. His conclusion about Slovakia's inherent Socialist character seems to me wishful thinking, and his statements also demonstrate his refusal to respect voters' rights *not* to vote for the KSČ.

After having accused the government coalition and the Prague parliament of orchestrating the KSČ's defeat in Slovakia, he concluded his text with a criticism: Czechoslovakia refused to acknowledge the Soviet Bolshevik government. Slovakia, as Clementis wrote ironically, had one advantage: she did not have in her small towns offices like Arkos or Amtorg, the trade organisations the Soviet government had established in London and New York.[65]

---

[64] Clementis, "Volebná porážka ...", 122. The lawyer Milan Ivanka (1876–1950) was interim Minister for Domestic Affairs in Šrobár's first government (1918-1920). He was an associate of Šrobár's from the times of *Detvan* in the 1880s and, like Šrobár, an Agrarian.

[65] *Vzduch našich čias I*, 454, footnote 91.

Those who were sabotaging negotiations about diplomatic relations or just normal trade relations with the Soviet Union should be reminded of the fact that "the number of Communists in Czechoslovakia is the highest worldwide, higher than in the Soviet Union".[66] Clementis concluded his Philippic with a sarcastic statement: "One still has to find an advantage in entertaining diplomatic relations with the Soviet Union."[67]

The meeting with the Soviet writer and journalist Ilia Ehrenburg (1891–1967), who visited Czechoslovakia in 1928, raised Clementis' curiosity about Marxism-Leninism in practice. In the autumn of 1929, he went on a first trip to the Soviet Union, followed by a second in 1930, when he attended the International Congress of Revolutionary Writers in Kharkov in Soviet Ukraine.[68] In 1929, he was twenty-seven years old, just about to accomplish his training phase and soon to be professionally independent. What did the young lawyer see in the workers' paradise?

I. 2. 1. 4   The Trips to the Soviet Union (1929, 1930)

Clementis described his impressions of the Soviet Union in 1931 in DAV, two years after his first trip to the workers' state. I selected three articles: "In the second year of the Five-Year Plan", "Potemkin villages built of concrete" and "A bowl of borsht and a glass of beer".[69]

In 1929, the first year of the first Soviet Five-Year Plan, he visited Moscow, Leningrad, Kharkov and Kiev, "the city that had suffered most from the attacks of the counterrevolutionary bands

---

[66] Clementis, "Volebná porážka …", 123.
[67] Clementis, "Volebná porážka …", 123.
[68] Holotíková a Plevza, 56.
[69] Clementis, "V druhom roku piatiletky", *DAV IV*, no. 1 (1931): 4-5; "Potemkinove dediny zo železobetonu", *DAV IV*, no. 2 (1931): 10-11; "Tanier boršču a pohár piva", *DAV IV*, no. 3 (1931): 12-13.

of Poles and mercenaries at the service of Imperialism".[70] He made new friends and experienced the enthusiasm of the Soviet people who explained their future to him in lengthy conversations:

> "'We are building: electrification, collectivization, sovkhozes, gigantic factories, socialist cities, a new culture, film.' [...] And, at one o'clock in the morning, one of my new friends, a poet and editor, invites me to visit with him the Lavra tower. [...] Later, I regretted not having gone, not because of the city, I had seen many, and not because of the monastery, which was the most famous destination of Orthodox pilgrimage, [...] but because of the enthusiastic words of my friend who so passionately described the iron bridge over the Dnieper that was illuminated by electric bulbs. This was not the enthusiasm of our bourgeois poets eager to 'civilize' the people [civilistických básnikov]. This was the emotional perception of human effort, of the building of victorious Socialism. It was the pathos of the *literati*, the engineers and the pathos of the small pioneers in their red bandanas."[71]

What difference between this Socialist pathos and the constructivist snobbery of the *literati* and intellectuals of the bourgeois countries! Clementis praised Soviet education and organisation of work: the workers were very well trained. The state institution "Protection of Work" (*Ochrana trudu*) had established a healthcare system, institutions of vocational, academic and professional training and organized also the cultural aspects of the new way of life.[72] Its principal goal was to make sure that the workers ruled the machines, not the other way round, not in the fashion of the "meaningless Americanism [*bezobsážný amerikanizmus*]" – this was evident to everybody who could tell the Capitalist and Socialist principles of social and economic organization apart.[73]

---

[70] Clementis, "V druhom ...", 4.
[71] Clementis, "V druhom ...", 4.
[72] Clementis, "V druhom ...", 4.
[73] Clementis, "V druhom ...", 4.

In 1930, a year later, Clementis returned to the Soviet Union to observe what had changed. It was the second year of the Five-Year Plan. He wrote in an enthusiastic tone, adding many exclamation marks, often using Russian words to render his text more authentic, to convey to his readers that there was a new society emerging, a new spirit ruling the vast country that spanned twelve time zones. To him, the Soviet Union was the shining beacon of Socialism, the future of mankind.

The city centres had completely changed, as he wrote: the Soviet government had established cultural institutions and administrative offices in the palaces of the former aristocracy. Now, workers' families lived in the houses of the former bourgeoisie. The suburbs, however, were badly connected with the city centre, the roads were dirty, and the houses, like old barracks, were oozing a depressing grey. Only the new Socialist towns were different; they truly embodied the Socialist spirit. Their architecture corresponded to the construction plans of a new society, a new way of life and a new culture.[74]

The old parts of the cities had changed: the last privately owned shops had vanished. Now, not even cigarette sellers were to be seen in the streets, only shoe polishers and the traditional horse carriages that sold apples from Georgia. The state grocery shops were not yet perfect: one was losing too much time in the "*ocheredi*" (queues).[75] Moscow was overpopulated; people had moved to the capital after WWI and the Russian Revolution, and the problems of the traffic system were not yet successfully resolved.

In view of the many queues, did the people of Moscow suffer from hunger? Clementis answered his rhetorical question with a decisive no: the state had established eateries and community

---

[74] Clementis, "V druhom …", 4.
[75] Clementis, "V druhom …", 4.

canteens (*jedálne*), which served good and nourishing food.[76] Meat was available, fish and poultry were still rare, but these problems would soon be tackled:

> "These are problems of transition and, compared with the last summer months, they are almost gone. [...] Therefore, one can see a firm and organized will to master them. These problems are but appearances [*zjavy*] that are going to vanish, much like the privately owned shops vanished, but what has also vanished is exploitation [*vykorisťovanie*] and the class of the bourgeoisie as its prime mover [*a jeho nositeľ buržoázna trieda*]."[77]

In his second article "Potemkin villages built of concrete",[78] Clementis referred to his first trip in 1929, when he had gathered information about the Soviet economic system. Back then, he had missed one important aspect of the new Soviet regime: besides the oil of the Caucasus and the coal of the Donets Basin, there was the "human material, these nameless millions marching towards world history with unwavering faith in a new society".[79] In 1929 he had visited Kharkov; he had had doubts whether the Five-Year Plan could be realized:

> "We went with friends to empty fields that were frozen, hollow and hopeless. Noisy Kharkov was behind us, on some plains only little huts, standing askew. One of the guides explained to me, with some courage, the plan of *Traktorbuda*. He was supposed to start building on 1 May 1930. The factory will produce tractors and agricultural machinery. It will be larger than the one in Stalingrad (that produces 50,000 tractors a year), and 50,000 workers are going to be employed here. On those

---

[76] Clementis, "V druhom ...", 4.
[77] Clementis, "V druhom ...", 4-5.
[78] Clementis, "Potemkinove dediny ...", 10. The title refers to the fake buildings Prince Grigorii Potemkin (1739–1791) had built in 1787 to impress Catherine the Great who visited her new Southern colonies in Crimea. For an interesting account see Michael David-Fox, "The Myth of the Soviet Potemkin village", on http://www.histoire.ens.fr/IMG/file/Coeure/David-Fox%20Potemkin%20villages.pdf; accessed 27 March 2016.
[79] Clementis, "Potemkinove dediny ...", 10.

plains they are going to build a city for the workers that shall be an expression of Socialist principles … shall … shall … shall! Can they do it? […] And in November 1930, I was there for the second time. One hundred delegates of the International Congress of Revolutionary Writers visited the plains of Kharkov. This time, the sun was shining. And they had done it!"[80]

On those formerly empty plains there now stood a huge brickyard with the capacity to produce eight million bricks annually for the construction of *Traktorbuda*. The Socialist city was almost finished: for each worker an apartment with two rooms, a bathroom and a small kitchen for warming up food, because the eateries and community canteens would cook the meals for the workers. Schools, theatres and cinemas – they would be finished soon. And the foundation stone of this complex had been laid only on 1 May 1930.[81] Clementis praised the Red Army: 10,000 soldiers and officers had worked on the construction site and dug canals for the water supply. Who would not want to become better acquainted with such an army?

When the Writers' Congress allowed some free time, the twenty-eight-year-old V. Ya. Furer, the chairman of Ukrainian Agitprop and a brigadier-general in the Red Army, led Clementis, Egon Erwin Kisch (1885–1948), Franz Carl Weiskopf (1900–1955) and Ernst Glaeser (1902–1963) through the barracks of the army corps of engineers.[82] A fortnight previously, Furer had received new recruits; some of them had travelled for the first time on a train, while others had to be taught how to use the toilets. The corps was raising pigs, poultry and rabbits, because the Soviet Army did not want to live off the workers and arranged for its own supplies. The revolutionary writers visited the library of the barracks; there, Clementis inquired about Czech literature and was

---

[80] Clementis, "Potemkinove dediny …", 10.
[81] Clementis, "Potemkinove dediny …", 10.
[82] Clementis, "Potemkinove dediny …", 10.

astonished to learn that they had ten copies of the famous *Švejk*.⁸³ In the libraries of the Czechoslovak army, *Švejk* was forbidden! The Red Army was closely connected with the political, economic and cultural aspects of the building of Socialism, and members of the hostile classes were not allowed to join. The spirit of the Red Army was particularly impressive. Furer explained to his writer friends how the Red Army was overseeing the induction of new recruits:

> "We start the training of the recruits with information: we inform them about our economic and political concerns, here in the Soviet Union and abroad. Once they have understood their duties and tasks for the building of Socialism, we teach them the Red Army's iron discipline [*ich budeme učiť železnej discipline rudej armády*]. After that, everybody understands why he is needed."⁸⁴

Clementis was concerned about the orphans, "the children who lost their parents in the Civil War and suffered hunger because of the embargo of the 'humanistic and civilized countries'".⁸⁵ He might find them in Moscow, he wrote. He had a look at the Lubyanka; the pseudo-baroque palace was a ghost of the past, "of the speculators from the NEP years [*nepamanov*]" ⁸⁶ and Europe

---

83 Jaroslav Hašek's *The Good Soldier Švejk* is the principal novel about the Czech national character. Švejk, a middle-aged catcher of stray dogs, survives WWI with his characteristic shrewdness.
84 Clementis, "Potemkinove dediny …", 11.
85 Clementis, "Potemkinove dediny …", 11.
86 Clementis, "Potemkinove dediny …", 11. NEP (*Novaia Ekonomičeskaia Politika,* New Economic Policy) was Lenin's economic policy in the Civil War years. NEP was launched in 1921; based on the re-privatisation of retail trade and small- and medium scale manufacture and services, NEP kept the state monopoly on heavy industry, banking and foreign trade. NEP's short-term goal aimed at the revival of the food sector that had suffered in the civil war. The conscriptions and requisition methods during wartime communism were no incentive for the farmers to increase production; the result was shortages and famines. NEP was a pragmatic step towards letting a modest market of consumer goods and food supply emerge. In the long run, however, the goal of Soviet command economy was the collectivization of agriculture:

alike. Now, it was the seat of the GPU (*Gosudarstvennoe Političeskoie Upravlenie*, State Political Directorate). There were no orphans to be found on the streets of Moscow, but he did finally find them in Kharkov. One hundred and fifty orphans lived in the Džeržinskii colony, established and managed by the GPU. The children lived in a modern building behind the aerodrome and could stay there until they reached the age of eighteen. They received education and vocational training and were excellently trained workers when they left the colony. Like every school in the Soviet Union, the colony was financed by state subsidies.

Clementis finished his text with praise for the Bolshevik revolution and the building of Soviet Socialism. In his view, there was nothing bad to be found in the workers' paradise, only economic and political successes that demonstrated the rightfulness and legitimacy of Marxism-Leninism:

> "A young commander of the colony guided us through the buildings. On the many *stengazety* in the corridors, one could see all the signs of the new spirit [*náznakmi nového ducha*], which was turning these orphans into pioneers of a new society, preparing them to build the future. This new spirit is also integrating the workers into an army of millions, the workers who are building 'Potemkin villages' of concrete, reaching from Negoreloie to Vladivostok in the Far East."[87]

In his article "A bowl of borsht and a glass of beer", Clementis described the activities of the Soviet artists and intellectuals. He began his text with a description of two events. He had received a letter from a person who had attended one of his many lectures about the Soviet Union. Apparently, as the author of the letter

---

the building of *sovkhozes* (large collective farms) and *kolkhozes* (collective farms); Geoffrey Hosking, *A History of the Soviet Union 1917-1991* (London: Harper Collins, 1992), 119ff. See also Oscar J. Baendelin, *Return to the NEP. The False Promise of Leninism and the Failure of Perestroika* (Westport, CT: Praeger, 2002).

[87] Clementis, "Potemkinove dediny ...", 11. *Stengazety* are wall newspapers; Negoreloie is Nieharelaie, today in Belarus.

wrote, everything in the Soviet Union was fine: the Five-Year Plan, the kolkhozes, the gigantic tractors, the machinery. Why did Clementis not "divulge more about the people, about their subjective lives [*o ich subjektivnom živote*], how they lived, loved, laughed, cried?"[88] An elderly gentleman had approached him after a lecture in Bratislava. He wanted to know if they were still eating borshtsh in the Soviet Union. But of course, Clementis replied, in the Ukraine they ate it with cream, in Moscow with milk. The elderly gentleman said with a smile that all was fine then, that the Five-Year Plan was working for them. These two events inspired him to write about his experience in the Soviet Union.

In Leningrad, Clementis and Ilia Gruzdev (1892–1960), a "*gorkiiolog* [Gorky scholar]", visited Grigorii M. Kosincev (1905–1973), the brother of Ilia Ehrenburg's wife; Kosincev was a film director at Sovkino, the largest film production company in the Soviet Union.[89] In the smoking breaks – Kosincev was shooting a new film – they gathered in the corridor and had an animated discussion. Kosincev explained his working method in detail, from the ideological conception of the film to the technical realization:

> "'We are not interested in abstract man, mankind with its past problems of 'good and evil'. We are not interested in the individual, isolated from his class. Our country is too big and has more pressing problems; we are helping to solve them in our professional field and with our means. We are analysing the social issues, society, applying the principles of the VKP (b) [*Vsesoiuznaia Komunističeskaia Partiia (bolševiki)*, All-Union Communist Party (bolševiks)]. The dialectical 'procedure', photography, sound, film and so forth.' [...] I walked through the wardrobe, where showcases protected the old Tsarist costumes from dust – the dust of history has already fallen on them. [...] I saw a little black bear, attached to the camera. As the film would be synchronized later, I asked

---

[88] Clementis, "Tanier boršču ...", 12. Gruzdev was Gorkii's biographer.
[89] Clementis, "Tanier boršču ...", 12.

Kozincev about the bear while he was shooting. 'Ach, it's just there, it's a lucky charm.'"⁹⁰

With drunken legs you won't march towards Socialism – that was probably the reason why the beer in the Soviet Union was so bad and expensive. Clementis learnt in Leningrad that beer could also be used as a means to fight alcoholism. The activities of a young Communist collective demonstrated to him a further aspect of the new spirit. During his visit to TRAM, the Theatre of the Young Workers, he met the team, some fifty actors and workers who lived together in a commune. TRAM was the most modern theatre in the Soviet Union and likely to become one of the most prestigious, since its members approached theatre in a Marxist way. Young workers, *Komsomoltsi* and Party members were not in the theatre to play or perform; theirs was the task of *agitprop*, to invoke the Socialist spirit:

> "The author receives a script, which he has to flesh out with words. The theme is taken from their lives off-stage, from the life of the Communist youth in the Party and the commune. [...] One example is the TRAMists' campaign against alcohol. In their understanding, it is not decent to agitate against alcohol on-stage and drink off-stage. They have all their meals together; one day, a lively discussion started, because one member insisted on having a beer with his lunch. He got his beer. On the first day, he drank it, ignoring the jokes of his comrades. On the third day, the beer seemed to taste bitter and he didn't drink it. But at every lunch over the next few days, there was a beer on the table for him. Finally he had had enough and poured it down the drain; since then he couldn't even stand the smell of beer."⁹¹

Compared with other professions, writers received the highest salaries in the SSSR; the state was in control of editorship, so naturally, the profession had lost its exploitative character. It was no surprise that many citizens felt that they were writers, trying to

---

90 Clementis, "Tanier borščudot;", 12.
91 Clementis, "Tanier borščudot;", 12-13.

cash in from the state. Clementis praised the Party's micromanaging of every aspect of life, the artistic one included; what amounted *de facto* to censorship, control of the press and the loss of freedom of speech was of no concern to him. Yet, to be fair, prior to the beginning of the Stalinist show trials and purges in 1936, not only Western leftist intellectuals were in awe of the new state; many Soviet citizens were enthusiastic about the government and the new spirit that ruled the country.

Clementis met Osip Maksimovič Brik (1888–1945); Brik was the leading leftist intellectual and married to Lilia Brik (1891–1978), a celebrated beauty of ProletArt and muse of the famous poet Vladimír Vladimírovič Maiakovskii (1893–1930).[92] Brik told Clementis two stories about the difficulties they had in rooting out the old ways. The first story was about greed and inflated self-esteem in literature.

Some citizen from a Western *gubernia* (province), let's call him Ivan Ivanovič, wrote poems and submitted them to a journal in Moscow; let's assume it was the famous *Ogoniok*.[93] So far, the editor-in-chief had thrown the one hundred poems and manuscripts of Ivan Ivanovič into the dustbin, but, in case the poet was a worker, why not publish the one hundred and first? He immediately paid the royalties, some twenty to thirty roubles. After two or three weeks, a man showed up in the editorial office, rudely leaving his wife standing in the hallway. Ivan Ivanovič had travelled to Moscow in the belief that he was already an eminent writer, acknowledged by a famous journal in the capital. Of course, he had brought with him further manuscripts – and his entire family, hoping that the journal would put them up in a nice apartment. And the desperate editor had no choice but to escort him back to

---

[92] Clementis, "Tanier boršču …", 13.
[93] *Ogoniok* is a weekly journal still published today; see http://www.pressreader.com/russia/ogonyok; accessed 28 March 2016.

the railway station, buy tickets for the whole family at the journal's expense and wait on the platform to make sure that they really left.

Brik's second story involved the class of the kulaks, the wealthy farmers and landowners, a class enemy of the ruling proletariat. Clementis was impressed with the friendly atmosphere and the lively discussion with the leftist writers:

> "Brik is speaking in beautiful German because of Glaeser. We are having tea at Aseev's house, discussing the forthcoming Writers' Congress in Kharkov. [...] When I asked Brik to recommend recently published books that describe the current situation, he answered immediately, recommending the *brožurky* written by some twenty workers, all former Kulaks. [...] Last year, the government had built a new factory in a remote village in western Siberia. There, the citizens were all former members of the Kulak class. And, indeed, it was really interesting to see how the proletarian ideology was conquering their minds. With few exceptions, these people had turned, in the space of six months, into self-aware and self-confident workers. That was the scientific conception of the extinction of the Kulaks as a class."[94]

The bowl of borsht and the glass of beer were Clementis' symbols for the Soviet successes in building Socialism. The Soviet people did not suffer hunger, and widespread alcoholism was a sign of Capitalist exploitation that had caused desperation and misery in the past. The young generation was fighting alcoholism; it understood the moral values of Socialist society: work, loyalty to the government, sobriety and proper class-consciousness.

Clementis would defend the Soviet Union against allegations published in the HSĽS press in 1935, flatly denying that there was a kernel of truth in the rumours about the Ukrainian famine seeping out from the workers' state.

---

[94] Clementis, "Tanier borščhu ...", 13. Nikolai Aseev (1889–1963) was a Soviet poet.

I. 2. 1. 5 The Anti-Soviet Press Campaign (1935)

An article entitled "*SLOVÁK* is looking at the SSSR"[95] appeared in DAV in 1935. Clementis referred to a quote from Karol Sidor (1901–1953), a devout Catholic and prominent politician of the HSĽS. Sidor was editor-in-chief of the daily newspaper *Slovák* from 1929 to 1938; on 15 December 1934 he had written:

> "The Slovak nation will not stand by indifferently and watch the spreading of Communism and its teachings here in our country. We shall fight not only Communism, but also those who are fraternizing with it, those who are trying to destroy our Slovak and Christian spiritual values. All of Slovakia will stand behind us in the next elections!"[96]

The autonomist press had become the chief instrument and principal organ of the campaign against Bolshevism. The campaign also involved the press promoting national unity, namely *Národ*, *Národní Listy*, *Polední List* and other centre-right newspapers. Naturally, as Clementis wrote in a sarcastic tone, a Slovak through and through could not be bothered with the fact that these newspapers were the organs of the strong Czech capital and Czech nationalism, which was already so whipped up that it was close to Fascism.[97] These were the organs of the people and institutions that had excelled "in mainstreaming the industry of Slovakia" [*že priemysel Slovenska bol tak dokonale 'zglajchšaltovaný'*].[98] In his article, he demonstrated the methods *Slovák* used in its anti-Soviet press campaign.

According to Sidor, the *Ľudáci* were not only nationalists, but their nationalism was also canonised by their Christian beliefs. Yet, even they had admitted that the Soviet nationality policy acknowledged the right to self-determination – which was in tune

---

[95] Clementis, "SLOVÁK sa diva na SSSR", *DAV 8*, no. 1 (1935): 8-11.
[96] Clementis, "SLOVÁK sa diva ...", 8.
[97] Clementis, "SLOVÁK sa diva ...", 8.
[98] Clementis, "SLOVÁK sa diva ...", 8.

with the *Ľudáci's* claim for Slovak autonomy. Yet, blind for the successes of the workers' state and so eager to protect the faithful from the virus of godless Soviet atheism, they had to come up with blatant lies. Clementis quoted from *Slovák* from 10 January 1934:

> "Everybody, who has read the Constitution of the Union of the Soviet Socialist Republics has the impression that Bolshevik Russia is the only state that has wisely and healthily solved the nationality issue. Hitherto unknown nations have built their republics [...] Stalin's regime is establishing a centralist policy that is Russifying the nations with the aim to create a uniform and indivisible Russia."[99]

To further justify the holy intentions of *Slovák*, the article continued with a description that only "an expert [*človek od fachu*]" could have written.[100] An expert, who knew how to instil into the people living in this world the fear of the next world, the terror of an after-life in hell. Clearly, Clementis hinted at the Catholic clergy, a principal enemy of the Communists and strong supporter of the HSĽS. For centuries, the Catholic clergy had been terrorizing the people with their horror stories, what appalling tortures the sinners could expect in hell. They had the imagination and ruthlessness to concoct horror tales and knew what buttons to push to arouse anti-Soviet feelings:

> "In the once-rich Ukraine, entire villages have vanished, the roads are overgrown with grass; where houses once stood, only ruins are to be seen now. The farmers are dying; if they resist [the collectivization enforced by the Stalin government, add. JB], they are shot. The newspaper Le Matin wrote on 31 August 1933 that cannibalism [*ľudojedstvo*] is a horrible reality in the Ukraine. In the evenings, the people stay indoors, afraid of being attacked, killed and eaten. In some cases, parents killed their own children and ate them. People are also eating those who recently died; they are digging out the dead from their graves. People's

---

[99] Clementis, "SLOVÁK sa diva ...", 8.
[100] Clementis, "SLOVÁK sa diva ...", 9.

bodies are bloated from nutritional oedema, the children are constantly crying."[101]

Clementis did not believe a word of the rumours about the artificially created famine and isolated cases of cannibalism in Ukraine, although *Slovák* had quoted the French *Le Matin*. He added pictures to prove the allegations of *Slovák* lies: on page 8 was the portrait of a happily smiling elderly female kolkhoz farmer in Ukraine, shouldering a bundle of wheat; on page 9 a picture of five young shock-workers from Minsk and on page 10 a picture of a workers' quarter in a Socialist city, a typical Soviet block of houses built in the style of constructivism.

The anti-Soviet campaign of *Slovák* included more lies: in the issue of 12 January 1935, the newspaper had claimed that the Slovak Communists were portraying themselves as autonomists fighting for the Slovak right of self-determination.[102] The Bolsheviks, as Clementis referred to his Party, fought, were fighting and would always be fighting, for the right of self-determination of every nation, but never for Slovak autonomy nor for any system intent on establishing a compromise brokered by the Czech and Slovak bourgeois elites. Such a compromise would be realised at the cost of the working people; it would only cement the interests of the Slovak and Czech bourgeoisie. *Slovák* was neither correct nor logically consistent in its musings about autonomy, the Communists and the relations between Czechs and Slovaks:

> "*Slovák* gave up on its own theory of national individuality [*téorie o samobytnosti slovenského národa*] a long time ago. How often do we

---

[101] Clementis, "SLOVÁK sa diva ...", 9. For information about the *Holodomor*, the artificially created famine in Ukraine in 1932 and 1933, see http://www.ncas.rutgers.edu/center-study-genocide-conflict-resolution-and-human-rights/ukrainian-famine; accessed 29 March 2016.
[102] Clementis, "SLOVÁK sa diva ...", 9.

read about 'Czechoslovak' teams in its reports about international athletic contests? They are using the concept 'Czechoslovak', even if there is not a single Slovak in the sport's team."[103]

After more quotes from *Slovák*, which Clementis condemned as hypocrisy and lack of humanism, he finished with a call that was a chilling portent of his way of thinking: Sidor was naïve to believe that the Slovak people would be united in their resistance against Communism. It was the other way round: nothing but their sympathy for the Soviet Union was uniting the Slovak working people and "save for the workers, nobody else matters [*Na tých ostatných -- nezáleží*]".[104]

Clementis had not become a radical after his trips to the Soviet Union – he had been a radical already in his early journalism of the 1920s, shutting out any criticism of the Soviet Union and the politics of the KSČ. He firmly rejected any news and rumours about the famine in Ukraine as anti-Soviet propaganda.

Naturally, we shall never know whether he was shocked to learn about the famine or believed that it was happening at all. Also, we can only speculate if he consulted English, French or German newspapers. If he had any, he did not express his doubts in public. I think it safe to assume that, had he indeed read international newspapers, he must have convinced himself that the press of the Capitalist states was mounting a campaign against the Soviet Union, envious of the successes of the Five-Year Plan. *Slovák* was only joining in the Western anti-Soviet propaganda. Defending his credo, Clementis fiercely rejected doubt and objectivity; in his way of thinking, everything fell into its logical place, consistent with the Soviet Party line. Not a shred of doubt would darken the rising dawn, the red horizon of the glorious Socialist future.

---

[103] Clementis, "SLOVÁK sa diva ...", 9.
[104] Clementis, "SLOVÁK sa diva ...", 11.

Clementis' exclusion of citizens who did not belong to the working class was most disturbing in terms of tolerance and democracy; to him, only the proletariat counted. His argumentation was logically consistent, which was not that great an achievement for a doctor of law and Party member trained in the principles of Marxism-Leninism. His thinking was radical: he knew only two intellectual camps, pro-Soviet and anti-Soviet. He did not acknowledge a middle way; in his thought, there was no room for compromise and no attempt to read the nuances of the situation. Clementis was no democrat, but he benefitted from the Republic's political tolerance to put forward his praise of the Soviet Union.

Four years earlier, in 1931, Clementis had demonstrated his dedication to Socialism in a trial that divided the Czechoslovak public into four parts: Communists, non-Communists, Czechs and Slovaks. Known in Slovakia as a Communist because of his journalism for DAV, the trial of Košuty would catapult him to fame – and notoriety. As a lawyer of the KSČ, he was the champion of the poor and oppressed, a Slovak Robin Hood with a doctorate of law. His political adversaries considered him a dangerously clever demagogue at the service of the godless Soviet Bolsheviks.

I. 3   Black Whitsuntide in Košuty (1931)

Czechoslovakia was not spared the harsh consequences of the world economic crisis in the 1930s. All Western economies suffered from the Great Depression.[105] Unemployment was on the

---

[105] See Roman Holec, "The Great Depression of 1929–1933 from the point of view of Czechoslovak financial experts and economists", on http://research.uni-leipzig.de/~eniugh/congress/fileadmin/eniugh2011/papers/Roman_Holec_TheGreatDepressionFromthePointofViewofCzechoslovak_2014-09-01.pdf; accessed 30 March 2016.

rise, social unrest, strikes and protest marches occurred; the politicians discussed in parliament the possibilities of government-subsidized labour and how to deal with the workers' protests. Children waited in front of soup kitchens with bowls in their hands, and queues of workers gathering in front of employment offices were a regular sight in the streets of Czechoslovakia's cities, towns and villages.[106]

The economic crisis strengthened the Communist movement all over Europe. The KSČ seemed to have the right approach to the social and economic crisis of the Capitalist system. Even the liberal democrat Ferdinand Peroutka, a close associate of President Masaryk and editor-in-chief of the revue *Přítomnost* (*The New Presence*), wrote that the Soviet Five-Year Plan was an important incentive to think about the recent harsh and unexpected blows of Capitalism.[107] Furthermore, one did not have to be a faithful Marxist to see that the economic crisis had, in its wake, also brought about the rise of Fascism in Italy and Spain and National Socialism in Germany, posing serious political threats to democracy. The crisis concentrated the minds of citizens all over Europe:

> "The blow of the economic crisis simplified the world and the people's opinions about it."[108]

In this desperate atmosphere, the shooting in the Western Slovak village of Košuty and the way the Czechoslovak government dealt with it seemed to confirm the view that Capitalism had never been, was not and would never be just. Capitalism was not about fairness and responsibility, but about exploitation and profit.

---

[106] Holotíková a Plevza, 59.
[107] Holotíková a Plevza, 59-60.
[108] Holotíková a Plevza, 60.

Many thought that Capitalism was a deeply inhuman economic order that could not compete with the successes of the Soviet economic system and the Five-Year Plan. Others thought that the Republic had the right to defend its democratic constitution by punishing Communist agitators who were time and again setting the workers against the government.

Košuty is a little village south of Trnava and Nitra, larger towns in western Slovakia; the violent incident gave Clementis the opportunity to put his profession at the service of his political beliefs. The defence in the trial of the KSČ delegate Štefan Major catapulted him into the public eye in both the Slovak and Czech parts of the Republic. It was a watershed in his political and professional life. What had happened in Košuty?

On 25 May 1931, a platoon of policemen (*četníci*) shot into a demonstration of agricultural workers led by delegate Major. Three workers died on the spot, six were gravely injured. Clementis and his friend Laco Novomeský visited the village two days later with a parliamentary delegation of the KSČ to investigate the details of the incident. DAV reported in a lengthy article about the tragedy, describing the miserable conditions of the agricultural workers in Slovakia. Nobody signed the article "Black Whitsuntide in Košuty",[109] but it is safe to assume that Clementis, as DAV's editor-in-chief, had put the information together and set the tone. Also, many text passages were held in a sarcastic tone, a particular rhetoric specialty of his.

The article showed a picture of Štefan Major making a speech, looking a bit like Lenin, with a hand raised above his head

---

[109] "Čierne Turice košutské", *DAV IV*, no. 5-6 (1931): 4-9. Anticipating that government censorship would affect their report, the editors asked the MP Kubač, a Party member, to "immunize" the text, that is, pro-active self-censorship, which he did on 2 June 1931. However, there are five text passages marked with "Konfiškované parlamentnou cenzúrou", indicating that parliamentary censorship had been applied.

and sporting a Lenin moustache; a caricature by the artist František Bidlo (1895–1945) was added, and four pictures of victims in white hospital garments showed their wounds. The text consisted of six parts: the main report; a description of Štefan Major, sarcastically titled "The Culprit"; a list of ten persons with a description of their wounds, titled "Ten persons lying in the dust of the streets"; an excerpt from the speech of the Agrarian politician and Interior Minister Juraj Slavík (1890–1969), entitled "Peace and order have returned to Košuty"; a comment by Julius Fučík (1903–1943), the editor of the Czech Communist journal for art and literature *Tvorba* (*Creation*), entitled "Here, children, democracy is in the making" and a comment by Dr Friedrich Bill, the chairman of the Czechoslovak League for Human Rights, entitled "The Slovak agricultural workers".[110]

The article began with the statement that one could not write about the shooting in Košuty without first clearing the air; the latter part of the sentence was censored, but one can assume that the editors had in mind something like 'clearing the air of the government's false information about the workers' living conditions'.[111] The people living in the little village in the Galanta district and its vicinity, wrote DAV, were mainly agricultural workers, very few were rich farmers. The owner of the sugar factory and the major part of the surrounding fields was a limited company that set the workers' salaries. Representatives of the Czech Živnobanka, the Prague Ministry of Agriculture and the "Viennese

---

[110] The titles in Slovak: Muž, ktorý je vinný, 4; Desať ľudí v prachu cesty, 6; Nyni je v Košutech klid a pořádek ..., 7; Zde se, děti, dělá demokracie, 8; Slovenskí zemerobotníci, 9. Fučík, tortured and executed by the Nazis in 1943, was a leading figure of the Communist resistance in the protectorate. The Gottwald government made Fučík a martyr of Communism.
[111] "Čierne Turice košutské", 4.

Capitalist Jews" Baron Kuttner and millionaire Guttmann were on the board of the company.[112]

These gentlemen, DAV continued, dictated the desperate living conditions of the workers: for a day of twelve to fourteen hours hard labour, a man received 7 crowns, a woman 6 crowns and a youngster 5 crowns. Since 1925, not a year had gone by without strikes and demonstrations in this district. Earlier in May, two thousand workers had gone on strike, but Mr Pfeffer and Mr Schiketanz, the directors of the sugar factory, simply refused to listen to the workers' complaints. Thanks to the intervention of a member of the district administration, who saw the desperation and poverty of the people, the directors finally caved in and signed a new contract with the workers. The male workers now received 1.30 crowns an hour, the women and young workers 1.10 crowns an hour.[113] Košuty was only the latest violent event in the workers' fight for a slice of bread: government violence had occurred in Krompach, Ardenov, Rumanov, Trenčín, Zvolen and Kereskyn.[114]

As it was widely known that delegate Major would speak at the demonstration, which the government had forbidden, police troops (*četníci*) were deployed to Košuty on 25 May; according to the number they had at their disposal, as DAV wrote, sixty gendarmes were deployed to the little village, not forty, as the government had claimed.[115] That preparation was certainly no coincidence! Around three o'clock in the afternoon, some forty people arrived in Košuty from the village of Hegy, among them delegate

---

[112] "Čierne Turice košutské", 4.
[113] "Čierne Turice košutské", 4. The authors did not present the figures of the daily salary, only the sum per hour. After the raise, the men received for a fourteen-hour day 18.20 crowns, women and youngsters 15.40 crowns, which is a rise in salary of almost 50%, compared with the 7, 6 and 5 crowns the authors mentioned earlier.
[114] "Čierne Turice košutské", 5.
[115] "Čierne Turice košutské", 5.

Major. A platoon of seven gendarmes stopped them. Officer Hocka asked to speak to Major. After some minutes, the group then continued its march through the village, accompanied by the gendarmes. Why did the platoon not stop them there and then? The government had no explanation for this detail. The group gathered in front of the Church in Košuty, a traditional meeting place. Some forty workers from the village joined them. The armed policemen formed a cordon, standing between the people and the church.[116]

According to Minister Slavík, the drunken mob, some one hundred and fifty persons, attacked the policemen and threw stones at them. Major was among the mob, inciting them to violence. This was not true, DAV wrote. Witnesses had told them that officer Janošík[117] had called up the delegate. Major had walked up to him, and was told that the demonstration was forbidden. Major, aware of the dangerous situation with the armed policemen standing in front of the masses, said they would disperse, turned around and wanted to walk back to the demonstrators – when officer Janošík hit him with his sabre on the back. The people saw Major on the floor and immediately attacked the policemen who then shot into the masses. The record of the tragic event: three

---

[116] "Čierne Turice košutské", 6.
[117] Janošík is a mythical figure in the Slovak collective memory, a proletarian Robin Hood who lives in the Tatra mountains and robs the rich to give to the poor; see Hana Hlôšková, "Národný hrdina Juraj Jánošík", in *Mýty naše slovenské* (Bratislava: Academic Electronic Press, 2005), 94-103, and my "Das Tatra-Gebirge als Symbol der slowakischen nationalen und politischen Identität", in *Berge* (Zürich: Chronos, 2009), 139-150. The unlucky platoon commander's name put a cynical spin on the tragedy: the Slovak Robin Hood shoots at his own people in the service of the exploitative bourgeois government.

dead and six seriously wounded. According to the first medical enquiry, four of the victims had been shot in the back, which was evidence that they had run away, not towards the policemen.[118]

The government's version substantially differed from DAV's version: delegate Major was the main culprit of the incident, a Communist agitator who deliberately provoked the violence, cold-bloodedly reckoning with dead and wounded. Officer Janošík had warned the masses three times in Slovak and Hungarian. When they did not stop throwing stones, he gave the firing order.[119] Major had thrown himself on the ground, simulating that he had been shot, which had enraged the masses to such extent that the *četníci* saw no other way of defending themselves than to shoot into the masses. Six policemen had been seriously wounded.

The appalling event, which reminded elderly Slovaks of the tragedy in Černova in 1907, when Hungarian policemen had shot into a group of Slovak Catholics, prompted the outrage of the Czechoslovak public. Some believed the official government version, others the version of the Communists. Some believed that Major had organized the masses and incited them to violence, deliberately provoking the shooting. Others believed that Major had wanted to disperse the demonstration, and officer Janošík had just lost his nerve. Some supported the state's self-protection from Communist agitation; others thought that the state was no democracy at all, since the workers' demonstration had been forbidden, which, according to the constitution, was a violation of their political rights. The constitution seemed to apply only to the rich and powerful, while the poor were not only shamelessly exploited, but also denied their political rights.

The editors of DAV and Clementis wrote open letters to the famous novelists Romain Rolland in Paris, Maksim Gorkii in

---

[118] "Čierne Turice košutské", 6.
[119] "Čierne Turice košutské", 6.

Moscow and Ernst Gläser in Berlin, asking them to spread the news: the world should see how Czechoslovakia was treating her workers.[120] They wrote also to Robert Seton Watson in London, a supporter of Czechoslovakia in Great Britain and personally acquainted with President Masaryk; similar letters were sent to *Le Monde* in Paris, *New Masses* in New York and other leftist newspapers in Moscow, Oradea Mare in Romania and Berlin.

The truth is probably somewhere in between the two versions. The incident was discussed in parliament on 2 June 1931: the Communist delegates presented their version, which the centre-right delegates rejected. In 1931, Clementis was living in Prague, working in a law office, but he regularly travelled to Bratislava to meet up with Dr Zoltán Weichherz, the defence lawyer of Štefan Major.[121] Major had been arrested on the evening of 25 May. The regional court in Bratislava charged him with "violent insurrection against the state"; the trial began on 30 June and ended on 13 July 1931.[122]

Clementis and Dr Weichherz mounted a successful defence: they presented new and convincing witnesses and gathered information from policemen, who had been in Košuty on the day of the shooting. These *četníci* wanted to remain anonymous, but told Clementis that first, the platoon had received instructions to load their guns with live ammunition before they marched towards the church and formed a cordon – which weakened the state attorney's version that the platoon had not been prepared and acted on the spur of the moment. Second, the *četník* Alois Joachimsthaler from Sabina had accidentally hurt himself while loading his gun,

---

[120] "Štyri dopisy", *DAV IV*, no. 5-6 (1931): 2-3.
[121] Holotíková a Plevza, 85.
[122] Holotíková a Plevza, 87.

he had not been hurt by the demonstrators as the government version claimed.[123] Most convincing was the statement of Ján Terebessy, a twenty-three-year-old graduate from the faculty of law, who was neither close to the Communists nor had any political interest in the trial; he just wanted to give a witness statement:

> "'Delegate Major left the group of people and walked up to the platoon commander, who was standing in front of the police cordon. [...] while talking to delegate Major, the commander already had a sabre in his hand, and the weapon was swinging over delegate Major's head. I saw this because the sun was reflecting on the blade of the sabre. I was eight paces away from them and could not hear what they were talking about, but I saw that, all of a sudden, the sabre came down. Then, delegate Major turned around and fell to the ground.'"[124]

The student described the shooting that immediately followed, the blood seeping into the ground, the women's cries, the panic and fear. The defence was gaining ground, but the state attorney did not give up easily: he wanted to know if Ján had heard Major shouting *Elöre* (onwards), calling the mob to attack the policemen. The student replied that he had heard no such command from Major.

For their closing statement, the lawyers agreed on a twofold strategy: Weichherz would prepare the legal and professional arguments, Clementis the political and ethical arguments of the defence. The Party and its legal organization Red Help (*Rudá pomoc*) had employed Dr Weichherz to defend Major; the Bratislava public did not know that he had been a member of the Hungarian Soviet Republic under Béla Kun in 1919.[125] People thought that lawyer Weichherz was a member of the Czechoslovak Social Democratic Party with no ties the Communists, all the more as he had defended the radical autonomist Vojtěch Tuka (1880–1946), who

---

[123] Holotíková a Plevza, 86.
[124] Holotíková a Plevza, 89.
[125] Holotíková a Plevza, 90-91.

stood trial for espionage for Hungary in 1929. Tuka had been found guilty and sentenced to fifteen years in prison.[126]

In his closing speech, Clementis accused the state attorney of nursing a political bias against Major and the workers. It was a political speech, full of sarcasm and irony. The trial of Major was a political trial, instigated by a government that smelled revolutionary upheaval behind every demonstration and strike.[127] On 17 December 1931, the Czechoslovak Press Agency informed the public that the court had revoked its first sentence of eight months and condemned Major to fourteen months' imprisonment, a fine of two thousand crowns and the abjuration of his parliamentary mandate.[128] Yet, in the political and legal context of the First Republic, the sentence was rather mild, since one Gabor Steiner had received eight months for leading a demonstration that had been conducted peacefully, hence could not be compared with the shooting in Košuty.[129] The state attorney's strategy to sentence delegate Major as the main culprit of the tragedy did not succeed.

DAV used Major's second sentence to criticize the government and the justice system; the article "A Conclusion and an Introduction" listed the procedural mistakes of the trial and quoted workers who had acted as witnesses in favour of Major. The text demonstrated the authors' view that bourgeois justice was no justice at all. The sentence was ample evidence of the state's corrupt

---

[126] Holotíková a Plevza, 91. Tuka was a lawyer, radical member of the HSĽS and Minister of Foreign Affairs in the Slovak State. He orchestrated the deportation of Slovakia's Jews as early as 1942, without pressure from Nazi Germany. US troops found him in Austria at the end of the war and extradited him to Czechoslovakia. The Czechoslovak government executed him on 20 August 1946. On Tuka's trial in 1929 see Maroš Hertel, "Vlastizrada alebo pomsta?", in *Storočie procesov. Súdy, politika a spoločnosť v moderných dejinách Slovenska* (Bratislava: Veda, 2013), 66-82.
[127] Holotíková a Plevza, 92.
[128] "Doslov, ktorý je úvodom", *DAV V*, no. 12 (1932): 2-3.
[129] Holotíková a Plevza, 93.

and unjust rule. Quite obviously, fairness and critical thinking in context were not DAV's characteristic features. The article ended with a sentence that expressed wishful thinking:

> "And under the watchful eyes of the court, the concluding speech [of Dr Vladimír Clementis, add. JB] in the trial about the incident in Košuty has evidently shown that the end of this world is near, and a new world is in the making."[130]

The defence of Štefan Major was Clementis' first professional success. He would continue to defend the workers, the poor and the disenfranchised.[131]

I. 4   Member of Parliament (1935–1938)

When the KSČ nominated Clementis to run as candidate for the district of Liptovský Svätý Mikuláš in the parliamentary elections of May 1935, the lawyer was already a well-known figure in Slovak political life. The citizens of his constituency elected him MP – he was their voice in Prague.[132] He had proved his loyalty to the Party with uncountable articles, speeches and, lately, the defence of Major in the trial of Košuty.

---

[130] "Doslov, ktorý …", 3. I have no means to prove it, but it is probable that the text contains parts of Clementis' closing speech at court, since it quotes Hurban Vajanský. He had quoted Vajanský in his speech.

[131] An interesting text is Karol Rezák, *30. výročie streľby do poľnohospodárskych robotnikov v Košútoch* (Bratislava-Vinohrady: Slovenský výbor Čs. Spoločnosti pre šírenie politických a vedeckých poznatkov a Osvetový ústav v Bratislave, 1961). This semi-scientific text informs the reader about the events in Košuty, but does not mention Clementis' name or his defence of delegate Major. In 1961, Clementis was still a *persona non grata*. One could not mention his name in public without getting into serious trouble.

[132] The results of the 1935 parliamentary elections in Slovakia: Autonomous bloc, 30.12%; Agrarians, 17.64%; the parties of the Hungarian-German coalition, 14.19%; and KSČ, 12.97%; *Chronológia Dejín Slovenska a Slovákov II*, 1203-1204.

Clementis had also proved his loyalty to Gottwald who had reorganized the Party leadership in 1929, introducing strict Bolshevik discipline. Seven older Party members, all writers and poets, had expressed their protest on 25 March 1929 in the so-called "manifesto of the seven", among them Stanislav Kostka Neumann (1875–1947) and the future Nobel laureate Jaroslav Seifert (1901–1986).[133] The seven reproached Gottwald and his followers with "terrorism of one faction and blind fanaticism";[134] they condemned the Bolshevization of the Party, which was in fact an act of Stalinization in tune with the directives of the fifth congress of the Comintern in 1924. To Stalin's way of thinking, the KSČ had to reorganize; it was too gullible, tolerant and naïve, unfit to face the challenges of the revolutionary fight for Socialism. The Soviet comrades had certainly learnt about Otto Bauer's (1881–1938) famous comment. The Austrian Social Democrat had said that he knew only two Social Democratic parties worth their name, first, the Austrian Social Democratic Party, and second, the Czechoslovak Communist Party.[135] The KSČ thus had to establish iron discipline, rid itself of Social Democratic thought and Social Democrats with that, and severely punish any criticism.

The day after the publication of their manifesto, the seven dissidents lost their membership and high positions at the Party's newspapers and publishing houses, and on 30 March 1929, *Tvorba* published an anti-manifesto, the so-called "letter of the twelve". Twelve loyal Party members condemned the seven, accusing them of going against the revolutionary workers' movement and the KSČ as its avant-garde. From now on, they would go

---

[133] Rudolf Vévoda, "Sedm našich kamarádů. Ke konfliktu mezi levicovými intelektuály v dobe bolševizace KSČ", in *Český a slovenský komunismus,* 24-31, 27.
[134] Vévoda, 27.
[135] RUPNIK, Jacques, *Dějiny Komunistické strany Československa. Od počátků do přezvetí moci.* Academia, Praha 2002, s. 65, quoted from Vévoda, 27.

separate ways. Prominent artists, poets and writers signed the anti-manifesto, among them Karel Teige (1900–1951), Vítěszlav Nezval (1900–1958), Konstantín Biebl (1898–1951), Laco Novomeský and Clementis.

The letter of the seven and the letter of the twelve demonstrated that an open discussion among comrades was no longer possible; Stalin's tight reins had wiped out Lenin's *democratic centralism*, the possibility of dissent among Party members, the intra-party tolerance. The Comintern's new directives drew a sharp line between the initiated, who were loyally following the Soviet Communist Party, and the doubtful, who no longer had a place or a voice in the Party.

In his three years as an MP, Clementis delivered nine speeches and made several interpellations in parliament; they were a further demonstration of his intellectual acumen and rhetoric.

I. 4. 1 On National Security (1936)

Clementis began his first speech in parliament with a reference to the past: in 1923, the Czechoslovak parliament had adopted the "Law on the Protection of the Republic [*Zákon na ochranu republiky*]".[136] In the name of the Republic's security, the law had it made possible to sentence hundreds of workers and peasants and also those who declared their sympathy for the Soviet Union with harmless words such as 'Long Live the Soviet Union'.

> "I am asking you, gentlemen, were these acts of protecting the Republic or acts of protecting something completely different? Today, I hope, not

---

[136] Clementis, "Prejav v poslaneckej snemovni 29. Apríla 1936", in *Vzduch našich čias II*, 151-162. Clementis' speech reflected the line of the seventh congress of the Comintern, e.g. the tactical move to build a united people's front to protect the Republic, which was a new ideological course opening up the possibility of co-operation with the government; *Chronológia Dejín Slovenska a Slovákov II*, 640.

even the Social Democratic section chiefs at the Ministry of Justice are insisting that the practice that sprung from this law, that is, the sentencing of antifascists and those sympathetic to the Soviet Union, were acts to the benefit of the Republic, or acts to protect the Republic."[137]

The press and the parliamentarians of the parties who had adopted this law rejected the suggestions of the KSČ for the simple reason that the Communists had submitted them.[138] Such was the mentality and thinking of the ruling masters!

Many voices, for example, today's *Lidové Noviny*, were now even comparing the Communists' views to those of the "Henleinists [*henleinovcov*]".[139] Clementis quoted Jaroslav Stránský (1884–1973), a doctor of law, parliamentarian for Beneš's National Socialist Party and founder of the *Lidové Noviny*. Stránský had pronounced his opinion very clearly in the constitutional assembly: it was understandable that the Communists were interested in the defence against Hitlerism. One had to believe them on this issue, although they otherwise used to fundamentally disagree. And today, as Clementis said in his outrage, Stránský's newspaper had come up with this primitive comparison – these gentlemen would not get away with such demagoguery.

This statement offers us an insight into Clementis' understanding of the freedom of the press: Stránský was the owner of the *Lidovky*, and his journalists were allowed to write articles and statements that were diametrically opposed to the bosses' opinion. Clementis' understanding of journalism was a Bolshevik one: the editor-in-chief had the last say, the final control, and his journalists were not to contradict him. His was no democratic view, but a totalitarian one.

---

[137] Clementis, "Prejav ...", 151.
[138] Clementis, "Prejav ...", 152.
[139] Clementis, "Prejav ...", 152. Henlein committed suicide in US captivity on 10 May 1945.

Recently, as Clementis said, comrade Gottwald had made a very important statement to the seventh congress of the KSČ: all members of the working class, Czechs, Germans, Slovaks, Ukrainians, Hungarians and Poles were suffering from the economic and social pressures of the Czech bourgeoisie. Yet, in spite of their fundamental and uncompromising resistance against the ruling Czech bourgeoisie, the Czechoslovak Communists were united in their stand to protect the Republic from both foreign and domestic Fascism.[140] Clementis described the current political situation in his native Slovakia:

> "Slovakia is the focal point of imperialist and revisionist threats, from Horthy as much as from colonel Beck. Slovakia is an important territory, not only because of strategic reasons, our state's control of the North, South, West and East, but Slovakia has also become the chessboard of gentlemen who are eager to change the map of Central Europe. We Communists have clearly stated in the past and we are clearly stating now that we shall not relinquish the nations of Slovakia [*národy Slovenska*] to Fascism. [...] Not a hut on our territory will fall into the hands of Horthy and colonel Beck."[141]

In view of the increasing danger of the barbaric militaristic and imperialist forces of Fascism that were gathering in the neighbouring states, one had to put up an equally strong defence. Words were not enough – real power was required now. Only the masses of workers of all nations in Czechoslovakia were self-confident, free, disciplined and united. They formed a huge potential for a military defence that was worthy of the name. The creation of such a defence was the KSČ's intention when submitting to parliament

---

[140] Clementis, "Prejav ...", 152-153.
[141] Clementis, "Prejav ...", 153. Míklos Horthy (1868–1957) was Hungary's regent in the interwar years. Józef Beck (1894–1944) was Foreign Minister of Poland in the 1930s. Both coveted parts of Slovakia's territory. Horthy wanted back territory in the south that had been assigned to Czechoslovakia in the peace treaty of Trianon in 1921, and Beck wanted the Těšín region on Czechoslovakia's North Eastern border.

the suggestions for amending the Law about the Protection of the Republic.[142] Clearly, Clementis had in mind the military might of the Red Army and the enthusiastic unity of the people he had witnessed five years ago in the Soviet Union.

Another problem was weakening the Republic. Clementis criticized the lack of effort to establish homogenous legislation, unifying both parts of the country in one legal system. Slovakia was still being ruled according to the old Hungarian legislation that denied the workers the freedom of assembly.[143] He referred to workers' strikes and demonstrations; on a regular basis, the regional administration did not issue permits for workers' demonstrations, which demonstrated a painful lack of democracy.

Clementis' words were a show of perfect Marxist-Leninist demagoguery: he focussed on the provincial and municipal legislation that was still in effect in some parts of Slovakia and executed by individuals who were not members of the KSČ. He refused to take in the whole picture: prior to 1918, the Budapest government had systematically oppressed all non-Magyars in Slovakia, the nationally conscious Slovak middle class as much as the Slovak workers – general franchise was one of the many democratic achievements of the First Republic. But to Clementis, only the

---

[142] Clementis, "Prejav ...", 153.
[143] He was not wrong, but not precise either: the creation of a unified legislation in both parts of the state was not a pressing issue, mainly because of Prague's lack of detailed knowledge about the Hungarian legislation and considerations of a political nature. Had the government presented to parliament a plan for the unification of legislation, that is, the remodelling of Slovakia's Hungarian legislation on the Czech (the old Austrian), it would have immediately provoked the opposition of the autonomists. The HSĽS would have been the first to condemn such a plan as further proof of Czech centralism, opposing it in parliament. The unification of legislation came into being only after the "victorious February of 1948". The Agrarian politician Šrobár, already ill and in his eighties, headed the insignificant Ministry of Unification of Laws until he died in 1950.

workers counted. As long as the government was oppressing the working class, as long as the workers' constitutionally granted democratic rights to organize demonstrations and strikes were being so gravely violated, the Republic was in danger. To him, only the power of the working class could unify the national groups of Czechoslovakia and mount a defensive force capable of protecting the Republic.

Clementis referred to the booklet that Emanuel Moravec (1893–1945),[144] a member in the general staff of the Czechoslovak army, had recently published. Moravec had praised the discipline of the Red Army from a military point of view, stressing the importance of moral values for a successful defence of the state. Clementis repeated his earlier warnings in a passionate tone:

> "In this situation, with Fascism at our doors that is threatening the life and future of the Czechs and Slovaks, it is high time to, once and for all, do away with the conditions that are dividing the working classes of our two nations. How to achieve this? Not in the way of our Czechoslovaks, neither in the way of our imitators of the Magyar National Party who had come up with the concept of state-building nations only to be able to speak about superior and inferior nations. That method has definitely crashed. But neither can the so-called autonomists accomplish the unification of the Slovak and Czech working classes [as the kernel of a future national defence, add. JB]. I am not referring to those autonomists who are certainly capable of shouting the biggest reproaches at a little Czech teacher in Slovakia, but to those who are going to Prague to confer with Messrs Stříbrný, Kramář and Preiss."[145]

After a passionate call for a military alliance with the Soviet Union, Clementis addressed the anti-Soviet attacks of the HSĽS press. By

---

[144] Moravec would switch sides after the Nazi occupation in March 1939; he served as Minister of Culture under Reinhard Heydrich. When the Red Army was close to Prague in May 1945, he shot himself.

[145] Clementis, "Prejav …", 156. Jiří Stříbrný (1880–1955) was a Social Democrat, politician and editor; Jaroslav Preiss (1870–1946) was the director of the Živnobanka, which had significant influence in financing Czechoslovakia's economy and industry.

now, Sidor had three times interrupted his speech with heckles, and I deem it very possible that Clementis wanted to get his own back, improvizing with a minor diversion from his main theme – which the brilliant orator took in his stride.

Clementis ironically referred to Sidor quoting Ľudovít Štúr in his recent speech in parliament. The lawyer demonstrated his excellent knowledge of Slovak history, addressing the political thought and activities of the father of the Slovak written language. It was an impeccable lesson of *applied historical materialism* and brilliant rhetoric alike. Clementis was in his element; like a shark, he swallowed up the little HSĽS fish in the sea of political theory, his domain. Assuring Sidor in biting irony that he would not delve into Štúr's Russophilia, nor mention Štúr's critical words about Catholicism, he insinuated to the assembly that the Autonomist had actually no clue about the political thought of the father of the Slovak language – then he moved on to target Sidor's jugular with historical facts:

> "I want to compare these gentlemen with Štúr, these gentlemen, who are now sporting themselves as adherents of Štúr's tradition, wanting to make politics in the name of Štúr. They have nothing at all in common with Štúr or with his legacy. In Slovak history, Štúr is a great person. When today there is so much talk about him, when today people are talking about his legacy, when today some gentlemen deem it necessary to celebrate Štúr by inspiring the young to throw stones at Jewish shops, by inspiring them to protest against some stupid film, when these gentlemen deem it necessary to hold empty speeches, while they so far have not been bothered with editing Štúr's works or analysing his historical tasks, then I allow myself a little lesson now, presenting you, at least briefly, with a comparison of Štúr's politics with the current situation of Slovakia. There is a clear analogy. We Communists, and I hope all Socialists in Slovakia too, acknowledge that Štúr accomplished a grand revolutionary task with the coinage of the Slovak written language, that he enabled the blossoming of the Slovak nation, that he created the foundations for the cultural and material development of the Slovak nation. However, his politics had a tragic error, which the nation paid for with its life. Štúr, this revolutionary of the people [*ľudový revolucionár*], this fundamentally anti-Feudalist revolutionary, tied the fate

of the Slovak nation to the most reactionary powers of Feudalism [*s najreakčnejšími mocnosťami feudálnymi*], the Austrian dynasty and Tsarist Russia. [...] And today, the Slovak nation is facing the same fateful question: should it ally itself with the reactionary forces as their appendage only to become their victim later, or should it join the progressive international forces that shall enable it to develop to the full its culture and social conditions? Since the *Sidorists* [*Sidorovci*] are answering this question with an even bigger error than Štúr's, it is quite obvious that their politics are a disaster, that their politics could lead the Slovak nation into a situation much worse than the one it had faced after 1848. (Delegate Sidor, shouting: You are talking like a Czechoslovak!) I would like to hear from you now what in my speech is Czechoslovak."[146]

---

[146] Clementis, "Prejav ...", 159-160. Clementis referred to the antisemitic rally of Catholic students that had taken place on the evening of 24 April 1936 in Bratislava. Students of the dormitory "Svoradov" had protested against the film *Golem* by French director Julien Duvivier (1896–1967), attacking it as anti-Christian and prosemitic. Some three hundred students demonstrated in the cinemas Tatra and Metropol, disturbing the show, gathered then in front of the cinemas and marched through the streets. Some went to the Jewish quarter close to the Old Town and smashed in the windows of Jewish shops. The local police arrested the ringleaders. The HSĽS press considered the protests that lasted until midnight as spontaneous expression of the Slovak national youth, while the Communists qualified them as antisemitic pogrom organized by the *Ľudáci*; Katarína Strapcová, "Bratislavská mládež kontra *Golem*", in *Storočie škandálov. Aféry v moderných dejinách Slovenska* (Bratislava: Spoločnosť Pro Historia, 2008), 161-170.
Clementis reproached Štúr with the alliance with Habsburg Austria during the revolution of 1848, which was a first grave mistake from the viewpoint of historical materialism, the Marxist interpretation of history. Štúr should have taken sides with the progressive Hungarian Liberals, fighting for civil and political rights against Austrian aristocratic and authoritarian rule. Clementis did not mention that Štúr had made his choice because of the Magyar assimilation; by siding with Austria, he had hoped to later submit Slovakia to the more liberal Austrian rule, tearing her away from the Hungarian kingdom. After the failed revolution, which Austria had been successful in oppressing only with the help of Russian troops, Štúr was deeply disappointed. The Slovaks had received no political reward from Vienna for their loyalty. Around 1850, Štúr, embittered and depressed, wrote *Das Slawenthum und die Welt der Zukunft* (*Slavdom and the World of the Future*), a political assessment of the Slavs in Central and South-Eastern Europe living under foreign-

He wanted, Clementis continued, to say a few words about the amendment of the law on espionage.[147] The Communists were drawing parliament's attention to the fact that, much like war, espionage was a characteristic element of the Capitalist order. As long as Capitalism existed, there was the danger of war; as long as war was threatening, there was espionage. It was grotesque that some poor and desperate fellow, who had stolen a little plan of a revolver, received a sentence of fifteen years' gaol, while stockholders, banks and factory directors were exporting thousands of these weapons abroad. The Communists had ample experience with the application of that law, how often the state administration had tried to construct a trial of espionage against a member of the KSČ.

Furthermore, as Clementis said, the version of the amendment of the law on espionage the government had submitted, presented a grave restriction of the freedom of defence in court. The politically and class-conscious defence lawyers were the only persons capable of fending off the various provocations coming from the Capitalist administration; according to the amendment, these lawyers were to be excluded from espionage trials.

Allegedly, this violation of the freedom to choose one's advocate should guarantee that the secret material of a trial would

---

political and alien-spiritual rule. His call was a passionate message of Panslavism: all Slavs should work towards a union with Tsarist Russia, since Russia was the only branch of the grand Slavic nation that lived in freedom, in self-government. In terms of historical materialism, Štúr's romanticist Panslavism was his second error. Either way, the Slovak nation did not have much political room to manoeuvre in 1848. Clementis' correct application of historical materialism to Štúr's thought proved that he had not only studied the history of the 1848 revolution, but also Štúr's grand last work. Sidor's accusation of 'Czechoslovak' demonstrates the radical thought of the Slovak Autonomists and their lack of loyalty to Masaryk's Republic.

[147] Clementis, "Prejav ...", 160.

not get into the hands of persons who had no security clearance.[148] Clementis claimed for the Communist lawyers the right to be included, the right to be subject to security clearance like the non-Communist lawyers. He used the concept of 'provocation', a word the comrades used for a perceived political threat from the forces of the Capitalist bourgeoisie:

> "All these elaborate texts only demonstrate that the intention behind the exclusion of lawyers from espionage trials to grant the state's security is a bluff. How is the secretary of the court controlled? How are the persons with security clearance controlled? For them, there is no control. But those lawyers are to be excluded, who, at least now, are the best guarantee that this law won't be misused for political provocations, and that various agent provocateurs won't be able to misuse it with their accusations."[149]

He finished his speech, warning all demagogues and rowdies, particularly those who were attacking them now, that the Communist Party would not let itself be terrorized, that it would stand firm in its beliefs.

On 13 May 1936, the National Assembly adopted law no. 131/1936 on the protection of the state, preparing the legal grounds for a call to arms; mobilization extended to all male citizens from the age of seventeen to the age of sixty.[150] Clearly, the Czechoslovak government ignored the appeal of the Communists, not only because it feared that the they would take over the army and hence pose a serious internal threat to the state's democratic order, but also because the KSČ did not reflect voters' preferences. The Party had never won a parliamentary election, neither in the Czech lands nor in Slovakia, and no party had ever expressed an interest in entering into a coalition with the Communists. Furthermore, the comrades had no domestic experts among their rank

---

[148] Clementis, "Prejav ...", 160.
[149] Clementis, "Prejav ...", 161-162.
[150] *Chronológia Dejín Slovenska a Slovákov II*, 640-641.

and file; they slavishly followed every directive of the Moscow-controlled Comintern.[151] And, if the Communists were so eager to protect the Republic, or so the centre-right politicians must have thought, why did they not co-operate with the government now, supporting the amendment of the law, instructing their members and voters?

From the Communists' viewpoint, the government was simply stupid, blind and selfish: in its petty clinging to the Capitalist order and protecting, first and foremost, the wealth of its voters, it did not see the reality: the Sudeten German alliance with Hitler posed a real threat. Neither did the government want to seriously consider the dangers from Poland and Hungary, both states ruled by regimes close to Fascism. The government's greed, selfishness and its contempt for the Soviet Union and the KSČ was only playing into the hands of the German Nazis and the Hungarian and Polish revisionists.

A year later, Clementis would reveal the ugly face of Autonomism, which he considered as much an enemy of the workers' movement as Capitalism. Yet, he correctly saw that there was one crucial element that distinguished the Capitalists from the Autonomists, the Slovak and Czech centre-right parties from the HSĽS: the *Ľudáci* were antisemites to the core.

---

[151] There was no capable economist in the Party who could have developed a sound economic strategy for Slovakia's industrialisation. Only in 1937, the Party published its plan for the socio-economic development and industrialization of Slovakia, focussing on electrification, improvement of the traffic system and the infrastructure. In 1945, the KSČ would offer the voters a plan for the country's economic reconstruction; Miroslav Sabol, "Sociálno-ekonomické koncepcie KSS v rokoch 1921–1948", in *Český a slovenský komunismus*, 32-40, 33, 35-36.

I. 4. 2   Lex Sidor – on Slovak Antisemitism (1937)

Among the HSĽS leaders, Sidor was Clementis' enemy number one, not Hlinka, who was already ill in 1937 and would die on 16 August 1938. In his article "Lex Sidor", Clementis reacted against Sidor's article "Let the Jews move to Palestine and Birobidžan"; he presented a summary of the history of Slovak antisemitism.[152] He explained to the reader the concept of Zionism and, most importantly, analysed how and why Hlinka's People's Party was creating an anti-Jewish mood in Slovakia.

The HSĽS was trying to stabilize its political course with statements that were in perfect accordance with the Berlin-Warsaw axis; they were also in support of Fascist Spain and did not criticize with one word the German murder of thousands of Basque people. Apart from their use of Fascist slogans directed against the Soviet Union, the leading party members had also adopted the antisemitic arsenal of Goebbels and Streicher:[153]

> "The Sidorists are defending themselves energetically against suspicions that their new slogans originate in Berlin. And, not that long ago, they even abused the anniversary of Vajanský's death, quoting his anti-Jewish remarks and trying to prove that their current antisemitism has historical and national roots, that they are just reviving Vajanský's legacy. Everybody with a little knowledge about the Jews' status in Slovakia prior to the *prevrat* is familiar with Jewry's social and political role in Hungary. The Jews' attempts to smash into pieces the ghettos – in the very sense of the word – had led the majority of them into the

---

[152] Clementis, "Vyhnať židov do Palestíny a Birobidžanu? Lex Sidor. Jeho smiešna demagogia tam, kde je 'vážne' mienený", *DAV 10*, no. 4 (1937): 3-5. Sidor published his article "Nech sa sťahujú židia do Palestíny a Birobidžanu!" in the HSĽS newspaper *Slovák*, no. 58, 12 March 1937, 3.
[153] Clementis, "Lex Sidor", 3. Julius Streicher (1885–1946) was the founder of the NSDAP's propaganda organ *Der Stürmer*. The Nuremberg trial sentenced him to death for his activities: https://www.jewishvirtuallibrary.org/jsource/Holocaust/Streicher.html; accessed 8 April 2016.

service of the ruling nation and class, that is, the ruling Magyar masters."[154]

Clementis explained to the reader the political situation of the Jews as entrepreneurial minority: before 1918, the Jews' dependence on good relations with the ruling Magyars had been even more important in Slovakia than in central Hungary. To receive a licence for the sale of alcohol in the countryside meant to be a servant of the local notary, usually a Magyar. To leave the Jewish ghetto implied that they had to renounce their traditions and fiercely advocate Magyar culture. The criticism of the Jews' positions and status prior to the *prevrat* was not home-grown, in particular not the anti-Jewish remarks of Vajanský: they originated in the most reactionary and black-clothed ideologies of the pogroms in Tsarist Russia.[155] The Slovak nation had never been antisemitic the way Vajanský had been:

> "The people's antipathy to the Jewish landowner, the Jewish leaseholder, the Jewish innkeeper and also the Jewish debt-holder had exclusively social roots. Had we at our disposal statistics of the revolutionary unrest and its 'victims' after the *prevrat*, we would probably find that the number of the expelled Arian notaries [*počet vyhnaných arijských notárov*] exceeded the number of the smashed Jewish inns."[156]

After the *prevrat*, the situation of the Jews in Slovakia changed fundamentally. Legionnaires, invalids, associations and farmers became the owners of inns and pubs. Farmer-notaries and district

---

[154] Clementis, "Lex Sidor", 3.
[155] Clementis, "Lex Sidor", 3. Clementis referred to the black cassocks of the Russian Orthodox priests who often initiated and sanctified anti-Jewish pogroms. He was certainly no admirer of Vajanský, whose antisemitism he criticised, but he opposed the unscientific way of the Ľudáci. By abusing the name of the nation's poet they wanted to create an unbroken tradition of Slovak anti-Jewish thought, rendering legitimate their Catholic antisemitism and the racist and pseudo-biological one imported from Berlin.
[156] Clementis, "Lex Sidor", 3.

secretaries replaced the Magyar notaries. The same changes occurred in business and banking. Quoting the census of 1930, which distinguished the adherents of the Israelite religion from the members of the Jewish national group, Clementis put forward figures: in 1930, approximately 400,000 Jews were living in Czechoslovakia, but only 204,779 declared themselves members of the Jewish national group, while 356,830 persons declared themselves adherents of the Israelite religion. In Slovakia, the number of Jews amounted to 4.11% of the population.[157] 136,737 persons were adherents of the Israelite religion, while 64,059 citizens considered themselves members of the Jewish national group.

These figures, Clementis stressed, were the only "'real' argument of the Sidorists" against the Jews in Slovakia.[158] The majority of those Jews who did not consider themselves members of the Jewish national group held a Magyar national identity, supporting the Magyar culture and press in Slovakia; they spoke Hungarian and kept their traditional ties with Budapest. By referring to the Jewish citizens who considered themselves Hungarians, he did not justify the Sidorists' antisemitism, but explained that the Ľudáci got at least one historical fact right in their otherwise despicable agitation modelled on the racist and pseudo-biological antisemitism in Germany. The Jews should not be blamed for the poverty and misery of the Slovaks, since Magyar rule had oppressed all non-Magyars. After listing statistics from 1921 about the employment of Jewish citizens in various economic branches, Clementis presented a brief explanation of Zionism:

> "The Jews' position in the social hierarchy is unstable: this is one of the most important arguments of the Zionists intent on building a compact territory for the Jewish people in Palestine and to rear there, first and

---

[157] Clementis, "Lex Sidor", 4.
[158] Clementis, "Lex Sidor", 4.

foremost, a strong class of workers and farmers [*vypestovať primerane silnú robotnicku a roľnicku triedu*]."[159]

The Sidorists in their pseudo-social demagoguery were focussing on the high economic status of the Jews – not because they wanted to understand Zionism or the oppression of the Jews, but for different reasons: to the petit bourgeois and half-educated, the Berlin-made antisemitism promised to be beneficial. The Sidorists' agitation was most successful among the citizens of the lower middle-class who envied the Jews their economic success and positions in educational institutions and publishing houses. Making a great show of seeming to care about the welfare of the poor Slovak Christians, the Sidorists, as Clementis stressed, were claiming that the Slovaks could improve their lives and economic possibilities if only the Jews were expelled either to Palestine or Birobidžan.[160] If the Jews were gone, the social and economic positions they had occupied would be open to Slovaks, which, Clementis wrote, was a simplistic 'solution' born of the typical demagoguery of the Sidorists. He did not want to enter into a polemic about the "democratic equality of citizens, nations and 'races'", but scrutinize the practical consequences of Sidor's suggestions.[161]

According to the statistics for 1933, the capital of the banks and financial institutions in Slovakia was divided into national groups. The first group of the so-called Slovak banks with their capital shares, reserves and financial deposits amounted to 3,054 million Czechoslovak crowns or 38% of the capital in Slovakia. Czech banks as the second group held 3,451 million or 44%

---

[159] Clementis, "Lex Sidor", 5.
[160] Clementis, "Lex Sidor", 5. Birobidžan was an autonomous *oblasť* in the Far East at the Russian-Chinese border. Stalin established the Jewish autonomous district in 1934: http://www.jewishvirtuallibrary.org/jsource/judaica/ejud_0002_0003_0_03013.htmland; accessed 9 April 2016.
[161] Clementis, "Lex Sidor", 5.

of the capital in Slovakia; the third group of the Hungarian-German banks, owned by Jews, held only 18% of the capital in Slovakia.[162]

The Sidorists were not only involved in Slovakia's economic situation by managing the Catholic Church's property, but their idea that the expulsion of the Jews would benefit the Slovaks was a naïve miscalculation. A look at the situation of the state healthcare system sufficed:

> "A large part of the adherents of the *Ľudáci* are medical students at the University of Bratislava; they are antisemites because of the Jewish competition in their field. We don't have any figures at our disposal about the number of Jewish doctors practising in Slovakia, but we think that the disparity of Jewish and non-Jewish doctors is a significant one. Yet, would it not be much better and more useful to ask: are there enough doctors practising in Slovak cities, towns and, most importantly, in the countryside? Is the network of hospitals already in such a perfect state that we have a surplus of doctors? We all know very well that it is not. We all know very well that Slovakia needs many more doctors, and we also know that different management of the healthcare system is needed, management that is different from the one practised by Tiso, the former minister and colleague of Sidor. Tiso has arranged for the building of palaces in Sliač, realizing the idiotic dreams of those who would like to see foreign and domestic conmen and gamblers gathering in the Slovak baths and spas."[163]

Now, considering the difficult state of the healthcare system, why would Mr Sidor like to expel Jewish doctors to faraway Birobidžan? Why did he not care to send them to the Slovak countryside? Even if one put oneself into the mindset of that barbaric, racist,

---

[162] Clementis, "Lex Sidor", 5.
[163] Clementis, "Lex Sidor", 5. Jozef Tiso headed the Czechoslovak ministry of health from 1927 to 1929. Under his guidance, large investments were made to reorganize the spas in Slovakia. Under his direction, the state built new hospital wards at the spas in Sliač and Smokovec in the Tatra Mountains, and attempts were made to revitalize smaller spas; Kamenec, *Tragédia politika, kňaza a človeka*, 58-59.

and medieval thinking, the Hitlerist antisemitism of Sidor's suggestions did not solve one iota of the fundamental social problems in Slovakia.

The Sidorists had come up with a further argument against the Jews: they were a disruptive band, undermining the fundamental order of Slovak society by spreading the bacillus of Bolshevism. The "*židoboľševici*" (Jews-Bolsheviks), they maintained, were an alien element,[164] poisoning the healthy body of the Slovak nation. Clementis finished with his usual conclusion, repeating his mantra: only a Socialist society could solve all contradictions and inequalities born of the class structure. Only a classless Socialist society could solve the Jewish question in a dignified and humane way.

I. 4. 3 A Farewell to President Masaryk (1937)

On 14 September 1937, Tomáš Garrigue Masaryk died in the presidential castle Lány at the age of eighty-seven. When a great personality dies, a person who has improved the lives of many, people are usually quick to make him immortal by remembering his legacy and gratefully paying their respects.[165] It seems to me that the attempts at 'occupying' a great person's legacy by claiming to speak in his voice, is a psychological need.[166] It was certainly a psy-

---

[164] Clementis, "Lex Sidor", 5.
[165] See the publication in honour of Masaryk and the centenary of his exile activities: Stanislava Kučerová et al., *Věrni zůstaneme. K 100. výročí československého odboje, korunovaného vznikem Československa* (Brno: Občanský a odborný výbor Brno, Pedagogická fakulta Masarykovy university Brno, Statutární město Brno, 2014).
[166] The psychological need to explain that which is inexplicable, life's unpredictability, can also prompt conspiracy theories, particularly in cases when the deceased person has died an unexpected, untimely and seemingly mysteri-

chological need of the Czechs and Slovaks, who sensed in September 1937 that their state was in danger, threatened from abroad as much as from within. After Masaryk's death, political debates about his legacy arose in Slovakia, and politicians of all parties interpreted Masaryk's legacy in their own particular way.

In 1920, Masaryk had prepared the political grounds to make Beneš his successor. According to the constitution, candidates had to be forty-five years old to be eligible for the senate and the presidency; in 1920, Beneš was thirty-six. Masaryk had pushed through in parliament a constitutional amendment that set the minimum age to thirty-five, making sure that his associate could run in future presidential elections.[167] Beneš had fought for the Republic with Masaryk in exile from 1914 to 1918 and was his close confidant, a kind of political son. In the early years after the *prevrat*, the young lawyer had not been well known to the general public in Czechoslovakia; when an adherent of Kramář had criticised Masaryk for his clear favouritism towards the young Beneš, the president had angrily reprimanded him:

> "You should not forget that without Dr Beneš, there would be no Czechoslovak Republic at all."[168]

In December 1935, Masaryk, already gravely ill, had stepped down, and the parliament elected Beneš president. He seemed to

---

ous death, for example, the deaths of John F. Kennedy, Marilyn Monroe, Princess Diana and Michael Jackson. See also the conspiracy theories about the 9/11 attacks on America, available on the Internet.

[167] Helmuth Slapnicka, "Die Rechtsstellung des Präsidenten der Republik in der Verfassungsurkunde und in der politischen Wirklichkeit", in *Die Burg. Einflussreiche politische Kräfte um Masaryk und Beneš, vol II* (Oldenbourg: München, Wien, 1974), 9-29, 13.

[168] Julius Firt, "Die Burg aus der Sicht eines Zeitgenossen", in *Die Burg, Einflussreiche politische Kräfte um Masaryk und Beneš, vol I* (Oldenbourg: München, Wien, 1973), 85-107, 91.

be the best guarantee for the integrity of the Republic, the continuation of Czechoslovakia's political orientation towards the West and integration in international organizations. Against all the difficulties of a state that was not only new but had also established a new political system from scratch, in view of the many political factions, delegates of the German and Hungarian parties attacking the Republic, infighting and corruption, Masaryk had kept the Republic together by the sheer force of his charisma. He truly believed that the Czech and Slovak people were capable of realizing democracy and defending their liberty. To him, politics was not the domain of Machiavelli's *Prince*, but the domain of liberty, equality and fraternity.

Probably one of Masaryk's most impressive talents was his gift for anticipating political changes, the global shiftings of power and the resulting crucial changes that could – but not necessarily must – affect the young Republic. Already in 1927 he had warned the parliament on the occasion of the Republic's tenth anniversary:

> "The foreign policy of our state [...] will require caution and a clear understanding of the political situation in Europe. [...] I have called to your attention already several times that we have to face a renewed and strong, not a defeated, Germany."[169]

Masaryk understood what was coming from Germany. Hitler would become a threat to democracy on a European scale. Back in 1923, he had read Hitler's *Mein Kampf* and published a review, a chilling portent of the future:

---

[169] Tomáš Garrigue Masaryk, "Projev Prezidenta Republiky", in *Cesta demokracie III. Projevy, články rozhovory 1924–1928* (Praha: Ústav T. G. Masaryka, 1994), 237-240, 239.

"Hitler is a fanatic and war-monger; his creed will achieve the status of a religion of the German people."[170]

To the Czechs and Slovaks, Masaryk's death seemed to mark the end of an era, a scary foreboding of the future. In December 1937 – DAV had ceased publication for good[171] – Clementis published a booklet to honour the founder of the Republic in his usual way: with an analysis of Masaryk's thought and politics.

The Slovak People and the Legacy of T. G. Masaryk"[172] is an impressive text, rich in detail and written in a scientific, reverent and matter-of-fact tone. No irony, no sarcasm. Clementis was deadly serious, and I had the impression that he was genuinely afraid of the future, of what was in the air. He had taken his time, almost three months, to study Masaryk's works; as always, he was correct with the historical facts, but he drew a conclusion the centre-right politicians certainly disagreed with – and Masaryk would have too.

After a quote from the official eulogy of the KSČ that promised that the working class would protect the Republic against the forces of reaction and defend democracy against Fascism, he quoted Zdeněk Nejedlý, the famous Czech philosopher, who was,

---

[170] Radovan Lovčí, *Alice Garrigue Masaryková. Život ve stínu slavného otca* (Praha: Opera Facultatis philosophicae Universitatis Carolinae Pragensis, 2007), 310, footnote 10. Masaryk published his review under a pseudonym in the German newspaper *Prager Presse* on 30 April 1923. His intention was to warn the Sudeten Germans about Hitler, to anticipate and prevent their becoming mesmerized by Hitler's aggressive National Socialism.

[171] According to Gustáv Husák, the rumours that Clementis had stopped the publication of *DAV* because he did not want to take a stand on the Moscow show trials, is unsubstantial; *DAV* simply ran out of money, and the KSČ had no funds to finance it; Viliam Plevza, *Vzostupy a Pády. Gustáv Husák prehovoril* (Bratislava: Tatrapress, 1991), 23.

[172] Clementis, "Slovenský ľud a odkaz T. G. Masaryka", in *Vzduch našich čias II*, 395-417; the booklet was published in December 1937 at the Zupka publishing house in Bratislava.

Clementis stressed, the only one who had really understood Masaryk's thought. Clementis mentioned Masaryk's activities in the times of the monarchy; with his involvement in the struggle of the manuscripts and the Hilsner affair, Masaryk had proved that he was dedicated to the truth, fighting the uncritical Czech nationalism and antisemitism then dominant in Prague. In contrast to the Czech lands, nobody in Slovakia had published a scientific study that scrutinised Masaryk's influence in Slovakia prior to the *prevrat*.[173]

This was not untrue, but not precise either: the Slovak Agrarians Anton Štefánek and Vavro Šrobár had written their memoirs about the foundation of *Hlas*. They had praised Masaryk's initiative and principal role in founding a progressive movement in Slovakia.[174] Štefánek was an economist and Šrobár a physician; their memoirs do not qualify as scientific analysis of Masaryk's thought, but they were certainly historical witnesses and personally acquainted with the founder of the state.

But in Clementis' way of thinking, their account did not do justice to the president's thought. He completely ignored Šrobár and referred to a letter from a certain Dr Smetana which Štefánek had published in his memoirs; according to Smetana, Masaryk was more a destroyer than a builder. One of his characteristic features was to be too critical, to tear things down.[175] Clementis drew his own conclusions:

---

[173] Clementis, "Slovenský ľud ...", 396.
[174] Anton Štefánek, *Masaryk a Slovensko* (Praha: Náklad spisovateľový, 1931); Vavro Šrobár, *Osvobodené Slovensko. Pamäti z rokov 1918–1920* (Praha: Náklad Gustav Dubského, 1922); Vavro Šrobár, "Československá otázka a 'hlasisti' (k 60. Narodeninám dra. P. Blahu), *Prúdy XI*, no. 5 (1927): 267-276.
[175] Clementis, "Slovenský ľud ...", 396. Holotíková, the editor of Clementis' texts, did not find the letter written by Smetana in the first edition of Štefánek's book. I do not deem it probable that Clementis had made up this letter; it was not his style to present faked documents, to deliberately lie and cheat. He was dedicated to serious academic analysis, naturally from the viewpoint of

> "From these quotes, it is obvious that not even persons very close to him understood what Masaryk wanted to achieve with his critical and rebellious activities. [...] We Marxists adhere to historical materialism, [...] our views about history are different from those of Masaryk, but we regard this fundamental statement of his as the truth: 'All that has been, teaches us about that, which will be. History is the art of predicting the future, to understand what one has to do.'"[176]

Clementis continued with a comparison of the economic situation in the Czech lands and Slovakia in the years prior to 1918, referring to the members of the Martin circle around Vajanský. Writers, priests, Protestant clergy teachers and notaries had been the scions of the Slovak national movement in the countryside. They had lived in a close-knit community, waiting for the nation's salvation, which they expected to come from the east, from the feudalist Empire of the Russian Tsar.[177] The Martin intellectuals did not understand that the fight for democracy and against the Hungarian feudalistic regime was the best, in fact the only, protection for the Slovak nation. They had had no contact with the working class, neither did they understand the needs of the people; cosily tucked away in Martin in their splendid isolation, they considered themselves the main representatives of the Slovak nation.

Clementis mentioned Masaryk's Slovak roots that explained his theory of Czechoslovakism and the constitutional construct of the Czechoslovak nation. Masaryk had been wrong in his statement of 1905 that two million Czechs were living in the Hungarian kingdom:

> "The Slovak nation is not and cannot be any longer the point of contention between our two nations. The Slovak nation is a reality. It exists. [...] In Slovakia, Masaryk's views were perceived as progressive. They

---

Marxism-Leninism. The author of the letter was probably Antonín Smetana (1863–1939), a Czech administrator and senator.
[176] Clementis, "Slovenský ľud ...", 400-401.
[177] Clementis, "Slovenský ľud ...", 403.

were directed not only against the reactionary Slavophilia of the Martinists, but also against a second danger – Clericalism."[178]

The backward-looking clergy in Slovakia had opposed Masaryk's ideas of democracy, equality of individuals and nations from the very first days of the Republic. It was remarkable that Andrej Hlinka had not been the first opponent to criticize Masaryk's thought. The professor had exerted significant intellectual influence on the priest, although the latter had a different interpretation of Masaryk's mottoes. The first opponent of the president in Slovakia was an author and member of the Catholic clergy, who had been hiding behind the pseudonym *Margin*, the author of *Modern Philosophy and the Slovaks*, a reactionary attack on rational thought and scientific inquiry. The author was František Jehlička (1879–1939), a creature of his Magyar reactionary masters, who had become an agent of Horthy and was now in the service of Goebbels, collaborating with the Gestapo![179]

What exactly was Masaryk's legacy in Slovakia? At the president's funeral, Beneš had called all citizens, regardless of their political views and national identity, to honour Masaryk's legacy by fulfilling his grand task – to continue on the path of progressive and humanist democracy. The Communists would follow Masaryk's call:

> "With our co-operation and support, we want to strengthen, deepen and develop Czechoslovak democracy, a democracy which has no room for reaction, Fascism, social injustice and national oppression. A democracy, supported by the working class and the masses, shall represent the will of the people in a better way. We are in full accord with the European and international political course that is moving towards a democracy of a higher state of development, a democracy that shall re-

---

[178] Clementis, "Slovenský ľud ...", 407-408.
[179] Clementis, "Slovenský ľud ...", 410. In the Czech and Slovak collective memories, Moravec and Jehlička are considered the biggest traitors in the histories of their nations.

place bourgeois democracy [*namiesto demokracie meštiackej*]. A democracy that will open the way towards the establishment of a better political, economic and social order for all mankind."[180]

Masaryk's legacy was the foundation of the state as a democracy. In Clementis' interpretation, the president had given the people a political system based on equality, which the Communists would further develop until they would reach the highest stage, a democracy in perfection. Although he did not express himself in clear words, it is safe to say that he must have thought of a people's democracy in a one-party system, naturally with the KSČ as the avant-garde of the working class. Clementis was careful not to mention the Soviet Union in this context or any other concept of Communist newspeak. But by mentioning the "democracy of a higher stage of development", he proved that his understanding of democracy had nothing in common with Masaryk's democracy. Clementis' message was clear to everybody familiar with the political goal and methods of the Communists: the political system he wanted to establish was the very contrary of Masaryk's democracy – a totalitarian state ruled by the KSČ that would follow Stalin's political course.

Clementis attacked the HSĽS for claiming Masaryk's legacy for themselves, for portraying themselves as those who continued in Slovakia the work Masaryk had begun, but the spirit in which they were acting was anti-democratic to the core. Drunk with admiration for Hitler and Mussolini, they were listening to Piłsudski in Poland and Franco in Spain.[181] Clementis' warning was a chilling portent of the future:

> "The autonomy which the current leaders of the Hlinka Party would love to instal would go against the people, against democracy [*protiľudová, protidemokratická*]. It would be an autonomy of the adherents of

---

[180] Clementis, "Slovenský ľud ...", 412.
[181] Clementis, "Slovenský ľud ...", 416.

Horthy and Goebbels, an autonomy that would suit the programme of foreign Fascism directed against the Czechoslovak Republic."[182]

To strengthen Slovakia and prevent the autonomy the Ľudáci wanted to establish, the KSČ, Clementis continued, had presented its programme of economic, social and cultural reforms.[183] This programme addressed not only the Slovak working class, but also the Czech workers; the Czech democrats should realize that they had to improve their relations with the Slovaks. Only a united working class would be able to defend the Republic against the threat of Fascism.

In tune with the Comintern's usage, Clementis avoided the concept of 'National Socialism' when referring to Nazi Germany's political system and thought; he strictly followed the Party's linguistic instructions. In terms of the Socialist fight against Hitlerism, the concept of 'National Socialism' was too close to 'Socialism'; uneducated persons might confuse German 'National Socialism' with the international Socialist movement led by the Soviet Union. The concepts of 'Fascism', 'Nazi regime' or 'Hitlerism' did no linguistic-ideological harm to the Socialist movement; thus Clementis used them consistently.

My former teacher Hermann Lübbe, professor emeritus of Political Philosophy at the University of Zurich UZH and a renowned philosopher in the German-speaking academic world, explained in an e-mail conversation on 30 June 2016 the importance of the Socialist element in both totalitarian regimes:

> "The adjective 'Socialist' in the name of the '*Nationalsozialistische Deutsche Arbeiterpartei*' was neither a coincidence nor a misconception and it was not born of an intent to deceive either. It is a banality that there was no transfer of the means of production from private property

---

[182] Clementis, "Slovenský ľud ...", 416.
[183] The delegates of the KSČ had adopted the reform programme at the Party congress on 16 and 17 May 1937 in Banská Bystrica; *Chronológia dejín Slovenska a Slovákov II*, 645.

to the property of the '*Volksgemeinschaft*'. But, in preparation for the war, the agricultural and industrial production had to fulfil the strict quotas of the so-called Four-Year Plans. Furthermore, the expressions of solidarity of National Welfare Socialism (*Volkswohlsozialismus*), as it could be called, were binding; one could not object them in public. The symbolic appeals for winter relief (*Winterhilfssammlungen*) obliged the very representatives of the political authorities and, in general, the well-off, to wander about on Sundays with their collecting boxes, demanding, for example, donations for maternity protection (*Mutterschutz*) or subsidized holidays for workers on comfort-ships under the Strength Through Joy (*Kraft durch Freude*) programme. As so-called *pimpfs*, that is, the 10- to 14-year-old compulsory members of the Hitler Youth, we had to get winter stocks of potatoes and coal to the houses of the elderly. [...] Soon after the beginning of WWII, we young German high school students received the book of a German Communist of the first hour who had returned to Germany as a consequence of the Hitler-Stalin Pact. Comparing the Soviet system with National Socialism, he celebrated Hitler as 'the greatest Socialist of all times' (Karl I. Albrecht: Der verratene Sozialismus. Zehn Jahre als hoher Staatsbeamter in der Sowjetunion. Berlin, Leipzig, 1941). [...] The Marxist-Leninist definition of German National Socialism as dictatorship of the bourgeoisie was equally consistent when addressing the desperate final phase of the rule of the bourgeois class; its linguistic politics demanded the strictest avoidance of the concept of '*Nationalsozialismus*', dictating the usage of '*Faschismus*'. After the war, one had to stick to this usage when visiting the states of the Eastern bloc; otherwise one would have been interrupted and reprimanded. In my publications in the West, I used the concepts of '*Nationalsozialismus*' (National Socialism) for right-wing Socialism and '*Internationalsozialismus*' (International Socialism) for left-wing Socialism." [184]

---

[184] Hermann Lübbe, "Der Totalitarismus. Politische Moral als Anti-Religion", in *Forum für osteuropäische Ideen- und Zeitgeschichte 17*, no. 1 (2013): 27-43. According to Eckhard Jesse, the concept of '*Faschismus*' had an overbearing importance similar to a canonical law in the former GDR; the authorities had been eager to avoid the concept of '*Nationalsozialismus*'; Eckhard Jesse, "Antifaschismus in der Ideokratie der DDR – und die Folgen", in *Extremismus und Demokratie, Parteien und Wahlen* (Köln, Weimar, Wien: Nomos, 2015), 93-104, 100. I thank Hermann Lübbe for this reference.
The Slovak historian Juraj Benko, a specialist on the Communist regime, in our e-mail conversation of 17 August 2016: "The Soviet elite, when address-

With his interpretation of Masaryk's legacy in Slovakia, Clementis reproached the Ľudáci that they were now praising Masaryk with admiring words, while they had attacked him in the past. He was spot on with the analysis of his enemies – but he was guilty of exactly the same transgression: he considered the KSČ as the only legitimate heirs of Masaryk. In his view, only the Communists had

> ing Germany, often replaced the concept of 'National Socialism' with 'Fascism', which reflected the changing position towards Germany after 1935. In the first half of the 1930s, one can speak of a certain sympathetic perception of German National Socialism among the Soviet elite; they perceived some features of the German political system as close to the Soviet system. The concept of 'National Socialism' was an expression of that ideological closeness. In general, the Soviet and Comintern authors did not conceive of the concept of 'Fascism' as genetically tied to Italy. To a certain extent, they considered 'Fascism' as a superior term that included 'National Socialism' as much as 'Social Democracy', which they perceived as a wing of the Fascist movement. 'Fascism' was used widely; Trotskii referred to the German National Socialist regime as a Fascist dictatorship. On the occasion of the seventh party congress on 26 January 1934, Stalin, referring to the tasks of the CC, spoke of 'Fascism of the German type', which was an incorrect term, since 'even under the most basic scrutiny, not an iota of Socialism can be found there'. 'Не удивительно, что фашизм стал теперь наиболее модным товаром среди воинствующих буржуазных политиков. Я говорю не только о фашизме вообще, но прежде всего о фашизме германского типа, который неправильно называется национал-социализмом, ибо при самом тщательном рассмотрении невозможно обнаружить в нем даже атома социализма.' (Сталин И.В. Сочинения. – Т. 13. – М.: Государственное издательство политической литературы, 1951. s. 393.) The Russian author F. Ľas writes that, from the beginning of the Nazi movement, Stalin disliked the linguistic closeness to Socialism, and when the NSDAP assumed power, he dictated the usage of 'Fascism' and 'Fascists', when referring to the Nazis. The Soviet Communist Party adopted Stalin's directive at the seventh party congress in 1934 and also on the occasion of the eighth extraordinary all-Soviet Convention in December 1936. (Ľas, Fjodor. Pozdnyj stalinizm i evrei. [Поздний сталинизм и евреи] Jerusalem: Filobiblon, 2012, s 71.) In his speech about the new Soviet Constitution, Viačeslav M. Molotov (1890–1986) consistently referred to 'German Facism' at the eighth extraordinary all-Soviet Convention; http://fennougrica.kansalliskirjasto.fi/bitstream/handle/10024/90622/HMS_12_04_1936_124-125_646.pdf?sequence=1.

fully understood Masaryk's thought and plans for the future. Naturally, Clementis did not mention that the president had never thought of Marxism as a viable social order, let alone a convincing solution for mankind's economic and social problems. On the contrary: Masaryk had studied the various Socialist thinkers of the 19th century and rejected Marx's concept of class and the distorted logic of the collective:

> "If the individual is nothing, if his consciousness and conscience are bereft of meaning, why are thousands of individuals, all of a sudden something and, finally, everything?"[185]

If Clementis considered Masaryk's democracy the basis of a future People's Democracy, he was only being true to his Marxist-Leninist thinking. His credo also allowed him to warn his readers of the dangers the rule of HSĽS would pose to the common state. Only nine months later, the Munich Agreement would prompt the Slovak declaration of autonomy, which was the first step towards the Slovak state.[186] Clerical Fascism would rule in pseudo-independent Slovakia; it was a peculiar conglomerate of Christian anti-Judaism, radical Catholic doctrine, racist Antisemitism, radical Nationalism, Populism and anti-Czech Chauvinism.

I. 4. 4 On Slovak Autonomy (1938)

When Neville Chamberlain, Edouard Daladier, Benito Mussolini and Adolf Hitler signed the Munich Agreement on 30 September

---

[185] Tomáš Garrigue Masaryk, "Socialism", in *Ideály humanitní* (Praha: Melantrich, 1990), 13-22, 17.

[186] I refer to Slovakia from 1939 to 1945 as the 'Slovak state', not as the First Slovak Republic, the official name adopted in the constitution of 1939. Slovakia was a totalitarian state ruled by the HSĽS and modelled on Nazi Germany. The uniforms of the Hlinka Guards, the military branch of the HSĽS, were literally identical to those of the SS. An excellent portrait of the Slovak state is given in the Czechoslovak film *Obchod na korze* (*The Shop on Main Street*) on http://www.imdb.com/title/tt0059527/; accessed 12 April 2016. It won the Oscar for best foreign film in 1965.

1938, many hoped that the German leader would be appeased. But the Munich agreement was but a stepping stone. In August 1939, with plans for the invasion of Poland already laid, Hitler would tell his generals that their enemies were small worms; he had seen them in Munich.[187]

Czechoslovakia lost the Sudeten lands to Germany, while the radicals of the HSĽS pursued their own plans. The Žilina Agreement (*Žilinská dohoda*) on 6 October 1938[188] established Slovakia's autonomy. Czechoslovakia's status changed to a federation with the new official name *Czecho-Slovakia*; Slovakia was now called *Slovenska krajna*. The government in Prague was responsible for international affairs, defence, currency, the state budget, customs, public traffic and the post.[189]

In March 1938, seven months before the Munich Agreement, Clementis described the political situation in Slovakia in his article "Autonomy?".[190] The Communists who counted two hundred and ten thousand members were firm in their rejection of the current political development the leaders of the Hlinka Party were pushing forward. The *Ľudáci* were claiming that autonomy would solve the national problem of the Slovaks within the common state, improve the economy and strengthen Catholicism. Their thinking was a tragic error:

> "The popularity that Berlin, revisionist Pest, imperialist Warsaw and the domestic agents Henlein and Count Eszterházy are enjoying, are strengthening the leading party members' efforts to establish autonomy. [...] And only a pathetic fool, who is blind in politics, can consider autonomy a positive development, or that our nation can continue to

---

[187] Ian Kershaw, *Hitler* (London: Penguin, 2008), 445.
[188] The text of the Žilina Agreement in Rychlík, *Češi a Slováci I*, 144.
[189] Kováč, *Dejiny Slovenska*, 210.
[190] Clementis, "Autonómia?", *Svět v obrazech*, 20 March 1938, no. 10, 4-5, in *Vzduch našich čias II*, 427-430.

exist in an autonomous Slovakia protected by the German *hakenkreuzler*, the Polish imperialists or the Hungarian feudalist revisionists."[191]

One did not have to be a Communist to predict how the *Ľudáci*, in conjunction with the German Nazis and the Hungarian Feudalists, would treat those who did not share their creed. Clementis warned his readers of the authoritarian regime that would be established if Slovakia became autonomous and Prague no longer had a say in political matters. There was no doubt, as Clementis wrote in a sharp, cynical and very angry tone, that autonomous Slovakia would turn into a colony of the foreign Fascist and Imperialist powers; the foreign powers would rob the country, and Slovakia would end as a tourist attraction because of her primitive backwardness.

The only issue raising some doubts was the question of whether the Catholic Church would gain in strength, i.e. would become even stronger than it already was. That was an issue the Catholics should decide for themselves, considering the particularly unfortunate position of Catholicism in Germany and the fate of the Austrian Catholics. But the arguments of the HSĽS leaders who favoured autonomy were but a smoke screen that was hiding other plans. Did the leaders of the Hlinka Party really believe that they could lie to the people? Did they not see that the foreign Imperialists did not even bother to conceal that they, by the sheer force of their size and military might, enjoyed privileged status, exerting their right to conquer not only Slovakia, but also Austria, Romania rich in oil, Ukraine and other countries?[192]

---

[191] Clementis, "Autonómia?", 427-428.
[192] Clementis, "Autonómia?", 428-429.

The current status of Slovak culture, lately discussed at the conference of young Slovak writers in Trenčianské Teplice,[193] demonstrated that the Slovak nation was a reality and that the intellectuals wanted to co-operate with the top representatives of Czech culture as equals and side by side.[194] Clementis spoke of "*rovný s rovným* [to be equal with the equal]", which would turn into a political principle of the post-war negotiations with Beneš about the future status of Slovakia in reconstructed Czechoslovakia. *Rovný s rovným* meant complete equality of Czechs and Slovaks in all matters of politics, culture and economics and self-government in Slovakia. The Slovak intellectuals, to Clementis' way of thinking a united group, needed the Czech intellectuals for their future cultural development, but they also demanded that the Czechs respected the distinct Slovak characteristics:

> "We are welcoming the representatives of Czech culture because we need them, especially for tackling several scientific problems – and we are grateful for their support. [...] But we reject the attitude some Czechs have towards Slovak culture; the attitude of considering us as periphery, as a mere province of the Czech cultural centre."[195]

In their efforts to solve the economic and social problems, the Czechs and Slovaks were concentrating on the liquidation of the separatist provincialism and lower level of quality of life in Slovakia. In their economic reform programme of May 1937, the Slovak Communists had laid the grounds for future co-operation with the Czechs, which was supposed to overcome the economic, social and cultural inequality between the two nations. It should also

---

[193] Clementis had participated at the conference of young Slovak intellectuals (*sjazd mladej inteligencie Slovenska*) on 25 and 26 June 1932. Some five hundred intellectuals had discussed Slovakia's status in the Republic and the social order. The majority was critical of centralism, thinking about a change of the political system; *Chronológia dejín Slovenska a Slovákov II*, 624-625.
[194] Clementis, "Autonómia?", 429.
[195] Clementis, "Autonómia?", 429.

promote the protection of the workers and, lastly, the Republic threatened by international Fascist aggression.

I. 4. 5 Munich 1938 – The End of the Republic

Clementis wrote his last article in Bratislava on 18 September 1938. On 6 October 1938, a week after the Munich Agreement, he and his wife Lída left for Prague. He was a realist and could foresee that one of the first tasks the HSĽS government would set itself would to be declare the KSČ illegal, rendering the persecution of Communists legal with a constitutional amendment.

In his article "Yes, yes – no, no!"[196], one can sense Clementis' anger, inner turmoil and distress. The doctor of law who never mentioned his emotions, who was always dedicated to matter-of-factness, began his article with a description of himself – a description that offers us an insight into his psyche. No Communist newspeak; no bashing of the centre-right parties; no praise for the Communist Party; only facts now – the Republic was in grave danger:

> "It is Thursday evening, 15 September. The editorial office of *Slovenské zvesti* in Prague has just called me, reminding me of my promise to hand in a feature article for the Bratislava issue. […] They need it by seven o'clock. A promise is a promise – it has to be kept. That's why I am sitting now in front of my typewriter, listening on the wireless to the latest news from Prague, Vienna and Budapest. And I am learning that Mr Chamberlain, who never before set foot on an airplane, has happily landed in Munich and is now on his way to the Führer's residence. In their broadcasts, Budapest and Vienna are repeating, over and over again, the brazen lies and slogans of the blood-stained putschists of the Henlein Party. They are also quoting, over and over again, Mussolini's letter to Runciman, published in the *Popolo d'Italia*: 'All nations in the Czechoslovak Republic have the right to decide about their citizenship by means of a plebiscite (naturally, not the Slovenes and Germans in

---

[196] Clementis, "Ano, ano – nie, nie!" *Slovenské zvesti III*, no. 182, 18 September 1938, 3, in *Vzduch našich čias II*, 464-466.

Italy). Mussolini's letter ends with the conclusion that since a Czechoslovak nation does not exist neither does the Czechoslovak Republic."[197]

The latest news offered ample material to write a series of feature articles, and Mr Chamberlain's reasons for his trip would enlighten the readers of the *Slovenské zvesti*. But, as Clementis wrote, all of Czechoslovakia was still under the shock of the news from the Sudeten lands, where Czech and German democrats were bleeding, where policemen and members of the Czechoslovak state security service had been murdered with foreign weapons of a well-known provenance while executing their great responsibity of protecting the state.[198]

No, he did not want to enter into a polemic with a certain Mr Kaláč, who had just yesterday in the *Slovenský denník* commented on Hitler's speech, admiring the German leader's clear standpoint on the Sudeten German issue. Hitler demanded an agreement for the Sudeten Germans – what a surprise!

The article of Mussolini was also a great initiative, Clementis wrote with acerbic sarcasm. The Duce's call for a plebiscite in the Sudeten lands was in tune with the declaration of alliance between Henlein and Sidor; the broadcasts from Budapest and all German radio stations were repeating that alliance over and over again. Allegedly, Mussolini was gravely concerned about the Slovaks, a nation he had not that long ago called "a nation of swineherds and servants, living in the Tatra Mountains [*národ pastierov*

---

[197] Clementis, "Ano, ano – nie, nie!", 464. Chamberlain visited Hitler at his residence Berghof in the Bavarian Alps close to Berchtesgaden. Walter Runciman (1870–1949) was a member of the British Liberal Party and mediator in the crisis of the Sudeten lands. He recommended to Prime Minister Chamberlain supporting the Sudeten Germans' secession from Czechoslovakia, thereby caving the way for the Munich Agreement.
[198] Clementis, "Ano, ano – nie, nie!", 465.

svín a slúžok spod Tatier]".[199] Henlein was clear at least now: he wanted to join the Sudeten lands to the Reich.

> "Yes, that Henlein, the leader of the Sudeten Germans, the party Sidor is embracing, the party that started the violent putsch. Now, is this putsch not reason enough for appealing to the conscience of those functionaries of Hlinka's People's Party who are still wavering, who are still refusing to see that Sidor's way will be the end, the extinction of the Slovak nation?"[200]

The situation was changing from hour to hour; Clementis was nervous and also desperate. He was trying to instil hope, encouraging his readers to stand firm, to defend the Republic. The attack on the Republic was based on the assumption that Czechoslovakia would cave in, that the Republic was too weak, that her Western allies were neither reliable nor quick enough – that was what the enemies' propaganda wanted to make the people believe. Clementis interpretation was spot on: very soon, the foreign attack would break up the Republic. Czechoslovakia's enemies were intent on dividing the Slovaks from the Czechs. He hoped that Czechoslovakia would defend herself in a war against Germany that he thought was imminent. In these dire and difficult days, the Slovak nation had to understand very clearly that only the closest co-operation with the Czechs would save both nations from the looming abyss. The stout atheist was so distressed that he even mentioned a Christian concept:

> "In these dire days, every Slovak, the entire Slovak nation has to speak up with clear words, not with the evasive willy-nilly words of diplomacy, but in biblical and clear terms: yes, yes – no, no. Together with the Czechs – yes! Together with the boys – yes! With the Republic's enemies – no, never, ever!"[201]

---

[199] Clementis, "Ano, ano – nie, nie!", 465.
[200] Clementis, "Ano, ano – nie, nie!", 466.
[201] Clementis, "Ano, ano – nie, nie!", 466.

Let down by the allies France and Great Britain, Beneš and his government would leave for Paris in October 1938 and form the Czechoslovak exile government in London in 1940. Gottwald and Slánský would find refuge in Moscow. Husák, who had worked with Clementis in his lawyer's office in Bratislava, would be arrested and interned in the notorious Ilava prison, from where he would flee and organize the Communist resistance movement. With the occupation of the Czech lands cynically referred to as a protectorate and the creation of the Slovak state, a puppet state at Hitler's beck and call, Masaryk's Republic ceased to exist on 15 March 1939.

"I asked him if he was aware that the KSČ leadership in Moscow had ousted him; he should have no illusions about that. He replied that he was certain that had he only fifteen minutes with Gottwald he could convince him of the rightfulness of his decisions, explaining his plans in France in 1939. [...] I delivered a message from Husák, who criticised Peter Hron's broadcasts about the Slovak nation. He just laughed. It was a long, truthful and quiet conversation that lasted from lunch at the new Czech restaurant on Edgeware Road to a walk in Maida Vale. [...] We were never close. [...] Our opinions were diametrically opposed. [...] Some said that he was arrogant, I don't know, I would rather describe him as unapproachable."[1]

"H. G. Wells at a luncheon at the London Pen Club: 'He is a gentleman. If all Communists are like that, then it's alright.'"[2]

"Clementis was the most important Slovak in the Czechoslovak exile in Britain. His radio broadcasts had the biggest effect at home. [...] The voice of Vlado Clementis cut through the English fog. He offered not only his intellect, but also his Slovak and Slavic heart to the resistance fighters who, in those dire days, did not need lectures on tactics, but a maximum of moral and material support. Clementis gave his moral bravery to the holy battle, which was not being fought in the ether or in thoughts, but in our mountains and valleys, against an enemy more than cruel and powerful. That's why the Slovak workers and farmers came to Banská Bystrica to look for Vlado Clementis. When they didn't find him there, they held out fighting for eight months. Because they knew that he was fighting with us."[3]

---

1. Prokop Drtina, *Československo, můj osud*, svazek I, kniha 2 (Toronto: Sixty-Eight Publishers, 1982), 721. Prokop Drtina (1900–1980) was a member of the London exile government and Minister of Justice in the short-lived post-war Republic (1945–1948) under President Beneš. During the war, he and Clementis worked at the Czechoslovak broadcast at the BBC. Peter Hron was Clementis' pseudonym.
2. Holotíková a Plevza, 237.
3. Dr. G. Husák, "O boj a spolubojovníkovi", in *Odkazy z Londýna*, V-VIII, VII. Husák referred to the Slovak National Uprising that had started in Banská Bystrica and lasted two months. Husák spoke of eight months, extending the resistance activities to April 1945, when the Red Army liberated Eastern Slovakia. He was not wrong, but not precise either: the partisans' resistance did not cease after the crushing of the uprising, but they were single, isolated activities, not an organized campaign.

II. In Exile (1939–1945)

II. 1   From France to Great Britain (1939–1940)

The government of autonomous Slovakia declared the KSČ illegal on 9 October 1938. The ties of the Czech and Slovak Communists ceased to exist; so did all Party journals and newspapers. Clementis and his wife Lída left for Prague on 6 October 1938, came back to Slovakia, and left again for Prague on 14 March 1939, this time for six years in exile.[1] They applied for exit visas to France, but only Lída received one. On instructions from the Party, Clementis had to join Party members in Paris; he left Czechoslovakia illegally through Poland, the Soviet Union and Sweden. His first attempt was unsuccessful, because he committed a mistake, which offers us an insight into his behaviour and character. Did he feel too safe in Poland? He obviously did not want to walk and took a short cut, probably pressed for time. Was he arrogant and spoiled? Or was he simply naïve, an impractical intellectual in an autistic bubble, unaware of the dangerous reality?

> "After he had passed the Slovak-Polish border, he was happy to have behind him the first phase of his journey; [...] he ordered a fiacre. Thus, the Communist refugee rode in a fiacre [the way a wealthy entrepreneur would have, add. JB] and soon, a Polish border patrol stopped him. The soldiers asked him about his profession, and Clementis answered truthfully, mentioning his Party membership and position as parliamentary delegate. Could he not have lied, telling them that he was a businessman, a civil servant or a hat maker? He could not. Because of his Party membership, the Polish patrol sent him straight back to Slovakia."[2]

---

[1]   Holotíková a Plevza, 198.
[2]   Holotíková a Plevza, 198-199.

The second attempt was successful; in Moscow, Clementis received a Swedish visa and arrived in Paris by plane from Stockholm at the end of June 1939. Prior to France's occupation by Germany on 22 June 1940, Paris was the centre of Czechoslovak refugees. Clementis was in steady contact with Milan Hodža and Štefan Osuský (1889–1973), the former Czechoslovak ambassador to France.[3] Moscow had given the KSČ clear instructions: Clementis was supposed to leave for the USA to organize an antifascist movement in the Slovak expat community. Yet, Beneš, who had been in London since 22 October 1938, advised Hubert Ripka (1895–1958) to prevent Clementis' trip to the USA; he obviously thought that the Communist lawyer would pose a serious threat to the exile government then being formed among the *krajane* in the USA.[4]

In the months prior to his leaving for Britain, Clementis tried to improve the living conditions of the *interbrigadisty*, the Czechoslovak Communists who had fought in Spain and were gathering in Paris after Franco had won the Civil War; they were interned in POW camps. He was an active member of the *maison de culture tchécoslovaque*, the intellectual and political centre of the Czechoslovak refugees in France.

When the news about the German-Soviet Nonaggression Pact broke on 23 August 1939, Clementis, ever truthful and committed to Socialism, expressed his opinion about the alliance. This was a grave mistake that would lead to his arrest and execution in 1951. He criticized the Ribbentrop-Molotov pact in a small circle

---

[3] On Hodža see Pavol Lukáč, *Milan Hodža v zápase o budúcnosť strednej Európy v rokoch 1939–1944* (Bratislava: Veda, 2005); Miroslav Pekník, ed., *Milan Hodža. Statesman and Politician* (Bratislava: Veda, 2007). Hodža's texts have been translated to Slovak from their English originals: Milan Hodža, *Federácia v strednej Európe* (Bratislava: Kalligramm, 1997). Excellent on Osuský is Slavomír Michálek, *Diplomat Štefan Osuský 1889–1973* (Bratislava: Veda, 1999).

[4] Holotíková a Plevza, 200.

of Party comrades he believed he could trust: Viliam Široký (1902–1971), Bruno Köhler (1900–1989) and Jan Šverma (1903–1944).⁵ He also criticized the Soviet aggression against Finland. Gottwald expelled him for lack of faith in the Soviet Union, the Comintern, the Communist movement and lack of Party discipline:

> "Clementis is opposing the Soviet-German Pact. He has opposed the Soviet Union on the issue of Finland. He is siding with English-French Imperialism against Germany. He is siding with Beneš for the oppression of our Party. [...] He is co-operating with Hodža and Osuský. We have excluded him from the Party. [...] Klemo."⁶

There is no document available that can inform us about Clementis' exact wording and tone, but in view of his loyalty to the KSČ and Moscow, his characteristic truthfulness, intellectual acumen, courage and straight-forwardness, one should not be surprised. I think that Clementis, like many European Communists who hoped that Moscow would join in the fight against Nazi Germany, was truly and deeply shocked about the Soviet-German alliance. In regard to his talent for political analysis, it was no surprise that he rejected the pact. German National Socialism embodied everything Marxism-Leninism was fighting against: the self-appointed superiority of the German *Volk* and the Arian race; Hitler's aggressive and anti-Slavic foreign policy; racism and antisemitism justified with pseudo-scientific explanations; the shameless cooperation with German capitalist enterprises such as IG Farben, Thyssen-Krupp and the textile fashion company Boss under the

---

5 Holotíková a Plevza, 202.
6 Bareš, G. – Janeček, O (ed.): Depeše mezi Prahou a Moskvou 1939–1941. Příspěvky k dějinám KSČ 1967, č. 3, s. 417, quoted from Jan Němeček, "Vladimír Clementis a československý zahraniční odboj", in *Vladimír Clementis. 1902–1952. Zborník ...*, 46-53, 47.

thin disguise of a German National Socialist revolution[7] and, lastly, the tradition of Prussian militarism and a particular hatred of Bolshevism.

A further consequence of the Ribbentrop-Molotov Pact was the persecution of Communists, French or foreign: on 25 August, the French government declared the French Communist press organ *L'Humanité* illegal, and on 26 September 1939, the French Communist Party was forbidden.[8] Because of the German-Soviet Nonaggression Pact, France considered the Soviet Union an ally of Nazi Germany that had attacked Poland on 1 September; the French government was afraid that the Communists and the disciplined *interbrigadisty* would try to establish Bolshevik rule in France. The government thus arrested French and foreign Communists and interned them in camps. According to President Beneš, Clementis was supposed to meet him secretly in Paris together with the Communist parliamentarian Jan Šverma on 10 October 1939 to organize the future exile government and the Czechoslovak army in France.[9] But on that day, the French police raided the *maison de culture tchécoslovaque*, and Clementis and other Czechoslovaks were arrested and interned at the Stade Roland Garros.[10]

Thanks to his wife Lída, who asked ambassador Osuský for help and the foundation of the Czechoslovak exile army on 2 October, Clementis was able to leave the camp after signing up with

---

[7] About the NSDAP's revolution see Leni Riefenstahl's (1902–2003) film *Triumph of the Will* (1935) on http://www.imdb.com/title/tt0025913/; accessed 7 May 2016.

[8] Holotíková a Plevza, 204.

[9] Edvard Beneš, *Paměti II. Od Mnichova k nové válce a k novému vítězství* (Praha: Academia, 2008), 150.

[10] Holotíková a Plevza, 205. About the dark past of the famous tennis court see http://edition.cnn.com/2011/SPORT/tennis/06/03/tennis.roland.garros.war.camp/; accessed 2 May 2016.

the Czechoslovak army, which was sent to Great Britain in June 1940.[11] Lída followed and found a room in London.

II. 2 In Great Britain

A principal source about Clementis' life in Great Britain is the correspondence with his wife Lída. The exact date when Lída and Vladimír met for the first time is shrouded in mystery.

According to Zora Jesenská, the editor of Clementis' *Unfinished History* (*Nedokončená kronika*), the young doctor of law met Lída Pátková (1910–?) in Bratislava at a reception in honour of Ehrenburg.[12] Lída was Czech and studying at the Academy of Music and Drama in Bratislava.[13] Vladimír approached Lída for the first time in the late 1920s; she was waiting at the tram station in front of the Manderla House in Bratislava's city centre.[14] Lída mentioned in her touching last posthumous letter to Vladimír in 1968 that he had first addressed her at the tram station close to the famous café *Štefanka*, which is ten minutes away from Bratislava's main railway station.[15] I deem it more probable that Lída is right – which is a psychological argument that I cannot confirm with

---

[11] Holotíková a Plevza, 209.
[12] Zora Jesenská, "Slovo na Záver. Drahá Hádička", in *Nedokončená kronika* (Bratislava: Slovenské vydavateľstvo krásnej literatúry, 1964), 161-173; 162.
[13] The Slovak film *Smrť ministra* premiered on 10 December 2009 on STV 1. The actors were very well chosen with Ján Kroner jun. as Vlado and Miroslava Pleštilová as Lída; http://www.noviny.sk/c/slovensko/vcera-odpremiero vali-slovensky-film-smrt-ministra; accessed 26 November 2015. Ľuboš Jurík is the author of the screenplay, a fictitious account of Clementis' last night in prison. In 2011, Jurík published a novel under the same title (Martin: Matica Slovenská, 2011).
[14] Holotíková a Plevza, 115.
[15] Clementis a Clementisová, *Listy z Väzenia* (Bratislava: Tatran: 1968), 73. See the famous meeting point of artists and intellectuals on http://www.cafestefanka.sk; accessed 20 May 2016.

documents. But I think that a woman does not forget the location and circumstances when her future husband addressed her for the first time. Apparently, they knew each other from afar, but had never spoken. Both shared an interest in the arts, music and literature. Lída Pátková and Vladimír Clementis had a civil marriage in Bratislava on 24 March 1933.[16]

The beautiful Czech artist-singer and the handsome Slovak lawyer were not only a match made in heaven because of their cultural interests. They were a beautiful couple, aesthetically contrasting each other: Vladimír had piercing green-blue almost turqoise eyes, brown hair and a stocky, broad-shouldered body, the body of a boxer-athlete. Lída's petite frame, deep blue eyes, ivory skin and delicate, classical features would have enabled her to follow a career in modelling in the 21st century.

In her letters, she addressed him as *Vlado* and *Hádik*; he called her *Hádička,* the feminized form of his nickname *Hádik*. The nickname originated in Vladimír's childhood: his little sister Božena (Boža) was very close to him. As Boža could not yet properly pronounce the short form *Vladik* for Vladimír, she called him *Hádik* instead – he called her *Veštúr*, seeress, prophetess, sybil and *Štúrča*, little sybil, obviously thinking that his little sister had the gift of seeing.[17]

Vladimír felt a deep, almost telepathic connection with his wife. In his letters, he would time and again stress that she was his closest comrade, the only person who really understood him – Lída was his other half.[18] Their correspondence amounts to 47 letters; the first note from Vladimír is dated on 21 December 1939, Lída's last letter on 1 January 1941. This is the collection of letters available to us, that is, the letters Lída had decided to publish after

---

[16] Holotíková a Plevza, 117.
[17] Clementis, *Nedokončená kronika*, 52.
[18] Clementis and Clementisová, *Ďaleko od Teba* (Bratislava: Tatran, 1972), 86.

Vladimír's rehabilitation in 1963. We don't know if she kept some letters to herself or whether some got lost, but both husband and wife mentioned letters that are not included in the published collection. He was interned at the POW camp in Sutton Coldfield, near Birmingham, and from 10 October 1940, in the POW camp in Scotland, "Glenbranter Comp., Argyll".[19] He wrote her 10 letters, she wrote him 37.

Lída wrote to Vlado more frequently; there were longer periods of time between his letters. He started with a brief note on 21 December 1939, then wrote on 15 February 1940, 24 July, 2 October, 4 October, 6 October, 7 October, 9 October, and 14 October. Most probably, he was not allowed to send letters in the spring of 1940 because of war censorship; I deem it also probable that Lída did not want some letters published because of their intimate or politically dangerous content.

---

[19] Clementis and Lída Clementisová, *Ďaleko od Teba*, 105. 'Comp' was a typo; it should be 'Camp'. For a list of POW camps in Great Britain see http://www.theguardian.com/news/datablog/2010/nov/08/prisoner-of-war-camps-uk#data; accessed 19 December 2015. Mrs Iseabel Thomson is a member of Glenbranter History Society; she kindly provided me with the following information: "The locals would not have any contact with the prisoners and I do not think the soldiers would be out and about in the village as there would be no social life. Everything was in short supply and petrol could only be used for journeys of national importance. Glenbranter camp had been a labour camp before the war and it was enlarged - it had a double perimeter barbed wire fence with a walkway and sentry posts every so often and one main gate. My father was the local builder and he was involved in the building of Glenbranter and other camps in the area, we were lucky to see him every three or four weeks because of the travel restrictions. The Germans from the Lofoten Islands were brought to Glenbranter, then the Italians and finally it was HMS Pasco a naval camp. After the war two German brothers stayed here and worked in the forestry. I am not sure if either of them had been in Glenbranter. Their surname was Berndt and the younger one Helmut used to come to the dances. The older brother married and took his wife's name of Cameron but I cannot remember his first name."

Their letters reveal not only the couple's deep love for each other, but tell us also about Great Britain in the months of the *Blitz*, the battle of Britain, in 1940 and 1941.[20] At first glance, the letters are rather boring, as love letters not addressed to oneself usually are. On a second glance, however, reading them with a historical eye, they reveal interesting details about first, Lída's living conditions as a refugee and her psychological state, and, second, Vladimír's care for her and a crucial political decision of his.

II. 2. 1 Lída's Living Conditions

In his letter of 15 February 1940 from Paris, Vladimír wrote that he was expecting her; he was optimistic that she would join him soon. Referring to a previous letter from her, he asked her to stop taking sleeping pills: they were not good for her nerves.[21] He certainly did not want to tell her what to do, patronizing her was not his intention, but he was concerned about her health.

On 17 August, Lída wrote that they had been separated for more than two months now. She described her living conditions in London: the Czechoslovak Refugee Committee paid her £1 a week, but her room cost 15 shillings a day. London was terribly expensive, but she would stay at this address; after the turbulent and noisy days on the steamer, where she never had a minute to herself, she was now enjoying her quiet room and the opportunity of playing the piano. I think that she chose this room because of the piano that reminded her of their happy life together in Bratislava. She would rather not eat than move to another place.[22] Also,

---

[20] For an account of the Blitz see http://www.bbc.co.uk/history/events/the_blitz; accessed 27 November 2015.
[21] Clementis and Clementisová, *Ďaleko od Teba*, 18.
[22] Clementis and Clementisová, *Ďaleko od Teba*, 23.

she kept refusing all loan offers from friends and had only accepted £10 from the parliamentarian Jan Bečko (1889–1972) as a salary for the concert she had given on the steamer.

On 21 August, she thanked Vlado for his letter, but expressed her regret that he had returned £1 she had sent him. She apologized for her bad English: she had thought he needed the money. She was fine, but the lonely nights were particularly hard; she was thinking of him all the time. Most of the nights, she stayed in bed, also during the bombings.[23] She had contracted a catarrh of her lungs on the steamer, which the physicians were treating with injections.

From her letters it transpires that Lída's psychological state was worsening the longer she and Vladimír were separated. In early September, she wrote to him on a daily basis, but starting from 29 September, she wrote twice daily.[24] I have the impression that she was keeping herself alive by writing – her letters were the only connection to him. In her first letters, she sounded calm and composed, although she expressed her sorrows in an emotional tone – who would not in such a situation? Her letters from October and November are painful, displaying her desperation, loneliness, emotional dependence and incapability of dealing with practical matters of daily life.

In many respects, Lída's situation in Britain was worse than Vladimír's: she was on her own in a foreign country, whose language she barely spoke. She did not have a structured day; as a refugee, she was not allowed to work. She could have gone out to meet other refugees or volunteer for the Czechoslovak war effort, but she preferred spending her days on her own. She was ill and in a deplorable financial situation. Lída had arrived in London with the barest necessities she could carry; she had had to leave

---

[23] Clementis and Clementisová, *Ďaleko od Teba*, 32.
[24] Clementis and Clementisová, *Ďaleko od Teba*, 71-73.

the major part of her belongings in France, hurrying to reach the steamer. She felt ashamed about her poverty and did not want people to see that she didn't have the funds to buy herself a winter coat.[25]

I think we would do her a grave injustice if we blamed her for the choices she made – and those she would refuse to make. Not everybody is psychologically strong and pragmatic, capable of optimism in the dire situation of a war. An artist might have more difficulties adapting to such a cruel change of life than a person who is used to dealing with difficulties on a daily basis in their profession, such as, for example, a physician, a soldier, a farmer, a nurse or a high-school teacher. Lída kept to herself; isolation, shutting out reality was her way of dealing with the new situation she found herself in.

Vladimír, on the other hand, was interned with other Czechoslovaks; he spoke perfect English, was fed, had company, the physical and psychological structure of the daily routine in a POW camp and knew how to occupy himself. He wrote for her. He did not have to deal with issues such as how and where to get food, finding a place in the shelter during the nightly bombings, how to keep your room heated and arrange for a hot bath.

I get the impression that Lída was emotionally dependent on her husband; in her letters, it transpires that she was not a practical person and had a hard time dealing with life's issues, in particular improving her financial situation. On 25 September, she wrote that she was concerned about Vlado's health. He was suffering from chronic sinusitis. Should she sell her gold bracelet?[26] Her life was difficult; she experienced her stay in Great Britain as social decline. She did not want to borrow money and became very

---

[25] Clementis and Clementisová, *Ďaleko od Teba*, 71.
[26] Clementis and Clementisová, *Ďaleko od Teba*, 63.

angry when she saw how certain persons lived a grandiose lifestyle, while he, a former parliamentarian after all, was forced to live in poor conditions.[27] Thank God that the family at home did not know about their living conditions – they would be horrified! Certainly, she was often invited out and had a few good friends, but the feeling of being a poor relative was terrible.[28]

Lída's complex mental state consisted of anxiety, fear, a deep feeling of sadness that bordered on depression and, on top of that, a bad conscience tormenting her: she often thought that her letters would put a psychological burden on her husband. In the evening, she wrote an apology to Vlado for having written such a sad letter that morning; then the next morning, she felt better and was now afraid that her descriptions of her state of mind might cause him sorrow.[29] She was also constantly worried about his health and the reasons why he did not write to her. She often wrote that she did not want to worry him, but then, in the next paragraph, completely irrational, she described the nightly bombings and her cold. She was trying to suffocate her pain and deal with her sleeplessness: she used to play cards all night long with people visiting her. Also, she was smoking heavily. Completely unaware of how this information might affect Vlado, she wrote that she would lay hands on any narcotics she could get – if only the opportunity arose.[30] Their separation was such injustice! At home, with their families, it would be bearable, but here, lost among strangers ... But she kept hoping for the best.[31]

On 2 October, Vlado wrote that he wrote as often as he was allowed to; he had also tried to call her, but the camp did not give

---

[27] Clementis and Clementisová, *Ďaleko od Teba*, 63.
[28] Clementis and Clementisová, *Ďaleko od Teba*, 71.
[29] Clementis and Clementisová, *Ďaleko od Teba*, 61.
[30] Clementis and Clementisová, *Ďaleko od Teba*, 69.
[31] Clementis and Clementisová, *Ďaleko od Teba*, 69.

him permission for private calls.[32] First and foremost now, she should not be anxious if she didn't hear from him – he was safe and healthy. His sinusitis had not broken out, and he had enough warm underwear. He was concerned only about her: she should sell some of her jewellery and buy everything she needed. He would find a solution to their financial situation with the help of some American friends. Also, he would try to arrange for her visit at the camp. In case some of their friends would offer her a loan, she should accept it. He would take care of their finances as soon as possible.[33]

The very same day, Vlado wrote a second letter, providing Lída with information about a Mrs Vavrová who would approach her with the offer of a loan.[34] He had already arranged for a plan to pay Mrs Vavrová back, so Lída should accept the money. As for her visit: Mrs Vavrová and a certain Mrs Schwartzová would also come to visit, it would be better if they all came together. He was sure that the change of environment would improve her health. If the money would not be sufficient, she should sell her gold bangle and use the money for herself. He would not need any money once out of the camp.[35]

Vladimír's love for Lída can be felt in his letters that focus on pragmatic issues; his love for her is visible between the lines. Beneath his rational sentences, one can feel a deep commitment to protect her. I think that Vladimír, brought up by his parents in a loving, traditional and psychologically stable environment, considered it his male honour to be a provider, the classic role of a man taking care of and protecting his wife. Although Lída was emotionally dependent on him, her letters gave him great comfort,

---

[32] Clementis and Clementisová, *Ďaleko od Teba*, 81.
[33] Clementis and Clementisová, *Ďaleko od Teba*, 83.
[34] Clementis and Clementisová, *Ďaleko od Teba*, 85.
[35] Clementis and Clementisová, *Ďaleko od Teba*, 86.

since she was his closest ally and friend, the only person he confided in. Lída comforted Vladimír in his most dire situation, giving him strength when she knew that he was suffering from having lost all influence and political power. Both of them kept themselves alive with their letters; each letter of the loved one provided the other with strength, instilling the hope that they would be soon together again.

II. 2. 2   A Political Decision

Why was Clementis interned in Great Britain? The answer is relatively simple, I think, but it is also rather complex. The reasons for his internment can be found in the context of the political factions of the Czechoslovak exile government, which, prior to its international recognition in the spring of 1942, tried to muster discipline and unity among the Czechoslovaks in British exile.[36]

In the summer of 1940, Clementis got into open conflict with the leadership of the exile *odboj*. Together with five hundred Czechoslovak soldiers, most of them *interbrigadisty* from Spain and interned in the POW camp in Cholmondeley, he demonstrated against the centre-right officers in command of the exile army.[37] Clementis demanded to speak with President Beneš in London, but was denied the trip. According to Prokop Drtina, whom he later confided in, the Communist lawyer had had a political discussion with an officer of the exile army in the POW camp. The officer told him that as a soldier, he had to obey his officers in command. Clementis insisted that he was as much a soldier as he was

---

[36] An excellent summary of Czechoslovak politicians imprisoned in Great Britian is Dušan Šegeš, "Internácia československých politikov vo Veľkej Británii v období druhej svetovej voiny ako prostriedok boja s opozíciou, alebo '... všichni musíme do jednotné fronty a intriky a malicherné pomluvy musí přestat.'" in *Adepti moci a úspechu. Etablovanie elít v moderných dejinách* (Bratislava: Veda, 2016), 231-246.

[37] Holotíková a Plevza, 212.

a delegate of the Czechoslovak parliament that had been democratically elected in 1935. Ever the astute lawyer, Clementis told the officer that President Beneš had in his recent speech at the camp stressed the legal and political continuity of Czechoslovakia.[38]

In protest against the violation of his civil and political rights, the lawyer quit the exile army in protest, and five hundred soldiers quit with him; the British authorities distributed the soldiers to several POW camps, dividing them. On 28 July 1940, Clementis was sent to the camp at Oswestry in Shropshire, and on 22 August, he arrived at the camp in Sutton Coldfield near Birmingham. The British War Office intervened: the Czechoslovak government in exile had no legal basis for the imprisonment of the soldiers. The Czechoslovak government decided to make an offer to the rebellious soldiers: if they joined the British Army, they would be released from the camp. Clementis refused. In the remaining months of 1940, he was interned in a camp in Scotland and then in Knapdale and Glenbranter in Argyll. In the spring of 1941, he finally arrived in London.

Members of the exile government did not trust the Communists, whom they suspected of having distinctly different plans about the re-construction of Czechoslovakia after the war. Although Clementis had criticised the Molotov-Ribbentrop Pact in August 1939 in Paris, albeit only to a close circle of comrades he thought were trustworthy, he still adhered to the post-war Socialist Czechoslovakia – and the centre-right politicians who knew him knew that he was still a believing Communist. His loyalty to the Marxist-Leninist cause, not Stalin's current foreign policy (!), was unfaltering. Yet, the very fact that the KSČ had thrown him out

---

[38] Němeček, "Vladimír Clementis a československý zahraniční odboj", 47-48.

made him more acceptable in the eyes of the exile government; although he was a Slovak, he was certainly no supporter of Tiso.

I think that members of the exile government considered the following: even if Clementis spoke out for a future Slovak autonomy in post-war Czechoslovakia, he was no adherent of an independent Slovakia, that is, a Slovak secession, a post-war Slovak state. One could work with him, for the time being – and a future Slovak autonomy in a Czechoslovak federation could be negotiated *doma*, after the war. For now, the intelligent and cultivated lawyer who spoke all the languages of the Allies was welcome to join the Czechoslovak war effort. He would be useful in mustering Slovak loyalty to the Beneš government and strengthening the resistance against the Germans and the Tiso government at home.

In Clementis' way of thinking, the post-war re-construction of Czechoslovakia would be a Socialist one, implementing the Marxist-Leninist system and, once and for all, do away with the decadent, conservative and nationalist democracy of the pre-war years. He was eager to commit himself to the war effort, to do his duty as a Czechoslovak patriot, but the chaotic situation of the first year of the war allowed him to join the exile government only in the autumn of 1941 – when Prime Minister Churchill declared the Munich Agreement null and void, prompting the alliance with the Czechoslovak exile government and army.

Vladimír mentioned his political decision to protest to Lída in his letter of 4 October. He did not understand why he was interned.[39] Back in Cholmondeley, the Czechoslovak soldiers had been given a choice: those interned who agreed to serve in the British army were released. Why should he join the British army? The Slovak people, the Slovak patriots in the USA, held him in high regard. Therefore, he had more right to speak for the nation than

---

[39] Clementis and Clementisová, *Ďaleko od Teba*, 81.

anybody in the Czechoslovak government in Britain. His political activities at home had always been more than simple Party politics. After all he had gone through, he just couldn't bring himself to join the British army, an activity he was not suited for – that would not only be to shirk responsibility, it would be treason![40] He believed in the reason of the leading British politicians, some of whom he knew personally. They would soon understand that his place was not in a POW camp, but elsewhere.

In his second letter of 4 October, he complained to Lída in a sarcastic tone about the exile government: by now, the unenviable situation he found himself in was clear proof how highly these gentlemen thought of him. One could only thank them for the mess they were in. As he had learnt from the exile journal *Čechoslovák* and some English friends, these gentlemen did not even shy away from the most despicable lies. But, if given the same choice again, he would decide exactly the same way he did in Cholmondeley. If that was the way these gentlemen projected the new Czechoslovakia – thank you very much![41] If the government in exile did not shy away from committing such grave violations of political and civil rights, of imprisoning patriots and elected parliamentarians for the simple reason that they were Communists, then it was not worth fighting this war.

Clementis' contacts with members of the British government finally resulted in his release. Prokop Drtina met him in March 1941 in London and wrote in his report:

> "He thinks that people are looking at him as if he is an exotic species and, sometimes, he even thinks that they want to show him off like a

---

[40] Clementis and Clementisová, *Ďaleko od Teba*, 82.
[41] Clementis and Clementisová, *Ďaleko od Teba*, 90.

dancing bear or involve him in some political shenanigans [*politické kšeftaření*]."⁴²

In response to Drtina's question whether the lawyer was in touch with his comrades from the Party, Clementis replied that one could not possible reason with them; only now, were they beginning to understand that they were at war. What should one think about persons he had seen the last time in Prague, now wanting to discuss with him Stalin's realization of Lenin's politics and Marx, whose works they obviously had not even read?⁴³ According to

---

[42] AÚTGM Praha, f. 40, sign. IV/28/1, kart. 15, Drtinův záznam o rozhovoru s Clementisem 14. 3. 1941, quoted from Němeček, "Vladimír Clementis a československý zahraniční odboj", 48.

[43] AÚTGM Praha, f. 40, sign. IV/28/1, kart. 15, Drtinův záznam o rozhovoru s Clementisem 14. 3. 1941, quoted from Němeček, "Vladimír Clementis a československý zahraniční odboj", 49. The KSČ members in London ignored Clementis; in their post-war memoirs, some of them claimed that they had worked with him, which is not true. Clementis was the only Slovak member of the Legal Council (*Právní rada*) the exile government founded on 30 January 1942; the council was a kind of high court in exile and consisted of five members. The centre-right politicians and President Beneš held him in high esteem. Gottwald, on the other hand, had instructed the Party to ignore Clementis, portraying him as a turncoat who had changed sides to Beneš and was thus no longer a representative of the Slovak Communists. When Beneš was in Moscow in December 1943 to attend the negotiations that would lead to the Soviet-Czechoslovak Treaty of Alliance, he said to Gottwald that Clementis "is very dear to me, he is an educated young person, the best of all the Slovaks in exile". Gottwald replied dryly that Clementis was no longer a member of the KSČ; Němeček, "Vladimír Clementis a československý zahraniční odboj", 50. About the Soviet-Czechoslovak Treaty of Alliance see http://www.jstor.org/stable/2213972?seq=1#page_scan_tab_contents; accessed 21 May 2016. Ladislav Holdoš (1911–1988), a veteran from Spain and survivor of the Buchenwald concentration camp, was accused of 'Slovak bourgeois nationalism' together with Husák and Novomeský in 1954. He remembered his meeting with Clementis in France in the spring of 1940: "I tried to avoid him, but I had to meet him at least once. I was reluctant to shake hands, because Široký had instructed me to ignore him, he was a traitor. [...] We met again after the war. [...] He told me about a meeting with Stalin and Molotov. Stalin asked 'Tovarišč Clementis, in France you were in prison, da? And, comrade

Drtina's report, Clementis strongly criticised the comrades for their cowardice and lack of loyalty: they knew about his expulsion from the KSČ, but did not dare to stay in touch with him, cautiously waiting to see how his status in the Party would develop. Drtina further wrote that he had the impression that the lawyer was sliding into a depression, which was no surprise: he was ousted by the Party and ignored by his former comrades, while trying to come to terms ideologically with the German-Soviet Nonaggression Pact and fighting the oppression of the British workers by their own government.

In the autumn of 1941, Clementis was in his element again. His spirits were restored: he joined the war effort in London, heading the Slovak section at the BBC. Until May 1945, he would broadcast for the exile government and the Allied cause, publish articles in exile journals and explain to his British and Czechoslovak audience the politics of the Slovak state and the history of the Slovaks.

II. 3   The BBC Broadcasts (1941–1945)

During his years in London, Clementis regularly broadcasted for the BBC's Czechoslovak service. [44] The range of themes he ad-

---

Clementis, you were also in prison in England?' Clementis answered truthfully. Molotov made a brutal joke: 'As allies of France and Britain, should we not imprison you too?' [...] Today, I consider Clementis the most capable person of the Slovak Communist movement. He had a talent for conceptual thinking, he was independent, no sectarian and he was thoughtful.'" Ladislav Holdoš and Karel Bartošek, *Svědek Husákova procesu vypovídá* (Praha: Naše vojsko, 1991), 114-115.

[44] For a brief summary of the Czechoslovak radio broadcasts during the war see http://www.radio.cz/en/section/one-on-one/london-calling-researcher-erica-harrison-on-fascinating-history-of-czechoslovak-exile-governments-wartime-bbc-broadcasts; accessed 3 May 2016.

dressed in his radio broadcasts was as wide as his former journalism for DAV: news from the Allies; Slovak literature and culture; the relations between Czechs and Slovaks; Slovak Catholicism and the propaganda of the Tiso government.

He contributed to the Czechoslovak war effort with his brilliant and passionate rhetoric, informing his listeners at home about the latest news from the Allies, explaining how the Tiso government was brainwashing the citizens with its clerical-fascist propaganda, and what unspeakable crimes Nazi Germany was committing against the Slavs and Jews in Eastern Europe.

With his sharp mind, he analysed the politics of the axis and the Western Allies. Avoiding Marxist-Leninist newspeak, he concentrated on instilling as much hope and resilience as possible into the minds of his listeners; his broadcasts never sounded sad, but always truthful, precise and optimistic, even in the months when Hitler was unstoppable and the Tiso regime at the peak of its power, in the months before the German defeat at Stalingrad in February 1943. Clementis always ended his broadcasts with an optimistic call for hope, anticipating the end of the war and stressing that the day of reckoning was close. Justice would be done soon.

In psychological terms, his contribution to the war effort was of immense importance: the Slovaks at home, whether they supported the Tiso regime or not or were politically indifferent and just trying to survive, knew that the exile government had not forgotten them, that their democratically legitimate government was fighting the Nazis together with the Allies. Clementis' broadcasts in Slovak were thus not only a beacon of hope, but also an independent source of information fighting Goebbels, Tiso and Mach's propaganda.

Compared with his speeches in parliament and articles for DAV, Clementis' language was different now: he used more colloquialisms, and his sentences were shorter, less academic but no less eloquent. His tone was as ever distinct and clear; there was no room for doubt, and he wanted to make sure that everybody, the silenced and the collaborating intellectuals, the uneducated workers and farmers, but also the Tiso government understood the politics of the exile government. At war, the exile government could not afford to broadcast lengthy and stylistically elaborate speeches the people did not understand – it was all or nothing, black or white, no grey zone, no compromise. One had to be perfectly clear and one had to take sides, with the Germans or against them.

Clementis' tone and wording were often rather rude when addressing the Tiso government or the Germans, but full of his characteristic logic; his statements were sharp and full of biting sarcasm, his information precise. He spoke to the people in their language – not as a lawyer, but as one of them. To him, the war was also a war of words, a war of political thought – one had to muster loyalty to the cause of the Allies with every word, every sentence. He often wove German concepts such as *Hakenkreuzler*, *Herrenvolk* and *Übermensch* into his broadcasts, and the sarcastic usage of these concepts gave his listeners a clear view of what the Germans with their *Schutzvertrag*[45] were really up to with the Slovaks, who were not yet officially declared Slavic *Untermenschen*:

> "From the outset, Hitler's particular hatred, and that of the Nazi leadership, was reserved for the so-called Slavic peoples, who were considered inferior and intended for the future slave class of Europe. [...] Where members of neutral or allied nations in (southern) Europe were concerned, of course, it was not possible to speak of inferiority; there-

---

[45] About the German-Slovak *Schutzvertrag* and the Slovak workers in Germany during the war see chapter II. 3. 5.

fore, these peoples were either classified as 'Southern Slavs', as 'Dinarians' and thus as racially related; or else *they were simply not counted among the Slavs at all.* [...] Members of enemy states, by contrast, were turned into 'racial foes' as a means of justifying their classification under special law. [...] Bolshevism and Jewry were flatly equated with one another, referred to as the 'Jewish-Bolshevist threat', and made out to be the very quintessence of all types of inferiority."[46]

The radicals in the HSĽS's leadership had no clue of Germany's true intentions and slavishly adopted Nazi thought and jargon.

I can vividly imagine how the gifted lawyer sat for hours at his typewriter in his London flat, smoking his pipe, Lída quietly reading a book, sitting on a sofa, at his side. I can see Clementis drafting his broadcasts, working over his texts time and again, chosing words that would prompt the greatest possible effect at home. Because every broadcast had to be perfect and convincing in this war of words that was a war of *Weltanschauungen*, of political systems, and lastly, a war of good versus evil, of Western liberalism against Nazi Germany's barbaric racism and militarism.

A particularly remarkable aspect of Clementis' rhetoric was the way he addressed the members of the Tiso government: he called them "the masters in Bratislava [*bratislavské páni*]", making sure that first, the Slovak citizens could tell the Nazis and the Slovak government apart and understand that Tiso and his government were responsible for the misery of the people – not

---

[46] Diemut Majer, *"Non-Germans" under the Third Reich. The Nazi Judicial and Administrative System in Germany and Occupied Eastern Europe, with special regard to Occupied Poland, 1939–1945* (Baltimore, London: Johns Hopkins University Press, 2003), 62, 63, italics by JB. Hitler had expressed his hatred of the Slavic people as early as the spring of 1934 in his conversation with the Prussian diplomat Hermann Rauschning (1887–1982), contending a future policy of depopulation: "What, you may ask, does depopulation mean? Do I propose to eliminate whole population groups? Yes, indeed something like that will have to be done;" Rauschning, Gespräche mit Hitler, 128 f., quoted from Majer, 624.

only the Germans. Second, the Slovak concept *pán* reminded people, particularly the older generation, of the harsh times of Hungarian aristocratic rule in the 19th and early 20th century and the brutal Magyar assimilation. Third, in the eastern part of Slovakia, many citizens, mostly farmers and workers, felt that Bratislava had been the executor of Prague's centralism, implementing policies that had let them down, that had not really improved their lives.

I think that Clementis cleverly played on the traditional Slovak opposition of town against country, signalling to the people in the countryside, his workers and farmers, that the evil Tiso regime was located in Bratislava, the city with a Hungarian and German population that had always looked down on and neglected the poor Slovak masses in the east. Here, one can see an aspect of Clementis' pre-war effort for the workers: I deem it possible that he projected an uprising against the Tiso regime, but such a revolt would not be planned or realized by Bratislava's intellectuals or civil servants, who were only benefitting from the new wealth and influence collaboration with the Tiso regime had brought them. If there ever was to be an uprising in Slovakia, the workers in the poor rural eastern parts would launch it. By hammering into his listeners' minds time and again that the masters in Bratislava were devout followers of Hitler, Clementis spoke to the Slovaks in the countryside who knew him well from the trial of Košuty.

His broadcasts followed a simple but effective and clever rationale: he was fighting the totalitarian brainwashing the Tiso government was conducting at home and, by reiterating that the Slovaks and Czechs were brotherly nations, he reminded his fellow countrymen of the liberty and democracy of the First Republic. He was trying to unite the Slovaks with the Czechs, while assuring the Slovaks that once the war would be over, they would negotiate with the Czechs their political status in post-war Czechoslovakia. The Slovaks would have a fair future, if they joined in now in the fight against Tiso and the Germans.

Furthermore, Clementis carefully and deliberately avoided mentioning President Masaryk, Jan Masaryk or Beneš – not only because Beneš and Jan Masaryk were making their own broadcasts on the BBC. I think that Clementis was aware that anti-Czech resentment was still strong in Slovakia. A further reason was his belief that after the war, the Slovaks would have equal status with the Czechs in a federation. To quote too often Czech politicians would give his listeners the impression that he was not speaking to them as an independent Slovak, but as a mere servant of the Czech-dominated exile government, promoting Beneš's centralist post-war plans. In terms of the war effort – and I deem it probable that the exile government and Clementis had drafted this strategy together – the slightest suspicion that Clementis would not stand for equal Slovak representation in the common state after the war had to be avoided. If the Slovaks at home gained the impression that nothing would change after the war, that Czech centralism would be renewed, their willingness to join the resistance would significantly lessen. From a Slovak viewpoint, fighting the Tiso regime and the Germans for the mere re-establishment of Prague's say in Slovak matters, for the *status quo ante* Munich, was not exactly an incentive to risk one's life and the lives of one's family.

From 4 November 1941 to 27 March 1945, Clementis broadcasted eighty-seven speeches and published forty-three articles.[47] I have selected nine radio broadcasts and one lecture he held in a series dedicated to Slovakia; they reflect not only the brutal life in the protectorate and the Slovak state, but also emphasize

---

[47] Dr Vladimír Clementis, *Odkazy z Londýna*, 519-521.

those events in the war that immediately affected the Slovaks and Czechs. His speeches and lecture demonstrate his brilliant rhetoric and profound analysis of history and current politics.

The war required black and white thinking – and now he was on the right side, on the side of good versus evil. His quick grasp of the situation, effective rhetoric and a particular diplomatic ability to convince adversaries to change sides and join the resistance, would earn him the position of deputy foreign minister under Jan Masaryk after the war.

II. 3. 1 Slovakia's Declaration of War on America (1941)

On 15 December 1941, eight days after the Japanese attack on Pearl Harbour, Clementis broadcast his speech "Slovakia has declared war on America".[48] The Führer revealed to the world that the diabolical Roosevelt had started this war – the Jews, the Jew-Bolsheviks and the plutocrats had moved down to the second level of Hitler's enemies, as Clementis sarcastically put it. The speeches of the masters in Bratislava were so full of claptrap that only one person could have written them: Šaňo Mach, the leader of the HG. Although the masters in Bratislava were falling over themselves to please Berlin, at least some of them were now aware that, in spite of all their evil and primitive deeds, they had to expect a serious reaction:

> "There is no country in the world that has so many family connections with Slovakia than America. There is not one Slovak village that doesn't have his 'American' living beyond the ocean. A third of the Slovak nation is living and working in America and they are now preparing to fight – for the freedom of their country and the support of their nation. All this is well known to our people at home; they know America's unrelenting military might. […] Only persons completely bereft of common sense [zbavení zdravého rozumu] can attempt to con the Slovaks the way the Hlinka Guards did. Whom in his right mind shall that gang of Bratislava

---

48 Clementis, "Slovensko vypovedalo vojnu Amerike", in *Odkazy z Londýna*, 12-14.

boneheads [*čvarga bratislavských šialencov*] convince that the Japanese who remember more than one bloody lesson taught to them by the Red Army in the Far East are now rushing to the defence of the Christian and Arian culture against America?!"[49]

The grandiose attitude of the masters in Bratislava prompted only a pitying smile in the wider world. The members of the exile government would have laughed heartily too, had they not been acutely and painfully aware that each of the regime's traitorous acts caused the people at home new suffering, greater poverty and more tears.

But it was not enough for the traitors in Bratislava and their Berlin masters to have subjected thousands of Slovak boys to the Horthy regime prior to the dissolution of Czechoslovakia.[50] Thousands of Slovak boys were dying in the fighting against the Soviet Union, a brotherly Slavic nation, while the Bratislava war profiteers were staying safely behind their walls. But the heroic Red Army was advancing on the eastern front, and once it had launched its attack, Hitler's army would collapse like sheaves of corn. Then, Mr Čatlos would no longer be able to publish communiqués about the Slovak platoons on the Russian front.[51] If the Slovaks at home still believed the lies of the Bratislava masters, there might soon be no Slovak platoon left. The Slovak mothers and orphans would be standing in vain in front of the notary's office in their village; nobody would tell them where their loved ones were buried.

---

[49] Clementis, "Slovensko vypovedalo vojnu Amerike", 13.
[50] Clementis referred to the Vienna Arbitrage of 2 November 1938, a consequence of the Munich Agreement: autonomous Slovakia lost strategically important southern parts on the Danube to Hungary, including the towns of Komarno, Nové Zámky and Košice.
[51] Clementis, "Slovensko vypovedalo vojnu Amerike", 14. Ferdinand Čatlos (1895–1972) was a professional soldier and had studied at the Czechoslovak military academy in Prague. He was Minister of Defence before he was appointed supreme commander of the Slovak army.

> "And just now, Mr Tiso declares war on America, thus war on a third of the Slovak nation that has found a new home in the USA. Yet, every evil has also its good side. Up to now, a handful of American Slovaks – save for the few paid agents – had not seen the crimes of the masters in Bratislava, not because of ill will but because of a lack of information. Now, they have opened their eyes. [...] And the American Slovaks shall deal with the agents of Tiso, Tuka, Mach and their cronies in their own way. And that is good! Because, after that blood bath, all liberated nations, purified from the plague that has drowned the world in violence and murder, shall march towards a new life. And the Slovak people will make sure that this purge will be a thorough one, down to the last man!"[52]

America's entry into WWII was the future: not even the Germans could win a war on two fronts. Clementis was not only an immensely talented orator, but he had a crucial psychological capability: empathy. Though he might seem secluded and unapproachable to persons who did not know him well, he was passionate and emphatic in his broadcasts – he knew what to say to his fellow Slovaks at home to raise their hopes and muster resistance. He described their situation in the Slovak villages, proving that he was one of them. Clementis was a theoretician, but also a political pragmatist: he knew how to compose effective political speeches. He must have seen with his inner eye the families in the countryside, how desperate the mothers, wives and children of the Slovak soldiers sacrificed on the eastern front were for news about their fathers, brothers and sons. He also must have thought a lot about his family in Tisovec – how were they surviving under the Tiso regime with him broadcasting with the exile government, being a traitor?

I think that Clementis pursued a consistent plan: first, to create intellectual resistance against the Tiso government at home and then, later, when the international situation would be ripe,

---

[52] Clementis, "Slovensko vypovedalo vojnu Amerike", 14.

call for military resistance. Yet, in 1941, before Stalingrad, Germany controlled Europe with the help of its allies. On 4 June 1942, the Czechoslovak officers Jan Kubiš (1913–1942) and Jozef Gabčik (1912–1942) executed *Reichsprotektor* Reinhard Heydrich in Prague. Operation Anthropoid demonstrated to the Czechs and Slovaks at home that the exile government in London was capable of planning and conducting an operation that was a symbol of the Czechoslovak spirit of resistance and democracy alike.[53] Much like Masaryk's *legia* in WWI, Operation Anthropoid convinced the Allies in WWII, that the Czechs and Slovaks were fighting on their side. The code name of the operation was rather telling: an anthropoid is not human. It just looks like a human, is something else in human guise. To the Czechoslovaks, at home and in London, Heydrich was an anthropoid; he had no heart or soul. To assassinate him would show the world that the Allies were fighting for humanity and human rights.

II. 3. 2 At the Grave of Vančura (1942)

Clementis broadcasted "At the Grave of Vančura" on 8 June 1942.[54] Shortly before Heydrich's assassination on 4 June, the Germans had arrested the famous Czech writer Vladislav Vančura (1891–1942); after the Gestapo had interrogated and tortured him, they

---

[53] On the attempt on Heydrich's life code-named *Operation Anthropoid* see http://www.holocaustresearchproject.org/nazioccupation/heydrichkilling.html; accessed 4 May 2016. See also http://www.bbc.com/news/world-europe-18183099; accessed 5 May 2016. The director Lewis Gilbert made a movie about the assassination of Heydrich: *Operation Daybreak* (1975) on http://www.imdb.com/title/tt0075019/?ref_=nm_flmg_dr_10; accessed 5 May 2016. A new movie called *Anthropoid* was released in September 2016: http://www.imdb.com/title/tt4190530/; accessed 28 November 2016.

[54] Clementis, "Nad rovom Vančuru", in *Odkazy z Londýna*, 25-27. On Vančura's significance for Czech literature see http://www.radio.cz/en/section/czechs/vladislav-vancura; accessed 4 May 2016.

shot him on 1 June for his resistance activities. Clementis honoured the famous writer, comparing his heroic death to the activities of Slovak writers who had achieved wealth and influence with their support of the Tiso regime.

The Germans were murdering loyal Czechs in cold blood and bestial cruelty, Clementis said on air.[55] The world would not be surprised if these *Übermenschen* in their distorted logic would take revenge on Czech soil for the killing of that mad dog Heydrich.[56] But during these tragic and heroic days for their Czech brothers, the Slovak press, controlled by Tido Gašpar, rushed to defend a position that was arousing the contempt and shame of the majority of the Slovak people:[57]

> "At the fresh graves of the Czech heroes, the *Gardista*, edited by Milo Urban, is boasting that they are neither fantasizing nor loosing themselves in illusions, but that they are in tune with reality. [...] That is the cowardly philosophy of slavery the masters in Bratislava would like to inject the entire Slovak people with."[58]

Who was fantasizing, so Clementis sarcastically asked: those who saw the near and final end of the rule of Nazism or those who saw Britain completely destroyed in the autumn of 1940, the Red Army completely destroyed in the autumn of 1941 or those who had not seen that America's entry to the war was a distinct possibility? And who was in tune with reality? Those who were leaping

---

[55] On 10 June the protectorate's authorities broadcasted that the Germans had destroyed the village of Lidice as an act of revenge for Heydrich's assassination. Lidice and Ležaky on http://www.lidice-memorial.cz/en/; accessed 4 May 2016.

[56] Clementis, "Nad rovom Vančuru", 25-26.

[57] Clementis, "Nad rovom Vančuru", 26. Tido Gašpar (1893–1972) was a Slovak journalist and writer and a prominent intellectual of the Slovak state.

[58] Clementis, "Nad rovom Vančuru", 26. *Gardista* was the newspaper of the HG. Milo Urban (1904–1982) was a Slovak writer and journalist and from 1940 on editor-in-chief.

on the creaking cart of Nazism, declaring the Reich's rule over Europe as a given reality, or those who were anticipating the rebellion of the enslaved countries that would end the rule of the Reich's agitators with terrible vengeance? Compared with the brutal activities of Hitler's executors, the shooting of Heydrich had been an act of sheer mercy![59]

Now, the reality was this: in spite of their different motives, Hácha and Tiso, Mach and Moravec would fall, together with all their cronies.[60] With whom would the Slovaks side in the near future to demonstrate that the current Slovak press was not speaking for them? That the activities of the Slovaks were not the same as those of Tiso, Tuka, Mach and the rest of the Bratislava masters? He, Clementis warned, was not speaking about the Slovak workers or farmers who were facing a real and uncompromising battle. But some Slovak intellectuals and writers would stand in court in the near future.

They – Clementis used the plural to put the focus on the exile government in London – had only recently read Milo Urban's editorial in the *Gardista*. Urban had warned of joining in the traitorous Soviet aggression against Poland; he denounced those who, in the name of Slavic brotherhood, refused to fight the Russians and ridiculed those who in the name of humanity and Christianity protected Jews from the regime's beasts:[61]

> "And the once-promising writer is now cravenly and devoutly praising these crimes only to please the Nazi thugs. He is praising them at a time when the Czech writer Vladislav Vančura, who is particularly close and

---

[59] Clementis, "Nad rovom Vančuru", 26.
[60] Emil Hácha (1872–1945) was Czech president from October 1938 until 9 May 1945. See http://ww2db.com/person_bio.php?person_id=217; accessed 5 May 2016. An interesting biography is Tomáš Pasák, *Emil Hácha (1938–1945)* (Praha: Rybka Publishers, 2007 (2)).
[61] Clementis, "Nad rovom Vančuru", 27.

dear to us Slovaks, has been murdered by the bullets of the Nazi criminals. […] Together with so many known and unsung heroes, Vladislav Vančura has entered Czech history as a hero of our tragic times. He has fallen for the freedom of the Czechoslovak people."[62]

One would hope, Clementis concluded, that neither Tido Gašpar nor Milo Urban would enter Slovak history as symbols of their times.

II. 3. 3   Hitler, Hlinka – One Line! (1942)

In 1942, the exile government arranged for a lecture series that informed the Czechoslovaks in London about Slovakia. To strengthen the ties between the two nations was part of the Czechoslovak war effort: the Czechs should learn more about the complicated history of Slovakia. In his lecture "Hitler, Hlinka – One Line!"[63] Clementis explained to his listeners the intellectual foundation of the Tiso regime and Hlinka's influence on Slovak politics.

He presented two quotes to begin his lecture. Tuka had said in 1940 in a speech in Nitra that Hlinka was spiritually akin to Hitler: "Hitler, Hlinka – jedna linka!" Mach had repeated the slogan the next day.[64] Clementis was in his element, delivering a precise analysis of HSĽS thought and activities:

> "Nazi thought – I would not call it an ideology, but a technique of ruling – is being realized in an even better form in current Slovak political life. The Slovak super-Nazi government is a system of one-party rule, organized in accordance with the 'Führer principle' [*vodcovského princípu*] and pushed forward by the 'revolutionary' activities of the HG 'stormtroops' [*údernými oddielmi*]. The regime is mirroring German Nazi rule also in the relationship of the HSĽS to the state apparatus, the HG's to the army, the executive's increasing dominance over the legislature, the abolition of democratic liberties and so forth. Nazi principles are also enshrined in social life: in the abolition of professional organizations

---

[62] Clementis, "Nad rovom Vančuru", 27.
[63] Clementis, "Hitler, Hlinka – jedna linka!", in *Odkazy z Londýna*, 222-225.
[64] Clementis, "Hitler, Hlinka – jedna linka!", 222.

and the Aryanization of business and people. However, German pressure can only partly explain why the Nazi 'spirit' was able to enter Slovakia's political and social life – the principal instigator has been that Führerlein Karmasin, the leader of the so-called 'Carpathian Germans' [*führeríka 'karpatských Nemcov'*] who, together with the ruling camarilla and instructed by the Nazis, has changed Slovak political life only to strengthen his position of power."[65]

But the soil for the implementation of Nazi rule in Slovakia had already been fertile; it had been prepared by the slogans and the propaganda of the People's Party, its radical follower HSĽS and, later, by Mach and Murgaš's storm-troopers.[66] Long before Munich, the People's Party had been cultivating the Führer principle with a totalitarian focus on Hlinka, praising his exceptional role in Slovak politics. The vulgar understanding and interpretation of Catholic universalism that included the teachings and ethics of Nazism had only strengthened these tendencies. In Tiso and Tuka's intellectually primitive and totalitarian world, Nazi thought was an integral part of Catholic universalism: one Shepherd – one Flock; one Führer – one Reich.[67]

---

[65] Clementis, "Hitler, Hlinka – jedna linka!", 222. Franz Karmasin (1901–1970) and János Esterházy (1901–1957), the leaders of the Carpathian German and the Hungarian parties in Slovakia, were, like Henlein in the Czech lands, Hitler's allies in breaking up the Republic.

[66] Clementis, "Hitler, Hlinka – jedna linka!", 222-223. Karol Murgaš (1899–1972) was a HG leader and main instigator of the pogrom in Piešťany in February 1939, when autonomous Slovakia was still a part of Czechoslovakia. His associates referred to him as "Charles the Terrible [*Karol Hrozný*]", which reminds everybody familiar with the Slavic World of the Russian Tsar Ivan the Terrible (1530–1584). For an account of Murgaš's adventurous political career characterized by a steady abuse of alcohol see Miroslav Michela, "Výčiny Karola Hrozného. Ukončil alkohol politickú kariéru?", in *Storočie skandálov. Aféry v moderných dejinách Slovenska* (Bratislava: Pro Historia, 2008), 171-178. About the pogrom in Piešťany see my *A life dedicated* ..., 202-210.

[67] Clementis, "Hitler, Hlinka – jedna linka!", 223.

The press of the People's Party had successfully copied its slogans from international reactionary forces; some issues of the newspapers *Slovák* and *Slovak Truth* looked much more like the organs of Dollfuss or Franco than those of Hlinka, the priest from Ružomberok.[68] The People's Party had laid bare its politics not only through its press: at the HSĽS meeting in Piešťany on 19 and 20 September 1936, the leadership had declared its membership of the "international front of nations against Jewish Bolshevism".[69]

Clementis was fair and decent enough to say that Hlinka had not read the text of the resolution composed by Durčanský and Mach.[70] He did not blame Hlinka for the deeds of his followers, which would have prompted a counterproductive response, since many Slovak Catholics considered Hlinka their liberator. Hlinka's followers had put the abominable theory of totalitarianism immediately into practice: the HSĽS radicals had incited the antisemitic demonstration of Bratislava students against the film *Golem*, and Tiso's government was responsible for the Nazi amendments to

---

[68] Engelbert Dollfuss (1892–1934) was an Austrian politician and chancellor from 1932 until 1934. Nazi agents assassinated him to clear the way for the *Anschluss* in 1938.

[69] *Chronológia Dejín Slovenska a Slovákov II*, 642. The leadership had adopted a resolution, which declared the principle "one nation, one party, one leader [*jeden národ, jedna strana, jeden vodca*]" as one of HSĽS' main goals.

[70] Clementis, "Hitler, Hlinka – jedna linka!", 223. Ferdinand Ďurčanský (1906–1974) was a radical member of the HSĽS. On 11 March 1939, Prague appointed Karol Sidor Slovak Prime Minister. Sidor refused to declare Slovakia's independence, resisting the pressure from the German delegates Arthur Seyss-Inquart (1892–1946) and Wilhelm Keppler (1882–1960). The Germans then concentrated their efforts on Tiso, who had moved to his parish in Bánovce nad Bebravou. On 13 March, Tiso met the party leaders in Bratislava to discuss the situation and left for Vienna, accompanied by Karmasin. From there, he and Ďurčanský flew to Berlin to meet Hitler and Ribbentrop. Tiso had no choice: "He was told the historic hour of the Slovaks had arrived. If they did nothing, they would be swallowed up by Hungary. Tiso got the message. By the following noon, 14 March, back in Bratislava, he had the Slovak Assembly proclaim independence." Kershaw, *Hitler*, 476.

the Slovak constitution. As soon as the Žilina Agreement of 1938 was put into effect, Tiso had ordered the abolition of the Communist Party, the Social Democratic Party, the Socialist organizations and associations and the *Gleichschaltung* of the press. Tuka too made his contribution; he had been a principal figure in forging the Fascist orientation of the People's Party; his activities reached back to the 1920s:

> "It was Tuka who had organized the *Rodobrana* association, introducing the Fascist storm-troops to Slovakia; in the First Republic's political conditions, he had masked the association with religious mystique. It was Tuka who had personal and political ties with Fascist and Hitlerist organizations, joining the HSĽS to the international forces of reaction."[71]

Hlinka, in his political naïvete and complete ignorance of international politics, had not been aware of how his politics and alliance with reactionary forces would end – neither had many *Ľudáci*. The slogan Tuka and Mach were promoting today, that is, Hitler, Hlinka – jedna linka!, was created in 1936; the HSĽS had joined Hitler's camp against Hlinka's political legacy.[72] Certainly, as Clementis stressed, without Munich and the international consequences it prompted, Fascism in the People's Party would have, after some lingering, died out:

> "But the topic of our considerations is neither that völkisch nor any other past of the People's Party – we have mentioned it only for the pur-

---

[71] Clementis, "Hitler, Hlinka – jedna linka!", 224.
[72] According to Eduard Chmelár, Clementis had invented the slogan "Hitler, Hlinka – jedna linka!" to make fun of Hlinka and his party. Allegedly, Hlinka had said at the party meeting in Piešťany that he was the Slovak Hitler; he would bring order to Slovakia like Hitler had in Germany. The Communist newspaper *Slovenské zvesti* published the slogan. There is no document available that confirms Clementis as the author of the slogan, but it was a political paradox that Tuka and Mach quoted the slogan; see Chmelar's statement on http://www.pluska.sk/plus7dni/rozhovor/otec-naroda.html; accessed 8 May 2016.

pose of thoroughness and proper analysis of the People's Party's connection with Hitlerism and Fascism. Our topic has been the dominance of the Nazi mindset in Hlinka's Slovak People's Party, or, in clearer words: the political, social and cultural programme of Tiso, Tuka and Mach's regime."[73]

As precisely as Clementis had described the regime's essential intellectual orientation, he would just as thoroughly address an issue particularly painful for every Czechoslovak who was loyal to Masaryk's idea of the Republic.

II. 3. 4 The Expulsion of the Czechs from the Slovak State (1943)

A consequence of the establishment of the Slovak state in 1939 was the expulsion of the Czechs from Slovakia. Lída's family, Czechs, had moved to Slovakia in the spirit of Masaryk's Czechoslovakia. After 1918, thousands of Czech teachers, engineers, civil servants, physicians, railway workers, academics and advocates had, in the spirit of Masaryk's Czechoslovakism, moved to Slovakia. They made a vital contribution to the building and running of administrative institutions, schools, hospitals, railways and courts. These Czech families had made Slovakia their home; two generations had lived in Slovakia when the Tiso government forced them to leave.

After the declaration of the Slovak state, national committees (*národné výbory*) had emerged all over the country; the long arms of the HSĽS had agitated in communities and towns, putting pressure on the local authorities. Some communities had started to expel Czech and Jewish citizens as early as in 1938, when autonomous Slovakia was still a part of Czechoslovakia.[74] The HG executed the commands of the national committees; its activities

---

[73] Clementis, "Hitler, Hlinka – jedna linka!", 225.
[74] Rychlík, *Češi a Slováci I*, 147.

had involved lies, defamation and also violence, stirring up anti-Czech and antisemitic feelings among the population. The HSĽS had justified the abolition of civil and political rights, freedom of the press and freedom of assembly with the need to preserve the unity of the nation. The Hlinka Guards in particular had become the "symbol of anti-Czech attitude",[75] but the Ľudáci were not alone in supporting the expulsion of the Czechs: sympathizers of the Slovak National Party, the Agrarians and those citizens who had had vested interests in replacing the Czechs in the administration had welcomed the expulsion. Because of the demagogic activities of the HG, it was also widely believed that the country's bad economic situation and the unemployment rate would improve once the Czechs had left.

At first, the Slovak government had been reluctant to implement the drastic measures the HG demanded, since it had needed Czech capital and the income from Czech tourists.[76] On 18 March 1939, the Tiso government had decided to expel all Czechs, since a former agreement with Prague about a gradual relocation of Czechs had become obsolete with the German occupation of Bohemia and Moravia. In the aftermath of Munich, an estimated 62,000 to 63,000 Czechs were expelled. At the end of the war, only 542 Czechs lived in Slovakia.[77]

Clementis addressed this particularly painful theme in his broadcast "The expulsion of the Czechs from Slovakia" on 20

---

[75] Čarnogurský, P. 14. Marec 1939. Bratislava, Veda 1992, s. 57. Čarnogurský, P. 6 október 1938. Bratislava, Veda 1993, s. 15, 34, quoted from Valerián Bystrický, "Vysťahovanie českých štátnych zamestnancov zo Slovenska v rokoch 1938–1939", in Od autonómie k vzniku Slovenského štátu (Bratislava: Prodama, 2008), 184-197, 190.
[76] Bystrický, "Vysťahovanie českých …", 191. Bystrický's figures include the entire families of the Czechs expelled from the Slovak state.
[77] Bystrický, "Vysťahovanie českých…", 197.

March 1943.[78] Tiso and Tuka had planned the expulsion, and Mach had carried it out – only the rotten brains of the Bratislava masters, infected with the German Nazi plague, could contrive such a heinous crime. Not only were they not content with their latest plan, the destruction of the livelihood of thousands of Czech brothers, they were not even afraid of robbing the Czech experts of the work they had done for Slovakia. The masters in Bratislava had also denounced Czechs to the Germans with allegations that they were dangerous agitators intent on disrupting the order of Tiso's state.[79] But Tiso was only a servant of Hitler, and he who was against the servant, was also against the master. That was the real reason of Mach's campaign against the Czechs in Slovakia:

> "Don't ask what they want to achieve with these actions. Don't expect from these lunatics any reasonable thinking, but only new crimes dictated by fear – and by the Germans. Note that this campaign began at the same time Hitler's work mobilization started, at the same time the massive aerial bombardment of Germany began. The expulsion of the Czechs from Slovakia means that much construction work is stopped, and so the Slovak workers are unemployed; together with the Czechs, they will be sent to the Reich to work in dangerous conditions there."[80]

Tiso, Tuka and Mach knew very well that they would gain nothing from the expulsion of the Czechs – on the contrary: the Slovak people's disgust was only growing. In their lack of any moral values and humanity, Tiso, Tuka and Mach were attacking the Czech brothers, without whom the Slovaks could have never freed themselves from the Magyar yoke back in 1918. This was a fact the masters in Bratislava could not efface from history – and the very reason for the expulsion of the Czechs:

---

[78] Clementis, "Vysťahovanie Čechov zo Slovenska", in *Odkazy z Londýna*, 40-42.
[79] Clementis, "Vysťahovanie Čechov zo Slovenska", 40-41.
[80] Clementis, "Vysťahovanie Čechov zo Slovenska", 41.

> "They are trying to burn the bridge on which the Slovaks can march towards a better future: the bridge formed by the unity of Czechs and Slovaks, who, together with the Allies and the victorious nations of the world, shall step over the abyss the traitorous masters in Bratislava are trying to create."[81]

The Slovaks, Clementis concluded, would keep this bridge safe and find a way of opposing the evil plans of the Tiso government. The Slovak workers in the Reich were a theme particularly important to him.

II. 3. 5 The Slovak Workers in Germany (1943–1944)

According to the German-Slovak *Schutzvertrag* (German-Slovak Treaty of Protection), Slovak workers enjoyed the status of a voluntary work force of an allied state, supporting the Reich's industry and agriculture.[82] Germany needed labour force to fill in the positions left by the soldiers fighting in the war. Unlike the *Zwangsarbeiter* (forced labourers) whom the Germans were abducting from the occupied countries, such as the protectorate of Bohemia and Moravia, Poland and the occupied parts of the Soviet Union,

---

[81] Clementis, "Vysťahovanie Čechov zo Slovenska", 42.
[82] Michal Schwarc et al., *Podoby nemecko-slovenského „ochranného priateľstva". Dokumenty k náboru a nasadeniu slovenských pracovných síl do Nemeckej ríše v rokoch 1939–1945* (Bratislava: HÚ SAV, Fakulta humanitných vied UMB, 2012), 15. The German authorities divided the foreign workers into four categories: first, voluntary foreign workers who could leave Germany any time during the war and contact the diplomatic representation of their country in Berlin. These workers were from the Nazi satellite states Bulgaria, Croatia, Hungary and Slovakia. Second, forced labourers with a part-time influence on their living conditions; these were mainly civil servants of the occupied countries, for example, Belgium and France. Third, forced labourers with minimal influence on their living conditions, such as civil servants from Poland, the Soviet Union and Polish and Italian prisoners of war. Fourth, forced labourers with no influence whatsoever on their living conditions, such as Polish and Soviet prisoners of war, Jews and everybody deported to labour and concentration camps; SPOERER, M. Nucené práce ..., s. 17, quoted from Schwarc et al., 15.

the workers of Bulgaria, Croatia, Hungary and Slovakia, the Reich's allies, received a monthly salary, holidays and, in view of the war shortages, relatively good housing and food.

The history of the Slovak workers in Germany can be divided into two phases: from 1939 to 1943, and from 1943 to 1945. In 1939, approximately 70,000 Slovak workers left for Germany; the high unemployment rate and the low salaries at home were the main reasons why work in the Reich was attractive for them.[83] From 1943 until 1945, the Slovak workers' conditions in Germany turned for the worse: Allied bombing was destroying German industry, and an increasing number of workers were not receiving their salaries, which threatened their families' survival in Slovakia. Also, many were not allowed to leave for their contractually granted holidays. The complaints of racist discrimination in the day-to-day contacts with the employing companies and the German administration increased.[84] After the German occupation of Eastern Slovakia that launched the SNP on 29 August 1944, the German authorities and army began to treat the Slovaks the way they had been treating the Slavic population of the occupied countries since 1939: they began to abduct Slovaks as forced labourers to the Reich, following their racist 'theory' of the Slavic *Untermenschen*.

The Slovak workers' status in the Reich thus mirrored the course of the war: when Germany was successful in her war campaigns, prior to the defeat at Stalingrad, the Slovak workers' status was a privileged one. According to the stipulations of the *Schutzvertrag*, however, the financial aspects of the treaty were, not surprisingly, to the overall benefit of Germany.[85] Yet, prior to the autumn of 1944, the Slovak workers cannot be considered victims of

---

[83] Schwarc et al., 17.
[84] Schwarc et al., 51.
[85] Schwarc et al., 18.

the Nazi regime.[86] From 1939 to 1945, a total of 200,000 Slovak workers were in the Reich's employment.[87]

Clementis encouraged the Slovak workers in his broadcast from 10 October 1943 to stay strong and not lose hope; victory was near, treating them as potential allies, not traitors.[88] The Germans had lost the battle of Stalingrad in February, a significant turn of the fortunes of war. But the suffering in Central Europe was going on:

> "Although you have found, in one way or another, a livelihood in Germany, a livelihood Tiso and Tuka's false independence [*tisovsko-tukovská lžisamostatnost'*] has not given you at home, yours is a hard lot to bear. And it is getting harder, day by day, and your life is getting more and more dangerous. Therefore, it is no surprise that you are using every opportunity to go home to Slovakia. But certainly not with the help of that so-called ambassador Černák, who just recently stuck a piece of metal on the chest of your gaoler, the murderer Himmler. That Černák also denounced to the Gestapo Slovak workers who wanted to save themselves, who tried to leave the bombed out German cities and go home. Now, you must use your own initiative and act with the support of your comrades."[89]

Not everybody could flee from slavery just now, but those who had to stay in Germany could do great service to their nation and the future Czechoslovak Republic. Post-war Czechoslovakia would grant the Slovak workers a new life in a new home. After this war, Clementis stressed, no Slovak would ever again be expelled from his home and sold into slavery as they were being sold to the Reich now.[90] The Slovak workers in Germany knew what their grandfathers and fathers, the emigrants of the 19th and 20th

---

[86] Schwarc et al., 15.
[87] Schwarc et al., 51.
[88] Clementis, "Slovenskí robotníci v Nemecku", in *Odkazy z Londýna*, 70-72.
[89] Clementis, "Slovenskí robotníci v Nemecku", 70. Matúš Černák (1903–1955) was for two months Minister of Education in the Slovak state. From 1939 to 1944, he was Slovak ambassador to Germany in Berlin.
[90] Clementis, "Slovenskí robotníci v Nemecku", 71.

century, had done abroad for their nation in WWI; the American Slovaks were doing exactly the same now, fighting Hitler as soldiers of the US army. The Slovak workers in Germany could immensely contribute to the war effort:

> "You know that the German army can murder, burn and force your brothers in Slovakia to die for the German masters only because millions of workers, violently abducted to Germany, are forced to make weapons. Thus, the fewer weapons you make, the sooner the murdering at home and your slavery will stop. Even in view of all that suffering, you are in a better condition than the millions of slaves from various countries. That's why you have the unique opportunity to sabotage and damage the German masters, whenever possible. You must help your comrades, whose conditions are much worse than yours."[91]

The Slovak workers at home, men and women working in the fields, were seeing with their own eyes what terrible fate their Slavic brothers in the Ukraine, White Russia and the occupied parts of the Soviet Union were suffering in Germany's munition factories. The Slovak workers had to help them, whenever possible. They had to demonstrate with actions that they were the rightful sons of the Slovak nation that had given the Slavic people and entire Slavdom so many excellent men.

Clementis appealed to the workers' class-consciousness and national identity. Insinuating that the Slovak workers in Germany were clever enough to see through Goebbels' war propaganda he slipped in an important item of information from home: they surely knew that "one hundred Slovak boys [*stá slovenských chlapcov*]"[92] had gone over to the Soviets. The boys were now fighting in the Czechoslovak platoon under General Ludvík Svoboda, a veteran of the *legia* of WWI, with the Red Army. And, one day in the near future, they would ask the workers what they had done for Slovak freedom, for purifying the nation's name the masters in

---

[91] Clementis, "Slovenskí robotníci v Nemecku", 71.
[92] Clementis, "Slovenskí robotníci v Nemecku", 71.

Bratislava had soiled with shame. Clementis was absolutely clear: every decent Slovak had to fight the Germans. Even the tiniest action would support the Czechoslovak war effort:

> "Slovak workers in Germany! In your own interests, in the interests of Slovakia and free Czechoslovakia, you, together with millions of other workers, must destroy Nazi Germany from within."[93]

Clementis' call for sabotage was in perfect tune with the Allies' war effort. He broadcasted four more speeches to the Slovak workers in 1943 and 1944, providing them with news from the eastern front. Their acts of sabotage in the German arms factories had to increase, but if ever the opportunity arose, they should go home and join the partisans who were waiting for the Red Army in the Tatra Mountains.

On 30 July 1944, roughly six weeks after the Allied landing in Normandy and a few days after Hitler had spoken on German radio, proving that he was still very much alive after the attempt on his life, Clementis broadcasted his last speech to the workers in Germany, addressing them now as Czechoslovaks.[94] He spoke Slovak, but the message addressed the Czechoslovak workers, signalling that victory was near – and therefore also the rebuilding of their home, their democratic Republic.

With regard to the Slovak workers' situation in the Reich and the course of the war, this broadcast was a call for co-operation – and, also, a last warning. In psychological terms, it was a cunning carrot and stick rhetoric that worked twofold: it put those Slovak workers under pressure who were still supportive of the Tiso regime and, at the same time, assured the Czech forced labourers that the Slovak workers were being offered a last oppor-

---

[93] Clementis, "Slovenskí robotníci v Nemecku", 72.
[94] Clementis, Československí robotníci v nemecku", in in *Odkazy z Londýna*, 144.

tunity. They could still join the right side, either by leaving Germany or helping their suffering Czech brothers with food and shelter and acts of sabotage. Clementis rationally, cleverly and deliberately left the door open for those Slovak workers who were close to the *Ľudáci* or were *Ľudáci,* telling them between the lines that if they joined the resistance now, no consequences would await them for volunteering for the German war effort. Furthermore, any Czech forced labourer who would, after this broadcast, experience help from Slovak workers, or the lack thereof, would give witness in court after the war.

Clementis started to speak to the Slovak workers only in 1943, exactly at the time when their situation in the Reich was getting worse. To appeal to them to support Beneš and the Allies prior to the German defeat in Stalingrad would have been futile, since, back then, their status in the Reich was good; they had had more to lose than to gain by committing sabotage. But now, with the Allied armies practically at the gates of Paris, it was high time and the last opportunity to switch sides. Slovak workers and Czech forced labourers should unite, since their union would render invalid the beginning of their misery, the principle of *divide et impera* the Germans had used to destroy their Republic. During their stay in the Reich, Clementis stressed, they had learnt what kind of *Volk* the Germans were:

> "Not even their ancestors were happy with the simple 'Deutschland'. They had to have 'Deutschland, Deutschland, über alles'. It was not enough for them to be human – they had to be superhuman – Übermenschen. And that's why you probably were not surprised that they, in their planning and execution, have declared total war and total mobilization, the latter, actually, for the fourth time now. That big gob Goebbels, the new administrator of the total war, began his speech last week with a declaration of the fifth total mobilisation – we could call it *übertotal* mobilization [*mobilizáciu übertotálnu*]. […] Not twenty-four hours after Goebbel's speech, Marshall Stalin broadcasted in five daily statements that the Red Army, pushing forward with lightening speed,

has liberated on Thursday Stanislawow, Lwow, Byalistok, Dvinsk and Šaulaj."[95]

Certainly, as Clementis said, Goebbels and his cronies could do much more damage to the living conditions of the German people, the people in the occupied countries and also the Slovak workers in Germany, but there was no way they could save Hitler's Germany. The Czechoslovak workers in Germany had to understand that in this crucial phase of the war every single blow to the German war machinery was only accelerating the advance of liberty and victory.

II. 3. 6 To the Slovak Women (1944)

On 4 March 1944, Clementis addressed the women of Slovakia. In his broadcast "To the Slovak Women",[96] he must have had in mind his mother, sisters, and Lída's mother. And the mothers, sisters, wives and sweethearts of the Slovak boys fighting with the partisans in the mountains, but also the mothers, sisters, wives and sweethearts of the Slovak soldiers who had been drafted into the Slovak army and had to fight at the side of the Germans against the Red Army. Clementis found the perfect words to console those who were mourning a loved one and those who were desperate because they had no news from the front. He put himself into the minds of Slovak women and tried to convince those still supporting the Tiso regime that they should switch sides now:

> "Slovak women, in these dire days you have heard from Moscow the messages of your sons – who are serving in the Czechoslovak army in the Soviet Union. They have left Čatloš and are now fighting with the Red Army for freedom. [...] They have spoken to you on the radio with

---

[95] Clementis, Československí robotníci v nemecku", 145.
[96] Clementis, "Slovenské ženy", in *Odkazy z Londýna*, 112-114. For a history of Slovak women's lives from the 19th to the 21st century see my *Seven Slovak Women. Portraits of Courage, Humanism and Enlightenment* (Stuttgart, New York: ibidem, Columbia University Press, 2015).

the courage of soldiers who have risked their lives many times and shall risk them again in new battles and the final battle for freedom. That's why their messages sound so different to you, different from the cynical comedy of the so-called greetings from and to the front [*cynická komédia takzvaných pozdravov z frontu a na front*] the masters in Bratislava are arranging on a daily basis."⁹⁷

On 30 October, the first Czechoslovak platoon had conquered the Ukraine together with the Red Army. The Slovak boys had shown with their military resilience and acumen that Čatloš' army was at the end of its tether. The Germans would retreat through Slovakia only if the traffic system was functional, the roads safe and food available to them – and no partisans around:

> "Slovak women! Your sons have spoken to you from Moscow. They know what a German retreat [*nemecký ústup*] through Slovakia means to the civilians, how the German army shall treat the civilian Slavic population. In the Ukraine, they have seen the burned-down villages and destroyed towns; they have seen the mass-murder of the innocent civilian population. They have seen how many hundred and thousands of Soviet citizens [*koľko státisícov sovietských občanov*] have been abducted to slave labour."⁹⁸

They, Clementis said referring to the exile government, were not calling on the Slovak women to commit senseless sacrifices. Once their sons and husbands would advance with the Red Army onto Slovak territory, they should not find burned villages. The Slavic women's legendary courage was a role model for the Slovak women; their sons and husbands needed their help and support. It was up to them now, if the boys advancing with the Red Army would have to face thousands of German bandits or the victorious Slovak partisans.

    I am no expert in military strategy, but I think that the following considerations make sense. In March 1944, at the time of Clementis' last broadcast to the Slovak women, there were as yet

---

97 Clementis, "Slovenské ženy", 113.
98 Clementis, "Slovenské ženy", 113-114.

no German platoons stationed on the territory of Slovakia. Clementis mentioned a German retreat from the eastern front through Slovakia. The Slovak women should make sure that, if such a retreat were to happen, they would muster the highest possible resistance by supporting the partisans and the Red Army with food, shelter and information. They should prevent a German retreat – which would have meant that the German platoons would be trapped on Slovak territory, thus incapable of joining the German army in the protectorate and on the Western front.

In his second and last broadcast to the Slovak women on 25 March 1944,[99] Clementis called the Slovak wives and daughters to stand firm. One of the most important tasks of women had always been the care of the family and the education of the children. In peace, this was a challenging task, but now, in war, it was a military task:

> "The fronts are clear. On the one side, there is the German army with their servants in Bratislava who want to make Slovakia a battlefield. The German army will destroy everything that can be destroyed when they retreat. On the other side, there are the Slovak soldiers in the Czechoslovak army, fighting at the side of their Russian brothers. They will bring not only freedom, but also safety from German ravage and murder. What Slovak man, what Slovak woman would not know their duty to the nation and not see what front will grant their safety?"[100]

By calling the Slovak women to battle, Clementis was trying to muster as much resistance in Slovakia as possible. He wanted the Slovak women to be prepared, to wait for their sons, husbands and fathers who were approaching from the east. As he had done in his broadcast to the workers, Clementis offered the women who still supported the Tiso government a way out: they should prove with their actions that they were good patriots. Again, he deliberately

---

[99] Clementis, "Slovenské ženy", in *Odkazy z Londýna,* 124-136.
[100] Clementis, "Slovenské ženy", 125.

avoided accusations of collaboration. What counted now was their support of the partisans.

I have no means to prove that Clementis knew about the situation of women in the Slovak state, but I deem it probable that he had information from the Slovak newspapers he received in London. Slovak women were increasingly angered by the food shortages and their discriminatory treatment in the healthcare system. In March 1941, the regime had issued constitutional law no. 66/1941 that forbade abortion.[101] To dictate how women had to spend their lives originated in the sexism of Catholic conservatism and Nazism alike: Slovak women were supposed to focus on the three Cs, that is, cooking, children and Catholicism. Women should produce more children for the fight against Bolshevism. Therefore, law no. 246/1939 issued immediately after the establishment of the Slovak state, had banned married women from work; they had to leave their positions in schools and the civil service.[102] It was thus no wonder that Slovak women took to the streets, protesting against the regime and its discriminatory policies.

These were the generations of women born in the last decades of the 19th and at the turn of the 20th century. Some had experienced the political change of the *prevrat* of 1918, while others had grown up in Masaryk's democracy that had established equal rights for women. Clementis appealed to their memories, how the Tiso regime had changed their lives for the worse, taken away their civil rights and liberties, banned them to the kitchen and pressed them into the production of children.

---

[101] Kováčiková, 9.
[102] Kováčiková, 7.

II. 3. 7 The Attempt on Hitler's Life (1944)

On 22 July 1944, Clementis broadcasted the latest news to his listeners at home: high officers of the Wehrmacht had tried to remove Hitler and assume power.[103] One might, as the lawyer said in his intelligent prognosis of the immediate future, learn the details and the whole truth of that operation only after the Allies' defeat of the Wehrmacht. But it was possible to draw some safe and uplifting conclusions now:

> "What has happened in recent days has been no isolated act or coincidence, but shows a characteristic feature of Germany's present situation. A situation caused by the victorious advance of the Red Army, the successful landing of the British-American forces in France and the overall superiority of the Allies; a superiority in military, material, moral and political terms. Thus, even if the murderous Himmler is successful in liquidating the decent officers, there is no power left in Germany that can extract itself from the final battle: the German army leadership is in chaos, and the Allies' bombers are systematically destroying Germany's industry."[104]

Himmler was not capable of turning around that power; by killing the rebellious officers he would not blot out the marks and consequences recent events had left on the morale of the German army and people. The attempt on Hitler's life originated in the calculations of experts in military technology; they knew that Germany could not win the war, and that Hitler with his dilettante leadership was only preparing the total extermination of the German army – yet, all this should be of no concern to the Allies now:

> "In the current situation, it makes absolutely no difference whether false illusions about a possible salvation of the army are ripe in the ranks of the German officers. The nations united in war know very well

---

[103] Clementis, "Atentát na Hitlera", in *Odkazy z Londýna*, 134-136.
[104] Clementis, "Atentát na Hitlera", 134-135.

that the Wehrmacht that had, some time ago, used Hitler as its instrument only to be instrumentalized by him later, is presenting the same danger to the peace-loving nations as Nazism itself."[105]

Nazism and Prussian militarism, the two evil forces of Germany were in an open fight. The shooting of some representatives of the traditional military caste on the one hand, and the continuation of Hitler's war strategy on the other did not change an iota of the current situation, of the Allies' superiority. Indeed, as Clementis said ironically, one had to be extraordinarily stupid and gifted with blind malice to interpret the recent events in Germany as a sign of Providence that was protecting Hitler. There was no doubt that the quislings, whether they called themselves Tiso, Hácha or Mach, showed these characteristic features of stupidity and blind malice. They were probably the only band in Europe Hitler had ever created to his own advantage:

> "And as the attempt on Hitler's life is foreshadowing the fate of all of Europe's quislings, it has been a call and signal for the decisive final battle to the enslaved nations of Europe united in their opposition, the final battle that will destroy, once and for all, Hitler's crumbling rule."[106]

Clementis was happy to present the goal of the Allies: the Reich's unconditional surrender. There would be no negotiations with the Germans who had brought so much suffering on Europe and the world, on Slovakia and the Czech lands. The Allied landing in Normandy on 6 June 1944 and the advance of the Red Army were decisive events in the grand theatre of the war. They prompted a military operation and a courageous endeavour that would go down in the nation's history as the most remarkable memoir of WWII, putting the Slovaks in the camp of the victorious Allies.

---

[105] Clementis, "Atentát na Hitlera", 135.
[106] Clementis, "Atentát na Hitlera", 136.

II. 3. 8 The Slovak National Uprising (1944)

In his broadcast of 31 August 1944, Clementis called the uprising that began on the same day the second grand uprising of the Slovak nation; the first one had happened in 1848.[107] Yet, there was a clear difference between the first and the second one:

> "This time – Slovakia is not only rising against the primitive interpretation of the Magyar nation [*proti divému mad'arstvu*] and for the liberation of the brothers enslaved by the Magyar yoke, but, first and foremost, against the even more primitive German nation and for the liberation of the Czechoslovak people [*za oslobodenie ľudu Československa*]. That's why this battle is going to be a brutal one. But – whatever the outcome – victory will be ours."[108]

Slovakia, Clementis stressed, knew that this time she was not fighting on her own and for herself, but she knew also that nobody else could fight this battle. The Slovak soldiers had risen in an open and all-national rebellion not because they wanted Slovakia to drown in suffering and desperation, but because they wanted her suffering to end.

Just yesterday, Tiso had committed the most revolting crime in his dark career: the outspoken support of the murderous attack of the German criminals against the Slovak people. Tiso had also said that a man judged a friend by his actions. Now then, as Clementis said with his sharp rhetoric, Slovakia was judging Tiso and his cronies by the actions of their German comrades, and neither sweet talk nor threats would deter the nation from its rightful path. With the uprising, Slovakia was taking an important and decisive step forward, gaining the admiration and respect of the whole world and the love of all Slavic nations. The soldiers had written Štúr's memorable words on their shields: "It is impossible

---

[107] Clementis, "Slovenské národné povstanie!", in *Odkazy z Londýna*, 151-153, 151.
[108] Clementis, "Slovenské národné povstanie!", 151.

to go back – one has to advance [*Cesta nazpät nemožna – napred sa íst musí!*]:[109]

> "Forward, this is the future of a free and happy Slovakia in a new and just Czechoslovakia. This shall be a world built by the victorious Allies and built by us. This shall be a world in which nobody will be able to toy with the fate of the Slovak nation."[110]

The uprising lasted two months; it was one of the largest anti-Hitler rebellions in Europe. The commanders Ján Golian (1906–1945) and Rudolf Viest (1890–1945) faced immense difficulties, since they were not familiar with the mountainous territory. Materiel support and troops could be sent in only by air.[111] The support and initiative of the local people was the decisive factor in gaining control of the territory around Banská Bystrica: 60,000 men were fighting in the resistance army and 18,000 in partisan platoons. The Germans could crush the uprising only with additional troops from Hungary. The centre of Banská Bystrica fell on 27 October. Viest and Golian were captured; the Germans interned them at the concentration camp Flossenbürg and executed them in 1945.

At the end of 1944, the Red Army liberated the Hungarian-occupied eastern and south-eastern parts of Slovakia. The Soviet offensive started in January 1945, and Bratislava was liberated on 4 April 1945. Tiso fled to Austria, where US soldiers found him and delivered him to the Czechoslovak authorities. He and Tuka would be found guilty of treason and collaboration and executed in 1947 and 1946, respectively. Mach received a prison sentence of thirty

---

[109] Clementis, "Slovenské národné povstanie!", 153.
[110] Clementis, "Slovenské národné povstanie!", 153.
[111] Kováč, *Dejiny Slovenska*, 237.

years, was amnestied in 1968 and died a free citizen in Bratislava in 1980.[112]

II. 3. 9   About the Future (1945)

In March 1945, the Germans were still in control of the larger part of the Czechoslovak territory. In his broadcast of 11 March 1945, entitled "About the future", Clementis drew the attention of his listeners to the political future; it was time now to think about the new state and its organization.[113] The new order demanded a new constitution and democratically elected delegates to the parliament. And it was also clear to everybody that a fundamentally important issue was the status of the Czechs and Slovaks in their common state, their political relationship. Another one was the basis of the future economic and administrative system:

> "In terms of our activities and considerations, we should already now start to develop the foundation of our new state. I am saying – a new state. In legal and international terms, Czechoslovakia has never ceased to exist; in international negotiations, she has been, even in these unhappy years, an equal and full partner [*rovnoprávný a plnoprávný partner*]. [...] After WWI, many of us experienced a distinct instability; a certain imperfection of the world oppressed us back then. Today, we know that the world is going to be safe. In the past, there had been things in our home we didn't like, things we were critical of. We wanted to improve our house. [...] But the storm came, blew off the roof above our heads and destroyed our home. That's why today, we are not facing the question where, what and how to build, improve and accomplish our home, but on what grounds and principles we shall rebuild it."[114]

The issue was a new Slovakia in a free Czechoslovakia. Clementis, who had been very restrained about Communist thought and concepts of political rule in his London broadcasts, announced what

---

[112] Mach was apparently astonished that his life was spared. The political circumstances that led to the verdicts on Tiso, Tuka and Mach have never been satisfactorily explained; Rychlík, *Češi a Slováci II*, 75-97.
[113] Clementis, "O veciach budúcich", in *Odkazy z Londýna*, 202-205, 202.
[114] Clementis, "O veciach budúcich", 202-203.

he believed would be to the benefit of the Slovaks. The future was the unity of the Czechoslovak Republic that respected the equality of her nations on the basic principle of a people's democracy. It was remarkable, as Clementis said with biting sarcasm, that the gibberish of the Bratislava geese was directed against those parts of President Beneš's speech that had stressed that their new people's democracy would be built from below. That was exactly the formula that would provide the Slovaks with important influence in the new Czechoslovakia:

> "Now – not even in Bratislava are they so stupid that they do not know and do not see that the Slovak nation today has a constitutional representation [*ustanovizeň*], the Slovak National Council [*Slovenskú národnú radu*], which is acting in the name of the Slovaks and shall participate in the negotiations with the Czechoslovak government. The Council will direct Slovakia's affairs until the democratic elections."[115]

The persons who had sold out Slovakia's liberty and sovereignty under the tutelage of their German overlords, and those who had driven the nation's fate along the German path, had certainly no legitimacy to speak for the Slovaks. Naturally, they criticized Beneš's principle of building from below, since they were used to governing from above; with their realization of the Führer principle they had buried the tiniest expression of the nation's free will. Already in the early months of Slovakia's autonomy, they had arranged the elections to parliament in such a way that the former Magyar electoral instructors in the 19th century would have turned pale with envy, as Clementis said with biting sarcasm. They had violated the rights of the villages, organizations and associations and appointed people to university professorships for their denunciations and other "scientific" services.[116]

---

[115] Clementis, "O veciach budúcich", 203.
[116] Clementis, "O veciach budúcich", 204.

Certainly, the *Führerprincipisti* were afraid of the principle of building from below, but the Slovak nation was not: with the assistance of the national committees, it was building the grounds of a new administration from below. The confiscation of the property of the German and Magyar oppressors would only reverse the crimes committed against the nation in the past. The new economic organization was not only in the interest of all Slovaks, but would also form the basis of a new structure of economic and social life, granting all citizens a basic income and improving their quality of life.[117]

Clementis announced the plan of a future land reform and, at the same time, justified the future expulsion of the Magyars from Slovakia. With his prognosis of the near future, Clementis instilled hope, appealing to his listeners to hold out and not to forget what they had gone through in the last five years:

> "The Tiso regime has left behind a terrible legacy. But thanks to the Slovak nation, which has built in the months of the uprising its organs and developed a national programme, we can look to the future with faith. Because we know that this programme will guarantee the safety of the Slovak nation in a new Czechoslovakia. And together with the victorious Soviet Union, the nation shall forge safety and stability, dedicating all its forces towards the quiet and happy construction of a new and free life."[118]

Clementis' optimism is visible in his words; in his way of thinking, the war was practically over. The devout Marxist-Leninist, whose membership of the KSČ would soon be restored, announced the building of a People's democracy, hoping that Slovakia's status in the new Czechoslovakia would be based on equal representation and self-government. He believed that Prague's centralism was a thing of the past, and that the Slovaks' claims for equal status would lead to a Czechoslovak federation. The Slovak National

---

[117] Clementis, "O veciach budúcich", 204.
[118] Clementis, "O veciach budúcich", 205.

Council and the Czech centre-right politicians had in their negotiations agreed on the principle of the National Front (NF). The Slovak position looked promising. By mentioning the people's democracy, Clementis officially supported Beneš's plans, but he thought of the people's democracy in Gottwald and Stalin's terms – the rule of the Party.

II. 3. 10   Banská Bystrica – Liberated! (1945)

In his speech of 27 March 1945, Clementis celebrated the liberation of Banská Bystrica. He was brief and jubilant; it was his last broadcast from London. He was preparing to go home after five years in exile and tremendously happy to inform his listeners that the Red Army had liberated a Slovak town close to where he had grown up, Banská Bystrica in Central Slovakia. Ever the intelligent and committed orator, Clementis' happiness and joy can be felt in his tone and wording. Finally, victory was near.

Thanks to the Allied offensive, the Germans would no longer be able to march into the heroic and beautiful centre of Banská Bystrica, where the Slovak National Uprising had started.[119] They, as Clementis said, speaking for the exile government, had never had any doubts that the Soviets would arrive one day; just yesterday, Marshall Stalin had declared the town liberated. They had always been fully aware, even in those tragic days when the Germans had crushed it, that the uprising showed the way out of the chaos the innocent nation had been thrown into. They also knew that their nation had not only wanted to protect its territory, but also lay the grounds for its future, fulfilling the people's wishes and needs. Clementis praised the heroic resistance of those who had withstood the Tiso regime:

---

[119] Clementis, "Banská Bystrica – zase slobodná!", in *Odkazy z Londýna*, 209-210, 209.

> "Not even the Nazi boots can trample down this grand idea. Only murderers can eliminate it – by killing those who believe in it. Those who believed in the Slovak National Uprising had to go underground [*do podzemia*] and flee in their thousands to the mountains – but the grand ideal, the great message of our uprising had been realized earlier, in the days before Banská Bystrica, the symbol of the uprising, was liberated."[120]

The new way of Slovak life was beginning in the east, with the plan of a new political regime. In Moscow, the negotiations of the Beneš exile government with Marshall Stalin were demonstrating the new, harmonious and brotherly relations of Slovaks and Czechs who would soon start building the new Czechoslovak Republic from scratch:

> "We know about the tremendous sacrifices Slovakia has made and is still making. Her enemies and collaborators have afflicted deep wounds on the nation. […] The liberation of Banská Bystrica has accomplished historical justice [*naplnuje sa kus historickej spravodlivosti*], as well as the liberation of Slovakia and the Republic. […] Justice will reach everybody who has helped to end poverty and suffering in Slovakia. […] Justice to those who deserve the honour and the love of all courageous people."[121]

The lawyer would arrive in Prague in May with his wife Lída after a long journey. Together with members of the exile government, they travelled on a steamer through the Mediterranean to the coast of Romania. From there, they took a train and arrived in Košice, liberated eastern Slovakia. Little did Clementis know in March 1945 that within just four years he would reach the peak of his political career; he could not know that his downfall would be ordered by two politicians and Party leaders he had admired since he had been a law student in Prague in the 1920s.

---

[120] Clementis, "Banská Bystrica – zase slobodná!", 209.
[121] Clementis, "Banská Bystrica – zase slobodná!", 210.

Vladimír Clementis' birthplace in
Tisovec, Central Slovakia,
© T. Winkler, 1966, Martin, Slovakia

The renovated birthplace
of Clementis is now a museum,
© Josette Baer, July 2016

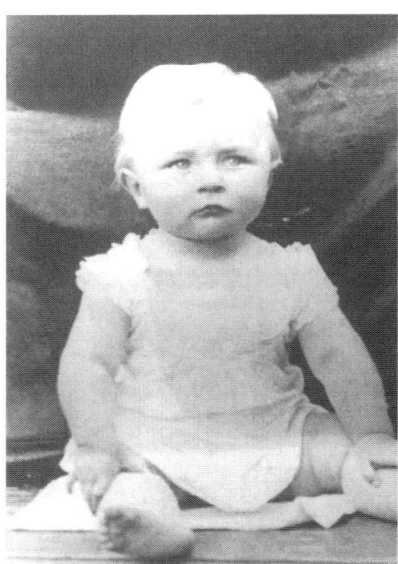

Little Vlado, SNK, Martin

Two-year-old Vlado in traditional
Slovak costume in 1904,
SNK, Martin

Vlado as a teenager with his father,
SNK, Martin

The student of law in the early 1920s,
© Muzeum V. Clementisa, Tisovec

Clementis and his friend Laco Novomeský in the 1920s,
SNK, Martin

Clementis in Dresden, Germany, in 1923,
© Muzeum V. Clementisa, Tisovec

The young Laco Novomeský,
SNK, Martin

Caricature of the editors of DAV by Ľ. Rambouský, from left to right: Novomeský, Clementis, Rybák, SNK, Martin

"Spirits that I've cited ... ?"

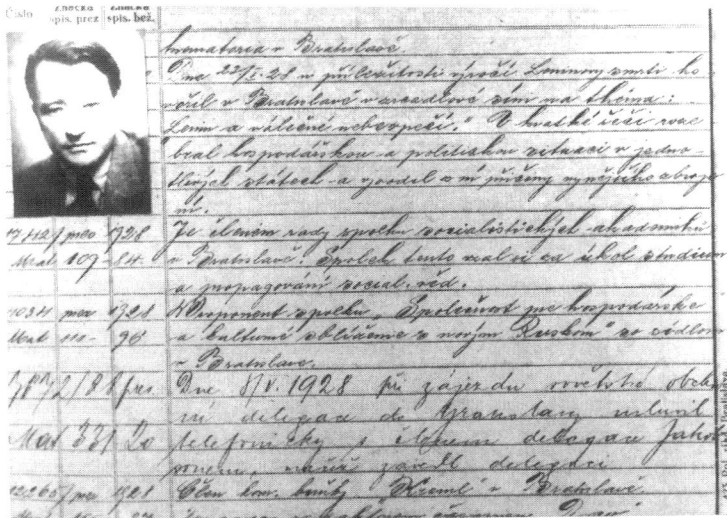

Clementis' file held by the Czechoslovak State Security Service, dated 1928, SNK, Martin

Lída Clementisová on the balcony of her husband's law practice in Bratislava on their wedding day, 24 March 1933,
© Muzeum V. Clementisa, Tisovec

Lída Clementisová in London exile during WWII,
© Muzeum V. Clementisa, Tisovec

A Czechoslovak girl in traditional costume gives flowers to a Czechoslovak sergeant. In the background a poster of Churchill: "Czechoslovaks, the hour of your liberation is near", © AMZV, Prague, Londýnský archiv, LA_F_151_020_001

Josip Broz Tito in Prague in 1945, from left to right: Karol Šmidke, Tito, Clementis, © TASR, Bratislava

Husák, Clementis' second-closest friend, SNK, Martin

The passionate politician speaking at festivities in Devín in 1945,
SNK, Martin

Festive reception of the Soviet delegation in the Czernín Palace in October 1946, SNK, Martin

The Czechoslovak delegation to the UN in 1948, Clementis is first from left, SNK, Martin

Foreign Minister Clementis on his way to the UN session in New York, autumn 1949, from left to right: Lída Clementisová, accompanying her husband to the airport, Clementis, his deputy Viliam Široký accompanying him to the airport and Theo Herkeľ Florin, his personal assistant at Prague Růzyně airport, SNK, Martin

The last picture of Lída and Vladimír Clementis before their arrest, SNK, Martin

Lída Clementisová received the Ľudovít Štúr prize on behalf of her husband 31 October 1968 from the chairman of the Association of Slovak Journalists. The SNR declared Clementis a national hero of the ČSSR, © TASR, Bratislava

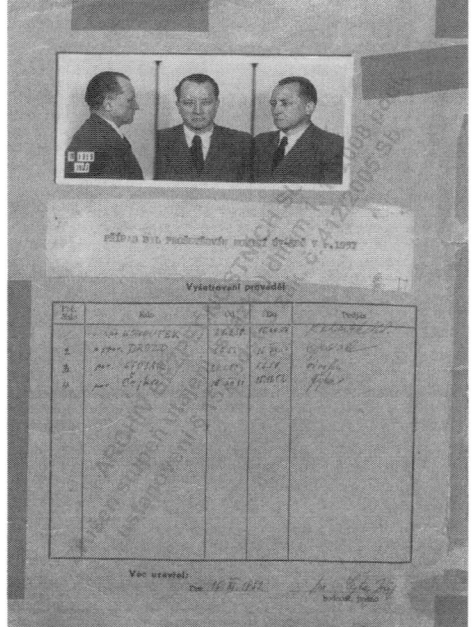

Clementis after his arrest on 28 January 1951,
© ABS USTRČR, Prague

The faked protocol of the house search of the Clementis flat in Prague
on 5 February 1951,
© ABS USTRČR, Prague.
Collection sorted files from the Ministry of the Interior secretariat, file code 319-34-13.

Out-of-court agreement of the Ministry of the Interior with Lída Clementisová, signed 23 April 1957,
© ABS USTRČR, Prague. Fund of the Ministry of National Security, archive code MNB-2 (file contains previous archive code number ZV-1-MV).

"The Boss received both delegations in the Kremlin in the cold February of 1948. He yelled at Dimitrow: 'You and the Yugoslavs never report on what you're doing.' The Yugoslav Kardelj, trying to smooth over the situation, told him that 'there are no disagreements between us'. This brought a furious outburst from Stalin: 'Nonsense! There are disagreements, and very profound ones at that.' [...] They resolved to consult each other regularly in the future. But the Boss had made up his mind to rid himself of Tito. He knew that 'one bad sheep can spoil the flock'. Tito would be now more useful to him as an enemy – as Trotsky had once been. [...] By anathematizing Tito, he would tighten the bonds of obedience within the camp."[1]

"Political conditioning should not be confused with training or persuasion or even indoctrination. [...] It is the battle for the possession of the nerve cells. [...] The simple man with deep-rooted, inner, freely absorbed religious faith could exert a much greater, inner resistance than could the complex, questioning intellectual. [...] The inquisitor knows that in the period of temporary relaxation of pressure, during which the victim will rehearse and repeat the torture experience to himself, the final surrender is prepared. During that tension of rumination and anticipation, the deeply hidden wish to give in grows. The action of continual repetition of stupid questions, reiterated for days and days, exhausts the mind till it gives the answers the inquisitor wants to have. [...] He yearns for sleep and can do nothing else than surrender. [...] At the moment faith and hope disappear, man breaks down."[2]

---

[1] Radzinsky, 517, 518.
[2] Joost A. M. Meerloo, M. D., *The Rape of the Mind. The Psychology of Thought Control, Menticide, and Brainwashing* (New York: Progressive Press, 1956), 8, 49, 85-86, 77.

III. The Ministry of Foreign Affairs (1945-1950)

In this chapter, I focus on the brutal politics at the beginning of the Cold War in the Eastern bloc:[1] a loyal Communist's power and loss thereof within the time span of two years. Clementis was appointed assistant secretary of state in March 1945 and minister of foreign affairs in March 1948. In May 1949, the Party elected him as a member of the Central Committee (CC), and in March 1950, the KSČ deprived him of all positions in Party and state. The StB arrested him on 28 January 1951. On 3 December 1952, he was hanged. President Gottwald, whom Clementis had known for thirty years, did not dare pardon his old comrades. He followed Stalin's directives to the letter and sacrificed his old buddy Slánský, with whom he had spent WWII in Moscow exile.

In the first part of this chapter, I shall present a summary of Clementis' activities as assistant secretary of state (*štátny tajomník*) and foreign minister (*ministr zahraničních vecí*), focussing on his speeches and lectures at international diplomatic meetings and to the public at home. Clementis' principal task was to realize the Kremlin's foreign policy directives.[2] He was in control of the

---

[1] On Czechoslovak politics from the Truman doctrine to the Vietnam War see Michal Štefanský and Slavomír Michálek, *Míľniky studenej vojny a ich vplyvy na Československo (od Trumanovej doktríny po Vietnam)* (Bratislava: Veda, 2015).

[2] Slavomír Michálek, "K niektorým otázkam československej zahraničnej politiky v rokoch 1945-1951 so zamieraním na činnosť Vladimíra Clementisa", in *Vladimír Clementis. 1902-1952. Zborník ...*, 38-45. Jindřich Dejmek holds that Clementis tried to keep room for manoeuvre in his decision-making until 1949, when the CC of the KSČ forced him to reorganize the ministry's structure according to the Soviet model. I disagree. Clementis was no independent Party member – he followed the Soviet line to the letter. His 'independence'

ministry, although Western politicians and diplomats believed that Foreign Minister Jan Masaryk was the boss. A personal success for Clementis was the negotiations with Hungary about the exchange of population that ended officially with the signing of the Czechoslovak-Hungarian Treaty on Friendship, Co-operation and Mutual Assistance in Budapest in 1949 under the auspices, that is, the pressure of the Soviet Union. Note that I cannot delve into all of Clementis' negotiations and speeches in detail – such a task would fill two large volumes in their own right. I can neither present a detailed history of the emerging antagonism between the Western Allies and the Soviet Union that led to the Cold War, but I shall focus on the events that were of principal importance for Clementis.

The second part deals with Clementis' fall from grace. The election of Yugoslavia as a non-permanent member of the UN Security Council in 1950[3] and not Czechoslovakia, as Stalin had planned, sealed Clementis' fate: he was no longer of use to the Soviet Union.[4] But he could perform a last service for the Party. My

---

was just a clever move, concealing his true intentions under the guise of good relations with the West, since Stalin's post-war strategy commanded him to act accordingly. The Christmas Agreement of 1943 had sealed Moscow's diktat in Czechoslovakia's foreign policy and domestic affairs. Portraying Czechoslovakia as a bridge between East and West from 1945 to 1948 was in tune with Stalin's geopolitical strategy, since US-Soviet relations were in a sensitive phase. The Soviet hemisphere of power had been decided in Yalta; by 1945, the national fronts were but a stepping stone to power for the Communist Parties in each country liberated by the Red Army; Jindřich Dejmek, "Ministr zahraničních věcí Vladimír Clementis, jeho úřad a jeho diplomatie", *Historický časopis 58*, no. 3 (2010): 497-531, 525.

3   For a list of members of the UN Security Council see http://www.un.org/en/sc/members/elected.asp; accessed 18 June 2016. For analysis of Czechoslovakia's role in the foundation of the UN and the election of Yugoslavia to the Security Council see Slavomír Michálek, *San Francisco 1945. Vznik organizácie spojených národov* (Bratislava: Veda, HÚ SAV, 2015), 105-126, 151-168.

4   Michálek, "K niektorým ...", 40.

brief analysis of Clementis' interrogation, trial and execution will show that it is impossible to find out in detail what happened to him in the interrogation room. Although we can make an educated guess, imagine in a speculative way what could have happened, we shall be left with more questions than answers.

III. 1 Assistant Secretary of State (1945–1948)

III. 1. 1 The Communist Coup d'Etat (25 February 1948)

I shall not delve into the context of the three Prague Agreements (*první, druhá a třetí Pražská dohoda*), because they are not important for our purpose: Clementis' domain was foreign policy, not domestic affairs.[5] Yet, a few remarks about the post-war political system are required here to explain Czechoslovakia's domestic affairs and foreign policy from 1945 to 1950.

In the months prior to the end of WWII, the majority of Czechoslovak politicians shared the view that the multi-party system of the First Republic had got out of control. Masaryk's Republic had been too generous with the minorities, the Sudeten Germans, the Carpathian Germans and the Hungarians in the South of

---

[5] For a summary of the three Prague Agreements in English see my *A Life Dedicated ...*, 244-250. The Slovak politicians of the SNR, among them also the Communists, tried to negotiate an equal status with the Czechs according to the principle of *rovný s rovným*. The SNR soon lost its influence, since the overall political atmosphere showed a tendency towards centralism. It was widely believed that a Slovak equal status would put an unnecessary burden on the reconstruction of the state. From 1944 to 1946, the Slovak Communists had, like their centre-right colleagues, favoured constitutional equality, which would have resulted in a federation. Because of the KSČ's change of course after the lost elections in Slovakia in 1946, Slovakia's equality with the Czech lands was no longer a principal goal. The Soviet NKVD consultants would use the efforts of the Slovak comrades for equality to accuse them of 'Slovak bourgeois nationalism'.

Slovakia – what had been the result? They had thanked the Republic's democratic generosity by weakening it prior to its destruction by Hitler. Therefore, a slimming-down of the party system was required. It was widely believed that Czechoslovakia's security was granted with the expulsion (*odsun*) of the Germans from the Czech lands and the Hungarians from Southern Slovakia. The latter would be a particularly important task for Clementis.

Post-war Czechoslovakia from 1945 to 1948 was neither a Republic nor a parliamentary democracy, but it was no totalitarian state either – not yet. In constitutional terms, the political system was a hybrid, a democracy limited by the stipulations of the Košice Agreement that had, under the psychological and political authority of Beneš and Stalin, secured the dominant position of the National Front (*Národní fronta*):

> "This fact was of key significance, and worked to the disadvantage of the non-Communist parties. These parties jointly shared in building up the new system, and they accepted the political conception of a regulated democracy. Beneš was the prominent advocate of the latter as a defensive measure taken to prevent a repetition of Munich. A regulated democracy was a limited democracy and was conditional on the fact that if one or more government parties were to try to take full power, it would limit the forces of democracy to acting in its own self-defence. A regulated democracy can be justified only when there is cooperation between democratic parties with equal representation in the coalition."[6]

Limited democracy is politically and ethically legitimate, if all involved parties agree on fair play, keeping to the rules of democratic procedure – which the KSČ blatantly did not. When the KSS lost the 1946 parliamentary elections in Slovakia to the DS, the KSČ changed its course: now, the comrades were preparing to assume power. From 1947 on, the Party stepped up its efforts; it was pressed for time, since the next parliamentary elections were

---

[6] Kaplan, *The Short March*, 189.

scheduled for 1948. The Communists had won the 1946 elections in the Czech lands with 41%; they began to orchestrate demonstrations of workers' unions and farmers' councils and increased their propaganda.

The resignation of 12 of 26 centre-right ministers in February 1948 demonstrated the pressure the KSČ put on the government with its maximalist demands for reforms. The most important issue was the involvement of the StB in the conspiracies against centre-right politicians. The secret service, already firmly in the Party's hands, had planned attempts on the lives of Prokop Drtina, Peter Zenkl (1884–1975) and Jan Masaryk. Gottwald simply refused to appoint an investigating commission. On 21 February, the Party called for a demonstration on Prague's Old Town Square. Gottwald accused the centre-right ministers who had stepped down of reactionary subversion – they had betrayed the National Front. The Czechoslovak citizens, exhausted after five years of war and occupation, wanted a change and believed the accusations of the KSČ.

The Party proceeded in a clever and subtle way: Gottwald promised that they would lead the country towards its own homemade Socialism, with no involvement of the Soviet Union. A homegrown Czechoslovak way towards Socialism suggested that the country's sovereignty, a very sensitive issue, would not be touched, but it had *de facto* ceased to exist with the Christmas Treaty in 1943 and the Košice Agreement in 1945.

On 23 February, Beneš, already gravely ill, promised the centre-right parties to refuse the resignation of their ministers, but on 25 February, he appointed a new government according to Gottwald's suggestions, caving in to the carpenter from Moravia. The government crisis the KSČ had artificially created seemed to be solved with the support of President Beneš – which suggested that the NF was working and Czechoslovakia was still a democracy.

On 29 July 1948, the KSS and the KSČ merged; from then on, the KSS was but an organ that executed the KSČ's policy directives in Slovakia, often to the disadvantage of the Slovak citizens. The KSS could not even independently issue the calls for the meetings of the CC and the CC's presidency – Prague had the last say in everything.[7] The Czech mistrust of the Slovak comrades, ever suspect of 'bourgeois nationalism' as a relic of the Slovak state and their former co-operation with the Slovak centre-right politicians in the SNR in 1943 was the main reason for the centralization of the Party. As soon as the KSČ was in control, it embarked on a brutal course of Sovietization:

> "The terror that was unleashed hit everybody. Even in the tiniest village citizens suspected of political opposition were found. The purges were carried out ruthlessly in all social strata. Privacy, a private life was completely eliminated, which hit the farmers and tradesmen particularly hard. Those who stood up against the terror had to expect that their families' fates were at stake."[8]

In the purges from 1948 to 1954, 250,000 to 280,000 citizens were imprisoned, and 23,000 sent to labour camps.[9] The rationale of the persecution and oppression unfolded in three phases: first, mass purges to terrorize the population; second, elimination of politicians of the oppositional parties, and third, a thorough purge of the Party's top ranks, demonstrating that not even high-ranking Communists could be trusted.

---

[7] Stanislav Sikora, "KSS a čiastočná liberalizácia režimu na Slovensku počas predjaria (1963–1967)", in *Český a slovenský komunismus*, 132-144, 132. The latest publication about Slovakia from 1945 to 1948 is *Slováci a ľudovodemokratický režim* (Bratislava: Literárne informačné centrum, 2016).

[8] Jan Kalous, "KSČ jako iniciátor a vykonavatel politických čistek a procesů", in *Český a slovenský komunismus*, 87-93, 89.

[9] Kalous, 91.

Endless propaganda and censorship eliminated any critical voice and created an atmosphere of mass hysteria. Enemies seemed to be everywhere. In 1950, the first *monstr process*, a show trial with several accused, would begin: the politician, feminist and doctor of law Milada Horáková[10] and three other prominent centre-right politicians would be accused of high treason and espionage for the Imperialist West. They would be executed by hanging. The show trial of Slánský, Clementis and co-accused would mark the peak, but not the end of the purges. The executed Party members had been prominent, while thousands of unknown citizens suffered in the radium mines in Jáchymov or were in prison for their class origins.

III. 1. 2 The Yugoslav-Soviet Split (29 June 1948)

The split between the Soviet Union and Yugoslavia was a decisive moment in Soviet post-war politics; by establishing clear ideological boundaries, the split marked a point of no return in the development of what soon would be called the Cold War. The show trials of prominent Party functionaries in Hungary, Czechoslovakia, Bulgaria and Romania were a direct result of the rift between Stalin and Josip Broz Tito (1892–1980), the leader of the Yugoslav Communists. The Cominform (Communist Information Bureau), founded in September 1947, played an important role in Stalin's decision-making: the Cominform's original task had been to speed up the Sovietization of Eastern Europe via *Gleichschaltung* of the Communist parties of the bloc states, France and Italy included.

In Stalin's view, Tito's activities to make Yugoslavia a regional hegemonial power in the Balkans threatened Soviet interests in Europe. Tito posed a danger to the Soviet bloc, since his

---

[10] For an account of Horáková's fate and the propaganda campaign during her trial see my "Milada Horáková (1902–1950) – executed for her belief in Democracy", in *Seven Czech Women,* 99-156.

Balkan policy could lead to a Western invasion of the region; a new war between the West and the Soviet Union was likely, especially in view of the US support of Turkey and the monarchists in the Greek civil war. Tito had ambitious plans: he planned to integrate Albania into Yugoslavia, merge the Albanian and Yugoslav armies and create a Balkan federation with Bulgaria. In terms of geopolitics, his support of the Communists in the Greek civil war was a risk the Soviet Union could not afford to take, [11] all the more as Greece had never been of strategical interest to the Soviet Union. The rift was not caused by ideological issues of Socialism, but Titos' attempts to create a Communist hegemonial power in the Balkans in defiance of Moscow's long-term plans in the region.

When US Secretary of State George C. Marshall (1880–1959) presented his plan for European reconstruction in June 1947, the states in the Soviet sphere of influence were not allowed to join. Yugoslavia's expulsion can thus be understood as the last act of a development that ended in the bi-polar world, the final act that cemented the Soviet Union's grip on its satellite states. After three brief post-war years, the ideological boundaries were officially defined. On 29 June 1948, the Cominform expelled Yugoslavia, thereby demonstrating to the leaders of the bloc states that the slightest deviation from Soviet foreign policy would no longer be tolerated.

Stalin ousted Tito because the Yugoslav leader was a danger to the goal of Soviet long-term foreign policy in Europe: to be on an even footing with the Capitalist West. Both Stalin and Tito were adherents of *Realpolitik*; their belief in Marxism-Leninism

---

[11] Jeronim Perović, "The Tito-Stalin Split: A Reassessment in Light of New Evidence", *Journal of Cold War Studies 9*, no. 2 (2007): 32-63. For a pdf version see http://www.zora.uzh.ch/62735/1/Perovic_Tito.pdf; accessed 17 June 2016. The latest and so far best biography of Tito is Jože Pirjevec, *Tito. Die Biographie* (München: Verlag Antje Kunstmann, 2016). I thank Nikola Todorovic for recommending this study to me.

and how to realize it was identical. Until February 1948, Yugoslavia was the Soviet Union's closest ally, sharing Stalin's plan to create a Communist bloc in Central and South-Eastern Europe.

The Yugoslav Communist partisans led by Tito had liberated their country on their own without the Red Army, which had boosted their confidence. Furthermore, Tito's increasing tendency not to inform the Soviets about his activities convinced Stalin that he had to get rid of him. Tito feared that he would lose all political influence if he caved in to Stalin's pressure; he decided to stand up against him when the Soviet leader ordered him to back down. Tito was as ruthless a leader as Stalin; after the split, show trials were arranged against the Cominformists, Tito's adversaries who supported Stalin.[12] What distinguished the Yugoslav trials from the Stalinist show trials in the bloc states in the 1950s was the simple fact that it was not Stalin who ordered them, but Tito.

Stalin used the expulsion of Yugoslavia from the Socialist bloc to tighten his power, reign and control: he created "a pretext and a precedent for the subsequent purges of Communist parties".[13] 'Titoism' was one of the principal accusations in the show trials and purges. As a consequence of the split, Bulgaria became the Soviet Union's strongest ally in the Balkans; Albania turned away from Belgrade and towards Moscow, and Yugoslavia stopped supporting the Greek Communists.

A detail in the history of the split offers us an interesting insight into Gottwald's pre-emptive and slavish obedience to Stalin and his lack of talent for strategic thinking. On 14 July 1948,

---

[12] Sabrina Petra Ramet, *The Three Yugoslavias: State-Building and Legitimation 1918–2004* (Washington, DC, Bloomington, IN: Woodrow Wilson, Indiana University Press, 2006), 178-179, 188-198. I thank Adis Merdzanovic for recommending this study to me.

[13] Perović, 62.

two weeks after Yugoslavia's expulsion from the Cominform, Stalin reacted to a suggestion of Gottwald's. Although Stalin expressed himself in a rather mild tone, Gottwald must have trembled with fear, as he knew from experience what consequences the slightest non-approval from Stalin could prompt:

> "I have the impression that you [Gottwald] are counting on the defeat of Tito and his group at the next congress of the KPJ. You suggest publishing compromising material against the Yugoslav leaders. ... We in Moscow are not counting on the early defeat of Tito and have never counted on it. We have achieved the isolation of Yugoslavia. Hence the gradual decline of Tito's Marxist groups is to be expected. This will require patience and the ability to wait. You seem to be lacking in patience. ... There will be no doubt that Marxism will triumph in due course."[14]

On 5 March, Stalin died, and on 14 March, Gottwald followed. A Slovak joke from 1953 demonstrates what ordinary citizens thought about the great leaders:

> "A citizen buys Pravda on a regular basis, day after day, year after year. He always looks at the front page and then throws the newspaper away in disgust. Finally, one day, the shop girl asks him what he is looking for. He replies: 'For an obituary.' 'But obituaries are always on page five', the shop girl instructs him. But the citizen knows better: 'The one I am waiting for will be on the front page.'"[15]

Once he had purged the Yugoslav Communist Party of the Cominformists, Tito would found the Non-Aligned Movement (NAM) in 1961. Yugoslav citizens would enjoy civil liberties Bulgarian, Czechoslovak, East German, Polish, Romanian and Soviet citizens could only dream of: they could travel to and work in the West.

---

[14] Dmitrii Volkogonov, *Sem' vozhdei: Galereya liderov SSSR v 2-kh knigakh*, 2 vols (Moscow: Novosti, 1995), Vol. 1, p. 246, quoted from Perović, 60.

[15] Marína Zavacká, "Whispered rumor as a kind of independent political news service in Slovakia in 1953: People and state reacting on the death of J. V. Stalin and Klement Gottwald", in *Slovak Contributions to 19th International Congress of Historical Sciences* (Bratislava: Veda, 2000), 229-240, 229.

Also, Yugoslavia became a coveted holiday destination for the citizens of the Eastern bloc. When Tito died in 1983, Yugoslavia began its slow disintegration, ending in the cruel civil war of the 1990s.

III. 1. 3 Czechoslovakia's International Relations (1945)

Clementis had to thank his friends Novomeský and Husák in the SNR for his position. The SNR had been founded in December 1943 in Moscow; it was composed of centre-right and leftist members. In the negotiations for the Košice Agreement in March 1945 in Moscow, Husák and Novomeský had suggested Clementis for the position of assistant secretary of state, praising his merits and efforts for the exile government.

Gottwald had expelled Clementis from the Party in 1939 for his criticism of the German-Soviet Nonaggression Pact; upon Husák and Novomeský's suggestion, he had inquired about the lawyer's activities in London. Loyal comrades such as Bruno Köhler ensured Gottwald that Clementis had never published his views about the pact nor discussed Stalin's politics in public.[16] Gottwald demanded a written explanation of his exile activities, which Clementis rushed to submit to him in March 1945. The gifted lawyer was now in a high position at the strategically important foreign ministry, and Gottwald renewed his Party membership on 3 July 1945. Upon nomination in late March 1945, Clementis immediately went to work.

On 8 June 1945,[17] the assistant secretary of state addressed the government, explaining Czechoslovakia's new foreign policy. As always, Clementis' descriptions were well structured,

---

[16] Holotíková a Plevza, 238-240.
[17] Clementis, "Prejav o medzinárodnej situácii z 8. Júna 1945", SNA, OF VC, carton aj 2, 34 pages, typewritten.

fact-based and logically coherent. His report was divided into two sections: first, the international situation after the Conference of Yalta in February 1945 with special regard to Czechoslovakia, and second, an assessment of the issues that immediately affected Czechoslovakia's foreign policy, including the most pressing tasks the ministry of foreign affairs had to deal with.[18] The history of the post-war treaties dealing with the Allies' division and control of Germany and the foundation of the UN in San Francisco in 1945 is well known.[19] I shall therefore focus on Clementis' activities at the MZV. In Czechoslovak terms, the post-war foreign policy was indeed new, since it was dictated by Moscow.

The basic principles of Czechoslovak foreign policy had been agreed upon in the Košice Agreement: first, the unity of the Czechs and Slovaks in their common state; second, friendly relations with the Soviet Union and the Soviet people, and third, friendly relations with the Slavic states and nations in Central, Eastern and South-Eastern Europe.[20] The path towards the future bloc of Socialist states was set, but it was not yet declared the country's official foreign policy in international forums, newspapers and the public arena. According to the assistant secretary of state, Czechoslovakia's military security was the most important issue now:

> "In the past, we could only search for our security, and we all know that we did not find it in the conditions back then. Today, we have it, and our task is to improve it and bring it to perfection, with all our effort. The pillar of our security is our treaty with the Soviet Union, which has also set the agenda of our foreign policy."[21]

---

[18] Clementis, "Prejav o medzinárodnej situácii z 8. Júna 1945", 1.
[19] The UN's official website http://www.un.org/en/index.html; accessed 9 June 2016.
[20] Clementis, "Prejav o medzinárodnej situácii z 8. Júna 1945", 22.
[21] Clementis, "Prejav o medzinárodnej situácii z 8. Júna 1945", 22.

It would be a mistake, Clementis continued, to assume that their foreign policy would now become less active than in the past – on the contrary: the great powers were the guarantee of international security, and Czechoslovakia's contribution would not be a small one. Very visible in Clementis' words was the opening rift between the West and the Soviet Union that would result in the division of the world into two ideological blocs.

Some reactionary states in the West had tried to instrumentalize Czechoslovakia to destroy the good relations between the Soviet Union and the other Great Powers, so the assistant secretary of state said. The Anglo-Saxon countries expected Czechoslovakia to establish a regime that was a kind of synthesis between Western democracy and Soviet Socialism.[22] But contrary to the beliefs of those Western diplomats, the experts at the MZV were convinced that the Soviet Union had the highest interests in Czechoslovakia's good relations with the West. Stalin had concluded the same treaty of friendship and co-operation with Great Britain and France as with Czechoslovakia. Czechoslovakia's friendly co-operation with the West would contribute to the good understanding between the Allies and thus further improve her security.

Clementis proceeded to states that were, due to problematic issues originating in the years after Munich, of particular importance for the new foreign policy. He began with Poland:

> "In the spirit of our government programme [*vládneho programu*, the Košice Agreement, add. JB] and the traditions of our nations, we want to make sure that our Slavic politics [*naša slovanská politika*] remain not only a slogan, but shall be put into practice. Therefore, preliminary difficulties shall not deter us from building good relations with the new and democratic Poland. [...] I remind you of the discussions of our delegate Hejret and our chargé d'affaires Hnízda with President Beruth and other representatives of the Polish government in Moscow, in

---

[22] Clementis, "Prejav o medzinárodnej situácii z 8. Júna 1945", 23.

which the Polish side has put forward, once more, the issue of the Tešin border."²³

In the Moscow negotiations in March 1945, Czechoslovakia had insisted on the inviolability of her borders prior to Munich, hence their full restoration; the Tešin border was thus no issue open to discussion with Poland. When a delegation of the Soviet deputy commissar Andrei Ia. Vyšinskii (1883–1954) had informed him that Moscow had sent troops to the region of Orava and Spíš,²⁴ he, Clementis said, had with a heavy heart asked the SNR to order the withdrawal of the Czechoslovak administrative organs to the border prior to Munich. The SNR had then explained to him that the Soviet troops were indeed in control of the border, but that Polish irregular troops were still terrorizing the Slovak citizens in the countryside, stealing their property.²⁵ He had informed Soviet ambassador Valerian A. Zorin (1902–1986) about the situation and sent ambassador Hejret as delegate of the SNR to negotiate with

---

23 Clementis, "Prejav o medzinárodnej situácii z 8. Júna 1945", 25. Referring to 'Beruth', Clementis' secretary had most probably made a typo. Bolesław Bierut (1892–1956) was Poland's President from 1947 to 1952; see http://www.president.pl/en/president/polish-presidents/boleslaw-bierut/; accessed 9 June 2016.
24 For a detailed account of the Czechoslovak-Polish border issue see Dušan Šegeš, "Orava: úvahy politických elit verzus realita sporného region v rokoch 1918–1947", in *Putovanie dejinami pod múrmi Oravského hradu* (Bratislava: Veda, HÚ SAV, 2015), 108-138. See further Jiří Friedl a Zdeněk Jirásek, *Rozpačíte spojenectví. Ceskoslovenské-polske vztahy v letech 1945-1949* (Praha: Aleš Křivan ml, 2008) and Marcel Jesenský, *The Slovak-Polish border 1918–1947* (New York: Palgrave Macmillan, 2014). I thank Dušan Šegeš for recommending these studies to me. Vyšinskii had been the Soviet Procurator General in the show trials of Sinoviev, Kamenev and Bukharin in 1936, 1937 and 1938. The only biography known to me is Arkady Vaksberg, *Stalin's Prosecutor. The Life of Andrei Vyshinsky* (New York: Grove Weidenfeld, 1990). The eminent British-American historian Robert Conquest (1917–2015), a specialist on Stalin, wrote the foreword.
25 Clementis, "Prejav o medzinárodnej situácii z 8. Júna 1945", 26. Clementis referred to the negotiations in Moscow in March 1945 that resulted in the Košice Agreement.

the Polish government. The Slovak citizens in the contested region should at least be allowed to leave with their movable property.[26]

A further problematic issue involving Poland were the towns and villages of Kladsko, Hlubčicko and Ratiborsko. The council of ministers knew that the foreign ministry had, in view of the information about the situation in Kladsko a delegation of citizens had brought forward, asked the Soviet government to send in troops. They had also learnt that the Polish authorities had declared the Czech population as "pre-Slavs but essentially Polish [*sa hovorí o českom obyvateľstve ako o obyvateľstve praslovanskom no poľskom*]".[27] The foreign ministry had informed Great Britain, the USA, France and Poland about these developments.

The situation in Ratiborsko and Hlubčicko was similar to the one in Kladsko. There, Polish platoons were forcing the citizens to declare themselves Polish, raise the Polish flag and attend the Polish Catholic mass. In many villages and communities, proclamations had been hung up: Ratiborsko and Hlubčicko would soon be a part of the Polish Republic. New announcements declared Ostravice and Opavice border towns of Poland. Polish commissars were already stationed in many villages and communities. The foreign ministry had to act:

> "I am calling to your attention that the population in this region, as it is well-known, is Czech, not Polish. According to paragraph 83 of the Treaty of Versailles, Hlubčicko would be ours, in case the majority of these districts would vote for Poland in a plebiscite. When they, however, voted for Germany, the stipulation of the Treaty of Versailles did not come into effect. Now, we have two possibilities: first, to ask the Soviet government for military assistance, as we did in the case of Kladsko. Or, second, to submit to the Allies a plan for the reconstruction of

---

[26] Clementis, "Prejav o medzinárodnej situácii z 8. Júna 1945", 26. Zorin was the Soviet ambassador to Czechoslovakia from 1945 to 1947.
[27] Clementis, "Prejav o medzinárodnej situácii z 8. Júna 1945", 26.

our borders and ask them for the right to occupy and control the territories that are in a similar situation to that of Kladsko."[28]

Clementis gave a brief presentation of Czechoslovak relations with the Vatican, Yugoslavia, Bulgaria, Albania, Greece, Romania, Spain and Turkey. Their relations with these countries were not problematic, since defined by the guidelines of European reconstruction the Allies had agreed on in Yalta. One state, however, demanded particular attention:

> "Our relations to Hungary are based on the armistice treaty the Soviet Union, Great Britain and the USA concluded with Hungary on 20 January 1945. According to this treaty, Hungary has to withdraw all her troops and administrative organs from Czechoslovak territory beyond the borders of 31 March 1939. The Hungarian government has committed itself to return to Czechoslovakia all valuables and materiel confiscated during the war, such as building and construction equipment, locomotives, traffic machinery, tractors, coaches, historical heritage and monuments, treasures from museums and other items. The Hungarian government has further committed itself to return to the Allies all vessels that are stationed at Hungary's shipyards on the Danube. The damage of Hungarian military operations and occupation of Czechoslovak territory amounts to one hundred million US dollars, which will be divided between Czechoslovakia and Yugoslavia. Also, the Vienna Arbitrage of 2 November 1938 has been declared invalid."[29]

According to the Soviet experts of the Allied Control Commission, Czechoslovakia and Yugoslavia had to agree, as a first step, to divide the 100 million dollars worth of the reparations between themselves. He had thus, Clementis explained, advised their representative to suggest to Yugoslavia a share of 50% each. In his view, this was more than just, since Germany and not Hungary had inflicted the material damage Yugoslavia had suffered in the war.

---

[28] Clementis, "Prejav o medzinárodnej situácii z 8. Júna 1945", 27. The armistice treaty with Hungary on http://avalon.law.yale.edu/wwii/hunga01.asp; accessed 17 June 2016.

[29] Clementis, "Prejav o medzinárodnej situácii z 8. Júna 1945", 32.

Belgrade had not yet replied, but he was sure that both countries would find a solution mutually beneficial for both.

A crucial question was how Hungary would pay the reparations? The country could export only oil, coal and hardware such as railway coaches and ships.[30] The Soviet Union had to agree with the export to Czechoslovakia, but, at the moment, the Hungarian factories were working at full capacity to send their hardware to the Soviet Union. He, Clementis said, had discussed this issue with Soviet ambassador Zorin and demanded that the Soviet Union, Yugoslavia and Czechoslovakia conclude a treaty about the organization of the reparation payments.

III. 1. 4 On Money (1946)

Clementis did not attend the inaugural meeting of the UN in San Francisco on 26 June 1945. Foreign Minister Jan Masaryk was the head of the Czechoslovak delegation; he arrived in San Francisco directly from Moscow. The government in Prague had issued no clear instructions; the delegation should attend all sessions and speak out only when Czechoslovakia's interests were at stake, following the rationale "to be seen but not to be heard".[31]

In his statement at the Foreign Affairs Committee on 31 October 1946 in New York,[32] Clementis mentioned the Paris peace negotiations, explaining Czechoslovakia's position. The peace negotiations seemed to confuse everybody and also seemed to deepen the rift between the East and West. However, as Clementis said, panic-mongers would not succeed, since the Allies could still find consensus. The Big Four, the foreign ministers of the USA,

---

[30] Clementis, "Prejav o medzinárodnej situácii z 8. Júna 1945", 33-34.
[31] Michálek, *San Francisco 1945*, 105.
[32] "Statement by Secretary of State Dr VLADIMÍR CLEMENTIS, delivered in the Foreign Affairs Committee of the Constituent National Assembly on 31 October, 1946", SNA, OF VC, carton aj 14, 21 pages, English, typewritten.

USSR, France and Great Britain, had demonstrated their unity and unanimity in three political areas. His tone was slightly sarcastic:

> "The first is Trieste and the complex of questions connected therewith, the second is the Danube, and the third consists of questions of an economic character. Of these three problems, only the problem of Trieste came exclusively within the competence of the Peace Conference and was settled, [...] whereas the question of the Danube could not be settled at the Conference where the peace treaties with defeated and ex-satellite States were under discussion and where it was, naturally, not possible to settle questions concerning, for instance, the sovereign rights of Czechoslovakia and Yugoslavia, as the states most interested in the Danube."[33]

At the peace negotiations, Clementis stressed, Czechoslovakia's principal interest was the conclusion of a treaty with Hungary. Czechoslovakia supported Yugoslavia's claims for the port of Trieste, since it would guarantee that both states could make maximum use of it for their trade relations. Also, Czechoslovakia did everything in her power to help Bulgaria and Romania, two former allies of Germany, to conclude fair peace treaties; Czechoslovakia had presented no special demands to Italy in order not to burden the country unnecessarily.

One did not have to be a fierce anti-Communist to suspect that Czechoslovakia's foreign policy was being made in Moscow, not in Prague. The agenda and rationale were in perfect tune with the Soviet Union's principal strategic interest in Europe: to keep the countries liberated by the Red Army under Soviet control and build up a Socialist bloc to counteract US influence in Europe.

In the second part of his statement, Clementis addressed Czechoslovak-US relations, in particular the position of the US

---

[33] "Statement by Secretary of State …", 3. The "ex-satellite States" Clementis referred to were Germany's former allies.

State Department about issuing credits to Czechoslovakia.[34] In the text of the Košice Agreement and Prime Minister Gottwald's note, one could find explicit thanks to the US support of the Czechoslovak struggle for independence. The Czechoslovak people were grateful for US economic support, in particular the UNRRA.[35] In view of the country's experience before and after Munich, the sincere and firm friendship with the Soviet Union was a fact. But this friendship did not have to interfere with maintaining good relations with the USA, certainly not from the Czechoslovak side. Yet, as the Czechoslovak delegation had experienced in Paris, members of the US delegation had shown no understanding for Czechoslovakia's most important demands: first, the population transfer of 200,000 Hungarians and, second, the return of the shipping on the Danube the US military administration was holding back:[36]

> "These conflicts with the American delegation resulted from the fact that we defended our principles, our requirements and our vital interests and that the aforesaid delegation defended her own conceptions and interests. It is a natural manifestation of international life, which, under normal conditions and in a normal atmosphere, would have not the slightest influence on inter-state relations. It would certainly be irresponsible to abandon one's vital interests for some absolute harmony or eulogy."[37]

Proof of Czechoslovakia's sovereignty was the fact that the delegation had voted against some suggestions the Soviet Union had put forward. Clementis did not elaborate, recapitulating briefly US-Czechoslovak trade relations.

The US had ended the trade agreement between the two countries in 1945; it had been suspended already in 1939. Since

---

[34] Excellent analysis of US-Czechoslovak economic relations from 1945 to 1951 is Slavomír Michálek, *Nádeje a vytriezvenia (Československo-americké hospodárske vzťahy v rokoch 1945–1951)* (Bratislava: Veda, SAV HÚ, 1995).
[35] "Statement by Secretary of State ...", 13.
[36] "Statement by Secretary of State ...", 14.
[37] "Statement by Secretary of State ...", 14.

the end of the war, Czechoslovakia had been trying to negotiate a new agreement. The USA had presented a draft, which contained an alteration of the principle of most-favoured nation treatment. Czechoslovakia had accepted the proposal, asking only for two points to be modified. The USA had rejected this demand, and a new round of negotiations had started in September 1946. Further negotiations included a credit of 50 million US dollars to purchase surplus war materiel from the USA; Czechoslovakia had already drawn 10 million US dollars against this loan, having bought cotton in the amount of 2 million dollars. Czechoslovakia had also started negotiations about a 50-million-dollar loan from the Export-Import Bank for the purchase of machinery and raw materials from the USA.[38] Both states had been negotiating about a new trade agreement, and things seemed to proceed well, when the USA, all of a sudden, stopped the sale of surplus war material on 14 September. On 28 September, the US State Department had also announced the suspension of the credit negotiations with the Import-Export Bank.[39]

In a careful, serious and diplomatic tone, Clementis explained that both governments would overcome the present difficulties. From the Czechoslovak viewpoint, there was no reason for the negotiations to stop. I think that the assistant secretary of state knew perfectly well why the USA had suspended the credit and the negotiations about a trade agreement – not so much because Czechoslovak diplomats had complained to the US ambassador of being "discriminated against" by US military authorities in their purchases of war material. The head of the economic department of the Czechoslovak mission had formally apologized to the US ambassador for the term 'discrimination'.[40]

---

[38] "Statement by Secretary of State …", 15.
[39] "Statement by Secretary of State …", 16.
[40] "Statement by Secretary of State …", 17.

The US authorities had told the Czechoslovak diplomats in clear words that they had stopped the sale because Czechoslovakia had sold to Romania a part of the war material she had purchased from the US, a clear sign of profit-making. The real reason for the difficulties with the USA were Czechoslovakia's relations with the Soviet Union and the states under Soviet control, Romania being one of them. Clementis must have also known that the USA had formulated its announcement in diplomatic terms; the US diplomats did not want to push the Czechoslovak government against the wall.

In 1946, Czechoslovakia was not yet an official member of the Soviet bloc. From the US point of view, the Cold War was just beginning, but Czechoslovakia was not yet lost.[41] The fact that US military authorities had stopped the sale can be seen as proof that they had suspicions that Czechoslovakia was acting as a kind of *economic Trojan horse*, buying sensitive material from the USA and then selling it to states in the Soviet sphere of influence, thereby strengthening their economy. I consider it very likely that

---

[41] Pavel Tigrid (1917–2003), the future founder of the Czechoslovak exile journal *Rozmluvy* that was published in Paris from 1960 to 1989, saw through the Party's smoke screen early on. On 14 July 1946, he published an article in the *Lidové demokracie* entitled "The perennial question of our times"', stating that the ČSR had joined the Soviet bloc and would, in case of war, stand with Stalin's army against the West, although Czechoslovakia and her people shared the West's political, cultural and religious traditions. The presidency of the NF convened the next day and discussed Tigrid's article. Gottwald criticized him, and Clementis, who knew Tigrid from London exile, said that 'such a damaging article had never been published before' and that 'the MZV, where the author (Tigrid) was employed, would immediately take disciplinary steps and dismiss him'." Quoted from Milan Drápala, "Na ztracené varte západu. Antologie české nesocialistické publicistiky z let 1945 – 1948" (Praha: Prostor, 2000), 166. Drápala referred to "Zápis o 2. schôdzi predsedníctva 3. vlády 15. júla 1946", Státní ústrední archiv, Praha, fond 100/24 (Klement Gottwald), archívna jednotka 1495. I thank Vlasta Jaksicsová for this information, the source and the archival source.

had Czechoslovakia sold the material, for example, to Italy or France, the USA would not have stopped the sale. With his smooth talk, cleverly creating a smoke screen, Clementis tried to quiet US suspicions of increasing Soviet influence in Central and Eastern Europe. He focussed on details, used a lawyer's way of expressing himself and deliberately ignored the real issue at stake:

> "The facts are as follows: – On September 14, 1946 an agreement was signed between Romania and Czechoslovakia concerning the re-sale to Rumania of the material bought by us, to the amount of 10 million Dollars. The agreement indeed contained the provision whereby Rumania shall be bound to pay us administrative expenses amounting to 7% of the purchase price, the agreement also providing for interest rates applicable in the event of non-payment which differed from the interest rate by which we ourselves were bound towards the United States. *According to the interpretation of our legal experts*, the stipulation concerning administrative expenses is a stipulation of actual outlays, i.e. the contracting party has a right to demand particulars of such outlays, thus making it impossible for any tendency to profit-making to be hidden under the cloak of the said stipulation; a stipulation of interest on unpaid balances surely cannot be qualified as a profit title."[42]

I am neither an economist nor an expert in Public International Law, but if we scrutinize this quote in the political context, it is obvious that Clementis presented to the Committee a legally and juridically flawless picture of Czechoslovakia's re-sale of materiel purchased from the USA with a US loan. The interest rates of the Romanian-Czechoslovak trade agreement were not the issue here – but Romania as the receiving end of Czechoslovakia's trade and credit activities with the USA.

The main reason for the suspension of the credit negotiations with the Import-Export Bank, as the US authorities had explained, was the fact that Czechoslovakia and the USA had not yet reached an agreement about the compensation of US property

---

[42] "Statement by Secretary of State ...", 18, italics by me.

that had been nationalized in Czechoslovakia.[43] Clementis argued with cleverly reserved emotion, appealing shrewdly to American generosity, pragmatism and sense of equality. He insisted that Czechoslovakia should be granted the credit:

> "In my opinion, it is due to the unequal distribution of the holding of raw materials and possibilities of production in the world that credit operations have become an essential part of the normal flow of international trade. [...] The question for the credit giver is whether he is not only sufficiently assured that his merchandise will be taken over and duly marketed, but also whether he has the guarantee that the credit will be duly paid for. I think it is open to no doubt that Czechoslovakia both in the past and now has always properly fulfilled her obligations, [...] In all her international negotiations concreted with matters commercial, financial and economic, irrespective of whether they are being conducted with Allied, friendly or other countries, Czechoslovakia is looking after her own interests and will accept only such agreements which in no way impair her sovereignty."[44]

Clementis portrayed Czechoslovakia as a sovereign country interested only in normal trade relations with the USA. He admitted that his country's economic situation was better than that of other European states, which had also received credits from the USA. The Czechoslovak government considered the halting of the credit negotiations as a "passing phenomenon, brought about partly by misunderstandings, partly by certain objective circumstances".[45] Unlike the press of other countries – Clementis did not name them – the Czechoslovak press reported the issue correctly, which was further proof of the common sense and sovereignty of Czechoslovakia.

The diplomatic tone and focus on Czechoslovakia's sovereignty Clementis used in his appeal to convince the UN Foreign Affairs Committee of his country's credit-worthiness, was one

---

[43] "Statement by Secretary of State ...", 19.
[44] "Statement by Secretary of State ...", 19.
[45] "Statement by Secretary of State ...", 20-21.

thing – quite another one was his speech about the new foreign policy to the Czechoslovak public, the people at home.

III. 1. 5 Czechoslovakia's New Foreign Policy (1947)

In a lecture on 17 February 1947 at the Socialist Academy in Prague,[46] Clementis delivered a summary of Czechoslovakia's foreign policy, its past, present, orientation and goals.[47]

Foreign policy was no longer the game of the aristocracy that had deeply affected the lives of the ruled. The worldwide trend towards democratization had resulted in a paradox: the people could follow domestic affairs and their development, but could not yet understand the new foreign policy. Yet, the years prior to Munich and the war had changed the public's perception of foreign policy, because the citizens had witnessed the changes of borders and political regimes in the region. The basic principles of the new Czechoslovak foreign policy had been formulated in exile during the war; specific acts, for example, the Treaty of Alliance with the Soviet Union, had fixed the state's new political orientation.

It was true, Clementis said, that under the leadership of Foreign Minister Beneš in the interwar years, the country had tried to establish its security by joining a system of collective security and improve relations with the Soviet Union. He spoke of 'objective conditions', a key concept of Marxist theory:

> "But, back then, no objective international conditions were given for a system of collective security to work, nor did objective conditions exist in domestic affairs. [...] Finally, with regard to the duties and rights of the people, the following has to be stressed: the political and economic

---

[46] In its zeal to educate workers and farmers in Socialist thought, the KSČ had established the academy in 1936 with Zdeněk Nejedlý as one of its prominent lecturers: http://www.cojeco.cz/index.php?detail=1&id_desc=88652&title= Socialistick%E1%20akademie&s_lang=2; accessed 19 June 2016.

[47] Clementis, *Naša zahraničná politika* (Praha: Orbis, 1947).

> building and rebuilding [*výstavba a prestavba*] of the post-war world are moving forward on two different tracks – in the framework of the peace conferences and the institutions that are preparing them – and in the framework of the United Nations."[48]

He would not delve into academic definitions about foreign policy; under consideration of the legal aspects of their new foreign policy, the government had decided to create two new ministries: the ministry of international trade and the ministry of information.[49]

Clementis addressed the Germans and the Hungarians. After lengthy explanations how these minorities had destroyed the Czechoslovak Republic, he defended Czechoslovakia's Slavic policy, criticizing Western politicians who were referring to the co-operation of Yugoslavia, Czechoslovakia and Poland as "Russia's satellites":[50]

> "I am deeply convinced that the co-operation of the Slavic nations is a decisive factor for stabilizing the world; it will ensure a lasting peace. Although they are often applying different methods, all Slavic nations are building political and economic systems today that are fundamentally just and progressive. [...] These systems are capable of mobilizing the nations' moral and creative forces [*mobilizovat morálne i tvorčie sily*] for the establishing of state institutions."[51]

He continued with brief explanations about Germany under Allied occupation. The "objective requirement" of the Allied administration was to make absolutely sure that Germany did not have the materiel to embark on a new campaign of military aggression; contrary to Western beliefs, a division of Germany into a western federalized part and a centrally governed eastern part would be the source of a renewal of German nationalism and Pangermanic thought.[52] Clementis defended the Soviet view: the Soviets were

---

[48] Clementis, *Naša zahraničná politika*, 6-7.
[49] Clementis, *Naša zahraničná politika*, 7.
[50] Clementis, *Naša zahraničná politika*, 12.
[51] Clementis, *Naša zahraničná politika*, 12.
[52] Clementis, *Naša zahraničná politika*, 16.

against a partition of Germany because they feared that the western part would become a member of a new Western military alliance. Stalin wanted Germany to become a neutral buffer zone between the Western and Soviet zones.

After the sad experience with the League of Nations in the 1920s, Clementis explained, every realistic statesman knew that the UN had to avoid the mistakes and misgivings that had led to the dysfunctional *modus operandi* of the League:

> "In the final phases of the war, in Dumbarton Oaks, at the Crimea conference with Roosevelt, Stalin and Churchill and, finally, at the conference of the United Nations in San Franciso, the Charter of the United Nations was born. It has solved, in a healthy and balanced fashion, the grave problems the peace-loving democratic states had faced. [...] As in a state, the Security Council [*bezpečnostná rada*] is the executive organ of the United Nations; it can act only with the consent of all five permanent members, that is, the unity and unanimity of the Great Powers. If one member refuses to consent, that is called the 'veto', so often spoken and written about recently, also in the sessions of the last UN General Assembly."[53]

The structure of the Security Council had been created to make it operational and effective, to avoid the shortcomings of the League of Nations, but it had resulted in misunderstandings, as Clementis elaborated. At the Paris Peace Concerence in 1946, the Anglo-Saxon Great Powers had tried to reject some of the Soviet Union's suggestions by voting. Or, in other words, the imperative of finding a friendly compromise had been replaced with, as they called it in Paris, "the mathematics of voting".[54]

Clementis accused the Western Powers of creating an anti-Soviet atmosphere; deliberately and subtly, he blended the Security Council's voting procedure with the negotiations at the Paris

---

[53] Clementis, *Naša zahraničná politika*, 19.
[54] Clementis, *Naša zahraničná politika*, 19.

Peace Conference – two completely different institutions and procedures. The Peace Conference's main task was to negotiate about borders and reparations; its main focus was the past, redressing the damage and injustices of war. The Security Council's task, on the other hand, was to prevent war, secure peace in the future and preside over the UN. Although some delegates thought that the stipulations of the UN should be applied to the peace negotiations, Yalta and Potsdam were the binding treaties for the Paris Peace Conference, not the UN Security Council's voting procedure.

The reparation demands of Great Britain and the USA and their dispute about it were not the same as a veto in the UN Security Council – but they seemed to be because Clementis presented them so. In the minds of his listeners and workers trying to get an education at the Socialist Academy, his lecture created great confusion, which was working to the advantage of Soviet foreign policy principles.

Clementis deliberately manipulated the facts. Adding the UN General Assembly to his explanations, he perfected his deliberate confusion of the public; as a lawyer, he could very well tell the difference between the procedures of the Paris Peace Conference and the stipulations of the UN Security Council, but he did not inform the public about this crucial difference. Therefore, I can call his lecture at the Socialist Academy only a deliberate misinformation. That the Western Allies had their own reasons was of no concern to him; he was obviously not interested in presenting a fair and balanced analysis of the Paris Peace Conference and the UN.

The assistant secretary of state concluded his lecture with a few words about criticism. The new Czechoslovak foreign policy had distinct aspects that the public should respect, and he was always open to constructive and creative criticism. The basis of any criticism, however, was profound knowledge of the facts and the good will to contribute to the cause without any ulterior, selfish and shortsighted interests.[55] Clementis quoted centre-right newspapers that criticized his lack of success in negotiating the expulsion of the Hungarians at the Paris Peace Conference. They had reproached him that Czechoslovakia's alliance with the Soviet Union was damaging the country's political interests. The centre-right journalists had written that the negotiations about the Magyar *odsun* would have been more successful if Czechoslovakia's foreign policy was oriented towards the West, hinting at the past politics of President Masaryk.

Clementis, with utter contempt for the freedom of opinion and the press, called the journalists' criticism naïve; he sounded arrogant, but he was spot on in political terms: [56] would the USA and Great Britain have agreed to the transfer of 200,000 Hungarians if Czechoslovakia had not been an ally of the Soviet Union? Certainly not – and Clementis had a point here: the transfer of the Hungarians from Slovakia was not an important issue for the Western Allies. They had no clue about what was going on between the Slovaks and the Hungarians. Stalin was not too interested in this issue either; if the Slovaks and Hungarians could not live peacefully together in Czechoslovakia, a population transfer was a rational solution. To the Americans, the transfer was a human rights issue – to Stalin, an issue of preparing the Communist take-over in both Czechoslovakia and Hungary. The Western Allies were much more familiar with the Sudeten German issue than Hungary's activities in Slovakia prior to and during WWII.

In 1947, freedom of the press still existed in Czechoslovakia, but not in Clementis' mind; as we have seen in his pre-war articles, tolerance towards views differing from the Party line was not a characteristic feature of his. I had the impression that he was

---

[55] Clementis, *Naša zahraničná politika*, 21.
[56] Clementis, *Naša zahraničná politika*, 22-23.

grateful that Gottwald had taken him back into the Party, his intellectual home. That was the reason why he excelled in following Stalin's policy of keeping good relations with the Western Allies, trying to lull them into believing that Czechoslovakia was a sovereign and democratic state oriented towards the West.

Clementis was not open to criticism – he just pretended to be. How more creative and constructive could criticism be than questioning the very principles of the country's foreign policy and suggesting a change of course? Where did constructive criticism begin and where did it end? In Clementis' mindset, the only criticism that was worthy of its name was Lenin's conception of inner-Party democracy; only a Party member could express constructive and creative criticism, within the limits of Marxism-Leninism, of course – and it was Stalin who dictated these limits. Class consciousness was everything: since centre-right journalists and politicians lacked proper class-consciousness in the Marxist-Leninist way of thinking, their criticism was neither creative nor constructive, it was nothing more than bourgeois anti-Soviet rhetoric.

On 10 November 1947, the assistant secretary of state spoke to a public that was better educated: the members of the Club of Lawyers, a professional association.[57] His theme was "The UN and some of its legal problems". After a few introductory remarks about the origins of the UN, Clementis addressed the legal aspects:

> "In terms of law, the UN Charter is organized on the basis of the principles accepted by international institutions; it is the most significant normative act in the area of international law, endowed with complicated and often far-reaching powers."[58]

---

[57] Clementis, "Prednáška v klube právnikov na tému: Spojené národy a niektoré z ich právnych problémov", SNA, OF VC, carton aj 21, 14 pages, typewritten.
[58] Clementis, "Prednáška v klube …", 1.

Legal norms and principles were one thing, Clementis said, but some states and the Great Powers, in particular, could always find ways to sidestep them, ignoring legal norms. The short history of the UN only confirmed this sad fact. The Great Troika, Roosevelt, Stalin and Churchill, had discussed all the consequences of the international situation at Yalta: the equality of military strength of the three had been the reason why they had agreed that the principle of unanimity should form the basis of the Security Council, the UN's most important institution.[59] Yet, the principle of unanimity had caused problems already at the first session of the General Assembly:

> "If article 108 and the following articles of the Charter exclude the possibility of a successful revision of the 'veto' in the General Assembly, a dangerous attempt has been made: the destruction of the principle of unanimity with the indirect subjection of the General Assembly by the 'little assembly' [the Security Council, add. JB]."[60]

Clementis criticized the stipulations about the voting in the UN General Assembly. Article 108 says: "Amendments to the present Charter shall come into force for all Members of the United Nations when they have been adopted by a vote of two thirds of the members of the General Assembly and ratified in accordance with their respective constitutional processes by two thirds of the Members of the United Nations, including all the permanent members of the Security Council."[61] In order to amend the articles of the Charter, all permanent members of the Security Council had to agree; thus, if one member put in his veto, it rendered invalid the votes of two thirds of the member nations of the General Assembly. This meant that the instrument of the veto in the Security

---

[59] Clementis, "Prednáška v klube …", 2.
[60] Clementis, "Prednáška v klube …", 3.
[61] http://www.un.org/en/sections/un-charter/chapter-xviii/index.html; accessed 21 June 2016.

Council had immediate consequences for the General Assembly – to amend the Charter was impossible because only the permanent members of the Security Council had the right to veto – not exactly a democratic procedure, in Clementis view.

Czechoslovakia was trying to defend the fundamental principles of the UN Charter in the current crisis. Often, the hostile discussions of the Great Powers had their origins in areas where the UN had no jurisdiction. The post-war world was built on two tracks, the peace conferences and the UN. The most pressing issues were Germany and Japan and therefore also the Far East.[62] A politician reasoning in a sober fashion had to count with all possible problems in the early phase of the UN that was organizing the new world order, but the Czechoslovak diplomats had not expected that a particular tendency would emerge: Western attempts at circumventing the UN, for example, Truman's support of Greece and Turkey, but, first and foremost, the so-called Marshall Plan:[63]

> "These are but variants of recent American foreign policy, which one can only characterize as attempts at a revision of the fundamental principles agreed upon during and after the war, as attempts at a revision of some fundamental treaties, for example, the Treaty of Potsdam."[64]

In Clementis' view, the US support of Greece and Turkey should have been discussed with the Allies, especially the Soviet Union; the USA, on the other hand, considered the support of Greece and Turkey a decision of its independent foreign policy. Thus, while the Western Allies considered Yalta and Potsdam as political treaties that focussed on what to do with Germany and Europe after the war, the Soviet Union conceived of Yalta and Potsdam as a guideline for future relations with the West, based on the equality

---

[62] Clementis, "Přednáška v klube ...", 4-5.
[63] Clementis, "Přednáška v klube ...", 5.
[64] Clementis, "Přednáška v klube ...", 5.

of the nations and armies that had defeated Germany. It was the different view of sovereignty and the economic system that finally led to the Cold War: the Western Allies acknowledged a limited sovereignty of what would become West Germany and supported it with the Marshall Plan, while the states in the Soviet hemisphere had lost their sovereign decision-making at the moment of liberation by the Red Army – no chance for them to join the Marshall Plan.

Clementis finished with his criticism of the UN Charter, referring to its "meta-judicial character" that was prompting political solutions and decisions to the West's advantage, although these decisions and solution would rightly belong to the domain of Public International Law.[65] The former Allies' different interpretations of the Charter were at the core of this problem.

Again, Clementis presented his public with a one-sided interpretation: as a lawyer involved in the sessions of the UN, he must have been aware that Public International Law changed after WWII, the UN being an attempt at creating a legal basis for the future of international relations. Since there was no supra-national institution above the UN Security Council, it operated according to the power of its members – and the former Big Three, the USA, the USSR and Great Britain, were now becoming increasingly divided, because of their different political systems and intellectual orientation.

III. 1. 6 On Germany and the Marshall Plan (1947)

From the Soviet Union's viewpoint, the Marshall Plan went against Soviet interests, facilitating the West's political and ideological intrusion into the Soviet sphere of influence under the guise of economic reconstruction and humanitarian aid. Clementis, naturally,

---

[65] Clementis, "Přednáška v klube ...", 7-9.

shared this view. Stalin and Gottwald had made sure that the National Front was keeping its pseudo-democratic face in domestic affairs as much as in international relations. But the moment of putting the cards on the table came when the USA presented a plan for the economic reconstruction of Europe.

After George C. Marshall had announced his plan on 5 June 1947 at Harvard University,[66] Stalin issued a clear order: the states in the Soviet sphere of influence were not to participate in the Marshall Plan talks scheduled for July 1947 in Paris. The British *Daily Telegraph* reported on 11 July 1947 that, in view of the fact that the Czechoslovak government had accepted the Anglo-French invitation to the conference three days ago, the pressure of the Soviet Union had made it back out now.[67]

On 2 December 1947, Clementis explained Czechoslovakia's foreign policy with regard to Germany and the decision not to join the Marshall Plan to the UN Foreign Affairs Committee.[68] The statements of Foreign Minister Masaryk and himself about Germany had not changed since the end of the war, as the assistant secretary of state said in his opening address. The main issue of Czechoslovakia's foreign policy was security, which could be achieved only with a significant change of Germany's economy, domestic affairs and, also, psychology:

> "We have consistently recommended such things as decartelisation, land reform, nationalisation of Nazi-owned enterprises, control of Germany's currency policy and foreign trade and the accelerated carrying out of her economic and, of course, her military disarmament in co-ordination with a thorough, consistent de-Nazification, demilitarisation,

---

[66] For the plan's details go to http://marshallfoundation.org/marshall/the-marshall-plan/; accessed 24 June 2016.
[67] *The Daily Telegraph*, 11. VII. 1947, SNA, OF VC, carton aj 1, 19.
[68] *Statement made by Dr. Vl. Clementis before the Foreign Affairs Committee of the Constituent National Assembly on December 2, 1947 on the subject of Germany* (Praha: Orbis, 1947).

re-education in democracy and the honouring on Germany's part of her reparation obligations."[69]

In principle, Czechoslovakia endorsed the economic and political unity of Germany, but recent developments were going in the wrong direction. The Western Allies had not kept to the political course agreed upon in Yalta and Potsdam,[70] and because the Soviet Union had insisted on keeping to those principles, the current political atmosphere among the Big Four was now displaying ideological tensions. One had to fear that Germany would be divided into two parts if the former Allies would not reconcile. The West had started this unfortunate development: it had arranged for the political conditions that a part of the reparations remain in Germany and, simultaneously, instigated an anti-Soviet press campaign, General Clay's so-called anti-Communist crusade.[71]

The West was also responsible for the meagre results of de-Nazification, because it had handed over control of the de-Nazification programme to the German authorities. Without the Soviet Union's consent, the representatives of the Marshall Plan considered the western part of Germany an integral element under the jurisdiction of the Western Allies. Thus, while the USA, GB and France, occupying the western zones, were interested in a quick economic reconstruction of what would soon be called West Germany, the Soviet Union and the states in her sphere of influence considered Germany's reconstruction a violation of the Allies' unity and unanimity, agreed upon in Yalta and Potsdam.

Clementis presented an example of the lack of fairness in distributing the reparations. The Potsdam Treaty was the basis of the Reparation Plan the Allied Control Commission had published

---

[69] *Statement made by Dr. Vl. Clementis* ..., 8.
[70] The text of the Potsdam Conference of 17 July to 2 August 1945 on http://avalon.law.yale.edu/20th_century/decade17.asp; accessed 24 June 2016.
[71] *Statement made by Dr. Vl. Clementis* ..., 12.

in March 1946. The Plan had defined the parts of German industry that had to be abolished and fixed the various branches of industry Germany needed for economic survival.[72] The plants that had already been liquidated and surplus equipment were destined as reparation payments, but the system did not benefit the states Germany had occupied, annihilated and plundered in the war – on the contrary:

> "Czechoslovakia had allocated up to the end of September 1947 industrial equipment to the value of slightly more than *19 million Reichsmark*, equal to almost 5 million pre-war dollars. Since our quota in Category B [ships and industrial equipment, add. JB] amounts to 4.3 per cent, our claim per September 30, 1947 figured roughly at 14.6 million Reichsmark. It means that we had an excess allocation of 4.5 millions or 31 per cent more than was due to us."[73]

In view of these figures, the assistant secretary of state said, Czechoslovakia had nothing to complain about; yet, in absolute figures, the reparations were much too low, considering the colossal damage caused by the war. Of the industrial equipment allocated, only 50% had reached Czechoslovakia from Germany, because dismantling and transportation were technically complicated, taking up much time. The West had unilaterally prepared and proclaimed the bizonal Marshall Plan, to which the Soviet Union had not given consent. Not only did the plan downsize the reparation material by keeping factories and equipment in the Western zones of Germany for the reconstruction of Germany's economy, but it was also putting Europe's peace in danger, since it was effectively raising the German standard of living at the expense of the countries Germany had destroyed and devastated in the war.[74] The Marshall Plan was therefore a violation and disrespect of the guiding principles of the Potsdam Conference.

---

[72] *Statement made by Dr. Vl. Clementis ...*, 13-14.
[73] *Statement made by Dr. Vl. Clementis ...*, 14.
[74] *Statement made by Dr. Vl. Clementis ...*, 16-17.

After brief words about the restitution of currency (mint gold) and the publication of German patents, Clementis addressed a theme that was of considerable concern to the Czechoslovak government: the activities of the Sudeten Germans in the Western zone, whom he called "the transferred Germans".[75]

According to Czechoslovak statistical data, 2,251,00 persons had been transferred to Germany; 1,464,00 went to the American zone and 792,000 to the Soviet zone. The legal basis for the transfer – Clementis avoided the word 'expulsion' (*odsun*) – had been fixed in the Potsdam Conference and the Czechoslovak agreement with the Allied Control Council. Czechoslovakia had submitted to the Council the governmental decrees no. 33/45 about state citizenship and nos. 12/45 and 108/45 about confiscation of enemy property to stress the transfer's legality and legitimacy.[76] The Germans transferred to the Soviet zone had been placed to work in the industry according to their skills and qualifications; because of the reforms in agriculture in the Soviet zone, the transferred Germans there had received land allotments. Their political status was equal to the Germans living there, and the formation of political organizations outside the existing political parties was prohibited.[77] Not so in the Western zone:

> "According to the findings of the American Information Control Division, 95 per cent of the transferees consider their removal from Czechoslovakia unlawful and unjust."[78]

Clementis listed four main goals of the Sudeten Germans' association, explaining their revisionist and irredentist activities. They wanted, first, to return to Czechoslovakia; second, they were put-

---

[75] *Statement made by Dr. Vl. Clementis ...*, 16-17.
[76] *Statement made by Dr. Vl. Clementis ...*, 21.
[77] *Statement made by Dr. Vl. Clementis ...*, 22.
[78] *Statement made by Dr. Vl. Clementis ...*, 22.

ting together lists of property that was left behind in Czechoslovakia with the intention of using these records for claims for financial compensation. Third, they were collecting personal memories of the transfer; their publication should demonstrate to the world the injustice they had suffered; fourth, they were informing the Germans still living in Czechoslovakia about their transfer, trying to instigate them to demand minority rights.[79] In view of the Sudeten Germans' activities, the West's ignorance and *laisser faire* policy was a violation of the principles of the Potsdam Conference.

At the end of his speech, Clementis expressed his hope that the Allies would find common ground for solving these issues. He warned the Foreign Affairs Committee of the Marshall Plan: it would allow Germany to rise again and become a danger to peace once more.

III. 1. 7 The Slovak-Hungarian Transfer of Population (1945–1949)

In this subchapter, I present an overview of the population transfer, highlighting the Slovak and Hungarian viewpoints that mutually excluded each other until 1949, when the Communist Parties of both countries had assumed power and thus had, by command of Stalin, found an agreement.

Although Czechoslovakia was on the victorious side, the transfer of Hungarians from Slovakia to Hungary and Slovaks from Hungary to Czechoslovakia proved to be more complicated than the expulsion of the Germans: the Allies did not approve of an *odsun* of the Hungarians because, unlike the former activities of the Sudeten Germans in the Czech part, the Hungarians' activities in Southern Slovakia were practically unknown to the international public. In the Vienna Arbitrage of 1938 and the Small War

---

[79] *Statement made by Dr. Vl. Clementis …*, 22.

of 1939 that had been immediate consequences of the Munich Agreement, Hungary had used Czechoslovakia's weakness to occupy territory in the south and south-east of Slovakia, where the Hungarian minority lived. After the Red Army had conquered Budapest, Hungary had signed the Armistice Treaty in January 1945, which Clementis had mentioned in his speech to the government on 8 June 1945.

With Minister of Defence General Ludvík Svoboda (1895–1975), the assistant secretary of state had gone on an inspection tour to the south; from 12 to 14 June 1945, they had visited Bratislava, Komárno, Nové Zámky, Levice, Lučenec and Rimavská Sobota.[80] In his report to the government that was classified *Tajné* (secret), Clementis described the political situation as unstable overall and potentially dangerous:

> "In many towns such as Komárno and Nové Zámky, troops have been stationed there only for a short time; the Hungarians form the majority of the population. That is the reason why taking control of the border region is very slow. In their unrestricted propaganda activities and provocative behaviour, the Hungarian citizens and deserters are using all means to create turmoil, insecurity and disruption among our people."[81]

While the representatives of the Czechoslovak National Committees and the local authorities had been either too weak or too indecisive to effectively counteract the Hungarian activities, the So-

---

[80] "Zpráva štátneho tajomníka v MNO o inšpekčnej ceste ministra NO a štát. tajomníka po južnom pohraničí Slovenska", AMZV, GS-A 1945-1954, carton no. 164, 6 pages, typewritten, 4-6. General Svoboda was a Czechoslovak national hero who had fought with the *Legia* in WWI. In 1944, he advanced with the 1st Czechoslovak Army Corps on the Eastern Front and liberated Eastern Slovakia with the Red Army. He would serve as Czechoslovak president after the invasion of 1968. For a short biography see https://www.hrad.cz/en/president-of-the-cr/former-presidents/ludvik-svoboda; accessed 29 June 2016.

[81] "Zpráva štátneho ...", 1.

viet troops stationed there lacked crucial information. The transfer of Hungarians from the Slovak part of Czechoslovakia to Hungary was proceeding very slowly. Members of the Hungarian Iron Cross and other fascist organizations had been systematically joining the Hungarian Communist Party, under whose protection they had continued their anti-Czechoslovak activities. This had been especially dangerous, since the uninformed Soviet authorities had allowed the new comrades to carry weapons and move around freely.[82] The co-operation of the local Slovak authorities with the Soviets, however, had been very friendly.

On 27 February 1946, Hungary and Czechoslovakia signed an agreement about the exchange of population;[83] in the protocol, Clementis was referred to as secretary of state, although he was assistant secretary of state. Jan Masaryk was acting secretary of state. The government chose Clementis for these difficult negotiations, because he understood Hungarian and was familiar with the Slovak-Hungarian problem; to be on an equal footing with the Hungarian Foreign Minister János Gyöngyössi, he had to be declared foreign minister.

ARTICLE 1 of the agreement fixed the basic principles of the transfer: voluntariness and reciprocity. Those citizens of Czech or Slovak nationality who wanted to leave Hungary would become Czechoslovak citizens by their act of immigration to Czechoslovakia; the same applied to Czechoslovak citizens of Hungarian nationality who wished to leave for Hungary. A special commission of Czechoslovaks and Hungarians would oversee the transfer (articles II, III, IV). According to law no. 33/1945, the Czechoslovak government had the right to transfer those Hungarians who had lost their Czechoslovak citizenship because of their

---

[82] "Zpráva štátneho ...", 3.
[83] "AGREEMENT between Czechoslovakia and Hungary concerning Exchange of Population", AMZV, GS-A 1945–1954, carton no. 164, 11 pages, type-written, 1.

anti-state activities before and during the war. The civil rights and duties pertaining to the state one left expired on emigration. Everybody willing to emigrate was allowed to take their movable property, and no taxes, duties or charges were imposed (article VI).[84] Manuscripts, documents, archives and other written material that was of essential interest for commerce, business, industry and agriculture of both states had to remain in the country the person emigrated from. The Special Commission would fix the sum of financial compensation for real estate property (article VII).

The detailed conduct of the transfer was listed in the supplement to the agreement. Persons wanting to leave Czechoslovakia had to submit a declaration of intention; parents, guardians and foster parents were allowed to sign on behalf of legitimate and illegitimate children under the age of 18, and married couples could sign on behalf of their spouse (paragraph 1). Paragraph 2 expressed the Czechoslovak trauma of Munich:

> "Refusal to allow entry into Czechoslovak territory as provided for in this paragraph may be justified in particular on the following grounds: *clear expression of an anti-democratic attitude*, hostile acts against the Slovak or Czech nation or any other of the Allied Nations, punishable offences of a grave nature falling within the provisions of criminal law."[85]

Contrary to her signature on the Armistice Treaty and the bilateral agreement on population exchange, Hungary tried to protract the population transfer, making it an international issue at the Paris Peace Conference. On 18 September 1946, Hungary's delegate Aladár Szegedy-Maszák explained his country's position; he said

---

[84] "AGREEMENT ...", 4.
[85] "AGREEMENT ...", 9, emphasis by me.

that Clementis, in his speech of 16 September, had based his arguments on "some erroneous and inexact facts".[86] According to the Czechoslovak Under-Secretary of State, 450,000 Slovaks were living in Hungary. The Hungarian census of 1930 had counted only 104,000 Slovaks. Clementis had also maintained that 570,000 Hungarians were living in Slovakia. The Czechoslovak Statistical Office had published the figure of 652,000 Hungarians in its bulletin of 1945.

By increasing the number of Slovaks living in Hungary and decreasing the number of Hungarians living in Czechoslovakia, Clementis's intention, Szegedy-Maszák said, was to demonstrate that an exchange of population at par was not only possible but also desirable and fair. The Czechoslovak government did not act in the spirit of the victorious Great Powers, which had declared that the peace negotiations should not be conducted in the spirit of revenge, but in the spirit of justice. The Czechoslovak delegation aimed at increasing the large number of war victims by "adding to them the victims of peace".[87] By wanting to expel 200,000 Hungarians from Czechoslovakia, the Czechoslovak delegation acted also contrary to the UN's principle that respected the relationship of the ethnic population to the territory. The Allies had confirmed the rightfulness of the transfer of the Sudeten Germans in Czechoslovakia to Germany because they had agreed about the German minority's fateful role in preparing Munich. But they had not supported a transfer of the Hungarians living in Slovakia.

---

[86] "SPEECH of Mr. ALADÁR SZEGEDY-MASZÁK, Envoy Extraordinary and Minister Plenipotentiary, Representative of the Hungarian Delegation in the Territorial and Political Commission for Hungary, September 18th, 1946", AMZV, GS-A 1945–1954, carton no. 164, 16 pages, typewritten, 1. Clementis' speech of 16 September 1946, untitled, AMZV, GS-A 1945–1954, carton no. 164, 13 pages, typewritten.

[87] "SPEECH ...", 2.

President Beneš, the Hungarian delegate said, had written in his memoirs that in 1938 he had had to fight the Sudeten Germans and the Slovaks in the country and Hitler outside of the country; Szegedy-Maszák quoted from Beneš's book in full, even citing the page.[88] Contrary to the assertions of the Czechoslovak delegation, the role of the Hungarian minority with regard to Munich had been negligible:

> "It should also be recalled that though the Munich decision contained no stipulations of any kind concerning the Slovaks, nevertheless on the 6th of October 1938 in Zilina all the Slovak political parties of that time met and officially proclaimed the autonomy of Slovakia, thereby repudiating the unity, that is the very basis of the Czechoslovak Republic. [...] We do not deny that the Hungarian population of Czechoslovakia did to a certain extent play the role of opposition in the State, because there were certain complaints the justice of which was recognized even by Seton Watson." [89]

Szegedy-Maszák quoted from Seton-Watson's book published in 1931; the distinguished British scholar and associate of President Masaryk had written that the situation of the Hungarian minority after the foundation of the Czechoslovak Republic in 1918 was not up to democratic standards. Why, the Hungarian delegate asked, would the Czechoslovak delegates who, neither in 1938 nor in 1943, had found any reason to criticize the behaviour of the Hungarians in Slovakia now try to make them a scapegoat for Munich? In citing 1943, Szegedy-Maszák was referring to a statement Clementis had allegedly made about the difference between the Sudeten Germans and the Hungarians; unlike the Sudeten Germans in the Czech part, the Hungarian workers and farmers in Slovakia had appreciated the political and cultural progress of the First Republic. Szegedy-Maszák did not indicate the source of the

---

[88] "SPEECH ...", 7.
[89] "SPEECH ...", 6, 7.

Clementis quote that must have been, if this text indeed existed, made from London.

Hungary believed that the Czechoslovak government wanted, first, to gloss over the Slovaks' role in the destruction of Czechoslovakia, and second, deprive the industrious Hungarians in Slovakia of their wealth and property.[90] Rather astutely, but nevertheless factually wrong, the Hungarian delegate accused the Czechoslovak government of selfishness; he was trying to cause a rift between the Allies and Czechoslovakia. With the plan to transfer the Hungarians from Slovakia to Hungary, the Czechoslovak government wanted to achieve "a revision of the Potsdam decision".[91]

Szegedy-Maszák mentioned the sensitive issue of war criminals. The Czechoslovak authorities were intent on declaring thousands of Hungarians war criminals to deprive them of their property and expel them to Hungary, but they were ignoring the Slovak war criminals, especially the Hlinka Guards and the leaders of the Hlinka Party. The Hungarian delegate further accused the Czechoslovak government of Fascist principles:

> "The so-called re-slovakization is equally a means which awakens queer and dangerous memories. The cohabitation of various nationalities necessarily involves natural assimilation. So far, it was only the fascism which has tried to change this natural process by mass means of pressure, when – on the basis of the racial principle – he laid claim to every person of German name or descent, irrespective of what nation that person belonged to. Reslovakization is based on the same idea."[92]

Szegedy-Maszák elaborated that Hungary could not possible take in 200,000 persons because of the country's difficult economic situation. Hungary was on her path to democracy and had carried through a land reform that had eliminated the large feudal estates.

---

[90] "SPEECH ...", 8.
[91] "SPEECH ...", 9.
[92] "SPEECH ...", 11.

While Czechoslovakia considered the transfer of 200,000 persons a condition for friendly relations with Hungary, the nine million Hungarians conceived of it as an act of hostility, subjecting the Hungarian people to "an unbearable political, moral and economic burden".[93] The government had accepted a Peace Treaty that was a considerable hardship for Hungary, but it did not deem acceptable that relations between nations could be settled "by surgical interventions".[94] Szegedy-Maszák implored the Allies not to forget the Atlantic Charter for which they had fought in the war.

Clementis reacted to Szegedy-Maszák's statement on 20 September 1946, setting the record straight; he presented to the Commission different figures and revealed "the notorious Hungarian statistics of nationality which figure even in international literature as a classic example for the falsification of facts."[95] He, Clementis said, had hoped that Hungary would change her revisionist politics once and for all. The Hungarian delegate had accused him of presenting false figures. Clementis replied that on the basis of the Czechoslovak census of 1930, the Czechoslovak statistical report of 1945, and under consideration of the uprising and the war, approximately half a million of Hungarians lived in Slovakia. After lengthy comments about the real figures, Clementis explained why Czechoslovakia insisted on the population transfer:

> "The Hungarian delegate deliberately distorts the facts when he says that the persons concerned here are leading war criminals, because the relevant clauses of the Czechoslovak-Hungarian Treaty give us the right to expel not only war criminals, but all those who took active part in preparing the dismemberment of the Republic in any form whatsoever and even in the years before the war. [...] We have not proceeded to

---

[93] "SPEECH ...", 15.
[94] "SPEECH ...", 16.
[95] "Řeč st. taj. Clementise v Maďarské komisi dne 20. Září 1946", AMZV, GS-A 1945-1954, carton no. 65, 23 pages, English, typewritten, 1.

mass condemnations simply because they are contrary to our understanding of justice."[96]

It was the Hungarian side that was not interested in the population exchange, using all its power to disseminate anti-Czechoslovak propaganda in Slovakia, trying to protract the transfer and internationalize a regional issue. Hungary was interested in significantly reducing the number of Slovaks living in Hungary and Hungarians living in Slovakia. Furthermore, Clementis said, Mr Szegedy-Maszák had stated that the Hungarian minority in Czechslovakia had had nothing to do with the dismemberment of the Republic, denying any connection with Henlein's Sudeten German movement in the Czech lands. Clementis quoted from a book by a Hungarian Press attaché in Washington, who had written in 1939 that the United Hungarian Party under the leadership of Jaross Andor and Ezsterházy János had followed the Sudeten Germans' *völkisch* principles.[97] Clementis finished his speech, reminding the assembly of a principal fact:

> "I should therefore consider it beneath the dignity of the Slovak nation which, considering its small number and difficult situation, took such an outstanding part in the struggle of the victorious nations, to reply to the accusations of the delegate of a state that was the first to take the road of Fascism, that stayed on that road the longest and put up the least resistance [...] On behalf of the Government and Delegation of Czechoslovakia, I declare that we commit ourselves in front of the Paris Peace Conference and the public opinion of the world to proceed with the transfer in a manner which will be in harmony with the humanitarian principles that made Czechoslovakia a bulwark of decency in Central Europe."[98]

---

[96] "Řeč st. taj. Clementise ...", 10-11.
[97] "Řeč st. taj. Clementise ...", 16.
[98] "Řeč st. taj. Clementise ...", 18-19. Clementis referred to the democracy of the First Republic.

At the opening of the peace negotiations in July 1946, Foreign Minister Jan Masaryk had presented the Czechoslovak viewpoint, reacting to the statement of the Hungarian Foreign Minister János Gyöngyössi. In contrast to Clementis' somewhat complicated lawyer's English, Masaryk's English was more elegant; his American mother Charlotte had brought him and his siblings up speaking American English. Note the difference in style and rethoric:

> "Who won this war – the United Nations or Hungary? [...] For twenty years Czechoslovakia did her best to prove to the world and herself that the idea of a transfer was alien to her idea of democracy. We had Germans in the Cabinet for several years and we gave to our Hungarian citizens not only what Mr Gyongossi calls 'les droits d' homme', but much much more. [...] Mr. Gyongossi tells us that the Hungarians wished for allied victory. That is not enough. How many Hungarian airmen did fly away from Horthy to join Roosevelt or Stalin? Not one. How many Hungarian volunteers joined the allied forces, formed bataillons, divisions and army corps alongside of the fighting units of the twenty one nations represented in this room?"[99]

On 16 April 1949, Czechoslovakia and Hungary, now in the firm hands of the Communist Parties, concluded the Czechoslovak-Hungarian Treaty of Friendship, Co-operation and Mutual Assistance (*Zmluva medzi Československou republikou a Maďarskou republikou o priateľstve, spolupráci a vzájomnej pomoci*). Moscow had its camp under control.

III. 2 Minister of Foreign Affairs (1948–1950)

III. 2. 1 The Mysterious Death of Jan Masaryk (1948)

On 25 February 1948, the KSČ assumed power. On the morning of 10 March 1948, Foreign Minister Jan Masaryk was found dead in the courtyard of the Czernín Palace, the Foreign Ministry in the

---

[99] Jan Masaryk, Untitled speech at the UN, AMZV, GS-A 1945-1954, carton 164, 8 pages, English, typewritten, 1-2, 3.

Prague Castle district. His body lay under the window of his bathroom. To this day, his death is shrouded in mystery, but the case has been officially closed.[100]

Masaryk's death has become the stuff of legend and given rise to many theories. I doubt that anyone will find a document in the Russian NKVD archives that proves Stalin's order to have Masaryk killed. But I also deem it safe to assume that Gottwald was too meek to order Masaryk's murder without asking the Soviets for permission. Therefore, I think that we shall never find out the whole truth nor the identity of the murderer(s). With hindsight, it is more likely that this operation was planned and executed by the experienced NKVD, since the StB was still under training in those years; I doubt that the Czechoslovak Security Service was up to a job of this magnitude at that time.[101]

In this subchapter, I present the two most prominent theories: first, suicide and second, murder. As a consequence of Masaryk's death, the Party appointed Clementis foreign minister, a top government position he would hold for roughly two years. It took the Party eight days to appoint him – rather a long time in such a sensitive situation, where leadership was paramount. The CC discussed if it should appoint Zdeněk Fierlinger (1891–1976), but finally gave the job to Clementis.[102] I cannot prove it with documents but I consider it very likely that Gottwald and Stalin, after

---

[100] On the strength of new evidence, Czech criminologists believe that Masaryk was murdered, see http://www.radio.cz/en/section/curraffrs/police-close-case-on-1948-death-of-jan-masaryk-murder-not-suicide; accessed 31 July 2016.

[101] For the development of the StB as the KSČ's instrument of power see Karel Kaplan, *Protistátní Bezpečnost 1945–1948. Historie vzniku a působení StB jako mocenského nástroje KSČ* (Praha: Plus, 2015). Kaplan's analysis ends with the StB's involvement and orchestration of the 'victorious February' in 1948, hence does not enlighten us about the StB's involvement in Masaryk's death.

[102] Holotíková a Plevza, 258.

'discussing the issue', came to the conclusion that, for the time being, Clementis was the best choice, since he would ensure continuity and was familiar with the international institutions, agreements and Western politicians. In terms of Czechoslovak domestic affairs and the Soviet Union's international relations, it was not a good time to introduce a new and unknown minister of foreign affairs. One had to have patience and the ability to wait ...

Some believe that Masaryk wanted to leave the country, and therefore, the NKVD murdered him on Stalin's orders.[103] With his famous name and reputation, Masaryk was a potential threat to Soviet long-term foreign policy, since he could form an anti-Communist movement abroad. As half-American and a Czechoslovak diplomat since the 1920s, he had good connections in the US Congress and the British government. With his considerable legacy, reputation and contacts in the West, Masaryk could potentially counteract Stalin's plan to increase Soviet influence in the UN Security Council with pseudo-democratic Czechoslovakia as a non-permanent member.

Others are convinced that Masaryk sacrificed himself as a last desperate act of protest against the Communist take-over.[104] The Gottwald government quickly insisted that it was suicide;

---

[103] For an analysis of Czech criminologists see http://pravyprostor.cz/smrt-jana-masaryka-ocima-kriminalisty-evidentni-vrazda/accessed 14 October 2016.

[104] Antonín Sum, *Osudný krok Jana Masaryka* (Praha: Nadace Janua, Masarykovo demokratické hnutí, 1996). Sum, one of Masaryk's personal assistants, was present at the forensic investigation of Masaryk's body on the afternoon of 10 March 1948 and summarized in his book the psychological and political reasons for Masaryk's suicide. An interesting article focussing on Masaryk's mental problems is Petr Zídek on http://www.lidovky.cz/pohnute-osudy-jana-masaryka-vysvobodila-az-smrt-ale-jak-to-s-ni-bylo-11m-/lide.aspx?c=A150924_214311_lide_ELE; accessed 31 July 2016. The best popular biography is Pavel Kosatík, *Jan Masaryk. Právdivý příběh* (Praha: Mladá Fronta, 2009 (2)).

there was no reason to kill Masaryk, because he supported the National Front and the KSČ's foreign policy – why murder him and draw unnecessary international attention to Czechoslovakia? Jan Masaryk was a useful puppet in the foreign ministry; he conveyed to the West the impression that the Communist coup d'etat was the democratic decision of the Czechoslovak people who were still oriented towards the West with the son of the President-Liberator as foreign minister, hence Czechoslovakia's symbol of democracy.

I can only speculate, taking into account Masaryk's state of mind and Stalin's psychology. Considering Stalin's talent for geopolitical strategy that was not limited by, in his way of thinking, the feeble concerns of humanity and justice, let alone fairness, I think it very probable that he wanted to play safe for the future. Jan Masaryk's mental problems and bohemian life style were well known in Czechoslovak and Soviet diplomatic circles. His elimination would thus kill two birds with one stone: first, Gottwald and the KSČ leadership would be rid of that 'troublesome son', that 'democratic nuisance', and second, Masaryk's death in Prague would prevent his emigration and future leadership of the Czechoslovak exile community in the West, especially in the USA.

On the other hand, it is also possible that Jan Masaryk, the weak son of a strong father, decided, perhaps in a split second, to make himself a martyr, to choose defenestration; his death would create a perennial myth, a symbol of the Czechoslovak nation, demonstrating to the world the brutality of Communist rule. Also, his sacrifice would prove *ex post* to his father, to the nation and to the democratic world that he was worthy of carrying the name Masaryk. Defenestration had been a Prague tradition since the Thirty Years' War (1618–1648), and a symbol of Czech democracy. The Czechoslovak citizens would understand his message.

An interesting coincidence: President Masaryk died on 14 September 1937 – Jan, his second son, was born on the same day in 1886. In psychological terms, this must have put considerable stress on Jan: every year on his birthday, he was reminded of his strong father who had created Czechoslovak democracy. I can imagine that Jan was under constant psychological duress, experiencing during his entire life how people always compared him with his father. Furthermore, all Masaryk's children, Alice, Olga and Jan suffered from bouts of depression; they had inherited that genetic make-up from their mother Charlotte. The date of President Masaryk's death reminded Jan constantly of his own shortcomings and deficiencies.

If Stalin gave the order to have Jan Masaryk murdered, he would not have left a written trace; he would have called the no. 1 NKVD officer in Prague. Comrade Klema (Gottwald) would have probably been informed after the murder – who was Gottwald, after all? In Stalin's eyes, a mere lackey. Furthermore, Stalin had tested Masaryk in July 1947 in Moscow: Masaryk had caved in to Stalin's pressure not to participate in the Marshall Plan, although he had had assured the centre-right politicians just a few days previously that Czechoslovakia would participate.[105]

According to Ferdinand Peroutka (1895–1978), a close associate of President Masaryk and friend of the family, Jan had promised his father "never to leave Beneš".[106] I think this was the reason, why Jan did not step down as foreign minister when the centre-right ministers resigned in protest in February 1948. That was a decisive moment when Jan could have taken action, leave the NF together with the ministers, leave the country and tell the world from his US or British exile what the NF in Czechoslovakia

---

[105] Slavomír Michálek, "Marshallov plan", in *Nádeje a vytriezvenia (Československo-americké hospodárske vzťahy v rokoch 1945–1952)* (Bratislava: Veda, 1995), 83-113, 94, 103-104.

[106] Ferdinand Peroutka, "O Janu Masarykovi", in *deníky, dopisy, vzpomínky* (Praha: Nakladatelství Lidové Noviny, 1994), 178, 179, quoted from Sum, 80-81.

was really up to, but his loyalty to Beneš and his father was stronger. Jan stayed on.

If we judge Jan Masaryk's behaviour, we should be fair and try to understand his situation. In psychological terms, he was in a *double bind*, a *catch-22* situation:[107] if he stood up against Stalin and left the NF or emigrated to the West, he would break his promise to his father never to leave Beneš. If he stood by Beneš and kept his promise to his father, he would betray his own political beliefs and his father's legacy, Czechoslovakia's democracy. For the sensitive and artistically talented Jan, who loved to play the piano and was no trained politician, this situation must have been psychological distress to the maximum – there was no way out. The

---

[107] A catch-22 is "a problematic situation for which the only solution is denied by a circumstance inherent in the problem or by a rule", http://www.merriam-webster.com/dictionary/catch-22; accessed 18 October 2016. The American Joseph Heller (1923–1999) coined the concept of catch-22 in his famous novel: "Yossarian came to him one mission later and pleaded again, without any real expectation of success, to be grounded. [...] 'You're wasting your time', Doc Daneka was forced to tell him. 'Can't you ground someone who's crazy?' 'Oh, sure. I have to. There's a rule saying I have to ground anyone who's crazy.' [...] Yossarian looked at him soberly and tried another approach. 'Is Orr crazy?' 'He sure is,' Doc Daneka said. 'Can you ground him?' 'I sure can. But first he has to ask me to. That's part of the rule.' 'Then why doesn't he ask you to?' 'Because he's crazy', Doc Daneka said. 'He has to be crazy to keep flying combat missions after all the close calls he's had.' [...] 'You mean there's a catch?' 'Sure there's a catch,' Doc Daneka replied. 'Catch-22 [...] specified that a concern for one's own safety in the face of dangers that were real and immediate was the process of a rational mind. Orr was crazy and could be grounded. All he had to do was ask; and as soon as he did, he would no longer be crazy and would have to fly more missions. Orr would be crazy to fly more missions and sane if he didn't, but if he was sane he had to fly them. If he flew them he was crazy and didn't have to; but if he didn't want to he was sane and had to. [...] Yossarian saw it clearly in all its spinning reasonableness. There was an elliptical precision about its perfect pairs of parts that was graceful and shocking, like good modern art." Joseph Heller, *Catch-22* (New York: Vintage, 1994), 61-63.

catch-22 can, at least partly, explain Masaryk's weakness, the reason why he did not stand up to Stalin.

I am inclined to think that Jan Masaryk was murdered, because of the interpretations and scientific explanations presented in a ČT documentary: Jiří Štrauss's forensic bio-mechanical reconstruction, Ilja Pravda's criminal investigation, the statements of the psychiatrist Cyril Höschl, Charlotta Kotíková, Masaryk's niece, and Libuše Paukertová-Lehárová, the daughter of Alice Masaryk's personal assistant.[108]

First, Masaryk's body lay further away from the building of the MZV as it would have, had he jumped; second, if the picture of his body was not tampered with, his feet show towards the building, not away from it, which means that he fell backwards. According to the psychiatrist, to let oneself fall backwards from a building is very unusual for people committing suicide: suicidal persons freely choose to end their life and face their death by jumping forwards. Masaryk must have tried to hide under the window, crouching on the window ledge when his murderers got hold of him and then pushed him down into the courtyard. Mrs Paukertová-Lehárová and Mrs Kotíková who both knew him personally stated that Jan Masaryk was always correctly dressed and cared about etiquette; he would have never jumped out of the window of his (own!) foreign ministry in pyjamas. Had he decided to kill himself, he would have done so neatly dressed in a suit.

Cui bono? Who benefitted from Masaryk's death? Clearly, the Soviet Union. Clementis, Moscow's loyal servant, was the perfect replacement for Masaryk, making sure that the Soviet Unions'

---

[108] The ČT documentary with the forensic bio-mechanical reconstruction, the psychiatric assessments, the criminal investigation and the statements of the two ladies on http://www.ceskatelevize.cz/porady/10354181410-krok-do-prazdna-jana-masaryka-aneb-dokonaly-zlocin/; accessed 16 October 2016.

foreign policy would be implemented without further complications. I am quite certain that Clementis, a decent person, was not involved in Masaryk's death; from a political point of view, Clementis was but a pawn on Stalin's ruthless board of chess – he had not trusted him since 1939 and his criticism of the Hitler-Stalin Pact. In the ČT documentary mentioned, an elderly gentleman, who had been employed as a guard at the MZV in 1948 insinuated that Clementis was involved in Masaryk's death because he directly benefitted from it. I think this is an absurd allegation; the criminologist Ilja Pravda proved that the statement was spurious, since it was not based on witness accounts. Also, the timeline was wrong.

On 11 March, Clementis addressed the employees of the Foreign Ministry, remembering Jan Masaryk's personality and activities. [109] To learn about the death of a person he had worked with for the last three years and whom he had known from their London exile must have shocked him. His language was rational and composed, but one can sense sadness in his words, remembering his last meeting with Masaryk:

> "In one of the last discussions with our Jan Masaryk we agreed to call you all together to clarify how the recent changes in our domestic politics will affect us and our work. I had no inkling that we would not inform you together, as we had planned."[110]

Masaryk's death shocked Clementis as much as the Czechoslovak people. The assistant secretary of state must have believed in Masaryk's suicide; I cannot prove this with documents, but, consid-

---

[109] "Prejav štátneho tajomníka Dr. Vl. Clementisa pri smútočnom shromáždení zamestnancov ministerstva zahraničných vecí dňa 11. Marca 1948", AMZV, GS-A 1945-1954, carton 67, 2 pages, typewritten.
[110] "Prejav štátneho tajomníka …", 1.

ering Stalin's distrust of Clementis, it is safe to assume that Clementis – if Masaryk indeed was murdered – had no clue what had happened on the night of 9 to 10 March at the Czernín Palace.

On 20 March 1948, the newly appointed foreign minister gave an interview to national radio.[111] He made a clear statement about his new position, answering the journalist's first question about Jan Masaryk. Yes, he and the former foreign minister had always been acting in agreement, although their political beliefs were different. And yes, he was missing Jan Masaryk. Czechoslovakia's foreign policy had a clear orientation, which provided the people with security and certainty.

In clear words, Clementis commented on the current political situation that was dividing the former Allies: "the hysterical war campaign" did not exactly foster international co-operation, but it was not as dangerous as it appeared.[112] The fact that Germany was being made into a platform against her former victims, albeit, for the time being, only in an economic form, was very dangerous. Clementis did not mention any Western state in particular, but his statement was clear: the West was pushing ahead the rift between the former Allies, enforcing the fear of a coming war:

> "The Soviet Union and her Allies shall never be the ones to attack. [...] And that so-called freedom of the press, abused to promote lies, untruths and concoctions that are keeping the Western world together, cannot endure forever. [...] But the campaign against the Soviet Union that had been mounted at the very beginning of her existence did not break her power, it only strengthened it, and after this war the campaign that is being mounted now against all People's Democracies [*všetkým ľudovo-demokratickým štátom*] shall never diminish their self-confidence and determination to build a peaceful world."[113]

---

[111] Clementis, "Prejav v rozhlase z 20. Marca 1948 o Janovi Masarykovi / interview/", AMZV, GS-A 1945-1954, carton 65, 6 pages, typewritten.
[112] Clementis, "Prejav v rozhlase ...", 3.
[113] Clementis, "Prejav v rozhlase ...", 3-4.

Note Clementis' usage of the key political concept "People's Democracy": the concept implied that the people voted for the rule of the Party. It was but another element of Marxist-Leninist newspeak that blurred the proper understanding of 'democracy'. The journalist's second but last question mentioned the Czernín Palace's tradition of optimism and the belief that eventually everything would turn out well. Did the new foreign minister share this tradition?

> "A good and just foreign policy must and should always be based on good and healthy domestic politics. And this is certainly the course of the government of Klement Gottwald. And thanks to this political course everything turned out well in our country. [...] And that is why Jan Masaryk's call is valid today more than ever before: Cheer up!"[114]

No, the Gottwald government would not change its foreign policy: it kept to the motto "loyalty for loyalty, friendship for friendship". Obviously, Clementis was eager to praise Comrade Gottwald, and we can only speculate whether he knew about the terror Comrade Slánsky was unleashing on the Czechoslovak people. If Clementis knew about the terror, he must have thought it was a necessary means to educate the people and exterminate the class enemy – or then, he shut it out from his conscience. He was certainly highly uncritical of the government's measures; his admiration for Stalin and Comrade Klemo did not falter. Happy that the Party had taken him back, he dedicated all his strength and talent to the workers' cause – not a word of criticism, not a hint of a doubt. The lawyer was in his element: proud to serve, happy to have power and use his admirable intellectual faculties to promote the building of the Communist paradise on earth.

I have found no information about the relationship of Clementis and Slánský in the years from 1945 to 1948, yet the

---

[114] Clementis, "Prejav v rozhlase ...", 6.

ruthless Czech Party functionary and the educated Slovak politician would stand trial together in 1952. Both were innocent of the charges brought against them, but in view of Slánský's activities after 'the victorious 25 February 1948', one does feel a bit of *Schadenfreude*. While in power, Slánský was merciless, trying to prove to Stalin that he was a reliable comrade in charge of purging Czechoslovakia of bourgeois elements, behaving as Stalin's eager little soldier:

> "A major impetus for this wave of arrests came from CP General Secretary Rudolf Slansky, who said in September, at Edvard Benes's funeral in Prague, that the country needed labour camps to deal with the class enemy and it made no difference that the West was going to complain about communist concentration camps in Czechoslovakia. Attempts at ideological education would be insufficient for dealing with enemies of communism."[115]

Clementis would fulfil Stalin's foreign policy in an area he was familiar with from his childhood: the longing for independence. As foreign minister, he was involved in the creation of an army that would defend the Jewish cause in Palestine: the building of the Israeli air force and army.

---

[115] Igor Lukes, *Rudolf Slansky. His Trial and Trials. Cold War International History Project Working Paper no. 50* (Washington, D.C.: Woodrow Wilson Center, 2008), on https://www.wilsoncenter.org/publication/rudolf-slansky-his-trials-and-trial; accessed 8 October 2016, pdf, 13-14. Lukes's paper provides important information: Slánský's task was to oversee the reconstruction of the Ruzyně prison complex in April 1949. The prison was ready in October 1949, and roughly two years later, Slánský and co-accused would be tortured in the very prison whose reconstruction he had overseen; Lukes, 13-14.

III. 2. 2 Operation Balak (1948)

> "In January 1948, Stalin [...] postponed the demolition of the Jewish Antifascist Committee. This was because the Boss was simultaneously watching with close interest the establishment of the state of Israel. [...] Already in May 1947 the USSR's United Nations representative, Gromyko, had announced to the UN General Assembly that the creation of an independent Jewish state in Palestine had the full support of the USSR. The Boss's plan was to use an Israeli state under Soviet influence in opposition to Britain, and to bar the way to the Americans. [...] It did not take Stalin long, however, to realize that ungrateful Israel was obviously leaning towards America."[116]

The Jewish emigration from Czechoslovakia to Palestine, and later, Israel, increased after the pogrom in the Slovak town Topoľčany and the KSČ's coup d'état;[117] from 1947 to 1949, 1,355

---

[116] Radzinsky, 530, 531, 532. For a history of the Jewish Antifascist Committee (JAK) in the Soviet Union see the excellent Frank Grüner, *Patrioten und Kosmopoliten. Juden im Sowjetstaat 1941–1953* (Köln, Weimar, Wien: Böhlau, 2008). A shorter version is Frank Grüner, "Jüdisches Antifaschistisches Komitee", in *Enzyklopädie jüdischer Geschichte und Kultur, Band 3* (Stuttgart: Metzler Verlag, 2012), 268-273. I thank Frank Grüner for the following recommendations: The YIVO Encyclopedia of Jews in Europe on http://www.yivoencyclopedia.org; accessed 27 September 2016; Joshua Rubinstein and Vladimir P. Naumov (eds.), *Stalin's Secret Pogrom: The Post-war Inquisition of the Jewish Antifascist Committee* (New Haven, CN: Yale University Press, 2001) and Kateřina Šimová, "'Nejnebezpečnější pozůstátek kannibalismu': Stalinský antisemitismus v letech 1948 až 1953", *Acta Universitatis Carolinae. Studia Territorialia* (Praha: Karlova Univerzita, 2013).

[117] Excellent accounts of the Topoľčany pogrom are Ivan Kamenec, "Protižidovský pogrom v Topoľčanoch v septembri 1945", in *Studia historica Nitriensia 8* (1999): 85-97; Robert Y. Büchler, *Židovská náboženská obec v Topoľčanoch. (Počiatky, rozvoj a zánik),* (Bratislava: Slovenské národné múzeum, Múzeum židovskej kultúry, 1996); Peter Salner (ed.), *Židovská komunita po roku 1945* (Bratislava: Ústav etnologie SAV, 2006). Jana Šišjaková a Michal Šmigel, "Protižidovské prejavy na východnom Slovensku v prvých povojnových rokoch (1945-1947)", in *Annales historici Presoviensis 8*, (2009): 197-217; Jana Šišjaková, "Židovská rodina v konfrontácii s povojnovou situáciou a antisemitizmom na Slovensku (1945-1946)", on http://forumhistoriae.sk/documents/10180/39170/sisjakova.pdf., accessed 15 October 2016 and Jana Šišjaková, "Rodina vo vojne", on http://www.forumhistoriae.sk/FH1_2009/texty

Czechoslovak Jews signed up for the secret training of voluntary soldiers organized by the Czechoslovak ministry of defence, using the opportunity for emigration to Israel.[118]

The Czechoslovak arms deals with the Jews in Palestine began in 1947, when the Jewish community, led by David Ben-Gurion (1886–1973), was preparing for war against the armies of Egypt, Iraq, Jordan, Lebanon and Syria. Czechoslovakia's military support should be understood in the post-war context of the Middle East and the emerging Cold War: Stalin's strategy was to support the building of a Jewish state in Palestine to counteract Great Britain's influence in the Middle East.

As usually, Clementis acted as expected; he had no room for manoeuvre, did not seek such and was also personally convinced that Stalin had sound geopolitical reasons for his strategy in the Middle East. Operation Balak[119] is the only arms deal Clem-

---

_1_2009/sisjakova.pdf; accessed 15 October 2016. For a literary account of Jewish life in Slovakia from 1945 to 1948 see Anton Baláž, *Krajina zabudnutia* (Bratislava: Slovenský spisovateľ, 2000) and *Transporty nádeje. Slovenskí Židia na ceste do novej vlasti* (Bratislava: Marenčin PT, 2010). I am indebted to Ivan Kamenec for recommending these studies to me.

[118] Tomáš Habermann, *Československo a Izrael 1947–1949: Léta přátelství* (Praha: Univerzita Karlova, Pedagogická Fakulta, Katedra Dějín a Didaktiky Dějepisu, 2001), 61. Habermann's Master thesis (*diplomová práce*) offers a good insight to the history of the Middle East and Czechoslovakia's involvement on the background of the beginning rift between the Allies. I thank Frank Grüner for recommending this study and the following publications: Jiří Dufek, Karel Kaplan a Vladimír Šlosár, *Československo a Izrael v letech 1945-1956: dokumenty* (Brno, Praha: Doplněk, Ustav pro Soudobé Dějiny AV ČR, 1993); Jiří Dufek, Karel Kaplan a Vladimír Šlosár, *Československo a Izrael v letech 1947-1953*: Studie (Praha: Ustav pro Soudobé Dějiny AV ČR, 1993).

[119] Tzvi Ben-tzur, "The Czechoslovak Arms Deals during the War of Independence", on http://www.palyam.org/English/ArmsShips/Czechoslovakia-en; accessed 10 October 2016, pdf, 6 pages.

entis was involved in: thanks to Czechoslovakia's training of military personnel and selling arms, ammunition and aircraft to the Jewish Agency, Israel won the War of Independence in 1949.[120]

> "Legal sources of arms in the U.S. and most European countries were blocked to the Yishuv (the Jewish community in Eretz Israel during the British mandate) due to arms embargo declared by the USA and Britain (and the UN as well once Israel became a state). The alternative was to engage in illegal arms procurement and to appeal to the Soviet bloc. Unlike the USA and Britain, the USSR, which enthusiastically supported the UN partition resolution, continued to stand behind the resolution, even after it led to the beginning of the armed conflict. One of the manifestations of the USSR's support was a 'green light' to broad scale arms deals between Czechoslovakia and the Yishuv/Israel."[121]

According to Habermann, Czechoslovakia was interested in the arms deals for economic, political and socio-cultural reasons. [122] Had Moscow openly sold arms to the Jews in Palestine, it would have risked an international scandal in the sensitive atmosphere of the Cold War, then just beginning. On Stalin's insistence, Czechoslovakia jumped in, taking on that risk, because the country needed foreign currency for its arms industry; it had to solve the economic problems resulting from not participating in the Marshall Plan.[123]

The arms industry had to find new markets – and the Middle East was such a new market. The Jewish Agency and the Vi-

---

[120] Israel's War of Independence lasted from 15 May 1948 to 20 July 1949; from February to July 1949, the five Arab states signed armistice agreements with Israel. For details see Bernard Reich and David H. Goldberg, *Historical Dictionary of Israel* (Lanham, MD: The Scarecrow Press, 2008 (2)), xxiv, 42-43, 528. A touching memoir of the War of Independence and the history of Polish Jews who immigrated to Palestine in the 1920s is Amos Oz, *A Tale of Love and Darkness* (Orlando, FL: Harcourt, 2003).
[121] Tzvi Ben-tzur, 1.
[122] Habermann, 61.
[123] Habermann, 64.

enna-born Ehud Avriel (Georg Überall) (1917–1980), a high-ranking member of the Haganah who would be elected to the Knesset in the 1950s, made the first contacts with the Czechoslovak government in 1947. The arms deal proved to be a win-win situation: the Czechoslovak arms industry could sell to the Jewish Agency the weapons and aircraft it needed so desperately to prepare for the war. Unlike the Arab states, the Jewish Agency was able to pay up-front and in hard currency – in US dollars and British pounds, which saved the Czechoslovak arms industry from collapse.[124]

In terms of politics, the arms trade with Israel made sense, since the USA had not yet formulated its policy in the Middle East; only the British opposed the Jewish state.[125] Israel came into being thanks to the emerging Cold War between the former Allies. The future political system of the fledgling Jewish state also played a role in Stalin's considerations:

> "Moscow [...] hoped that the support of the Jews would create a state that would promote Socialism in the Middle East and 'carry the flame of the revolution into the region'."[126]

A last factor was the social and cultural closeness of the Czechoslovak people and the Jewish Zionists: Foreign Minister Jan Masaryk especially considered it a moral and humanitarian duty to support the building of the Jewish state in view of the horrors of the Shoa. In the First Republic, the Jews adhering to Zionism and committed to a Jewish homeland had enjoyed the sympathies of President Masaryk and Foreign Minister Beneš. Czechoslovak citizens could relate to the Zionists' goal: they remembered their past in the Habsburg Monarchy, what it meant to live under foreign rule

---

[124] Habermann, 65.
[125] Habermann, 65.
[126] Habermann, 65.

and have no say in politics. They understood the Zionists' wish for a nation-state.[127]

Once Avriel had established the contacts with the Czechoslovak government, Jan Masaryk told him to talk to Clementis in case he encountered administrative difficulties. Avriel remembered what Masaryk had jokingly told him:

> "'For me it is enough that you defend yourself against your enemies. But Clementis will be happy to know, that by fighting for your life, you are undermining British imperialism in the Middle East.'"[128]

The contract was signed in mid-January 1949; the Jewish Agency purchased small arms from Zbrojovka in Brno and paid $750,000.[129] Since Israel could not buy American aircraft because of the embargo, the government decided to purchase ten fighter planes Avia S-199, a Czechoslovak variant of the German Messerschmidt.

> "Operation Balak – the airlift to transport arms from Czechoslovakia to Israel – began on March 31, 1948 [...] and continued until August 12, 1948, when Israeli activity at the Etzion base came to a sudden halt due to U.S. threats against Czechoslovakia. [...] The highlight of Balak Operation was the transfer of the 'Sakinim' ['knives', the Hebrew name for the airplanes, add. JB] to Israel. [...] The first airplane arrived on May 20, 1948 ('Balak-5') and the last on July 28, 1948."[130]

Thanks to the arms deal, every IDF soldier was equipped with a gun and ammunition; the jet fighters the Czechoslovak ministry of defence sold to the Israeli government stopped the advance of the Arab armies and their bombings of Jewish settlements. Without Czechoslovakia's military support, young Israel would have lost the war and perished.

---

[127] Habermann, 62.
[128] AVRIEL, E.: *Open the Gates! A personal story of "illegal" Immigration to Israel.* New York: Atheneum, 1975, s. 335, quoted from Habermann, 51-52.
[129] Tzvi Ben-tzur, 2.
[130] Tzvi Ben-tzur, 3, 4.

How much the political constellation in the Middle East changed in just three brief years is visible in the report written by a member of the Czechoslovak embassy in Tel Aviv dated 7 December 1952, summarizing the reactions in Israel to the trial of Slánský and co-accused. On 29 November, the governing party Mapaj called for a protest demonstration; deputy chairman G. Livné said in Nazareth that "the people's anger was not directed against the nation of the Presidents Masaryk and Beneš, but against their current Communist rulers."[131]

A spokesman for the Israeli Foreign Ministry said on 23 November that such a trial had so far been conducted only in Tsarist Russia and Hitler's Germany, but it would not negatively affect Israel's relations to the People's Democracies in Europe.[132] The liberal newspaper *Haarec* reported on 3 December that Dr Arieh Kubovi, Israel's envoy to Czechoslovakia, had left Prague with his family; his children were safe in Vienna. While in Prague, Kubovi had repeatedly informed the Israeli Foreign Ministry about the danger of arrest in connection with the Slánský trial.[133] Kubovi had returned home after the verdict was out and informed the Knesset about the trial; he refused to return to Prague.[134] *Kol Haam*, the newspaper of the Communist Party of Israel, wrote on 24 November 1952:

> "It is no surprise that the spy agencies of the Atlantic bloc are going systematically against the People's Democracies. The attempts of their press to deny the existence of the American secret services, which are

---

[131] "IZRAEL. REAKCE NA PROCES SE SLÁNSKÝM A SPOL. /Dokumentační přehled od 21. XI. – 7. XII.52/", AMZV, GS-A 1945-1954, carton 155, 14 pages, typewritten, classified *Tajné*, 7.

[132] "IZRAEL. REAKCE NA PROCES …, 1.

[133] "IZRAEL. REAKCE NA PROCES …", 12.

[134] Kubovi's report to the Knesset on 3 December 1952 on http://www.jta.org/1952/12/04/archive/israel-cabinet-holds-two-sessions-on-prague-trial-hears-envoy; accessed 17 October 2016.

organizing sabotage and counter-revolutionary operations, are just ridiculous."[135]

Delegate Wilner pronounced at a meeting of the CPI that the Prague trial demonstrated four facts: first, the conspiracy of the Imperialists against the camp of peace and Socialism; second, the traitorous services Ben Gurion was providing for American Imperialism; third, the real character of the world Zionist organizations that were acting in the service of the American warmongers; fourth, the connection of the Imperialists' spy services and their lackeys, in particular Ben Gurion, that were directed against the USSR and the Socialist camp.[136]

When a bomb exploded on the evening of 4 December 1952 behind the building of the Czechoslovak embassy in Tel Aviv, the MZV sent a protest note to the Israeli government.[137] Dr Nahum Goldmann, the chairman of the World Jewish Congress WJC, commented on the trial:

> "It will be a terrible tragedy if the Prague trial marks the beginning of a new policy in the Eastern bloc states. The Jewish people will not accept an antisemitic course and anti-Jewish demagogy from the People's Democracies."[138]

Very visible in this report is what Czechs and Slovaks were no longer able to enjoy: freedom of the press, democratic competition in a multi-party system and a rule-of-law state. Save for the Communists, the majority of the Israeli associations, political parties and interest groups were united in their condemnation of the Slánský trial and committed to the West.

In 1954, after Stalin's death, the Czechoslovak government under Prime Minister Viliam Široký began to improve relations

---

[135] "IZRAEL. REAKCE NA PROCES ...", 7.
[136] "IZRAEL. REAKCE NA PROCES ...", 9.
[137] "IZRAEL. REAKCE NA PROCES ...", 10-11.
[138] "IZRAEL. REAKCE NA PROCES ...", 11.

with Israel that had been on the brink of severing diplomatic ties because of the Slánský trial. A delegate at the Czechoslovak embassy in Tel Aviv summarized in his report to the Prague government the history of the young Israeli state, the political constellations in the Middle East, Israel's relations with the People's Democracies in Central and Eastern Europe, relations to Czechoslovakia and the general perception of the Slánský trial.[139]

The author of the report mentioned briefly the military support the conspirators and traitors colluding with Slánský had provided the young state with: back then, some 19,000 Czechoslovak Jews had emigrated, which had seriously damaged Czechoslovakia's economy.[140] The report suggested improving relations in five areas: diplomatic-political relations; family reunion; the issue of the convicted Israeli citizens Oren and Orenstein; liquidation of old debts and the adjustment of future economic relations and finally, co-operation in the areas of sport and culture.

Since the main task of Czechoslovakia's foreign policy was to support the Soviet political course, a normalization of Czechoslovak-Israeli relations was in tune with Soviet foreign policy. The state should thus send a chargé d'affairs to Tel Aviv and an ambassador at a later point in time, when relations would have improved. The problem of family reunion could be solved by allowing elderly and sick persons to join their relatives in Israel.[141]

In the case of the convicted Israeli spies Oren and Orenstein, [142] the author suggested to stand firm: the government

---

[139] "Návrh na úpravu vzájemních vztahů mezi ČSR a Izraelem", 5 July 1954, AMZV, GS-A 1945-1954, carton 155, 35 pages, typewritten, classified *Tajné*, 1.
[140] "Návrh na úpravu ...", 18.
[141] "Návrh na úpravu ...", 33.
[142] The Israeli citizens Mordechai Oren and Israel Shimon Orenstein were arrested in 1952 for espionage; see http://www.jta.org/1953/11/03/archive/oren-sentenced-in-prague-to-15-years-orenstein-gets-life-term; accessed 25 October 2016. Oren and Orenstein were tortured into confessing being

should not revise the verdict nor allow Oren and Orenstein to receive visitors.[143] Israel's president Chaim Weizmann (1874–1952) had submitted to the Czechoslovak government a claim for mercy. The authorities should neither grant mercy to the convicted, nor push Weizmann to the wall; a diplomatic formulation would leave room for future manoevring. To compensate for the negative trade balance of Czechoslovakia, the government should enter into new trade relations with Israel. Enhanced co-operation in the areas of sport and culture would further befit the relations; the organization of a festival of Czechoslovak film in the larger cities of Israel in the autumn would be well received. The Israeli Foreign Ministry had suggested arranging for concerts of Israeli conductors and orchestras to be held in Czechoslovakia the following year. The exchange of football and basketball teams could be scheduled as early as February or March 1955.[144]

The antisemitic character of the Slánský trial and the timing of the trial – planning started in 1949 – demonstrate not only Stalin's ousting of Tito, but also his punishment of Israel and the top Czechoslovak Party members of Jewish extraction. The Soviet Union had been the first state to diplomatically acknowledge Israel. Stalin had hoped that the young state in the Middle East would become a strong ally of the People's Democracies, since the leading Zionists, such as Chaim Weizmann and future Prime Minister Golda Meir (1898–1978), had grown up in eastern European Slavic countries and were Socialists. Weizmann was born in Poland, Meir in Kiev in Tsarist Ukraine. Stalin did not foresee that the Israelis had their own particular idea of Socialism. The majority of

---

Zionist spies and in the service of US Imperialism; in the show trial, their 'confessions' were used to 'prove' Slánský's guilt as the mastermind of the Zionist, Titoist and imperialist anti-state conspiracy.
[143] "Návrh na úpravu ...", 34.
[144] "Návrh na úpravu ...", 35.

Israeli citizens felt politically closer to the USA and the system of democracy, which must have given Stalin the impression that the Israelis were an ungrateful bunch who switched sides as soon as they could buy US military equipment. If Israel was lost to the Soviet bloc – fine. It was time now for punishment and then to change gear in Soviet foreign policy in the Middle East.

The Slánský trial also served another purpose, besides the ousting of Tito and the creation of mass hysteria among the Czechoslovak people who were taught that the ruthless warmongers of Western Imperialism had infiltrated even the top echelons of the Party: the Soviet Union and the Gottwald government rid themselves of the witnesses of the Czechoslovak-Israeli arms deal, sending a clear message to Israel that she could no longer count on the support of the People's Democracies in Eastern Europe. The message to the Czechoslovak citizens was antisemitic to the core: Jews could not be trusted – period.

Clementis experienced the peak of his political career, while the former Hungarian Foreign Minister László Rajk was standing trial in Budapest. On 24 September, Rajk received the death sentence for espionage for the Western Imperialists and Titoism. Did Clementis believe that Rajk was guilty? We shall never know. Rajk was executed on 15 October, while the Czechoslovak foreign minister was attending the UN summit in New York.

III. 2. 3 The UN Summit in New York (1949)

The year 1949 started well for Clementis; he could not possibly know that within the time span of one year he would lose his top positions in the Party and the state. On 20 January 1949, he held a speech to the MZV staff to honour the centenary of Lenin's birthday. He was in his element, talking enthusiastically about his credo. His love and talent for political theory was not affected by the pragmatic decisions he had to make in his position. In his view of the world, everything made sense; Marxism-Leninism had an answer to every problem. The scientific *Weltanschauung* of his credo was perfect.

Thanks to Lenin, a new era of mankind had begun, an epoch that Marx and Engels, the proletariat's great teachers, had prepared in the 19th century.[145] It was no easy task to summarize in a few words Lenin's gigantic personality and great work, but a characteristic element of Lenin's thought was the "organic unity of theory and practice, the unity of his theoretical work and his daily tasks".[146] The genius Stalin had built up Socialism in the Soviet Union; he was teacher and prophet to all nations that had chosen the path to Socialism. Clementis praised Lenin's fight against and oppression of the Russian Social Democrats; right at the beginning of the establishment of a Capitalist system that had been merging with the remainders of Russia's feudalist system, Lenin had clearly seen that the conditions in Russia had been ripe for revolution.

As we have seen above, Clementis always followed the party line. In the 1930s, he had believed that the rumours of the famine in Ukraine were concoctions of Western anti-Soviet propaganda. He had also believed that Sinoviev, Kamenev and Bukharin were guilty; it was convenient that DAV had run out of money back in 1937, which had spared him and Novomeský from the need to comment on the show trials of the Trotskyist conspirators and traitors. The chief prosecutor in the 1930s trials had been Andrei Vyšinskii, who would play a particularly nasty role in the scheme to make Clementis feel safe in the autumn of 1949 in New York. It is a brutal irony of Czechoslovak history that Clementis praised the Soviet Communist Party's prosecution of traitors,

---

[145] "Prednaška pána ministra k zamestnancom MZV u príležitosti výročia úmrtia V. I. Lenina", AMZV, GS-A 1945-1954, carton 67, 5 pages, typewritten, 1.
[146] "Prednaška pána ministra ...", 1.

whose fate was the exact blueprint of what he would have to endure himself very soon:

> "A journey, a long and instructive one to us, leads from the ideological unmasking of the so-called 'friends of the people' to the division of the Party into Bolsheviks and Mensheviks and [...] lastly, to the purge of the Soviet Bolshevik Party from the foulings of a Trotskii, a Bukharin and other factions [*až k očisteniu strany bolševíkov od Trozkistických, Bucharinovských a iných nánosov*]."[147]

The IX Party convention on 27 May 1949 was an important event for Clementis: he was elected to the CC KSČ, the highest Party organ. He held a brief speech, summarizing the Party's successes and praising Czechoslovakia's firm position in the Soviet camp that was fighting the "histrionic war propaganda" of the Capitalist West.[148] I think that he was overwhelmed with joy about this 'sign of trust' from Gottwald: as a member of the almigthy CC, he was now at the top of Party and state; his mistake in 1939 that had soured his political career was expunged. The Party finally trusted him and was grateful for his work at the ministry – or so he must have thought.

The enemy's camp was disunited, the foreign minister said; it was occupied with its own problems and rather perplexed in view of the liberation movement of the masses in the East, where bastions of peace were growing that neither atomic bombs nor hundreds of Western military bases could destroy.[149] Comrade Stalin was leading the camp of peace and progressive mankind and he was convinced, the foreign minister said, that comrade Gottwald would lead them to Socialism and peace.

Clementis truly believed that "the entire Czechoslovak people, both our nations" had wholeheartedly supported the

---

[147] "Prednaška pána ministra ...", 4.
[148] Clementis, "Prejav na IX. sjazde KSČ z 27. Mája 1949", SNA OF VC, carton a.j. 56, 11 pages, typewritten, 10.
[149] Clementis, "Prejav na IX. sjazde ...", 11.

Party and the Košice Government Programme after the war.[150] Not surpisingly, he referred to the centre-right politicians of the National Front in a negative fashion. He also used the emblem of Marxist-Leninist newspeak 'We know', which is not based on proven facts, but on the mere belief in the rightfulness of the CC's viewpoint. The linguistic emblem 'We know' is a phrase that embodies the dictate of Marxism-Leninism as a rational and 'scientific' system of thought:

> "*We know* that our forces of reaction [*naša reakcia*] rather unwillingly accepted the Košice Government Programme, because it predetermined the road to Socialism. A real Socialism, which is a step-by-step liquidation of the privileges of the exploiting classes [*postupné likvidovanie privilégií vykorisťovateľských tried*], thus also their social basis. And it is understandable that our forces of reaction, did they not want to commit premature political suicide, could not openly oppose the Programme [...] What they could not do openly, they did in hiding and scheming, choosing tactics that had a damaging effect on our foreign policy."[151]

Clementis described the alleged scheming of the centre-right politicians who had been eager to make Czechoslovakia a member of the Western camp. Not Stalin's policy directives were the reasons for the three years of protracted development towards Socialism, but the exploiting classes of the old system that had been boycotting the country's road to Socialism.

According to Husák, the StB began right after the ninth party convention to collect material to compromise Clementis. Široký was in command of the StB in Slovakia.[152] In connection with the Rajk trial in Hungary, the StB started building 'the case against Clementis'; his name was on a list of suspects the General Secretary of the Hungarian Communist Party Mátyás Rákosi

---

[150] Clementis, "Prejav na IX. sjazde ...", 1.
[151] Clementis, "Prejav na IX. sjazde ...", 1-2. Italics by me.
[152] Plevza, *Gustáv Husák prehovoril*, 64.

(1892–1971) had sent to Gottwald.[153] Clementis had not the slightest inkling of what was going on – had he realized he might have saved his life. His last appearance in public in the West was in the autumn of 1949 at the fourth session of the UN in New York. On the agenda was China.

Clementis and his delegation arrived in New York shortly before the start of the UN session on 29 September 1949. The Czechoslovak foreign minister stayed at Essex House, not far from Central Park.[154] The session of the UN General Assembly opened at 10.45 a.m. at Lake Success, New York, chaired by General Carlos P. Romulo from the Philippines; the session was registered as A/PV 230.[155]

The Chinese delegate Mr Tsiang had submitted a request: the assembly should discuss the Soviet threats to China's political independence and territorial integrity, which presented a violation of the Sino-Soviet Treaty of Friendship and Alliance of 14 August 1945.[156] Mr Tsiang said that he was not a delegate of the Chinese Communist Party. Not only had the Soviet Union violated the Chinese border, moved into Manchuria and stolen industrial equipment there, but Moscow was also giving moral and material support to the Communist insurrection. Tsiang accused Vyšinskii of using foul language in the UN assembly and stressed that China would use a language that reflected the dignity of the General Assembly.

Clementis was the first to speak after the Chinese delegate. Naturally, he spoke in favour of the Soviet viewpoint:

---

[153] Kaplan, *Report on the Murder* …, 61. Most of the Party members listed in Rákosi's letter had been in London exile during WWII.
[154] Holotíková a Plevza, 264.
[155] "Řeč min. dr. Clementise u Gen. Shromáždění", 29. Září 1949", AMZV, GS-A 1945-1954, carton 78, 46 pages, English, typewritten, 1.
[156] "Řeč min. dr. Clementise u Gen. …", 2.

> "The General Assembly is once again seized of a provocative proposal. [...] What kind of judgement is it that Mr. Tsiang expects to hear on the morals and the policy of the Kuomintang Government? Or was it perhaps his intention even more to promote publicity for the State Department's book on United States relations with China? I do not wish to quote too much from this book; I would give one quotation, pars pro toto. On page 68 of this book, in the section dealing with reports by General Stillwell, the General complains about the non-co-operation of Chiang Kai-Shek, and concludes with these words: 'I believe he (Chiang Kai-Shek) will only continue his policy and delay while grabbing for loans and post-war aid, for the purpose of maintaining his present position, based on one-party government, a reactionary policy, or the suppression of democratic ideas with the active aid of his Gestapo.'"[157]

The "wonderful resurrection of the great Chinese people" against the corrupt, exploitative and reactionary Kuomintang government was liberating the country from its external and internal enemies; the real China had already declared its adherence to the camp of peace, Clementis said.[158] The old China was disappearing. He rejected discussing Tsiang's request in the UN assembly, because the most important problem now was the Soviet proposal on atomic weapons and a new agreement of the five permanent members of the UN Security Council.[159] The delegates of Yugoslavia and Poland also expressed their rejection of Tsiang's request; then Vyšinskii began his long speech.

The former Soviet prosecutor general who had chaired the trial of Sinoviev, Kamenev and Bukharin in the 1930s, was extremely cynical – but also a talented and ruthless orator. Vyšinskii spoke in Russian, demonstrating the might of the Soviet Union:

> "The only motto seems to be: Against the Soviet Union. 'We want to slander someone, so let us do it against the Soviet Union. If anything bad is happening, let us ascribe it to the Soviet Union.' [...] This is as if

---

[157] "Řeč min. dr. Clementise u Gen. ...", 12.
[158] "Řeč min. dr. Clementise u Gen. ...", 13.
[159] "Řeč min. dr. Clementise u Gen. ...", 13.

the governmental authority in some state hailed an innocent person before the bar of justice without even informing him of the indictment. [...] The Kuomintang representative objected to the language I used. He reminded us of the cultural traditions of China. We all know these cultural traditions of China, and I shall say a few words about that, too, subsequently. But I must warn the representative of China -- excuse me, the representative of the Kuomintang -- that I shall call a 'spade' a 'spade'. [...] No, sir, Mr. Representative of the Kuomintang, I will say that you are not dealing with any distortion of the truth but merely lying and indulging in mendacious slander against the Soviet Union. [...] At the same time, however, you are slandering and libelling your own people who have turned away from your government, who have chased your government from the greater part of its territory and which people, I am quite deeply convinced, do not consider you to be its representative, the Chinese people's representative, here."[160]

In New York, Clementis was in his element, busy with the UN sessions and other official duties. He was on the phone with Gottwald and his deputy Široký on a daily basis, completely clueless that Comrades Klema (Gottwald) and Vilo (Široký) were scheming behind his back; Široký even paid Lída a couple of visits to lull her into a sense of security – the rumours about Clementis' arrest were just US Imperialist propaganda.[161] Yet, persons close to Clementis, such as the delegate of the Czechoslovak diplomatic mission Adolf Hoffmeister (1902–1973), warned him:

> "'I invited Vlado for a walk in the late morning. We went to Central Park, [...] I gave him the letter from Juhn. He read it. He was silent. Then he said that Juhn was just a frightened journalist, that this information was nonsense. We burnt the letter in a wooden dust bin.' From the very beginning, Clementis trivialized the warnings and made fun of the persons

---

[160] "Řeč min. dr. Clementise u Gen. ...", 21, 27. "Evidently, Stalin, who had shorthanded reports of Vyshinsky's speeches sent to him at the Kremlin by special courier, was impressed by the unusual language Vyshinsky used as he grew more and more incensed. Nothing quite like it had ever been heard in diplomatic circles anywhere in the world before; the matchless and unparalleled mixture of high-flown Latin and scurrilous abuse was his rhetorical style abroad as well as at home." Vaksberg, 282.
[161] Holotíková a Plevza, 266.

who submitted them. He was convinced that American propaganda was behind the news. [...] 'Once a week, we used to go to a pub in the countryside. [...] Somewhere in the vicinity of Mount Kisco, [...], Vlado showed us Sulzberger's letter. It was a draft article for the *New York Times*. The article described in very precise terms what awaited him in Prague, warning him that he should not go back home.'"[162]

Clementis laughed the warnings off; one might think that he was naïve or arrogant, yet Gottwald and the Soviets systematically undertook everything to make him feel safe. On 23 October 1949, Clementis called Gottwald and suggested Lída join him in New York.[163] Gottwald praised his foreign minister's idea: Lída's arrival in New York would certainly dispel the vile rumours the Imperialist camp was mounting against the Czechoslovak government. With Lída on her way, Clementis wrote a letter to the *New York Times*, thanking them ironically of taking such good care of him.[164]

It might be difficult for us to understand why Clementis fobbed off all warnings, but he truly believed that US propaganda was behind the rumours. As recently as May, the Party had elected him to the CC. Why would the comrades, his friends, want to get rid of him now – to Clementis, the rumours made no sense. The trap prepared for him was devilishly precise and psychologically astute, playing on his integrity, decency and loyalty. On 28 October, Czechoslovakia's national holiday, Vyšinskii sent him a telegram, acknowledging Clementis' importance to the Soviet government:

---

[162] Holotíková a Plevza, 266-267. Cyrus Leo Sulzberger (1912–1993) was a Harvard graduate and journalist for the *New York Times*; for more details see his obituary on http://www.nytimes.com/1993/09/21/obituaries/c-l-sulzberger-columnist-dies-at-80.html?pagewanted=all; accessed 31 October 2016. Hoffmeister was a famous Czech caricaturist and artist. Erich Juhn was a German who had fled to the USA.
[163] Holotíková a Plevza, 267.
[164] Holotíková a Plevza, 267-268.

> "I kindly ask you, foreign ministr, to accept my sincere congratulations [*priniat' moi serdečnie pozdravlenia*] for the thirty-first anniversary of the foundation of the Czechoslovak Republic, and also for the future strengthening of the friendship between the Soviet Union and Czechoslovakia. A. Vyšinskii."[165]

Lída's presence in New York had the effect Clementis expected: the rumours stopped.[166] Ever the dutiful and decent Party member, he sent his deputy Široký a telegram on 11 November, following the Party tradition:

> "Dear Comrade, I kindly ask you to submit to the CC of the KSS my best wishes and greatest admiration for its work. [...] The CC of the KSS has the grand task and the great responsibility of realizing our grand goals, goals that you mentioned in your speech at the ninth Party convention. [...] with comradely greetings Práci čest [honourable work] Vladimír Clementis."[167]

After the UN session in New York, Clementis and his wife returned to Prague and spent a happy Christmas together. It would be their last.

---

[165] AMZV, GS-A 1945-1954, carton 78, 1 page, telegram sent by Western Union on 28 October 1949, in Russian, 1. Congratulations from comrades to comrades for birthdays, the anniversary of the October Revolution, or important Party events were customary and a sign that one was safe. OKAPI, a group of high-ranking members of the Czechoslovak army and intelligence officers, who had fled in 1948, planned the operation *Great Sweeper* together with the American OSS immediately after Slánský's 50th birthday on 31 July 1951. An OKAPI officer noticed that there was no mention of Stalin's traditional birthday telegram in the Czechoslovak press. He drew the right conclusion: Slánský had fallen from Stalin's grace, and something was going on against him at the top of the Party. For details of the operation *Great Sweeper* see Lukes, *Rudolf Slansky* ... .

[166] Holotíková a Plevza, 268.

[167] Clementis, "Pozdravný telegram s. V. Širokým na zasedání ÚV KSS – 11. XI. 49", AMZV, GS-A 1945-1954, carton 78, 1 page, 1.

III. 3 The End (1950–1952)

At the beginning of 1950, Gusto (Husák) and Laco (Novomeský) visited their old friend Vlado in his apartment in the Czernín Palace. They had a splendid time together, drinking wine and singing Slovak folk songs. The three friends were in top government and Party positions; Czechoslovakia was firmly in the Soviet camp, and life was good. Husák remembered:

> "He returned from New York after a long session at the UN. He told us about the shindy they had kicked up in the West about his person [*aký bengál robili na Západe okolo jeho osoby*]. Allegedly, arrest awaited him, that's why he should not return home. At the ministry, where Široký acted as his deputy, they had arrested people. [...] He told us that he had informed Gottwald, how attentive Gottwald had been, and how they had laughed together about having outwitted Western propaganda. Clementis [...] believed that he had Gottwald's full trust. [...] He had a sincere and noble soul [*priamu a ušlachtilú dušu*] and liked it when people trusted him. [...] We had no idea that this would be our last friendly encounter."[168]

But Husák remembered also Clementis' bitterness about Široký's behaviour. Although he was in daily contact with his deputy while in New York, Široký had never mentioned the arrests at the MZV. The foreign minister had learnt about them from the US press, which was speculating about whether Clementis would return to Czechoslovakia. Husák understood his friend:

> "Clementis was an honest man and a loyal party member. Of course he returned home."[169]

---

[168] Plevza, *Gustáv Husák prehovoril*, 64.
[169] Husák, Gustáv, "Request for Full Party Rehabilitation, Addressed to the CC KSČ, 1 May 1963 (copy in author's possession), quoted from Kaplan, *Report on the Murder* ..., 61. According to Vlasta Jaksicsová, the workers' mistrust of the intellectuals in the Party originated from the times of the Social Democrats, that is, before the split of the workers' movement into Communists and Social Democrats. Široký's hatred and envy of Clementis was also caused by the lawyer's privileged position in the Party. While the labourers had to fullfil

On 11 March 1950, the Party made a move: the CC KSS criticized Clementis and sacked him from his position as foreign minister. Široký was appointed new foreign minister on 14 March. This must have been a brutal blow to Clementis – yet, he still did not understand the situation he was in, which is very easy to say with hindsight. Working as a clerk in a state bank in Prague, he thought that he had a chance to fend off the Party's criticism and rehabilitate himself.

At the ninth Party convention of the KSS in May 1950, he was given the opportunity to engage in self-criticism, after Husák and Novomeský who had lost their high positions too. Clementis believed in fairness between comrades – a characteristic trait of his Gottwald and Široký could not be bothered with. I think that Clementis hoped that by acknowledging his past errors, that is, his activities in exile with the Beneš government and his criticism of the German-Soviet Nonaggression Pact, he would convince the Party leadership of his unremitting loyalty.

On 26 May 1950, Clementis defended himself against the accusations; he stressed that he had always been loyal to the Party and said that his criticism of the Ribbentroop-Molotov Pact had been a personal failure – but he could not distance himself from his entire life, activities for Socialism and the Czechoslovak state.[170] He mentioned his trips to the Soviet Union and defended his editorship of DAV that had promoted the revolutionary Socialist movement in Slovakia in the First Republic:

---

    tough and clandestine tasks such as organizing the illegal press in the underground, the intellectuals were sent abroad, had money and wore expensive suits. Široký had had only basic school education; he was a railway worker. It is not difficult to understand, why he envied the elegant and educated Clementis who had never had to endure life's hardships.

[170] Holotíková a Plevza, 290.

> "Clementis' speech was brief, his voice firm, but not servile. Yet, the assembly felt that the chair did not like the tone and contents of Clementis' self-criticism. And that was why nobody applauded. [...] Viliam Široký rejected Clementis self-criticism [...], playing the role of the baffled inquisitor to perfection."[171]

The CC KSS also rejected the self-criticism of Husák and Novomeský. Slánský, still at the height of his power as General Secretary of the KSČ, sent Clementis a telegram on 15 September 1950 – another despicable little action that would raise Clementis' hopes, while the planning of the trial of the 'Slovak bourgeois nationalists' was in full swing.

Slánský's telegram gives us a good insight into how the KSČ's administration worked, particularly with regard to members who had fallen from the Party's grace. After the CC KSS had refused to accept Clementis' self-criticism at the May meeting, he had to submit a written account of his errors to the CC of the KSČ. Note Slánský's non-committal but sub-cutaneously threatening tone in his telegram that confirmed the Party's receipt of Clementis' self-criticism. Clementis should keep guessing what the CC's final verdict would be:

> "Dear Comrade, the presidency of the CC of the KSČ has received your self-critical letter of 27 June, taking into consideration that you shall prove with your future activities that you have drawn all the necessary lessons from your self-criticism. With comradely wishes, Slánský."[172]

In his last months of freedom, from June 1950 to January 1951, Clementis tried to come to terms with what was happening to him. He had, at least, his beloved Lída at his side, their dog Brok and their friends Gusto and Laco. The work at the bank was no chal-

---

[171] Holotíková a Plevza, 292, 293.
[172] Telegram from Slánský to Clementis, 15 September 1950, SNA OF VC, carton a. 9., 97, 1 page, typewritten. The directives for Clementis the CC KSČ issued in June 1950 in Kaplan, *Report on the Murder* ..., 62.

lenge for the passionate politician; the dull bureaucratic and administrative activity was neither intellectually stimulating nor interesting.[173]

Lída was busy furnishing their new apartment, since they had had to move out from the Czernín Palace. Clementis went on long walks with Brok through Prague; one day, he would not come back home.

III. 3. 1 Arrest and Interrogation (1951–1952)

The StB arrested Clementis on 28 January 1951:

> "He was kidnapped while taking a walk [with his dog Brok, add. JB] and driven off westward, until the car passed the stones marking Czechoslovakia's border. Clementis found himself at a West German police station. Officers in German and American uniforms welcomed him and inquired about the reasons for his defection. Clementis demanded to be taken back to Prague."[174]

The border officers and the police station were a fake.[175] Had Clementis walked into this trap, the little border scheme would have served the prosecutor to add a further accusation to his list: defection to the enemy camp of Capitalist Imperialism. I think that Clementis wanted to be brought back to Prague because of two reasons: first, he did not want to leave behind Lída. Second, he did not want to leave Czechoslovakia, his home. He truly wished to explain himself to the Party, hoping for rehabilitation. Naturally, the carpenter from Moravia found the little border scheme funny; Gottwald chuckled[176] when he read the details in the report about

---

[173] Holotíková a Plevza, 295.
[174] Kaplan, *Report on the Murder* …, 107.
[175] Fake 'Western' police stations equipped with agents in West German and US uniforms was a practice in the Communist satellite states bordering Germany; East German and Czechoslovak citizens who fled should be made to feel safe, which would give the prosecutors and the State Security Services a legal basis for condemning them for 'Republikflucht'.
[176] Kaplan, *Report on the Murder* …, 107.

Clementis' arrest – most probably in the presence of a glass of vodka, his steady companion.

Before I present parts of Clementis' interrogation and the material I have found in the archives of the Czechoslovak State Security Services in Prague, it is important to understand how the trial was planned – and changed on Stalin's orders. On 21 February 1951, roughly one month after Clementis' arrest, comrades Václav Kopecký (1897–1961) and Štefan Bašťovanský (1910–1952) informed the CC KSS about the "Clementis case".[177] The 'Husák-Novomeský group' – both had been arrested on 6 February – had imported into Slovakia the ideology of 'bourgeois nationalism'; the spy and conspirator Clementis was the ringleader:

> "First of all, it is proven beyond any doubt today that Husák and Novomeský gave up important positions in the leadership of the uprising to members of the Capitalist and reactionary parties during the Slovak National Uprising. [...] The interrogations have also confirmed that Husák, Novomeský and their band had planned to maintain the power apparatus of the Fascists of the Tiso state after the post-war reconstruction of Czechoslovakia. [...] Clementis said, and the latest results of the interrogation confirm this, that the Husák-Novomeský group had not committed only 'errors' or 'mistakes', but that they had been a well-organized anti-Party and reactionary band."[178]

Allegedly, Clementis had schemed against the Party as early as the autumn of 1944; while Novomeský was in London, both had secretly formed a reactionary platform, which they planned to establish in Slovakia after the war.

Let me briefly explain the meaning of 'Slovak bourgeois nationalism' in the context of Marxist-Leninist thought. The only

---

[177] *Zpráva súdruha Václava Kopeckého a Štefana Bašťovanského na zasadaní ústredného výboru Kommunistickej Strany Československa dňa 21. Februara 1951* (Bratislava: kultúrno-propagačné oddelenie sekretariátu ÚV KSS, no date mentioned, most probably 1951), 35.
[178] *Zpráva súdruha Václava Kopeckého a ...*, 36, 37.

feature of identity a Marxist-Leninist approves of and acknowledges is his identity as a worker: he is a proletarian, nothing else. He conceives of Nationalism and national identity as core elements of Capitalism; the bourgeois class uses Nationalism as an ideology to divide the workers, prevent their global solidarity and uprisings against their exploiters. Therefore, any attempt of Party members to pursue rights for their nation, for example constitutional equality of one's nation or national minority in a bi- or multi-national state, has to be condemned as reactionary.

Clementis, Husák and Novomeský were patriots, but their Slovak identity was closely connected to their belief in Marxism-Leninism. Their attempts to strengthen the Communist movement in Slovakia after WWII were not based on anti-Communist thought – on the contrary: in their opinion, the Slovaks who had just survived the Tiso regime would become loyal Communists only if the Prague government would arrange for a constitutionally granted equality with the Czechs. The DS had won the parliamentary elections in 1946 in Slovakia, because the centre-right politicians had promised to negotiate for Slovak self-government within the common state. The KSS had lost the elections, because it had been under the tight control of the KSČ and was not allowed to speak out for negotiations; it had to keep to the strict Party discipline dictated by Moscow and the CC KSČ. One could speak of an intra-Party centralism, which forbade the KSS to co-operate with the centre-right parties to negotiate Slovak equal status and self-government – which actually went against the stipulations and the fundamental idea of the National Front.

In the Slovak Communists' way of thinking, the KSČ should not make the same mistakes as the bourgeois governments in the First Republic; they had ruled Slovakia in a centralist fashion from Prague. Clementis and his friends truly believed that the common state's future was Socialism; to achieve this goal, the Slovak citizens had to be convinced that the Communist credo was the way toward a new and better life. They thought and acted rationally: promoting Socialism in Slovakia would only improve relations between Czechs and Slovaks that had still been suffering from mistrust, grievances and contempt ever since the 1938 Munich Agreement. If the Communist Party established a Slovak equal status with the Czechs, gave the Slovaks what they wanted, it would create loyalty to Marxism-Leninism and the Gottwald government. Equality with the Czechs and regional self-government was thus a first step towards overcoming nationalism; Socialism could be realized only if all citizens, Slovaks and Czechs, would enjoy equal status and a fair amount of local and regional self-government, within the political confines of the Party's unchallenged monopoly of governmental rule, of course.

The view of the Gottwald government, which had taken over the centralist policy from the first post-war government from 1945 to 1948 under President Beneš, was diametrically opposed. Czech and Slovak Party members of the Gottwald government thought that Slovakia had to be ruled with a tight centralist fist, not only because the centrally planned economy demanded Prague's control. To give the Slovaks what they wanted, would only create ideological unrest and sow the seeds of anti-Communist rebellion. Particularly the Catholics and bourgeois elements in Slovakia would be trying to drive a rift between the two nations and split the state. They had done it before, or so the CC KSČ must have thought. After the lost 1946 parliamentary elections, the CC KSS had no more say in Slovakia in terms of independent policy-making.

Had Czechoslovakia's capital been Bratislava and the Slovaks the more powerful and numerically larger nation, Stalin would have instructed them to accuse leading Czech comrades of

'Czech bourgeois nationalism' – the result, that is, the show trial, would have been the same. Had the KSS been the more powerful Party, Stalin would have dictated that they get rid of the Czech Party members who had had fought in Spain, spent WWII in London exile, and were intellectuals and Jews. Every comrade who had come into contact with the Imperialist West was, in Stalin's brutal logic, infected with the virus of Capitalism, Titoism and Imperialism. Thus, the Soviet camp had to rid itself of these potentially dangerous individuals.

An important aspect of the planned show trial that added to Titoism the accusation of Zionism was not only Stalin's antisemitism, but also the hatred working class members felt towards their privileged comrades. The majority of the accused in what would become the *monstr proces* of Slánský and co-accused had a bourgeois background, were Jewish and had enjoyed university education. They were no real proletarians like Gottwald, a carpenter, Novotný, a blacksmith and Široký, a railway worker.

The NKVD and StB's original plan was to train the arrested Slovaks to act as 'witnesses' in the trial of top Czech Party members, at the time Otto Šling and Marie Švermová (1902–1992). Yet, in the course of 1951, the script was changed:

> "Husák and the other Slovak prisoners accused of 'bourgeois nationalism' were brutally interrogated. But at the beginning of 1951, views were appearing within the StB that the real leader of the conspiracy was not Šling, but somebody higher up in the Party's ranks. [...] When a new batch of Soviet advisors arrived, the original plan of the trial changed. The Slovak bourgeois nationalists no longer fitted into the new plan since they were not important enough [...] Rudolf Slánský was now the ringleader of the anti-state conspiracy."[179]

---

[179] Pešek, "Nepriateľ so ...", 219-220.

The change of the trial's concept, but also Husák's resilience saved his and Novomeský's lives. The lawyer and ruthless former government trustee (*povereník*) for Slovak affairs drove his interrogators literally to despair: he signed nothing, entangled the interrogators in legal details and revoked what he had confessed earlier. The interrogators decided to separate Husák and the Slovaks from the Slánský trial and arranged for a trial in Bratislava, which would be held from 21 to 24 April 1954.

In view of the change of plan, why did the interrogators keep Clementis in the Prague trial? I think for two reasons: first, they had him already well prepared – he would co-operate. Second, Clementis would act as a witness of Slánský's traitorous activities, which would render the accusations even more convincing, since he had been in the top rank of Party and state, thus personally close to Slánský. Furthermore, the trial was scheduled for November 1952 – it had to be conducted now. I can only speculate, but one explanation why the interrogators were pressed for time might be Stalin's health. He was ill and might have sensed that he did not have much time left: he wanted to make sure that the CPs of the Eastern bloc would be safely purged of unreliable Party members.

The StB prepared another scheme for Clementis, just to be on the safe side with enough incriminating 'evidence' – they faked reports of Western newspapers and broadcasts, among them Radio Free Europe: according to information gathered by Soviet organs, Clementis and his wife had allegedly left Czechoslovakia on 8 January 1951 in their car, passing Graz on their way to Tito's Yugoslavia, where they were believed to have asked for political asylum.[180]

---

[180] ABS USTRČR, YSGŠ, sign. a. č. 9479 Vlado Clementis.

In 1951, Austria was still under Soviet occupation; at first glance, it thus made perfect sense that the Soviet *kommandatura* in Vienna or Graz would inform the comrades in Prague. But: there are no records that prove that Lída and Vlado owned a car. As foreign minister, he had had a car with a chauffeur, but lost this privilege when the Party fired him. It was also quite impossible for Clementis to be arrested by the StB on 28 January 1951 in Prague and, twenty days earlier, drive to Austria with his wife. Had he wanted to ask for asylum in Yugoslavia, why would he return to Prague – just to get himself arrested? And how could Radio Free Europe possibly know that the couple was heading for Yugoslavia? They could have driven to Italy, Switzerland or Germany – or Turkey.

The faked document demonstrates that the StB, under the guidance of the Soviet NKVD officers, made sure they had all the angles covered, to have enough 'evidence' to accuse Clementis of Titoism and high treason. The trial's plan could always change, and the scheme was immensely clever: since people knew that Clementis was a Slovak, they must have assumed that he lived in Bratislava, particularly after he had lost his position at the MZV. The shortest way to Yugoslavia from Bratislava was through Vienna and Graz. The alleged flight of Clementis to Yugoslavia would not be mentioned in the trial.

Clementis was being 'prepared' for the show trial from January 1951 to November 1952 – twenty-three long months of physical and psychological torture. Before the StB arrested Lída on 24 February 1951, they executed a thorough search:

> "Protocol of the house search of V. Clementis' flat in Prague IV, Na Valech 16/283, conducted on 5 February 1951 in the presence of Clementis' wife and her brother Václav Pátek, academic painter, and her father, Jan Pátek, editor. The mentioned relatives confirm with their signature that nothing was damaged or stolen. The following items were found:

> 3 suitcases with various documents
>
> 1 suitcase with ammunition for a hunting rifle
>
> 1 pistol, calibre 7.65, with a silencer
>
> 1 leather attaché case with documents
>
> 1 key to a bank vault
>
> 1 weapon, calibre 22x26, Ho ZKW, 465 001 with a telescope ... "[181]

According to the protocol, the StB found seven (!) weapons, among them a US Smith & Wesson, and enough ammunition to kill the population of a large Czech or Slovak village with some thousand citizens. Clearly, the StB had made up the 'protocol': there is no hint in the literature that Clementis liked hunting[182] – on the contrary: he loved animals. Why would he have seven weapons and ammunition in his flat? But, as a 'Slovak bourgeois nationalist' intent on betraying the government and the Czechoslovak people and conspiring to overthrow the People's Democracy, he had to have weapons hidden in his flat, Western currency paid into a bank safe and documents. Every detail was taken care of in this grand scheme of the anti-state conspiracy of the Slánský group. Lída, her brother and her father signed the protocol of the house search; most probably, the StB told them to sign, or otherwise your dear Vlado shall ...

From Kopecký and Bašťovanský's report to the CC KSS it transpires that Clementis must have decided early on to co-operate. One month after his arrest, the interrogators had already made him 'confess' to a Slovak conspiracy he had allegedly planned while in London exile. Clementis did not put up much resistance. Why? I think, because of Lída.

---

[181] ABS USTRČR, MNB 2_1_35_00004_jpg.

[182] In psychological terms, I find it interesting that the Communist leaders Brežnev, Honecker and Ceaușescu, all from proletarian background, loved hunting and took photos of their bounty of shot deer.

The interrogators' psychological astuteness was devilishly clever; they knew exactly which buttons to push to make the former foreign minister co-operate. I deem it safe to assume that Clementis sacrificed himself in the hope of saving Lída. His wife sent him beautiful letters, giving him the impression that she was free and in steady contact with his beloved sister Boža in Tisovec, that the Páteks in Prague and the Clementis family in Slovakia were unharmed – while she was imprisoned and forced to write these letters.[183] The StB put Lída under pressure: write these letters or else, you cannot imagine what we can do to your husband ... The StB and their NKVD advisors were free to do anything to achieve their goals; they acted without compunction, placing themselves above the law.

Looking at Clementis' last picture, the official identification photograph taken in Růzyně prison shortly after his arrest: I can see anger, humiliation, fear and disbelief in his face. He must have thought that his arrest was a major error, that he could still explain himself to the Party, that the comrades would see that he was innocent. Yet, he would learn very soon that he had to co-operate, if he wanted to save his life and his wife. Clementis was forced to go through two training sessions and one final rehearsal, the protocol for the court (*soudní protokol*).[184]

Even if one is fairly familiar with the administration in the Socialist states of the Eastern bloc, one is baffled by the meticulous procedure and enormous effort involved: the archive material relating to Clementis' interrogation amounts to hundreds of files and thousands of typewritten pages. The NKVD officers went to

---

[183] Holotíková a Plevza, 297.
[184] The first protocol is filed as ABS USTRČR, MNB 2_1 Z_1480 podsvazek 43; the second as ABS USTRČR, MNB 2_1 Z_ 1480 podsvazek 44 and the protocol for the court can be found under the signature ABS USTRČR, MNB 2_1 Z_1480_podsvazek 65.

great lengths to prove him guilty of crimes he had never committed. The three statements prepared for the 'court' consist of witnesses' statements 'confirming' the principal accusation of Slánský's conspiracy, lengthy indexes of alleged Western spies in alphabetical order, lists of dates when Clementis was in contact with them, and lists of alleged conspiratorial meetings of the Slánský *banda*. The NKVD and StB furthermore collected articles, speeches and books Clementis had published at home and abroad; these newspaper-clippings were filed in chronological order as 'evidence' of his treason.[185]

Citizens of a democracy and rule-of-law state are used to being treated according to the constitution – they have rights. The authorities have no right to beat them, let alone torture them, and the assumption 'innocent until proved guilty' is a fundamental principle of the Western legal system. Every violation in the interrogation, every trespassing of the interrogator has to be put on record. A citizen in Communist Czechoslovakia had no such rights. We know about the torture only from the memoirs of those who survived, London, Husák and Holdoš. From the texts of the official records, a Western reader gets the impression that the interrogations had been conducted in a civilized manner on a normal question-answer basis, signed by the accused, probably with a coffee and a cigarette. The records do not mention the beatings, the cold prison cells, the sleep deprivation and the endless questioning. The rationale of the interrogations: first, get the accused to co-operate; second, get him to sign all the statements including the final one; and third, make sure he sticks to his text in court.

The practice of law and the judiciary had undergone a 'revolutionary' change after the 'victorious February 1948': the Party conceived of the law as instrument of bourgeois Capitalism that

---

[185] ABS USTRČR, MNB 2_11, MNB 2_10, MNB 2_9, MNB 2_8.

had served only the ruling class. Now, the jurisdiction of the People's Democracy served the people: in the first two years after the coup d'etat, the Party was careful not to change the text of the law, but exchanged the judiciary's personnel and instructed it to apply the legal practice of the new regime.[186] The law had to be interpreted as an instrument of the proletarian class that was fighting the old ways. The legal codex of 1920 was still officially the basis of jurisdiction – but the text of the laws had nothing to do with how the law was applied. The law was an instrument of the class struggle.

Alexej Čepička, Gottwald's son in law and minister of justice, had said in parliament, quoting Marx and Engels, that the equality of the citizens was a legend that had only oppressed the people. The idea of a justice system that stood above the classes went against the truth and reality of the class struggle. The unbiased objectivity of the judges was a "stupid and impractical lie and deception [*objektivní soudce, jaký to stupidní a nepraktický klam, podvod*]", since it limited the power of the legislator, that is, the Party, hence the avant guard of the proletariat.[187] The Party's po-

---

[186] Ota Ulč, *Komunistická justice a třídní boj* (Praha: Stilus Press, 2016), 95. Ulč wrote his excellent analysis of Communist legal practice as a PhD thesis at Columbia University in New York in the 1960s, hence used sources from those years, conveying to the reader the academic atmosphere in the Cold War. He had studied law in the 1950s and fled to the USA, where he decided to study the new subject political science that was just emerging. The Czech text is an abridged version of his PhD thesis with an afterword by Pavel Molek. For a recent analysis of the legal practice under Communism see Michal Bobek, Pavel Molek a Vojtěch Šimíček (eds.), *Komunistické právo v Československu: kapitoly z dějin bezpráví* (Brno: Masarykova univerzita, 2009).

[187] Alexej Čepička, *Právní prakse*, prosinec 1948, s. 283, quoted from Ulč, 96. The concept 'impractical' demonstrates the subordination of the law to the Party's political decisions.

litical needs determined jurisdiction. According to Ulč, the principles of "ambiguity and flexibility" dominated the legal system; special consideration was given to international relations, that is, how the class enemy would interpret the Commmunist practice of law.[188] It was therefore no surprise that Prime Minister Antonín Zapotocký at a conference of the Czechoslovak bar association in 1949 said that *justitia* in the People's Democracy was not blind, on the contrary: aware of her crucially important function for the class struggle, she had to have her eyes wide open.[189]

Under psychological and physical torture, Clementis signed all three statements; he admitted to having schemed against the Party since his youth. Every action on behalf of his beloved Marxism-Leninism and the Party was turned into an activity against the Party – save for his trips to the Soviet Union in 1929 and 1930, which made perfect sense in Stalin's mind: if I want to get rid of Party members infected with the virus of the West, I naturally do not mention their visits to the beacon of the workers' movement. Slánský and Gottwald had spent WWII in Moscow; Gottwald was obedient, reliable and from proper proletarian stock. Therefore, or so Stalin must have thought, the Jew Slánský had to die.

Let us have a brief look at the court records, the final version after months of 'training' and the change in the trial procedure mentioned above. I have selected brief parts of the judicial transcript I think are particularly important, since they give an insight into the trial's meticulous planning. The statement the accused was to give before the court was dated 17 October 1952, that is, roughly one month before the start of the trial scheduled

---

[188] Ulč, 97.
[189] SCHMIDT, 1952, s. 172, quoted from Ulč, 96.

for 20 November 1952. Once Clementis had signed the final statement, the authorities fed him up, because he had to look healthy and composed; the audience in the courtroom should see no signs of distress, let alone torture:

> "'Explain why you are guilty!' – 'I admit to being guilty of affiliation to the French espionage service 'Sûreté Nationale', when I became an agent of the Western Imperialists in 1939. [...] I was a co-conspirator with Slánský and Geminder and other conspirators in the service of the Western Imperialists. We undertook anti-state and disruptive activities against the Czechoslovak People's Democracy, with the intention to liquidate the government of the People's Democracy and restore Capitalism in the country [*na likvidaci lidově demokratického zřízení a restauraci kapitalismu v zemi*]."[190]

On the second page of the court protocol, Clementis 'admitted' that he had met up with André Simone (Otto Katz) in 1946, known to him as a close associate of Slánský's; he had given him secret information and provided him with financial means for his espionage activities.[191] It must have been particularly hurtful for Clementis that the authorities portrayed him as a traitor ever since he had joined the Party in 1925:

> "'That means that you and your employees who worked for the journal DAV committed anti-democratic activities!' – 'Yes, my activities at DAV were directed against the Party. With my considerable influence, I drew DAV and the Davists away from the Party and the working class. Later, I began to promote the politics of bourgeois nationalism in Slovakia; as a consequence, our group formed a secret platform with the Slovak people's main enemies, the Hlinka Fascists. Like Tuka, I directed our DAV group against the progressive forces in Czechoslovakia [*Tukovým spôsobe, jsem usměrňoval své přívržence ze skupiny DAV proti pokrokovým silám Československa*].'"[192]

---

[190] ABS USTRČR, MNB 2_1 Z_1480 podsvazek 65_0003.jpg; ABS USTRČR, MNB 2_1 Z_1480 podsvazek 65_0004.jpg
[191] ABS USTRČR, MNB 2_1 Z_1480 podsvazek 65_0004.jpg.
[192] ABS USTRČR, MNB 2_1 Z_1480 podsvazek 65_0006.jpg.

In London exile, Beneš had employed him, Clementis added, because they both shared anti-Soviet and pro-Imperialist beliefs:

> "'Is it right to say that you became an enemy of the Czechoslovak people like your friends who shared your beliefs? – 'Yes, I admit to this. In England, the reactionary forces consolidated, and some members of the Czechoslovak Communist Party were under their influence.'"[193]

After the war, Slánský had, with the support of Clementis, placed Western spies at the Foreign Ministry, while Clementis, then assistant secretary of state, had used the negotiations with Hungary about the population transfer to build up his own network of spies in Hungary.[194] Clementis answered the interrogator's last question on page 52 of the court statement:

> "'Would you like to add something to your confession?' – 'I have confessed everything, I have admitted that I betrayed the Czechoslovak people as an agent of Imperialism, that I committed actions against the Czechoslovak people to support the Western Imperialists. I have admitted that I engaged in subversive activities as a member of the Beneš band and the anti-state spy ring led by Rudolf Slánský. All my activities and the activities of Slánský's conspiratorial spy ring were aimed at the liquidation of the government of the Czechoslovak People's Democracy, the restoration of Capitalism and the republic's subordination to Western Imperialism.'"[195]

In the trial's cruel logic, the authorities also had the 'witnesses' sign their 'statements'. On 18 November 1952, two days before the start of the trial, Novomeský signed:

> "'Explain, how you, in post-war Czechoslovakia, set about realizing the hostile plan you had hatched with Dr Clementis in London.' – 'After Dr Clementis had returned home from London in 1945 and until his resignation from the government, I was secretly meeting up with him and Dr Gustáv Husák in Bratislava on a regular basis.'"[196]

---

[193] ABS USTRČR, MNB 2_1 Z_1480 podsvazek 65_00014.jpg.
[194] ABS USTRČR, MNB 2_1 Z_1480 podsvazek 65_0033.jpg; ABS USTRČR, MNB 2_1 Z_1480 podsvazek 65_0026.jpg.
[195] ABS USTRČR, MNB 2_1 Z_1480 podsvazek 65_0054.jpg.
[196] ABS USTRČR, MNB 2_1 Z_1480 podsvazek 65_0058.jpg.

The three friends's plan was, allegedly, to realize in the state institutions Slovak plans in the spirit of 'bourgeois nationalism'. The last part of the court protocol is the statement of the Israeli citizen Mordechai Oren (Markus Orenstein) given on 6 November 1952.[197] Oren's role was to prove Clementis' support of Zionism, the last item on the prosecutor's list of accusations:

> "'What did Clementis' activities to promote Zionism look like in detail [*V čem se konkrétně projevovala činnost CLEMENTISE v prospěch sionismu*]? – 'Clementis provided significant support for the foundation of the independent Jewish Capitalist state, which the Imperialists, mainly the USA, were directly supporting and promoting. […] During the war [the Israeli war of Independence, add. JB], economic support and full freedom of action was given to all Capitalist elements who emigrated from Czechoslovakia to Israel, taking with them values, goods and property.'"[198]

Oren further 'confessed' that Clementis had collaborated with Avriel to such an extent that Israeli Prime Minister David Ben-Gurion had praised the Czechoslovak foreign minister: the Zionists had no better friend in the People's Democracies than Clementis, who was pursuing the old politics of Masaryk and Beneš. Oren also said that as Slovak bourgeois nationalist, Clementis had a good understanding of Zionism, the embodiment of Jewish bourgeois nationalism.[199]

III. 3. 2 Show Trial and Execution (1952)

In the West, namely in France, the Communists found themselves in a dilemma: what to think of the Rajk trial in Hungary and the news of the arrests of Clementis, Slánský and top Czechoslovak Communists? Some French comrades had quite an intense New Year's Eve in Paris:

---

[197] ABS USTRČR, MNB 2_1 Z_1480 podsvazek 65_0071.jpg.
[198] ABS USTRČR, MNB 2_1 Z_1480 podsvazek 65_0073.jpg.
[199] ABS USTRČR, MNB 2_1 Z_1480 podsvazek 65_0074.jpg.

"'Psychodramas' weren't much talked about at the end of 1951. I turned up with Claire toward midnight on New Year's Eve, coming from one family party at my relatives' to this other family party at Pierre Courtade's house. [He was a Communist journalist and writer.] Everyone was very happy. In fact, everyone was quite drunk. 'You're the one we were waiting for,' said all my friends. They explained the game to me. Jean Duvignaud [an art historian and sociologist] said that every epoch invents its own literary genre or form: the Greeks had had tragedy, the Renaissance the sonnet, the classical age the five-act play in verse with the three unities, etc. The socialist age had invented its own form: the Moscow show-trial. These partygoers, who were all slightly the worse for drink, had decided to play at being on trial. All they needed was an accused, and as I had come last I was the obvious choice. Roger Vailland [a Communist writer] was the prosecutor, Courtade was the defense lawyer. I had to take my place in the dock. I resisted rather feebly, and then decided to go along with it. The charges were very serious, as I had broken ten different articles of the Code, and was accused of sabotaging the ideological effort, collaborating with the cultural enemy, plotting with international spies, philosophical high treason, etc. When I wanted to argue during the examination, the procurator, lawyer, witnesses, etc. all got quite angry. My lawyer's address to the court was terrible, and he pleaded that there were attenuating circumstances, but that I should be relieved of the burden of life as soon as possible. Thanks to the alcohol, the clowning around soon became quite nightmarish, and what was supposed to be a parody really began to hurt. When the sentence was passed (I got the death sentence, of course), two women there, including my wife, really began to get quite upset. Everyone was shouting and crying, looking in the cupboards for indigestion tablets, putting cold compresses on heads, etc. We all – judge, lawyer, and accused– attended to these people and tried to calm them down. I think I was the only one who wasn't drunk; but I wasn't the only one to feel ashamed. No doubt about it, looking back on it now we were all quite mad. There must be a point past which madness diminishes your responsibility. But before you get to that point, madness doesn't relieve you of of the burden of your responsibility. You choose madness to escape the noose that is closing around your neck, which you don't dare slip. Our insanity was the consequence of the insanity of the moment. We were rationalizing and internalizing a sort of general dementia."[200]

---

[200] Claude Roy, *Nous* (Paris: Gallimard, 1980), 389-390, quoted from Karel Bartošek, "Central and Eastern Europe", in *The Black Book of Communism*, 394-456, 406-407.

The show trial of Slánský and co-accused was scheduled for 20 November 1952. The protocol of the political commission of the secretariat of the CC KSČ offers us an insight into the final touches of the trial's conduct. The commission with Široký, Alexej, Bacílek, Čepička, Novotný, Rais and Prchal convened on 17 November.[201] The programme of the meeting had six points: last corrections of the text of the indictment; provisions for the public in the courtroom; security plan of the trial; suggestions about invited guests from the People's Democracies; working procedure of the trial and instructions for the press.

Especially interesting is the careful selection of members of the public invited to the courtroom: 300 to 350 members of the KSČ; 150 to 200 members of the army, security service and the department of justice and 50 seats for the press.[202] The intention was to ensure that the people selected to attend the trial should come from every district of the country; it was therefore necessary to arrange for hotel reservations for those who lived outside Prague. The StB should send coded invitations to the CPs in Poland, Hungary, Romania, Bulgaria and the GDR.[203]

The trial would last eight days. The verdict, which would be proclaimed at five o'clock on the last day, would be formulated

---

[201] "Zápis ze schůze pol. Sekretáriatu ÚV-KSČ k procesu s protistátním centrem, dne 17. listopadu 1952", AMVZ GS-A 1945-1954, carton 96, 5 pages, typewritten, addressed to Široký, 18 November 1952, classified *Príšně tajné* (top secret), 1.

[202] "Zápis ze schůze ...", 1. Save for a few details related to the Party and the bloc states, the show trial and the propaganda campaign were organized in a fashion similar to the trial of Milada Horáková and co-accused in June 1950. An excellent study about the propaganda campaign during the Horáková trial is Pavlina Formánková and Petr Koura, *Žádáme trest smrti! Propagandistický kampaň provázející proces s Miladou Horákovou a spol. (historická studie a edice dokumentů)* (Praha: Ústav pro studium totalitních režímů, 2008). The campaign's main goal was to unite the people in their hatred for the accused.

[203] "Zápis ze schůze ...", 2.

according to the Soviet model: first, the opinion of the court, then the sentence.²⁰⁴ The accused would be heard in the following order: Slánský, Geminder, Clementis, London, Hajdů, Simone, Frejka, Frank, Löbl and others; then Reicin, Švab and Šling. The StB had to oversee the written translations of the indictment; planned were written translations into Russian, German, English and French. During the trial, an interpreter would simultaneously translate directly from the courtroom, but only into one language: Russian. Some correspondents of the Western brotherly Communist Parties would have a personal translator at their disposal.²⁰⁵

To keep up the façade of a rule-of-law state, the authorities arranged for defence lawyers; their main task was to suggest to the domestic and international public that the accused had a fair trial. Five (!) defence lawyers took care of the fourteen accused.²⁰⁶

Did the majority of the people believe the accusations? Given the Party's propaganda machine that controlled the press and broadcast media, the citizens were bombarded with one-sided news. Yet, the trial did arouse some suspicions. The psychologically astute view of a critical person:

> "The one night I heard a nurse speaking behind a partially closed door. 'Back home in my village', she was saying, 'when a thief stole a goose, he denied he had done it to the end – even if he had been caught red-handed. These poor people are standing up confessing to all kinds of horrible crimes and accusing themselves of things nobody's even asked them about! Who knows what they did to them? The whole thing stinks to high heaven!'"²⁰⁷

Heda Margolius Kovály who had heard the nurse while in hospital was the wife of the accused Rudolf Margolius. Heda's fate was particularly cruel: as a teenager, she was deported with her parents

---

[204] "Zápis ze schůze ...", 2.
[205] "Zápis ze schůze ...", 5.
[206] Holotíková a Plevza, 302.
[207] Margolius Kovály, 140.

from her native Prague to the Lodz ghetto in Poland, from there to Auschwitz. Heda survived and escaped from the death march to Germany. Back in Prague in 1945, she witnessed how former friends refused to help her, learning that she was the only one of her family who had survived the Shoa. Her memoirs are an excellent source about the frightening atmosphere the Party created to indoctrinate the people, and how the families of the accused were made to suffer. After her husband's arrest, Heda lost their government apartment, was moved into a flat that lacked basic facilities such as running hot water and heating; she struggled for years to find work to feed her son. The people were afraid of the StB and did not dare to speak to the relatives of the accused, let alone help them. The social apartheid created in this atmosphere of hatred and hysteria would isolate the relatives for years to come.

All defendants had met Minister of Defence Karol Bacílek (1896–1974) a few days short of the trial:

> "All defendants promised to follow the script. Thus Clementis said, 'I'm a lawyer and a politician, I know what to expect. I have no illusions in this respect. I will behave in court so as to give no pretext for any campaign against the party or the public.' [...] Hinting that the sentence and the fate of the families would be influenced by discipline in the courtroom was a particularly strong psychological weapon. On the other hand, it gave the defendants some hope that they might be spared."[208]

On the concluding day of the trial, the accused were given the opportunity for a last word. Clementis said: "The verdict of the nation's court was just, however harsh it may be."[209] Most of the accused still hoped that their lives would be spared as long as they were co-operating, but the Party had made up its mind long before. On 2 December, President Gottwald signed the nine death

---

[208] Kaplan, *Report on the Murder* ..., 224.
[209] Kaplan, *Report on the Murder* ..., 232.

sentences. The other three 'lucky ones' were sentenced to life in prison. The execution date was 3 December.

Hours before his execution, the StB allowed Clementis to say good-bye to Lída and write a last letter to his sister Boža. He could put on his civilian clothes, and Lída received a makeover so that Vlado would not suspect that she had been in prison. Her hair was done, make-up applied to make her look healthy, and she wore her own clothes.[210] After their good-bye – they could see and speak to each other through a grille for an hour – he wrote her a last letter:

> "I am drinking lots of black coffee, I have rested for a few minutes, I am writing, taking breaks [...] my dear Hadička, I know that you will be surrounded by the love and tenderness of your father and mother and all our family. They will help you get through the worst. I am smoking my last pipe. I am listening, and I can clearly hear your voice, singing the songs of Smetana and Dvořák. I am with you now and and will always be with you. Vlado."[211]

Why did Clementis drink lots of black coffee? I think he wanted to be alert, thinking about Lída and his relatives in Tisovec and Prague, to breathe in life until the last second.

Clementis was hanged at five o'clock in the morning of 3 December 1952. His last words were "Thank you".[212] He died the gentleman he had always been: dignified, not bitter, nor revengeful or sarcastic, with elegance. I think the reason for thanking his executioners was gratitude: his ordeal was over, at last, and Lída would live.

Slánský was the last to die, forced to watch how one after the other of his comrades were hanged – a last cruel punishment from the Party. The bodies of the nine were cremated and the ashes dispersed in the countryside near Růzyně prison. The value

---

[210] Clementis a Clementisová, *Listy z Väzenia*, 74.
[211] Clementis a Clementisová, *Listy z Väzenia*, 69.
[212] Kaplan, *Report on the Murder* ..., 234.

of Clementis' personal belongings was estimated at five hundred crowns.²¹³

Clementis had accepted his fate early on. His love for Lída and his belief in Socialism that could not be broken, not even by the beatings and the humiliation, had carried him through the interrogations. In his penultimate letter to Lída, dated 2 December 1952, Vlado wrote that he hoped that she would live long enough to witness a Socialist Europe, perhaps in ten or fifteen years.²¹⁴ She should stay strong and greet Socialist Europe from him.

To question his faith, to understand that he had served a cruel and inhuman theory and regime would have been too much to bear for him. He had doubted once, back in 1939, and that was the reason why the Party punished him now. Clementis died in the belief that the future would prove his innocence. Socialism was a faultless and scientific theory with a humanist goal, but man was prone to mistakes. But, man could learn, with the help of the Party. One day, or so he must have thought, the Party would see the error of its ways and rehabilitate him *ex post*. He would prove right.

III. 3. 3 Rehabilitation (1963–1968)

After she was released from prison on the morning of 3 December 1952, Lída began a fight for justice that would last years. In her letter to Minister of National Defence Karol Bacílek from 7 December 1952, she demanded that the authorities return her husband's wedding ring and the letters they had written to each other while in prison.²¹⁵ As the wife of a traitor, people were reluctant to employ her, because everybody was afraid of the almighty StB. Lída stayed at her sister Božena's flat on Jungmann Square in Prague II.

---

[213] Holotíková a Plevza, 308.
[214] Clementis a Clementisová, *Listy z Väzenia*, 69.
[215] ABS USTRČR, Fond 319, sign. 319-34-13, letter from Lída Clementisová to Karol Bacílek, 7 December 1952, hand-written, 3 pages.

On 1 May 1953, she was finally employed at the department of music at the National Library Klementinum in Prague.[216] On 13 February 1957, she wrote to general prosecutor Dr Bartušek:

> "The imprisonment has wreaked havoc on my health. I have been damaged in social terms, especially because of the liquidation of my home, which happened in my absence, even before the beginning of the trial. As a loyal and honest working person, I have, to this day, no place on my own nor the financial means to establish a new home for myself, which a 46-year-old working woman certainly has a right to."[217]

Under Chruščev, the political atmosphere changed. The authorities finally agreed to an out-of-court agreement: the ministry of the interior payed Lída 15,000 Czechoslovak crowns as compensation for her time in prison on condition that she acknowledge all her claims were met with this single payment.[218] After Lída and Vlado had been arrested, the authorities had stolen the couple's entire property: furniture, linen, porcelain, kitchen equipment, carpets, music instruments, a radio, a typewriter, books, dresses, suits, coats, shoes, jewellery – even the couple's wedding rings.

The year 1963 brought a caesura to Czechoslovak domestic politics: the Kolder and Barnabite commissions presented the results of their investigations of the show trials of the 1950s.[219]

---

[216] ABS USTRČR, Fond 319, sign. 319-34-13, letter from the Ministry of Higher Education to the Ministry of National Security, 1 page, typewritten, classified *Tajne* (secret).

[217] ABS USTRČR, Fond 319, sign. 319-34-13, letter from Lída Clementisová to Dr Bartušek, general prosecutor, 13 February 1957, hand-written, 4 pages.

[218] ABS USTRČR, Fond 319, sign. 319-34-13, confirmation from Lída Clementisová, signed by her and two witnesses on 23 April 1957, 1 page, typewritten.

[219] The Kolder commission was named after its chairman Drahomír Kolder (1925–1972) who would be one of the signatories of the letter submitted to the Brežnev government, asking the Soviet Union for military assistance against the reformers in August 1968. The Barnabite commission was named after the former monastery of the Barnabite order in the Prague district Hradčany, where the commission was in session; Valerián Bystrický a kol., *Rok 1968*, 28.

The reports led to a slow thawing of the totalitarian ice. Chruščev's criticism of Stalin's personality cult had left behind a "vacuum of ideas": the old ideological norms and rules had collapsed, but new ones were not yet in sight.[220] The Party's somewhat reluctant acknowledgement that injustice had been done in the past prompted the barrier of fear to crumble – the citizens were no longer afraid. The early 1960s were the years of the Czechoslovak *nouvelle vague* in cinema, and journals and newspapers published hitherto unthinkable essays. The theatres showed daring new performances – and the KSS stood up to the KSČ.

The reports of the Kolder and Barnabite commissions also prompted changes in personnel in the highest echelons of the Party: members compromised in the show trial, such as Bacílek, lost their positions. Against the will of President Novotný, the CC KSS elected the young Alexander Dubček First Secretary on 8 April 1963 in a courageous and emancipatory move.[221]

Novomeský and Husák had been released in 1960 in Novotný's amnesty in honour of the 15th anniversary of Czechoslovakia's liberation in 1945. Clementis' friends openly criticized the Stalinist methods they identified as the roots of the trials of the 1950s. The Slovak journal *Kultúrny život* (*Cultural Life*) became the platform for the critical voices of artists and writers.[222] Lída anwered the request of Dr Miloš Ruppeldt (1922–1967), the editor-in-chief of *Cultural Life*, on 20 August 1963; he had asked her about details for his article about Clementis:

---

[220] Sikora, "KSS a ...", 133.
[221] Sikora, "KSS a ...", 134.
[222] Kováč, *Dejiny Slovenska*, 281. About the journal and the intellectual atmosphere in the years of the harshest oppression see Vlasta Jaksicsová, "'Pokolenie v útoku': *Kultúrny život* v zrkadle ideologickej (ne)kultúry v rokoch 1948–1953", in *Slovensko v labyrinte Európskych dejín. Pocta historikov Milanovi Zemkovi* (Bratislava: HÚ SAV a Prodama, 2014), 424-441.

> "Question: The date of Clementis' arrest? Answer: Clementis was arrested in Prague on 28 January 1951. I was arrested two weeks later and was in custody until December 1952, that is, until after Clementis' execution. [...] In this situation, with the rehabilitation not yet fully accomplished, I do not want to give you Clementis' last letters. They are too intimate."[223]

After the CC KSČ rehabilitated the victims of the Slánský trial in December 1963, Lída published her and Vlado's letters from exile in 1964 with the help of Novomeský. In 1968, in Dubček's liberal atmosphere in Slovakia, she could publish his letters from prison. They are dated from 29 October 1951 to 2 December 1952; for nine long months, Clementis had feared for his wife's safety. He received her first letter on 18 November 1951 and was allowed to write to her for the first time on 5 December 1951. I think that the StB told him that as soon as he co-operated, he would be allowed to receive letters – but they kept him waiting for nine cruel months.

Her letters made him believe that she was safe – and allow us to speculate: considering the total censorship, I think that Clementis wrote to his wife in code. On 5 December 1951, he wrote that he had gained weight and lost one of his orthodontic bridges.[224] Most probably, the interrogators hit him when he did not have his answers right in the 'training sessions'. I also seriously doubt that he had gained weight in prison – not under the conditions of sleep deprivation, continuous psychological stress and physical torture. Lída wrote Vlado a last letter in November 1967, a last word to the book that would be published in 1968:

> "Together, we lived through beautiful and hard years, the hardest. [...] I sat for a while in my cell, in prison clothes again. I could not stand the silence and asked for cleaning tools; the entire night, I cleaned my cell

---

[223] "Letter from Lída Clementisová to Dr Miloš Ruppeldt", SNA OF VC, sent from Prague to Bratislava, 20 August 1963, 2 pages, typewritten, 1-2.
[224] Clementis a Clementisová, *Listy z Väzenia*, 20.

like in a fever. [...] In the morning, they brought me to the prison director; he told me that you had been executed. Apparently, you had been courageous, the execution had lasted five minutes and you had died without pain. [...] He gave me your letters [...], your pipes. Then, they released me. [...] And now, I am saying good-bye to you for a second time with this book, which I hand over to the public as a document of your character – you were truthful [...] Could you speak up now, you would confess your belief in Communism and tell us that to die for the right cause, for a happy future, is not for nothing."[225]

Husák published five long articles in *Cultural Life* in 1967, remembering Vlado's life and ordeal. [226] Little did Husák, in the happy months of the Prague Spring, know what cruel fate Moscow had in store for Czechoslovakia. Like his friend Vlado, he would not lose his belief in Socialism, not even in November 1989, when the Berlin Wall came down, and the Czechoslovak citizens would liberate themselves from the rule of the Party that had promised them paradise on earth and had created quite the opposite.

---

[225] Clementis a Clementisová, *Listy z Väzenia*, 74-75.
[226] Gústav Husák, "Spomienky na Vlada Clementisa", *Kultúrny Život XXII*, no. 31 (1967): 1-2; "Búrlivé roky", *Kultúrny Život XXII*, no. 34 (1967): 3; "Svetlá a tiene", *Kultúrny Život XXII*, no. 36 (1967): 3; "Prípad na zamyslenie", *Kultúrny Život XXII*, no. 38 (1967): 1, 10.

"The remarkable thing about the Spanish war – about all ideological wars, I suppose – was the fiery single-mindedness, that it produced in otherwise quite sophisticated people. All doubts were banished, all questions answered, all quibbling done with." "Why did you spy for the Russians? How did you get away with it? What did you think you would achieve by betraying your country and your country's interests?' ... 'Not the Russians,' I murmured. I could feel her blink. 'What?' 'I did not spy for the Russians,' I said. 'I spied for Europe. A much broader church.'"[1]

"Historia vero testis temporum, lux veritatis, vita memoriae, magistra vitae, nuntia vetustatis, qua voce alia, nisi oratoris, immortalitati commendatur?"

(By what other voice too, than that of the orator, is history, the evidence of time, the light of truth, the life of memory, the directress of life, the herald of antiquity, committed to immortality?) [2]

"Hindsight is the foresight one lacked at the time."[3]

---

[1] John Banville, *The Untouchable* (London: Picador, 1997), 106, 29. Victor Maskell, the hero in Banville's fiction, tells the story of the Cambridge Four from the perspective of the fourth man Anthony Blunt. An excellent movie portraying a West German writer and former activist of the 1968 generation who believes in Lenin until the very end is *No place to go* (*Die Unberührbare*) (2000) by Oskar Roehler, http://www.imdb.com/title/tt0235841/; accessed 10 January 2016. The movie's heroine Hanna Flanders lives in Munich and shops at Christian Dior; her novels are published only in Honecker's East Germany because of their unfaltering belief in Socialism. With the fall of the Berlin wall, Hanna's life is completely uprooted. Roehler's movie is a sensitive portrait of his late mother. Interestingly, both Banville and Roehler describe their heroes with the same word: Victor Maskell and Hanna Flanders are referred to as 'untouchable', as persons who are out of touch with the political realities of their times, incapable of critically questioning their beliefs.

[2] Marcus Tullius Cicero, *De Oratore*, II, 36; https://archive.org/stream/cicero deoratore01ciceuoft/cicerodeoratore01ciceuoft_djvu.txt; accessed 26 April 2016. The English translation of Cicero's *Oratory and Orators* by J. S. Watson (New York: Harper & Brothers, 1860), on http://archive.org/stream/cicero onoratoryo00cice#page/92/mode/2up; accessed 26 April 2016. Watson translated *magistra vitae* with 'directress of life'; today, we might say 'history is the teacher of life' or 'the guiding hand of life'.

[3] Peter Thomas Hill, "History", in *Half-Life. The Dictionary of Hidden Meaning*, work in progress, Zurich 2016. I thank the author for allowing me to quote this *bon mot* from his unpublished manuscript.

Conclusion – and a few questions

Under what conditions can we pass judgement? Can we learn from history?

Anthony Blunt (1907–1983), Guy Burgess (1911–1963), Donald Maclean (1913–1983) and Kim Philby (1912–1988) achieved notoriety in the West as the Cambridge Four. They were all British civil servants, educated at Cambridge University and communists since their student years. They betrayed their country, passing political and military information to the Soviet Union during WWII and the Cold War. Upon detection in 1951, Maclean and Burgess defected to Moscow; Philby followed in 1963. Until his memoirs were released in 1984, Blunt, an art historian, was the Surveyor of the Queen's Pictures.[1] The Cambridge Four, and as we know now, the Cambridge Five with John Cairncross (1913–1995)[2] believed in Marxism-Leninism, convinced that their activities were saving the world from a third world war that would be a nuclear one, extinguishing mankind. According to UK legislation, the Cambridge Three were traitors who fled to evade their country's justice. Blunt was a traitor too, but remained in Britain; after his detection, the government stripped him of his position and knighthood.

---

[1] Anthony Blunt: Confessions of spy who passed secrets to Russia during the war on http://www.telegraph.co.uk/news/uknews/5889879/Anthony-Blunt-confessions-of-spy-who-passed-secrets-to-Russia-during-the-war.html; accessed 26 April 2016.

[2] The alleged fifth spy was John Cairncross; see http://www.independent.co.uk/news/people/obituaries-john-cairncross-1576877.html; accessed 19 March 2017.

Clementis, on the other hand, did not betray Czechoslovakia or the Party; he fell victim to a show trial of immense proportions, because Stalin decided so. Clementis was a decent and honest man and loyal Party member; as the former minister of Foreign Affairs and a Slovak, he was an ideal figure to act in the trial that should discipline the Czech and Slovak citizens. If the people could not even trust top Party members, only strict vigilance, iron discipline and total obedience would secure the future of the People's Democracy.

Comparing the Cambridge Four with the former Czechoslovak foreign minister is just one example of the Cold War and its ideological and political paradoxes, but it also demonstrates the spell Marxism-Leninism had had on European intellectuals born at the turn of the 20th century.

The Cambridge Four grew up in an Empire with longstanding democratic traditions, were from privileged families and, after the victory of WWII, could look forward to a bright and quiet future as well-paid civil servants in Her Majesty's service. Clementis, on the other hand, was born into a family of lower gentry in Central Slovakia. His family was well off, and he grew up in Czechoslovakia, a democratic island in a sea of authoritarian Central European regimes. While the Spanish Civil War had mobilized the Cambridge Four to secretly join the Communist cause, Clementis had openly joined the Party in 1925 as a privileged student of law at Prague's prestigious Charles University. In spite of their different social class, upbringing and lifestyle, the Cambridge Four and Clementis shared one characteristic feature: they unremittingly believed that Socialism, steered by the Soviet Union, would establish a better world.

Today, this fierce dedication to Socialism of European intellectuals in the first half of the 20th century seems to us a grave error of judgement, or perhaps even a moral fault of individuals who were blinded by the intellectual beauty and appealing social ethics of Marxism-Leninism. This is very easy to say with hindsight. Vlasta Jaksicsová on the difference between Western European and Central European intellectuals:

> "While the Western intellectuals perceived their political engagement as autonomous and born from free decision (which they could, after some deliberation, always freely revoke), Czech and Slovaks intellectuals (as members of small modern nations that were emancipating themselves from the former political threats in the geopolitically sensitive region of Central Europe) conceived of political engagement primarily as a mission, as a kind of holy duty towards the nation or the class they had chosen to represent."[3]

Considering the significant experience of liberty and unthreatened sovereignty that was a much older aspect of life in Western Europe than in the young Czechoslovak Republic, the British, German and French intellectuals were more critical of their states after WWI. The Czech and Slovak intellectuals, regardless of their political orientation, were bound to Masaryk's Republic by what they conceived as their duty to the nation: they had, first and foremost, to secure their independence. The loyalty to Masaryk's Republic was a shared and almost visceral duty, certainly a psychological one: by 28 October 1918, for the first time ever, Czechs and Slovaks could vote and elect their government in a democratic environment and in a state that orientated itself towards the West and its political ethics.

The Slovak and Czech intellectuals born at the turn of the 20th century were the first generation to enjoy political liberty and equality, the right to vote and the freedom of the press. Some of them, overwhelmed by the possibilities the new system granted, namely, political competition, forgot about one crucial Western value: humanity.

---

3   Jaksicsová, "Komunistický intelektuál ...", 66.

For the Communists, only the workers and their fight against exploitation by the bourgeois regime counted. Clementis was one of them. But unlike the working-class boys Gottwald, Slánský and his Bratislava adversary Široký, the Slovak doctor of law had one advantage: he had remarkable intellectual faculties the Party was in dire need of, especially for the negotiations at the Paris Peace conference and the UN sessions. Clementis was the only Slovak who was fluent in all the languages of the Allies: English, French, German, Russian – and Hungarian, which enabled him to conclude the agreement on the Slovak-Hungarian transfer of population.

In their enthusiasm for Marxism-Leninism and their belief in a new and just world, I do not see a big psychological or theoretical difference between Western and Central European intellectuals in the 1930s. They were all concerned with the Spanish Civil War and Hitler's rise to power. One had to take sides: with Fascism and National Socialism or against both movements, which catapulted one into the powerful anti-Fascist camp of the Comintern or the British, French and American Allies.

There was, however, a third option, the path of Churchill: Liberalism, a current of thought based on the conviction that whatever political thought you adhere to, there will always be room for compromise, since democratic politics is the art of the compromise. If you cannot make compromises, if you are bound by defence agreements such as Britain was in 1939, you have to muster resilience, fighting for the future of the compromise, of democratic politics. In a nutshell: I agree that you adhere to a different line of political thought – and we shall never convince each other that one of us is right, the other wrong, since there is no supra-individual institution that could pass judgement on our beliefs. Therefore, we have to compromise: we agree to disagree, while we are working to resolve pressing political and social issues. But Clementis had no interest in compromise and he was no democrat.

After the Communist coup d'état of 25 February 1948 in Czechoslovakia, there was one crucial difference between Western and Central European intellectuals: a Western Communist could always leave his country and emigrate to the Soviet Union, the GDR or any People's Democracy in East Central Europe,[4] while a Czech or Slovak citizen could not. Leaving the People's Democracy was a criminal offence in each state of the Socialist bloc: in the GDR, it was called '*Republikflucht*'.

The German film '*Das Leben der Anderen*' (The Lives of Others) won the Oscar for the best foreign film in 2007; in the first scene, Stasi officer Wiesler, portrayed by the great actor Ulrich Mühe (1953–2007), who was born in East Germany, instructs young Stasi trainees in interrogating citizens arrested while attempting to flee to the West.[5] In view of the absence of liberty in the Eastern bloc and the harsh punishment of those who wanted to leave, I can only praise Vlasta Jaksicsová's superbly informed judgement of Jean-Paul Sartre (1905–1980); she considers the French philosopher a 'useful idiot', correctly interpreting Lenin's anti-Individualism and revolutionary ruthlessness.

With the foundation of NATO in 1949, the Cold War was a fact, dividing the world into two ideological camps. The Polish Nobel laureate, novelist and poet Czesław Miłosz (1911–2004) described the mindset of the East European intellectual:

---

[4] See the insightful Kathleen Geaney, "At Home among Strangers. The Extraordinary Year 1950 in the Life of an Ordinary American Family in Communist Czechoslovakia, *COMENIUS. Journal of Euro-American Civilization II*, no. 1 (2015): 25-42.

[5] *Das Leben der Anderen* on http://www.imdb.com/title/tt0405094/; accessed 24 September 2016.

> "More than the West imagines, the intellectuals of the East look to the West for *something*. The something they look for is a new great writer, a new social philosophy, an artistic movement, a scientific discovery, new principles of painting or music. They rarely find this *something*. The people of the East have already become accustomed to thinking of art and society on an organizational and mass scale. [...] The Eastern intellectual is a severe critic of everything that penentrates to him from the West. He has been deceived so often that he does not want cheap consolation, which will eventually prove all the more depressing. The War left him suspicious and highly skilled in unmasking sham and pretense. [...] The work of human thought should withstand the test of brutal, naked reality. If it cannot, it is worthless."[6]

From 1867 to 2016, over roughly one hundred and fifty years, Slovaks and Czechs lived through seven (!) political regimes. Western European citizens never had to live through change on such a massive scale, over such a protracted period: governments, systems, wars, occupation and terror. Do we Westerners have the right to stand in judgement on a politician who had found his intellectual home and acted according to his beliefs? Is it fair to condemn Clementis as a champagne Socialist? Or should we avoid passing judgement at all?

To judge, one has to be informed. Raymond Aron (1905–1983), the great French philosopher, a friend of Sartre's from their student years at the Paris *école normale superieure* in the 1930s, had witnessed the Nazi rise to power while studying in Germany in 1933. Aron had fought in the French Army after the German attack on France; he was not afraid to pass judgement in the heightened intellectual climate of Paris in 1955. His former friends and colleagues attacked him in public for his critical views of the French Communists. Here we have Aron about on the intellectual atmosphere in France:

---

[6] Czesław Miłosz, *The Captive Mind* (New York: Vintage International, 1990), 37, 39.

> "The astronomer can foretell an eclipse of the sun with faultless precision: neither the economist nor the sociologist knows whether humanity is progressing towards an atomic holocaust or Utopian peace. That is where ideology comes in – the longing for a purpose, for communion with the people, for something controlled by an idea and a will. The feeling of belonging to the elect, the security provided by a closed system in which the whole of history as well as one's own person find their place and their meaning, the pride in joining the past to the future in present action – all this inspires and sustains the true believer, the man who is not repelled by the scholasticism, who is not disillusioned by the twists in the party line, the man who lives entirely for the cause and no longer recognises the humanity of his fellow-creatures outside the party."[7]

Clementis lived entirely for the cause; to him, only the workers and their future counted. The Marxist-Leninist credo was attractive to him because of three main features. First, Marxism-Leninism was based on *atheism*, thereby breaking the power of the churches and, above all, the strong Catholic clergy in Slovakia that was not really interested in social change and reform, consoling the poor and weak with the phoney promise of a future life in paradise – if they behaved on earth. Second, Marxism-Leninism was *egalitarian*, breaking down the hierarchy of the social classes and the concomitant privileges of the middle class and the aristocracy. Third, it was *international-universal-global*, hence modern and oriented towards the future, ignoring national identities and focussing only on the human aspect of the suffering workers. If the workers of the world united, a new era of global peace would come. Clementis conceived of the citizens who did not believe in Marxism-Leninism simply as class enemies; they were doomed because of their failure to understand the 'scientifically proven' rightfulness of the workers' movement.

---

[7] Raymond Aron, *The Opium of the Intellectuals* (New Brunswick, London: Transaction Publishers, 2005), 323. The best biography of Raymond Aron known to me is Nicolas Baverez, *Raymond Aron. Un moraliste au temps des ideologies* (Paris: Perrin, 2006).

To European citizens who had survived WWII, these three principles of Marxism-Leninism seemed to promise a better future – and to those who had witnessed WWI, Socialism was a truly humanist movement that would bring about a new era of justice, freedom and equality.

A further crucial feature of Marxism-Leninism was its call for loyalty, obedience and discipline – virtues and psychological features that had not only liberated the Nazi concentration camps but were also required for the building of a Socialist society after 1945. Hermann Lübbe convincingly argued that what German politicians in the 1980s had called "*KZ-Wächter-Tugenden* (the discipline of concentration camp overseers)" was no different from the discipline of the Red Army soldiers who liberated the occupied countries and the Communist citizens who were building the Socialist society: punctuality, obedience and courage.[8]

Writing Clementis' political biography, scrutinizing his way of thinking and acting is one thing, to pass judgement on his thought and activities quite another. How and when should we pass judgement? The brilliant German born political theorist Hannah Arendt wrote in her famous *Eichmann in Jerusalem*:

> "The argument that we cannot judge if we were not present and involved ourselves seems to convince everyone everywhere, although it seems obvious that if it were true, neither the administration of justice nor the writing of history would ever be possible."[9]

---

[8] Hermann Lübbe, *Politischer Moralismus. Der Triumph der Gesinnung über die Urteilskraft* (Berlin: WJS Corso, 1987(2)), 62-63. I consider Professor Lübbe's criticism of political correctness one of the most important contributions to political philosophy of the 20th century.

[9] Peter Baehr, ed., "Banality and Conscience: The Eichmann Trial and its Implications", in *The Portable Hannah Arendt* (New York: Penguin, 2000), 313-408, 386. On Arendt's theory of judgement see Seyla Benhabib, *The Reluctant Modernism of Hannah Arendt* (Lanham, MD: Rowlamn & Littlefield, 2003), in particular chapter 6. I thank Valentina Welser for this recommendation.

Arendt's theory of judgement consists of two models: the actor's model, who is judging in order to act, and the spectator's model, "who is judging in order to cull meaning from the past".[10] For the purpose of this conclusion, it is obvious that we can pass judgement on Clementis only from the perspective of the spectator. Let me now answer my research questions.

1. Democracy: Why did Clementis not join a different party after WWII, in view of the fact that the KSČ had expelled him in 1939? Why did he return to the Party after five years of working with and for the London exile government? Was Party membership a stepping stone to political power, or was he naïve in terms of the dictatorship of the Party? Was he ambitious, naïve or both?

Clementis had joined the Party at a time when the Czechoslovak authorities had a careful eye on the Communists. The Party was his intellectual home and, although he was a rather reclusive person, he had close friends: the poet Laco Novomeský and Gustáv Husák who had trained as *koncipient* in Clementis' law office in the 1930s. Clementis enjoyed being the most important Slovak in the exile government; he could not imagine changing sides, joining a centre-right and, in his way of thinking, bourgeois party. To him, such an act would have been treason of the worst sort. He could not leave the Party, not so much because it was, indeed, a stepping stone to political power, especially after the end of WWII, but because the Party was an almost intimate expression of his inner self, his intellectual home. To betray Marxism-Leninism would have equalled betraying his wife Lída or his sister Boža.

All his life and thought was centered on the principles of Marxism-Leninism. Yet, as an intelligent and educated person who loved the good things in life such as art, food and fashion, he lacked

---

[10] Hannah Arendt on http://plato.stanford.edu/entries/arendt/#AreTheJud; accessed 26 April 2016.

two crucial psychological features: the instinct for political survival and a particular sense for intrigue the working-class boys Gottwald and Široký had. Clementis was truth to himself and the Party and he could not imagine lying or betraying for his personal advancement or survival. Vlado believed in fairness. He could not imagine that Comrade Klema, the Party, his intellectual home, his family, would be so *irrational* as to destroy its top echelons, all of the accused being faithful Communists.

During WWII in London, Clementis was depressed because heterogeneity dominated his life: the split between him and the Party must have created an immense feeling of loneliness and desperation. A characteristic feature of the totalitarian mind: everything has to be homogeneous, rounded, fulfilled and brought to logical and rational perfection. Clementis could not bear the slightest doubt, a nagging voice in the back of his mind – if he had doubts, he supressed them. After the war, Gottwald renewed his Party membership, and Clementis' personal homogeneity, the unity of his life with the Party, was reinstated. Had he been a selfish careerist, an ambitious individual, or a realist, he would have switched sides in 1939, after the KSČ had ousted him. He had had every opportunity to join a political party represented in the exile government.

In terms of the Party's dictatorship, I cannot but judge Clementis's activities naïve and ignorant at the same time. He did not say a word against the mass terror Slánský and Gottwald orchestrated – if he expressed criticism of the purges that were beginning after the 'victorious' 25 February 1948 in private conversations, we shall never know. But he certainly did not publicly condemn or criticize the Party's terror. Warned in New York in the autumn of 1949 that there was something in the making against him, he made fun of the rumours, which demonstrates characteristic features of his: loyalty, trust and a distinct self-confidence, born from his life-long hard work as an intellectual and a politician. Indeed, everybody who had achieved what he had could be proud; he had made a stellar career as a lawyer and politician. The little boy from Tisovec had become Czechoslovakia's Foreign Minister.

Clementis just could not believe that Gottwald would scheme behind his back. As an intellectual and politician, he should have taken the warnings seriously – but then, the Soviet and Czechoslovak authorities did everything to lull him into a sense of security. Gottwald consented to have Lída sent to New York to dispel the rumours the *New York Times* published. Vyšinskii sent him a telegram to New York, congratulating him on the anniversary of the foundation of Czechoslovakia, thus signalling that the Soviet Union was grateful for his work.

Vanity was perhaps a weakness in Clementis' character. He was certainly ambitious and naïve, but not stupid; his naïveté was born of his loyalty to the Party, to Gottwald and Stalin. He was a truthful and decent man, and he fell victim to those whose nature was to lie, betray and scheme – the Party members who survived the purges of the 1950s.

2. Constitutional status of Slovakia within Czechoslovakia: what constitutional arrangement did he pursue for Slovakia? Autonomy, federation or centralism, that is, Slovakia ruled from Prague with no Slovak self-governing institutions?
Clementis was a Slovak patriot and, albeit in London exile and in contact with Czech centre-right politicians, he advocated a new constitutional arrangement for Czechoslovakia after the end of WWII. After all, the SNP was ample evidence that the Slovaks wanted Czechoslovakia back, but with a new constitutional arrangement that would grant them self-government from Brati-

slava, hence the end of Prague's centralism that had not really improved their lives in the First Republic – at least, in economic terms.

Had Clementis not been executed in 1952, I deem it very probable that he would have supported Alexander Dubček's reforms – or initiated reforms himself as elected Prime Minister, with Dubček as his minister of domestic affairs. Much like Husák, Novomeský and the Slovak patriots in the Party, he would have certainly supported a federation.

After three years of studying archive material, Clementis' texts and broadcasts, I have come to the conclusion that he was guilty in ideological, not criminal terms. Clementis did not himself execute orders to have centre-right politicians arrested after the 'victorious February 1948', nor did he send citizens of the wrong class background and members of the clergy to the Radium mines in Jáchimov, but he supported the Gottwald government as foreign minister and did everything in his power to make Czechoslovakia a member of Stalin's Soviet bloc. In the crucial years from 1945 to 1948, he represented the Party's concealed interests at the Paris Peace Conference and the UN.

Clementis had joined the KSČ in 1925. He firmly believed in Marxism-Leninism and criticized the Soviet Union only once: for Stalin's decision to conclude the German-Soviet Nonagression Pact and the Soviet attack on Finnland, because these decisions were not pure in Marxist-Leninist terms. As a Socialist state, you don't enter into a pact with the ideological enemy, nor do you send your army to attack a weaker and smaller state. Clementis had no talent for strategic thinking, because he was a decent person – and moral values and decency significantly undermine one's strategic options. Stalin could not be bothered with these moral niceties, which made him the embodiment of Machiavellian thought in the 20th century.

In exile, Clementis suffered from having been ousted from the Party, but he never doubted. Sir Isaiah Berlin described the totalitarian mindset with his unrivalled insightfulness:

> "If I know that I am right, if I know that what I seek is the true good, then people who oppose me must be in error about what it is that they themselves seek. No doubt they too think that they are seeking the good, they assert their own liberty to secure it, but they are seeking it in the wrong place. Therefore I have a right to prevent them. In virtue of what have I this right to prevent them? ... It is because if they knew what they truly wanted, they would seek what I seek. The fact that they do not seek this means that they do not *really* know – ."[11]

Clementis never had any doubts about the rightfulness of his credo, although he had grown up in a country that had sustained a high level of civil liberties: in the 1930s, he flatly refused to investigate the news about the artificially created famine in the Ukraine. He had no understanding of tolerance and believed that only Soviet Socialism could right the wrongs of the Capitalist system. Why did this highly intelligent and university-educated man join the Party in the first place? I think the answer might be found in Clementis' psychology. The psychiatrist Joost A. M. Merloo, a specialist in brainwashing and menticide:

> "Increasing attention has been given to the various psychological motivations leading to political extremism and a totalitarian mentality in men and women who have been brought up in a democratic atmosphere, but who have voluntarily chosen to associate themselves with some totalitarian ideology. Psychologists who have come into contact with the totalitarian attitude and have studied those who are easily influenced by it agree, by and large, that in the free, democratic countries the option for totalitarianism is nearly always determined by an inner personality factor – frustration, if you will. It is usually neither poverty nor social idealism that makes a man a totalitarian, but mostly internal factors such as extreme submissiveness and masochism on the one

---

[11] Isaiah Berlin, *Freedom and its Betrayal. Six Enemies of Human Liberty* (London: Pimlico, 2003), 45-46.

> hand or a lust for power on the other. Unsolved sibling rivalry plays a role too."[12]

Since there are no indications of masochism and submissiveness in the literature about Clementis, it is safe to assume that he was driven by a lust for power and also a distinct need to join an intellectual elite, to be a member of the avant-garde. What could have been the origins of this psychological need? What had made Clementis tick?

After careful study of his texts and broadcasts, I think that Clementis was driven by his ambition to be somebody significant, to prove himself. With regard to Merloo's findings, we could thus ask the following questions: Was Clementis jealous of his older half-brother Dušan, although he grew up in a loving family? How hard did grandfather Vrány's rejection hurt him? How much did he want to please the Czech teenager-friend who had introduced him to Marxist-Leninist theory at the Skalica high school back in 1918? Did he want to prove to his father that he, like his father before him, who had joined the *Hlas* movement in Slovakia, was capable of joining a movement that would, one day, be victorious and establish a new political system?

The tragedy of Clementis is that the spirits he had called on himself with his Party membership never obeyed him – on the contrary: he was the Party's slave out of his own free will. He had had ample opportunities to leave, stay in Great Britain in 1945 or find refuge in the USA in 1949. He could have embarked on a lawyer's career in New York or joined Ferdinand Peroutka in California, founding a journal for the Czechs and Slovaks in exile, like Pavel Tigrid would do after 1968 in Paris. He could have become a lawyer on behalf of the Slovak workers in the rust belt, strengthening the US Communist Party and defending it against the anti-

---

[12] Merloo, 180.

Communist hysteria whipped up by Senator Joseph M. McCarthy (1908–1957) in the early 1950s.

Yet, Clementis could not imagine a life away from his beloved Czechoslovakia. His last duty as a Party member was to play-act in the show trial. Stalin and his NKVD agents made sure that the majority of the accused lost everything: power, influence, self-respect and, lastly, their lives.

But the StB could not take away his belief in Socialism and the love and loyalty of three persons who held him dear and spoke up as soon as they could: his wife Lída and his friends Laco Novomeský and Gustáv Husák. In his last letter to Lída, Clementis expressed his hope and belief that Socialism would not only prevail, but also offer a better future to the generations to come. To admit that he had dedicated his entire life to an inhuman and cruel regime, a body of thought that promised to liberate the people but enslaved them to a hitherto unprecendent degree would have been unbearable to him.

Given Clementis' unfaltering belief in Marxism-Leninism, his criticism of the Hitler-Stalin Pact and his eagerness to join the Party's rank and file again in 1945, I think that he truly believed in his credo until the last minute. Aberrations were man-made; man was not perfect, but Marxism-Leninism was. In a couple of years, or so he must have thought, the Party would see its gross error and correct it. He would be right: in 1963, he was rehabilitated.

Let me conclude with a quote from a friend who has taught me a lot about life under Communism. She has the characteristic black humour of the Central European citizen:

> "JB: 'So, what you are saying is that we shall never find out what really happened in that interrogation room?'
>
> XY: 'That was the point!'"

Oral History Interview with Mr Antonín Liehm (*1924)

12 January 2017, Prague, 2.30 pm to 3 pm. The interview was conducted in Czech. English translation by me.

JB: Dear Mr Liehm, thank you very much for your time. From Francis Raska, our common friend, I learnt that you knew Vladimír Clementis.

AL: Yes, I met him first at the theatre of Burian in Prague. That was after the war; he was assistant secretary of state. We immediately liked each other – as we say in Czech: we fell into each other's eyes. Some time later, he asked me – I was a young Party member, some twenty years younger than him – would I like to work at the Czechoslovak Foreign Ministery. I did, and he gave me a position at the MZV. One year after the trial of Slánský, who was not a very kind person, they fired me. Then, they hired me again and fired me again, because I was not reliable in political terms.

JB: What kind of person was Clementis in psychological terms?

AL: He was quiet, respectful and very intelligent, well educated, a decent man. Once I learnt from the broadcast and the news about the trial of Slánský and co-accused, I immediately knew that the trial was a fake. Clementis would have never betrayed the Party or Czechoslovakia. He was warned in America that he should not go home, but he did not believe the warnings. He came back home.

JB: Could you explain to the Western reader why so many intellectuals at the beginning of the 20th century believed in Marxism-Leninism?

AL: Marx's *Das Kapital* is still one of the best books about politics and economics. What Lenin and Stalin did, their Marxism-Leninism, was quite another issue. The leftist intellectuals agreed that Capitalism was a rotten system, that the bourgeoisie was exploiting the workers. They believed that only a workers' revolution could get rid of Capitalism.

JB: Did you meet Clementis also in private – how would you describe your relationship?

AL: No, we met only at the theatre, that is, socially. We did not meet in private.

JB: We Westerners are always in awe about the political instinct of the Central European citizen. What do you think about the reforms of 1968 under Alexander Dubček?

AL: The day after the Warsaw Pact troops invaded our country, I left for France, because I feared that they would arrest me. My wife and I stayed in Paris until 2013, when we moved back to the Czech Republic.

JB: A last question: Mr Liehm, you have experienced Communism and the Western democratic system in France. You are fluent in English, French and German. What do you think about the current international political situation?

AL: I don't understand what is going on now in politics.

JB: Dear Mr Liehm, I thank you very much for this interview.

Appendix

Clementis in Data

Education	*Maturita* at the Czechoslovak high school in Skalica (1921)
	Doctor of Law (JUDr.), 1925, Charles University, Prague
Books, journalism, broadcasts	See bibliography in the appendix
Political Thought	Czechoslovak state theory (political Czechoslovakism); Marxism-Leninism
Editorships	*DAV* (1924–1935)
Political regimes	Hungarian Kingdom, 1902–1918
	First Czechoslovak Republic, 1918–1938
	Second Czechoslovak Republic, limited by the National Front, 1945–1948
	Communist Czechoslovakia, 1948–1952
Political Parties	Czechoslovak Communist Party KSČ, Slovak Communist Party KSS: 1925–1939, 1945–1950
Political positions	Member of Parliament for the KSČ (1935–1938)
	Assistant Secretary of State (Deputy Foreign Minister) (1945–1948)
	Foreign Minister (1948–1950)
Trips abroad	Dresden, Germany, 1923, training of German
	Aix-en-Provence, France, 1924, training of French
	Soviet Union, 1929, 1930

	WWII: exile in France and Great Britain
	From 1945 in the diplomatic service: USA, Great Britain, France
Wars, armed conflicts	WWI, 1914–1918
	WWII, 1939–1945 in exile in France and Great Britain
Punishment for political activities	Expulsion from the KSČ (1939)
	Arrest, show-trial and execution (1951–1952)
Confession	Brought up a Slovak Lutheran, atheist Marxist-Leninist

Chronology

Pseudonyms and pen names: Vladimír Sopko (*DAV*), Petr Hron (BBC).

1902, 20 September	Born in Tisovec in Central Slovakia to Ľudovít and Mária Adela, née Vraný. His mother was of Czech descent, his father was a school teacher and of Slovak Lutheran confession. Vlado had four siblings: half-brother Dušan, Miroslav, Božena, Viera and Olga. Lída (Ludmila) Pátková was born 4 July 1910 in Prague. Her family moved to Bratislava, where she met her future husband. Lída Pátková studied music and song at the Bratislava conservatory.
1918, 28 October	The Slovak physician Vavro Šrobár (1867–1950) signed the Czechoslovak Declaration of Independence as representative of the SNR.
30 October	The Declaration of Martin, signed by all prominent Slovak politicians of the SNR, expressed the free will of the Slovaks to live in a common state with the Czechs, thereby announcing Slovak secession from the Hungarian kingdom.
November	After an unsuccessful stint at the Hungarian high school in Skalica, where Vlado had enrolled in 1912, he studied at the same high school from November 1918 on. Šrobár's preliminary Czechoslovak government in Slovakia established the gymnasium as a Slovak speaking school. Czech professors moved to teach at the newly founded high schools, replacing the Magyar teachers.

1919, 18 January	Pressburg / Poszony declared the seat of the Czechoslovak government in Slovakia, the Slovak capital.
27 March	Pressburg / Poszony named Bratislava.
1921, October	After graduation with an A grade at Skalica high school on 20 June, Vlado enrolled at the Faculty of Law at Charles University in Prague. First contacts with members of the patriotic Slovak students' association *Detvan* and the Communist students' fraction (*Študentská kommunistická frakcia*).
1922, January	With equally-minded leftist students, Vlado founded the Free Association of Slovak Socialist students (*voľné združenie študentov-socialistov zo Slovenska*).
1923, spring	Perfected his command of German at Dresden university in the spring term.
1924	Visiting stay at Aix-en-Provence to perfect his command of French. In the autumn, he founded the journal *DAV* with friends: the first issue of *DAV* was published in early December. It was planned as a quarterly, but because of financial difficulties only two issues could appear in the first year. Clementis would be editor-in-chief of *DAV* until 1935. The revue would cease publication in 1937.
1925, May	Final exams at the Faculty of Law.
22 December	Promotion as doctor of Law. Clementis was a member of the KSČ since the beginning of the year. Anticipating that he would have difficulties finding a position because of his Party membership, he applied for a job in Chicago, USA, but was rejected. He was fluent in English, French, German, Hungarian, and was studying Russian.

1926, February	Employed at the district court in Bratislava, but given notice when his political orientation became known. Employed at the legal office of advocate Dr. Kuba, where he accomplished his practical training as *koncipient* in 1931.
1927	Held lectures and speeches about leftist art in various cultural clubs and associations. In December, he met the Soviet writer Ilia Ehrenburg (1891–1967).
1928, autumn	Accompanied Ehrenburg, his wife Ľuba Kozincevová and the linguist Roman Jakobson (1896–1982) on a tour through Slovakia. With non-Communist intellectuals, he founded the Society for the economic and cultural rapprochement with the new Russia (*Spoločnosť pre hospodárske a kultúrne zblíženie s novým Ruskom*), in which he held the position of executive secretary.
1929	*DAV* issued a survey about the cultural orientation of Slovakia, which non-leftist intellectuals received with interest. *DAV* was a respected intellectual forum and significant part of modern Slovak cultural and political life.
25 March	"Letter of the Seven", protesting against Gottwald's new authoritarian style of leadership of the Party. Stalinization of the KSČ. Clementis and eleven comrades protested against the seven in their "Letter of the twelve" on 30 March.
October-November	First trip to the Soviet Union. Clementis attended the festivities of the October Revolution in Moscow.
1930, autumn	Second trip to the Soviet Union. Clementis participated at the International meeting

	of revolutionary and proletarian writers in Kharkov, the Ukrainian Soviet Republic.
1931, 25 May	Whitsuntide massacre in Košuty, Central Slovakia.
30 June – 13 July	Clementis defended Štefan Major at his trial in Prague.
September	Moved back to Bratislava and opened his own law firm in the Central Passage. He later moved his office to the Namestie Republiky (The Square of the Republic).
1932, 25 -26 June	Meeting of young Slovak writers and intellectuals in Trenčianské Teplice. The Davists participated in a principal role.
1933, 24 March	Vladimír Clementis and Lída Pátková had a civil marriage in Bratislava.
1935, May	As candidate for the KSČ for the county of Liptovský Sv. Mikuláš, Clementis was elected MP to the Prague parliament under Prime Minister Jan Malypetr.
18 December	Edvard Beneš elected Czechoslovak president. The KSČ voted for him, forfeiting their ususal opposition because of the threat of German National Socialism in the Sudeten lands.
1936, 24 April	Antisemitic student rally in Bratislava, incited by radicals of the HSĽS. Catholic students protested against the film *Golem*.
31 May -1 June	Congress of the Slovak writers in Trenčianské Teplice. Clementis spoke out for a wider understanding of the tasks of their times that were related to the Fascist threat growing in Europe.
1937, 14 September	President Masaryk died in Lany Castle. *DAV* stopped publication for good.
1938, April	The KSČ sent Clementis to Paris for a fact-finding stay. The Party ordered him back

	to support the election campaign in July. Gustáv Husák finished his practical training at Clementis' law firm.
19-22 May	From Paris, Clementis left for London, where he met with delegates of the Labour Party and gave interviews to British newspapers.
22 July	Participated at a peace conference in Paris and returned to Bratislava at the beginning of August.
16 August	Andrej Hlinka died.
30 September	Munich agreement. ČSR lost the Sudetenland and Silesia to Germany. President Beneš and the Czechoslovak government left for London in October, where they would establish the government in exile. Milan Hodža, Prime Minister from 1935 to 1938, left for France and later joined Beneš in London.
6 October	Declaration of Slovakia's autonomy. HSĽS and the Hlinka Guards in power. Clementis and his wife left for Prague, but came back to Bratislava.
2 November	German-orchestrated Vienna Arbitrage (*Viedenská arbitráž*); ČSR lost territory in the South to Hungary.
1939,	
9-10 March	Czechoslovak President Emil Hácha ordered the occupation of Slovakia, referred to as the Homola putsch (*Homolov puč*).
13 March	Slovak President Jozef Tiso in Berlin, pressed into declaring Slovakia's sovereignty.
14 March	Tiso declared Slovakia's sovereignty in the Bratialava Parliament. Clementis and his

	wife left for Prague. Lída received an exit visa and left for Paris.
15 March	Hácha signed the Czech capitulation. German troops occupied the Czech lands, referred to as protectorate (*Reichsprotektorat Böhmen und Mähren*).
18 March	Beginning of the expulsion of Czechs and their families from Slovakia.
23 March	In the Small War (*malá vojna*), Slovakia lost more territory in the south-east to Hungary.
29 March	First deportation of Slovak citizens critical of the Tiso regime to the Ilava prison in North-Central Slovakia.
End of June	Clementis arrived in Paris and was politically active in the Czechoslovak exile community.
23 August	German-Soviet Nonaggression Pact. Clementis criticised the alliance in a close circle of Party comrades. He never published his critical view in a journal or newspaper.
1 September	Beginning of WWII with the German attack on Poland.
10 October	The French authorities arrested Clementis and interned him at the Stade Roland Garros until October, when he joined the Czechoslovak exile army as a soldier.
1940, 22 June	German occupation of France. The Czechoslovak exile army in France was transferred to Great Britain. The soldiers were interned at the POW camp in Cholmondeley.
28 July	Clementis transferred to the camp in Oswestry, Shropshire.
22 August	Interned at the POW camp in Sutton Coldfield near Birmingham. Until the early

	months of 1941, he was interned in several POW camps in Scotland.
1941, spring	Released from the POW camp, Clementis arrived in London.
9 September	Adoption of the Jewish codex in the Slovak constitution, infringing the Jews' civil and religious rights.
4 November	Clementis began his broadcasts for the BBC that would last until 27 March 1945.
7 December	Japanese attack on Pearl Harbour. US President Roosevelt declared war on Japan and Germany.
1942,	
31 January	The exile government founded the Legal Council (*právní rada*), a kind of High Court in exile; its task was to supervise and evaluate the legal aspects of the exile government's decisions. Clementis was the only Slovak in the Council that consisted of five members.
April	On Clementis' suggestion, the Slovak Seminar (*Slovenský seminar*) was founded and immediately started its activities; it published articles and arranged for a lecture series about the current political conditions in the Slovak state. The writer and intellectual Theo Herkel' Florin (1908–1973) acted as the seminar's secretary; he would serve as Clementis' personal secretary at the Foreign Ministry after the war.
15 May	Adoption of the constitutional law that deprived the Jews of their Slovak citizenship and legitimated their deportation to concentration camps in Poland and Germany. By October 1942, 60,000 Jews had been deported.

4 June	Czechoslovak officers Jozef Gabčik and Jan Kubiš shot *Reichsprotektor* Reinhard Heydrich in Prague. The Germans took cruel revenge with the destruction of the villages Lidice and Ležaky.
1943, 12 December	Stalin and Beneš signed the Soviet-Czechoslovak Treaty of Alliance in Moscow. Christmas agreement of the Slovak political parties and resistance groups, followed by the foundation of SNR.
1944, 6 June	Allied landing in Normandy.
20 July	Failed attempt on Hitler's life by Wehrmacht officers.
29 August	German occupation of Slovakia, called in by the Tiso government. Start of the Slovak National Uprising (SNP).
27 October	Fall of Banská Bystrica, end of the uprising.
1945, 20 January	Armistice Treaty of the Allies with Hungary.
4-11 February	Conference of Yalta. Roosevelt, Stalin and Churchill met on Crimea to discuss the progress of the war and the reconstruction of Europe after the war.
22–29 March	Moscow negotiations, which led to the Košice Agreement (*Košický vládny program*). The negotiating parties were the members of the London exile government, Czech centre-right parties (*občiansky blok*), the SNR and the Communist exile in Moscow, represented by Gottwald and Slánský. Beneš and the Soviets did not directly intervene in the negotiations. Clementis and his wife left London on a steamer; after a long journey that brought

	them from Iceland to Gibraltar, the Mediterranean Sea and the Bosporus, they arrived in Constanța in Romania. From there, they drove to Trebišov and arrived in Košice by train. On the steamer, Clementis learned from the Moscow broadcast that the SNR had appointed him Assistant Secretary of State.
5 April	Declaration of the Government Program (Košice Agreement) and the National Front as its executive in Košice.
8 May	With Germany's unconditional surrender, WWII ended in Europe.
9 May	Liberation of Prague by the Red Army.
10 May	Czechoslovak government moved to Prague. Clementis and his wife arrived in the capital a few days later.
2 June	First agreement of Prague. The Slovak attempt to establish an equal status in the state failed.
26 June	Inaugural UN Conference in San Francisco, USA, adoption of the UN Charter.
3 July	As Clementis was a member of the Czechoslovak government, Gottwald had his party membership officially restored.
17 July – 2 August	The Big Three (USA, GB and SSSR) met in Potsdam. They agreed to create the Interalllied Council that coordinated the administration of the four occupation zones. The International War Crimes Tribunal was to organize the Nuremberg trials.
2 August	President Beneš issued the constitutional decree no. 33/1945 about the abolition of Czechoslovak citizenship of Germans and Magyars, rendering the *odsun* legal.

1946,

27 February	ČSR and Hungary signed in Budapest the Treaty about the Transfer of Population (*Dohoda medzi ČSR a Maďarskom o výmene obyvateľstva*). Hungary tried to prevent the transfer with various interventions at the UN, protracting the population exchange until 1949.
11 April	Second agreement of Prague. Slovaks unsuccessful.
26 May	First Czechoslovak post-war parliamentary elections to the Constitutional Assembly. In Slovakia, DS won 62% of the vote, KSS 30%, SSl 3.73% and SP 3.1%. In the Czech part of the country, the Communists won the majority with 41% of the vote.
2 July	President Beneš appointed Klement Gottwald Prime Minister.
27 July	Third agreement of Prague. Slovaks unsuccessful.
29 July – 5 October	Peace Conference in Paris, which led to the Peace Treaties signed on 5 February 1947.
20 November	Start of the Nuremberg Trial.

1947,

10 February	Twelve states including Czechoslovakia signed a peace treaty with Hungary in Paris. The Vienna Arbitrage was invalid and the borders restored to the status quo of 1 January 1938.
25 February	Great Britain turned the Palestine issue over to the UN. The General Assembly adopted resolution 181 III that led to the partition of Palestine into an independent Jewish state and and an independent Arab state.

5 June	US Secretary of State George C. Marshall announced his plan for Europe's economic recovery and US humanitarian assistance in his speech at Harvard University.
4 July	ČSR received the official invitation to the conference of the Marshall Plan.
7 July	Foreign Minister Jan Masaryk instructed the Czechoslovak ambassador in Paris to attend the preparations for the conference of the Marshall Plan.
9 July	Foreign Minister Masaryk, Premier Klement Gottwald and Prokop Drtina negotiated with Stalin in Moscow about Czechoslovakia's participation in the Marshall Plan. Stalin pressed them into revoking their delegation in Paris.
11 July	Clementis declared to the world press that Czechoslovakia would not join the Marshall Plan.
22-27 September	Delegates of the Communist Parties from the Soviet Union, Eastern Europe, France and Italy founded the Cominform (Communist Information Bureau, *Informbyro*), an organization that should coordinate the strategies of the Communist Parties in Europe.
17-18 November	Dress rehearsal for the coup d'état: the pressure of the KSS in Slovakia forced three DS *poverénici* (government trustees with executive power) to resign. Husák established KSS control in Slovakia.

1948,

10 February	Yugoslav-Soviet negotiations in Moscow; expulsion of Yugoslavia from the Cominform on 29 June, providing the pretext for the show trials of the 1950s in the Soviet bloc.
25 February	President Beneš dissolved the democratically elected government and appointed a new government according to Gottwald's suggestions. The KSČ in control of the country, referring to the events as the 'victory of 25 February'.
10 March	Mysterious death of Jan Masaryk who was found dead in the court yard of the Czernín Palace, the building of the Foreign Ministry in the Prague Castle district.
18 March	Clementis succeeded Masaryk in office.
14 May	Declaration of Independence of the state of Israel; David Ben-Gurion elected Israel's first Prime Minister. On the next day, Arab armies from Egypt, Iraq, Jordan, Lebanon and Syria invaded, as the British mandate ended; beginning of the War of Independence.
24 June	Berlin Airlift as reaction of the Western Allies to the Soviet Union's blockade of Berlin. Until the end of 1949, the US, GB and F flew in supplies to West Berlin, demonstrating that they would not give up on the Western zone of the divided city.
3 September	Edvard Beneš died in Sezimovo Ústi; state funeral in Prague on 8 September.
31 December	Formal end of the population transfer between ČSR and Hungary.

1949,

5-8 January	Foundation of the COMECON (RVHP) in Moscow.
4 April	Foundation of NATO in Washington, DC.
16 April	ČSR and Hungary signed a Treaty on Friendship, Co-operation and Mutual Assistance in Budapest. The treaty signalled the normalisation of relations between the two states.
11 May	Israel became a member of the UN after her victory in the War of Independence.
25-29 May	At the IX KSČ Party Congress, the Party elected Clementis member of the CC.
24 September	The People's Court in Budapest condemned former Foreign Minister László Rajk to death for Titoism, high treason and conspiracy with the Imperialist West.
15 October	László Rajk executed in Budapest.
Autumn	Clementis participated at the UN plenary session in New York. He ignored the warnings and rumours about a trap the Party had prepared for him after his return and suggested to Gottwald that these rumours could be dispersed if Lída joined him in New York. After the end of the UN session, they returned to Prague in mid-November.
16 December	Traicho Kostov executed for Titoism and espionage in Sofia, Bulgaria.
1950	Yugoslavia elected non-permanent member of the UN Security Council
11 March	Meeting of the presidium of the CC; the highest organ of the Party criticised Clementis' past in London, his activities as foreign minister and stripped him of his position. Clementis' adversary Viliam Široký

	(1902–1971) succeeded him in office on 14 March.
6-7 April	Široký accused Clementis, Husák and Novomeský of 'Slovak bourgeois nationalism' at a meeting of the CC KSS.
24-27 May	IX Congress of the KSS. On 26 May, Clementis acknowledged his errors and committed self-critique, like Gustáv Husák and Laco Novomeský before him. The Party accused the Slovak members of 'bourgeois nationalism' and rejected their self-criticism. Bereft of all functions in Party and state, Clementis found employment as clerk at a state bank.
31 May – 8 June	The first Stalinist show trial of Milada Horáková (1901–1950) and co-accused took place in Prague. The four centre-right politicians were sentenced to death for espionage, conspiracy with the Imperialist West and high treason. They were executed on 27 June.

1951,

28 January	StB agents arrested Clementis, while he was walking his dog Brok. He was imprisoned in the newly built prison complex Ruzyně near the airport.
5 February	The StB executed a search warrant of the Clementis flat.
6 February	Husák and Novomeský arrested.
24 February	Lída Clementisová arrested and imprisoned in Ruzyně.

23 November	Arrest of Rudolf Slánský, the former General Secretary of the KSČ and closest confidant of Gottwald.
1952, 20 November	The show trial of Slánský and co-accused started. They were accused of Titoism, Zionism, conspiracy with the West and high treason. The trial concluded on 27 November. Gottwald confirmed the death sentences on 2 December.
3 December	Clementis and the ten sentenced to death were executed by hanging; he died at 5 am. Their bodies were burnt and the ashes dispersed in the countryside close to Ruzyně prison. Lída Clementisová released from prison. She would have to wait until the early 1960s to receive her husband's last letter.
1953, 5 March	Stalin died.
14 March	Gottwald followed. The CC KSČ elected Viliam Široký (1902–1971) Prime Minister and Antonín Zápotocký (1884–1957) President.
1954, 17 April	Lucreţiu Pătrăşcanu executed in Bucarest.
21-24 April	Trial of the 'Slovak bourgeois nationalists' in Bratislava. Husák, Okali, Holdoš and Ivan Horváth received long prison sentences.
1955, 14 May	Foundation of the Warsaw Pact in Warsaw, Poland.
1960, 9 May	At the occasion of the 15th anniversary of Czechoslovakia's liberation, President Novotný announced a general amnesty. 5,601 prisoners were released, among them Husák and Novomeský.

1963, 8 April	The CC KSS elected Alexander Dubček First Secretary of the Party.
22 April	At the III congress of the Slovak writers' association, Novomeský and others criticised the findings of the Kolder commission that had not fully rehabilitated Clementis and the comrades imprisoned for 'Slovak bourgeois nationalism'.
18-19 December	At the meeting of the CC KSČ, the Slovaks accused of 'bourgeois nationalism' were partly rehabilitated. The Barnabite commission admitted that the accusation had been constructed, but the political future of the accused, their return to the Party, remained unclear.
1964	With the support of Laco Novomeský, Lída Clementisová published her late husband's memoirs of his childhood and their letters written in France and Great Britain in exile.
1968	Lída Clementisová published their letters from prison.

Bibliography

Foreword by Vlasta Jaksicsová

"Sartre a de Beauvoir v Bratislave". *Kritika & Kontext VII*, no 1 (2002): 17.

"Úvodník". *Listy*, no. 15, 17 April 1969.

Clementis, Vladimír. "V centre päťročnice". In *Vzduch našich čias. Články, state, prejavy, polemiky 1922-1934, vol. I*. Bratislava: Vydavateľstvo politickej literatúry, 1967.

Judt, Tony with Timothy Snyder. *Thinking the Twentieth Century*. New York: Penguin, 2013. The Czech edition: *Intelektuál ve dvacátém století. Rozhovor Timothyho Snydera s Tonym Judtom*. Praha: Prostor 2013.

Jungmann, Milan. *Literárky můj osud. Kritické návraty ke kultuře padesátých a šedesátých let s aktuálními reflexemi*. Praha: Atlantis, 1999.

Klíma, Ivan. *Moje šílené století I*. Praha: Academia 2009.

Novomeský, Ladislav. "Aký si (How you are)". In *Svätý za dedinou (Patron Saints for the Country)* (1939). Bratislava: Literárne informačné centrum, 2005.

Šalda, František Xaver. "Gidovo zklamání ze Sovětskeho Ruska". *Zápisník IX* (1936-1937): 109-120.

Urban, Milo. *Kade-tade po Halinde. Neveselé spomienky na veselé roky*. Bratislava: Slovenský spisovateľ, 1992.

Introduction, Chapters I, II, III, Conclusion

"Boj proti Bolševizmu". *Národný denník*, 6 December 1928.

"Doslov, ktorý je úvodom", *DAV V*, no. 12 (1932): 2-3.

"Na cestě k moci a ovládnutí státu". In *Český a slovenský komunismus (1921–2011)*. Praha: Ústav pro studium totalitních režimů, 2012.

"Štyri dopisy". *DAV IV*, no. 5-6 (1931): 2-3.

1948. Únor 1948 v Československu: Nástup komunistické totality a proměny společnosti. Praha: Ústav pro soudobé dějiny AV ČR, v.v.i., 2011.

Arendt, Hannah. "Antisemitism". In *The Origins of Totalitarianism*. San Diego, New York, London: Harcourt Brace & Company, 1973.

Aron, Raymond. *The Opium of the Intellectuals*. New Brunswick, London: Transaction Publishers, 2005.

Baehr, Peter, ed. "Banality and Conscience: The Eichmann Trial and its Implications". In *The portable Hannah Arendt*. New York: Penguin, 2000.

Baendelin, Oscar, J. *Return to the NEP. The False Promise of Leninism and the Failure of Perestroika*. Westport, CT: Praeger, 2002.

Baer Josette. "Milada Horáková (1902–1950) – executed for her belief in Democracy". In *Seven Czech Women. Portraits of Courage, Humanism and Enlightenment*. Stuttgart, New York: ibidem, Columbia University Press, 2015.

Baer, Josette. "The Genesis of Czechoslovakism. An Interdisciplinary Inquiry into the Influence of Rousseau's Réligion Civile". In *East European Faces of Law and Society: Values and Practices.* Leiden: Brill Nijhoff, 2014.

Baer, Josette. "A Man Motivated by Power". *New Eastern Europe 4*, no. 5 (2014): 156-160.

Baer, Josette. "Das Tatra-Gebirge als Symbol der slowakischen nationalen und politischen Identität". In *Berge*. Zürich: Chronos, 2009.

Baer, Josette. "Ein Catch-22? Die slowakischen Sozialdemokraten zwischen nationaler Identität und internationaler Arbeitersolidarität (1905–1918)". In *Arbeit. Philosophische, juristische und kulturwissenschaftliche Studien*. Basel: Schwabe, 2014.

Baer, Josette. "Svetozár Hurban Vajanský (1847–1916). Messianism, Panslavism and the superiority of art". In *Revolution, Modus Vivendi or Sovereignty? The Political Thought of the Slovak National Movement from 1861 to 1914*. Stuttgart: ibidem, 2010.

Baer, Josette. "Thomas G. Masaryk and Svetozár Hurban Vajanský. A Czecho-Slovak friendship?" *KOSMAS. Czechoslovak and Central European Journal 26*, no. 2 (2013): 50-62.

Baer, Josette. "Twilight of the Idols in Slovakia – or using Nietzsche's hammer to strenghten the nation". In Kapitoly z histórie stredoeurópskeho priestoru v 19. a 20. storočí. Pocta k 70-ročnému jubileu Dušana Kováča. Bratislava: Historický ústav Slovenskej Akademie Vied SAV, 2012.

Baer, Josette. "Vertrauen ist nichts, Macht ist alles. Gustáv Husák (1913–1991) und die tschechoslowakische Normalisierung. Versuch eines politischen Psychogramms". In *Vertrauen*. Basel: Schwabe, 2015.

Baer, Josette. *A Life Dedicated to the Republic. Vavro Šrobár's Slovak Czechoslovakism*. Stuttgart, New York: ibidem, Columbia University Press, 2014.

Baer, Josette. *Politik als praktizierte Sittlichkeit. Zum Demokratiebegriff von Thomas G. Masaryk und Václav Havel*. Sinzheim: Pro Universitate, 1998.

Baer, Josette. *Revolution, Modus Vivendi or Sovereignty? The Political Thought of the Slovak National Movement from 1861 to 1914*. Stuttgart: ibidem, 2010.

Baer, Josette. *Seven Czech Women. Portraits of Courage, Humanism and Enlightenment*. Stuttgart, New York: ibidem, Columbia University Press, 2015.

Baer, Josette. *Seven Slovak Women. Portraits of Courage, Humanism and Enlightenment*. Stuttgart, New York: ibidem, Columbia University Press, 2015.

Baláž, Anton. *Krajina zabudnutia*. Bratislava: Slovenský spisovateľ, 2000.

Baláž, Anton. *Transporty nádeje. Slovenskí Židia na ceste do novej vlasti*. Bratislava: Marenčin PT, 2010.

Banville, John. *The Untouchable*. London: Picador, 1997.

Bartlová, Alena. "Posledné parlamentné voľby v máj 1935". In *V medzivojnovom Československu 1918–1939*. Bratislava: Veda, 2012.

Bartošek, Karel. "Central and Southeastern Europe". In *The Black Book of Communism. Crimes. Terror. Repression.* Cambridge, MA, London: Harvard University Press, 1999.

Batscha, Zwi. *Eine Philosophie der Demokratie. Thomas G. Masaryks Begründung einer neuzeitlichen Demokratie.* Frankfurt a. Main: Suhrkamp, 1994.

Baverez, Nicolas. *Raymond Aron. Un moraliste au temps des ideologies.* Paris: Perrin, 2006.

Bažantová, Ilona. "Zapomenutý ekonom Karel Havlíček Borovský". *Politická Ekonomie 5*, no. 2 (1999): 621-629.

Beller, Steven. "'Pride and Prejudice' or 'Sense and Sensibility'? How reasonable was Anti-Semitism in Vienna, 1880-1939?" In *Essential Outsiders. Chinese and Jews in the Modern Transformation of Southeast Asia and Central Europe.* Seattle: University of Washington Press, 1997.

Beller, Steven. *Antisemitism. A Very Short Introduction.* Oxford, New York: Oxford University Press, 2007.

Beneš, Edvard. *Paměti. Vol. II Od Mnichova k nové válce a k novému vítězství.* Praha: Academia, 2008.

Beneš, Edvard. *Paměti. Vol. III Dokumenty.* Praha: Academia, 2008.

Benhabib, Seyla. *The Reluctant Modernism of Hannah Arendt.* Lanham, MD: Rowlamn & Littlefield, 2003.

Berlin, Isaiah. "The Origins of Israel". In *The Power of Ideas.* Princeton, NJ, Oxford: Princeton University Press, Oxford University Press, 2002.

Berlin, Isaiah. *Freedom and its Betrayal. Six Enemies of Human Liberty.* London: Pimlico, 2003.

Berlin, Isaiah. *Karl Marx.* Princeton, NJ: Princeton University Press, 2013 (5).

Bernáth, Viliam. *Spomienky na Vladimíra Clementisa.* Bratislava: T.R.I MEDIUM v spolupráci s vydavateľstvom Spolku slovenských spisovateľov v edícii *SocietaS*, 2002.

Bihl, Wolfdieter. "Die Juden". In *Die Habsburgermonarchie 1848–1918. Die Völker des Reiches, vol III/2*. Wien: Österreichische Akademie der Wissenschaften, 1980.

Bilková, Hana a Jan Hančil, eds. *Antisemitismus v posttotalitni Evrope. Sbornik z Mezinarodního seminare o antisemitismus v posttotalitni Evrope*. Praha: Nakladátelství Franze Kafky, 1993.

Bobek, Micha, Pavel Molek a Vojtěch Šimíček, eds. *Komunistické právo v Československu: kapitoly z dějin bezpráví*. Brno: Masarykova univerzita, 2009.

Büchler, Robert, Y. *Židovská náboženská obec v Topoľčanoch. (Počiatky, rozvoj a zánik)*. Bratislava: Slovenské národné múzeum, Múzeum židovskej kultúry, 1996.

Bystrický, Valerián a kol. *Rok 1968 na Slovensku a v Československu*. Bratislava: HÚ SAV, 2008.

Bystrický, Valerián, Dušan Kováč, Jan Pešek a kol. *Kľučové problémy moderných slovenských dejin 1848–1992*. Bratislava: Veda, 2012.

Bystrický, Valerián. "Vysťahovanie českých štátnych zamestnancov zo Slovenska v rokoch 1938–1939". In *Od autonómie k vzniku Slovenského štátu*. Bratislava: Prodama, 2008.

Chirot, Daniel and Anthony Reid, eds. *Essential Outsiders. Chinese and Jews in the Modern Transformation of Southeast Asia and Central Europe*. Seattle: University of Washington Press, 1997.

Čierny, Ján. *Vladimír Clementis. Diplomat*. Bratislava: Literárne informačné centrum, 1999.

Courtois, Stéphane, Nicolas Werth, Jean-Louis Panné, Andrzej Paczkowski, Karel Bartošek and Jean-Louis Margolin. *The Black Book of Communism. Crimes. Terror. Repression*. Cambridge, MA, London: Harvard University Press, 1999.

Dangl, Vojtech, Valerián Bystrický a kol. *Chronológia Dejín Slovenska a Slovákov, vol I a II*. Bratislava: Veda, 2014.

DAV I, no. 1 (1924): 49.

Dejmek, Jindřich. "Ministr zahraničních věcí Vladimír Clementis, jeho úřad a jeho diplomatie". *Historický časopis 58*, no. 3 (2010): 497-531.

Detvan. 50 rokov v Prahe. Rozpomienky, štúdie, úvahy. Praha, Turčiansky Sv. Martin: Matica Slovenska, 1932.

Drápala, Milan. "Na ztracené varte západu. Antologie české nesocialistické publicistiky z let 1945 – 1948". Praha: Prostor, 2000.

Drtina, Prokop. *Československo, můj osud*, svazek I, kniha 2. Toronto: Sixty-Eight Publishers, 1982.

Drug, Štefan. *Vladimír Clementis. Život a dielo v dokumentoch*. Martin: Osveta, 1993.

Dubček, Alexander. *Leben für die Freiheit*. München: Bertelsmann, 1993.

Dubova, Alice. "War experiences with Slovakian partisans (1958)". Yad Vashem Archives, Israel, Wiener Library Collection, record group 0.2, file no. 668.

Dufek, Jiří, Karel Kaplan a Vladimír Šlosár. *Československo a Izrael v letech 1945-1956: dokumenty*. Brno, Praha: Doplněk, Ustav pro Soudobé Dějiny AV ČR, 1993.

Dufek, Jiří, Karel Kaplan a Vladimír Šlosár, *Československo a Izrael v letech 1947-1953*: Studie. Praha: Ustav pro Soudobé Dějiny AV ČR, 1993.

Firt, Julius. "Die Burg aus der Sicht eines Zeitgenossen". In *Die Burg. Einflussreiche politische Kräfte um Masaryk und Beneš, vol I*. Oldenbourg: München, Wien, 1973.

Formánková, Pavlina a Petr Koura. *Žádáme trest smrti! Propagandistický kampaň provázející proces s Miladou Horákovou a spol. (historická studie a edice dokumentů)*. Praha: Ústav pro studium totalitních režimů, 2008.

Friedl, Jiří a Zdeněk Jirásek. *Rozpačíte spojenectví. Ceskoslovenské-polske vztahy v letech 1945-1949*. Praha: Aleš Křívan ml, 2008.

Funda, Otakar. *Thomas Garrigue Masaryk. Sein philosophisches, religiöses und politisches Denken*. Bern: Peter Lang, 1978.

Furst, Alan. *Night Soldiers*. London: Weidenfeld & Nicolson ebook, 2011. Loc. 813, kindle edition.

Galandauer, Jan. *Vznik Československé Republiky 1918*. Praha: Svoboda, 1988.

Geaney, Kathleen. "At home among Strangers. The Extraordinary Year 1950 in the Life of an Ordinary American Family in Communist Czechoslovakia". *COMENIUS. Journal of Euro-American Civilization II*, no. 1 (2015): 25-42.

Grüner, Frank. "Jüdisches Antifaschistisches Komitee." In *Enzyklopädie jüdischer Geschichte und Kultur, Band 3*. Stuttgart: Metzler Verlag, 2012.

Grüner, Frank. *Patrioten und Kosmopoliten. Juden im Sowjetstaat 1941–1953*. Köln, Weimar, Wien: Böhlau, 2008.

Guelton, Fréderic, Emanuelle Braud a Michal Kšiňan. *Milan Rastislav Štefánik v archívnich dokumentov Historickej služby francúzskeho ministerstva obrany*. Paris, Bratislava: service historique de la Défense, Vojkenský historický ústav, Ministerstvo obrany SR, 2008, 2009.

Habermann, Tomáš. *Československo a Izrael 1947–1949: Léta přátelství*. Praha: Univerzita Karlova, Pedagogická Fakulta, Katedra Dějín a Didaktiky Dějepisu, 2001.

Hain, Radan. *Staatstheorie und Staatsrecht in T. G. Masaryks Ideenwelt*. Zürich: Schulthess, 1999.

Hanák, Harry, ed. *T. G. Masaryk (1850–1937). Statesman and Cultural Force*. Basingstoke: MacMillan, SSEES, University of London, 1990.

Harding, Neil. *Leninism*. London: MacMillan, 1996.

Heller, Joseph. *Catch-22*. New York: Vintage, 1994.

Hertel, Maroš. "Vlastizrada alebo pomsta?" In *Storočie procesov. Súdy, politika a spoločnosť v moderných dejinách Slovenska*. Bratislava: Veda, 2013.

Hill, Peter Thomas. "History". In *Half-Life. The Dictionary of Hidden Meaning.* Unpublished manuscript. Work in progress. Zurich 2016.

Hlôšková, Hana. "Národný hrdina Juraj Jánošík". In *Mýty naše slovenské*. Bratislava: Academic Electronic Press, 2005.

Hodža, Milan. *Federácia v strednej Európe.* Bratislava: Kalligramm, 1997.

Hoensch, Jörg K. *Geschichte der Tschechoslowakei*. Stuttgart, Berlin, Köln: Kohlhammer, 1992 (3).

Hoffmann, Roland J. *Thomas G. Masaryk und die tschechische Frage.* München: Oldenbourg, 1988.

Holdoš, Ladislav a Karel Bartošek. *Svědek Husákova procesu vypovídá*. Praha: Naše vojsko, 1991.

Holec, Roman. "Uvahy k fenoménu maďarizácie pred rokom 1918". In *Kľučové problémy moderných slovenských dejin 1848–1992*. Bratislava: Veda, 2012.

Holotíková, Zdenka a Viliam Plevza. *Vladimír Clementis*. Bratislava: Vydavateľstvo politickej literatúry v edícii Postavy slovenskej politiky, 1968.

Holubec, Stanislav. "Léta 1948–1949". In *Ještě nejsme za vodou. Obrazy druhých a historická paměť v období postkommunistické transformace*. Praha: Scriptorium, 2015.

Hope Dies Last. The Autobiography of Alexander Dubcek. London: HarperCollins, 1993.

Hosking, Geoffrey. *A History of the Soviet Union 1917-1991*. London: Harper Collins, 1992.

Hronský, Márian a Miroslav Pekník. *Martinská deklarácia. Cesta slovenskej politiky k vzniku Česko-Slovenska*. Bratislava: Veda, 2008.

Hurban Vajanský, Svetozár. *Nálady a výhľady.* Turčiansky Sv. Martin: Kníhtlačiarsko-účastinarský spolok, 1897.

Husák, G., Dr. "O boj a spolubojovníkovi". In *Odkazy z Londýna*. Bratislava: Obroda, 1947.

Husák, Gústav. "Spomienky na Vlada Clementisa". *Kultúrny Život XXII*, no. 31 (1967): 1-2; "Búrlivé roky", *Kultúrny Život XXII*, no. 34 (1967): 3; "Svetlá a tiene", *Kultúrny Život XXII*, no. 36 (1967): 3; "Prípad na zamyslenie", *Kultúrny Život XXII*, no. 38 (1967): 1, 10.

Jablonický, Jozef. *Z ilegality do povstania. Kapitoly z občianskeho odboja*. Banská Bystrica: Muzeum SNP, 2009 (2).

Jaksicsová, Vlasta. "Kommunistický intelektuál – víťaz a porazený hodnotového sporu v 'medzičase' pred kommunistickou diktatúrou". *Historický časopis LXII*, no. 1 (2014): 61-89.

Jaksicsová, Vlasta. "'Pokolenie v útoku': *Kultúrny život* v zrkadle ideologickej (ne)kultúry v rokoch 1948–1953". In *Slovensko v labyrinte Európskych dejín. Pocta historikov Milanovi Zemkovi*. Bratislava: HÚ SAV a Prodama, 2014.

Jesenská, Zora. "Slovo na Záver. Drahá Hádička". In *Nedokončená kronika*. Bratislava: Slovenské vydavateľstvo krásnej literatúry, 1964.

Jesenský, Marcel. *The Slovak-Polish border 1918–1947*. New York: Palgrave Macmillan, 2014.

Jesse, Eckhard. "Antifaschismus in der Ideokratie der DDR – und die Folgen". In *Extremismus und Demokratie, Parteien und Wahlen*. Köln, Weimar, Wien: Nomos, 2015.

Judt, Tony with Timothy Snyder. *Thinking The Twentieth Century*. New York: Penguin, 2012.

Jurík, Ľuboš. *Smrť ministra*. Martin: Matica Slovenská, 2011.

Juza, Peter, ed. *Vlastenec a Európan Vladimír Clementis. Zborník príspevok zo spomienkovej konferencie 20. 9. 2012 v Bratislave*. Bratislava: Institút ASA, 2012.

Kalous, Jan a Jiří Kocian, eds. *Český a slovenský komunismus (1921–2011)*. Praha: Ústav pro studium totalitních režimů, 2012.

Kalous, Jan. "KSČ jako iniciátor a vykonavatel politických čistek a procesů". In *Český a slovenský komunismus (1921–2011)*. Praha: Ústav pro studium totalitních režimů, 2012.

Kamenec, Ivan a Eduard Nižňanský, eds. *Holokaust na Slovensku: Prezident, vláda, snem SR a štátni rada o židovskej otázke*. Zvolen, Bratislava: Klemo, nadacia Milana Šimečka, židovská náboženská obec, 2003.

Kamenec, Ivan. "Novohlasistická skupina a robotnická akadémia na Slovensku v rokoch 1933–1937". In *Slovensko v labyrinte moderných europských dejín. Pocta historikov Milanovi Zemkovi*. Bratislava: HÚ SAV, 2014.

Kamenec, Ivan. "Protižidovský pogrom v Topoľčanoch v septembri 1945". In *Studia historica Nitriensia 8* (1999): 85-97.

Kamenec, Ivan. *Po stopách tragédie*. Praha: Archa, 1991.

Kamenec, Ivan. *Tragédia politika, kňaza a človeka. Dr. Jozef Tiso, 1887–1947*. Bratislava: Premedia, 2013 (2).

Kann, Robert A. *A History of the Habsburg Empire 1526–1918*. Berkeley: University of California Press, 1974.

Kaplan, Karel. *Protistátní Bezpečnost 1945–1948. Historie vzniku a působení StB jako mocenského nástroje KSČ*. Praha: Plus, 2015.

Kaplan, Karel. *Report on the Murder of the General Secretary*. Columbus: Ohio State University Press, 1990.

Kaplan, Karel. *The Short March. The Communist Takeover in Czechoslovakia 1945–1948*. London: Hurst & Co, 1987.

Kershaw, Ian. "Biography and the Historian". In *Biography between structure and agency. Central European lives in international historiography*. New York: Berghahn, 2008.

Kershaw, Ian. *Hitler*. London: Penguin, 2008.

Kołakowski, Leszek. *Main Currents of Marxism*. New York, London: Norton , 2005.

Kořalka, Jiří. "Nationsbildung und nationale Identität der Deutschen, Österreicher, Tschechen und Slovaken um die Mitte des

19. Jahrhunderts". In *Ungleiche Nachbarn. Demokratische und nationale Emanzipation bei Deutschen, Tschechen und Slovaken (1815–1914)*. Essen: Klartext, 1993.

Kosatík, Pavel. *Jan Masaryk. Pravdivý příběh*. Praha: Mladá Fronta, 2009 (2).

Kosta, Jiří. "Systemwandel in der Tschechoslowakei. Ökonomische und politische Aspekte". *Osteuropa 41*, no. 9 (1990): 802-818.

Köstler, Arthur. *Darkness at Noon*. London: Vintage, 2005.

Kováč, Dušan. *Dejiny Slovenska*. Praha: Nakladatelství Lidové Noviny, 2007 (2).

Kováč, Dušan. *Slováci. Česi. Dejiny*. Bratislava: AEP, 1997.

Kováčiková, Terézia. "Ženy v národnooslobodzovacom zápase (1939–1945)". In *Zborník múzea Slovenského Národného povstania 7*. Martin, Múzeum SNP v Banskej Bystrici: Osveta, 1982.

Kozák, Jan B. *T. G. Masaryk a vznik Washingtonské deklarace v říjnu 1918*. Praha: Melantrich, 1968.

Krajčovičová, Natália. "The Programme and Objectives of Slovak Agrarianism in the Works of Milan Hodža". In *Milan Hodža. Statesman and Politician*. Bratislava: Veda, 2007.

Křešťan, Jiří. *Zdeněk Nejedlý. Politik a vědec v osamění*. Praha: Paseka, 2012.

Kučerová, Stanislava, Jaroslav Hroch a kol. *Věrni zůstaneme. K 100. výroči československého odboje, korunovaného vznikem Československa*. Brno: Občanský a odborný výbor Brno, Pedagogická fakulta Masarykovy university Brno, Statutární město Brno, 2014.

Langer, Jo. *Convictions. My Life with a Good Communist*. London: Granta, 2011.

Lässig, Simone. "Introduction: Biography in Modern History – Modern Historiography in Biography". In *Biography between structure and agency. Central European lives in international historiography*. New York: Berghahn, 2008.

Londák, Miroslav, Stanislav Sikora a Elena Londáková. *Predjarie. Politický, ekonomický a kultúrny vývoj na Slovensku v rokoch 1960–1967.* Bratislava: Veda, 2002.

London, Artur. *On Trial.* London: Macdonald, 1970.

Lovčí, Radovan. *Alice Garrigue Masaryková. Život ve stínu slavného otca.* Praha: Opera Facultatis philosophicae Universitatis Carolinae Pragensis, 2007.

Löwenstein, Shimona. *Emanuel Rádl. Philosoph und Moralist 1873–1942.* Frankfurt am Main: Peter Lang, 1995.

Lübbe, Hermann. "Der Totalitarismus. Politische Moral als Anti-Religion". In *FORUM für osteuropäische Ideen- und Zeitgeschichte 17,* no. 1 (2013): 27-43.

Lübbe, Hermann. *Politischer Moralismus. Der Triumph der Gesinnung über die Urteilskraft.* Berlin: WJS Corso, 1987(2).

Lukáč, Pavol. *Milan Hodža v zápase o budúcnosť strednej Európy v rokoch 1939–1944.* Bratislava: Veda, 2005.

Luža, Radomír with Cristina Vella. *The Hitler kiss. A Memoir of the Czech resistance.* Baton Rouge: Louisiana State University Press, 2002.

Macho, Peter. *Milan Rastislav Štefánik. V hlavach a v srdciach.* Bratislava: HÚ SAV a Prodama, 2011.

Majer, Diemut. *"Non-Germans" under the Third Reich. The Nazi Judicial and Administrative System in Germany and Occupied Eastern Europe, with special regard to Occupied Poland, 1939–1945.* Baltimore, London: Johns Hopkins University Press, 2003.

Mannheim, Karl. *Ideology and Utopia. An Introduction to the Sociology of Knowledge.* San Diego, New York, London: Harvest Harcourt, 1936.

Margolius Kovály, Heda. *Under a Cruel Star. A Life in Prague 1941–1968.* London: Granta, 2012.

Marzík, Tomas D. "The Slovakophile Relationship of T. G. Masaryk and Karel Kálal prior to 1914". In *T. G. Masaryk (1850–1937). Thinker and Politician.* London: SSEES, 1989.

Masaryk a myšlenka evropské jednoty. Praha: Filosofická Fakulta Univerzity Karlovy FFUK, 1992.

Masaryk, Tomáš G. "Proststředky národa malého". In *Ideály humanitní.* Praha: Melantrich, 1991.

Masaryk, Tomáš, G. "Slavjanofilství. Mesianismus právoslavné teokracie. Slavjanofilství a Panslavismus". In *Rusko a Evropa. Studie o důchovních proudech v Rusku, vol. I.* Praha: Ústav T. G. Masaryka, 1995.

Masaryk, Tomáš, G. "Projev Prezidenta Republiky". In *Cesta demokracie III. Projevy, články rozhovory 1924–1928.* Praha: Ústav T. G. Masaryka, 1994.

Masaryk, Tomáš, G. "Socialism". In *Ideály humanitní.* Praha: Melantrich, 1990.

Merloo, Joost A. M., M. D. *The Rape of the Mind. The Psychology of Thought Control, Menticide, and Brainwashing.* New York: Progressive Press, 1956.

Michálek, Slavomír, Miroslav Londák a kol. *Gustáv Husák. Moc politiky. Politik moci.* Bratislava: Veda, 2013.

Michálek, Slavomír. *Diplomat Štefan Osuský 1889–1973.* Bratislava: Veda, 1999.

Michálek, Slavomír. "K niektorým otázkam československej zahraničnej politiky v rokoch 1945–1951 so zamieraním na činnosť Vladimíra Clementisa". In *Vladimír Clementis. 1902–1952. Zborník príspevkov z konferencie 28. 5. 2002 v Bratislave.* Bratislava: Ministerstvo zahraníčných vecí Slovenskej republiky, Slovenský inštitút medzinárodných štúdií, 2002.

Michálek, Slavomír. "Marshallov plan". In *Nádeje a vytriezvenia (Československo-americké hospodárske vzťahy v rokoch 1945–1952).* Bratislava: Veda, SAV HÚ, 1995.

Michálek, Slavomír. *Nádeje a vytriezvenia (Československo-americké hospodárske vzťahy v rokoch 1945–1951).* Bratislava: Veda, SAV HÚ, 1995.

Michálek, Slavomír. *San Francisco 1945. Vznik organizácie spojených národov*. Bratislava: Veda, HÚ SAV, 2015.

Michela, Miroslav. "Výčiny Karola Hrozného. Ukončil alkohol politickú kariéru?" In *Storočie skandálov. Aféry v moderných dejinách Slovenska*. Bratislava: Pro Historia, 2008.

Mikulášek, Alexej. *Antisemitismus v česke literatuře 19. a 20. stoleti. Teoreticka a historicka studie*. Praha: Votobia, 2000.

Miller, Daniel E. *Forging Political Compromise. Antonín Švehla and the Czechoslovak Republican Party 1918–1933*. Pittsburgh, PA: University of Pittsburgh Press, 1999.

Milosz, Czesław. *The Captive Mind*. New York: Vintage International, 1990.

Němeček, Jan. "Vladimír Clementis a československý zahraniční odboj". In *Vladimír Clementis. 1902–1952. Zborník príspevkov z konferencie 28. 5. 2002 v Bratislave*. Bratislava: Ministerstvo zahraníčných vecí Slovenskej republiky, Slovenský inštitút medzinárodných štúdií, 2002.

Neudorflová, Marie, L. "Karel Havlíček, T. G. Masaryk a demokracie". In *Spisovatelé, společnost a noviny v promínách doby*. Praha: Literární Archiv Národného Písemnictví, 2006.

Nižňanský, Eduard. "Deportácie v roku 1942". In *Nacismus, Holokaust, Slovenský Štát*. Bratislava: Kalligramm, 2010.

Novák, Jozef, ed. *On Masaryk. Texts in English and German*. Amsterdam: Rodopi, 1988.

Opat, Jaroslav. *Filozof a politik T. G. Masaryk, 1882–1893*. Praha: Melantrich, 1990.

Oz, Amos. *A Tale of Love and Darkness*. Orlando, FL: Harcourt, 2003.

Padevět, Jiří. *Průvodce protektorátní Prahou. Místa – události – lidé*. Praha: Academia, Archiv hlavního města Prahy, 2014.

Pasák, Tomáš. *Emil Hácha (1938–1945)*. Praha: Rybka Publishers, 2007 (2).

Patočka, Jan. *Die Bewegung der menschlichen Existenz*. Stuttgart: Klett Cotta, 1990.

Pauer, Jan. *Prag 1968. Der Einmarsch des Warschauer Paktes. Hintergründe – Planung – Durchführung*. Bremen: Edition Temmen, 1995.

Pekník, Miroslav, ed. *Milan Hodža. Statesman and Politician*. Bratislava: Veda, 2007.

Pekník, Miroslav, ed. *Slovenské národné povstanie 1944. Súčať európskej antifašistickej rezistencie v rokoch druhej svetovej vojny*. Bratislava: Veda, 2009.

Peroutka, Ferdinand. "O účasti na revoluci" (1924). In *Kdo nás osvobodil?* Praha: Náklad Svazu národního osvobození, Tisk 'Pokrok', 1927.

Pešek, Jan. "Najbrutálnejšie obdobie komunistického režimu (1948–1953)". In *Štátna moc a spoločnosť na Slovensku 1945 – 1948 – 1989*. Bratislava: HÚ SAV a Prodama, 2013.

Pešek, Jan. "Nepriateľ so straníckou legitimáciou. Proces s tzv. Slovenskými buržoáznymi nacionalistami". In *Storočie procesov. Súdy, politika a spoločnosť v moderných dejinách Slovenska*. Bratislava: Veda, 2013.

Pirjevec, Jože. *Tito. Die Biographie*. München: Verlag Antje Kunstmann, 2016.

Plevza, Viliam. *Vzostupy a Pády. Gustáv Husák prehovoril*. Bratislava: Tatrapress, 1991.

Prúdy V, no. 9-10 (1919): 399-567.

Pynsent, Robert B., ed. *T. G. Masaryk (1850–1937). Thinker and Critic*. Basingstoke: MacMillan, SSEES, University of London, 1989, 1990.

Radzinsky, Edvard. *Stalin*. New York, Toronto: Anchor books, 1996.

Ramet, Sabrina Petra. *The Three Yugoslavias: State-Building and Legitimation 1918–2004*. Washington, DC, Bloomington, IN: Woodrow Wilson, Indiana University Press, 2006.

Reich, Bernard and David H. Goldberg. *Historical Dictionary of Israel*. Lanham, MD: The Scarecrow Press, 2008 (2).

Reinfeld, Barbara K. *Karel Havlíček (1821–1856). A National Liberation Leader of the Czech Renascence.* New York, NY, Boulder, CO: Columbia University Press, 1982.

Rezák, Karol. *30. výročie streľby do poľnohospodárskych robotníkov v Košútoch.* Bratislava-Vinohrady: Slovenský výbor Čs. Spoločnosti pre šírenie politických a vedeckých poznatkov a Osvetový ústav v Bratislave, 1961.

Rubinstein, Joshua and Vladimir P. Naumov, eds. *Stalin's Secret Pogrom: The Post-war Inquisition of the Jewish Antifascist Committee.* New Haven, CN: Yale University Press, 2001.

Rybářová, Petra. *Antisemitizmus v Uhorsku v 80. rokov 19. Storočia.* Bratislava: Pro Historia, 2010.

Rychlík, Jan. *Češi a Slováci ve 20. století. Česko-slovenské vztahy 1914–1945.* Bratislava, Praha: AEP, Ústav T. G. Masaryka, 1997.

Rychlík, Jan. *Češi a Slováci ve 20. století. Česko-slovenské vztahy 1945–1992.* Bratislava, Praha: AEP, ÚTGM, 1998.

Rychlík, Jan. *Rozdělení Česko-Slovenska, 1989–1992.* Praha: Vyšehrad, 2012.

Sabol, Miroslav. "Sociálno-ekonomické koncepcie KSS v rokoch 1921–1948". In *Český a slovenský komunismus (1921–2011).* Praha: Ústav pro studium totalitních režimů, 2012.

Salner, Peter, ed. *Židovská komunita po roku 1945.* Bratislava: Ústav etnologie SAV, 2006.

Salner, Peter. "Die Juden in der bürgerlichen Gesellschaft der Slowakei". In *Bürgertum und bürgerliche Gesellschaft in der Slowakei 1900–1989.* Bratislava: AEP, 1997.

Schwarc, Michal, Ľudovít Hallon a Peter Mičko. *Podoby nemecko-slovenského „ochranného priateľstva". Dokumenty k náboru a nasadeniu slovenských pracovných síl do Nemeckej ríše v rokoch 1939–1945.* Bratislava: HÚ SAV, Fakulta humanitných vied UMB, 2012.

Sedm pražských dnů. 21–27. srpen 1968. Dokumentace. Praha: Academia, 1990.

Šegeš, Dušan. "Internácia československých politikov vo Veľkej Británii v období druhej svetovej voiny ako prostriedok boja s opozíciou, alebo '... všichni musíme do jednotné fronty a intriky a malicherné pomluvy musí přestat.'" In *Adepti moci a úspechu. Etablovanie elít v moderných dejinách.* Bratislava: Veda, 2016.

Šegeš, Dušan. "Orava: úvahy politických elit verzus realita sporného region v rokoch 1918–1947". In *Putovanie dejinami pod múrmi Oravského hradu.* Bratislava: Veda, HÚ SAV, 2015.

Sidor, Karol. "Nech sa sťahujú židia do Palestíny a Birobidžanu!" *Slovák*, no. 58, 12 March 1937, 3.

Sikora, Stanislav. "KSS a čiastočná liberalizácia režimu na Slovensku počas predjaria (1963–1967)". In *Český a slovenský komunismus (1921–2011).* Praha: Ústav pro studium totalitních režimů, 2012.

Šimová, Kateřina. "'Nejnebezpečnější pozůstátek kannibalismu': Stalinský antisemitismus v letech 1948 až 1953". *Acta Universitatis Carolinae. Studia Territorialia*, Praha: Karlova Univerzita, 2013.

Šišjaková, Jana a Michal Šmigel. "Protižidovské prejavy na východnom Slovensku v prvých povojnových rokoch (1945-1947)". In *Annales historici Presoviensis 8,* (2009): 197-217.

Skilling, Gordon H. *Czechoslovakia's Interrupted Revolution.* Princeton, NJ: Princeton University Press, 1976.

Slapnicka, Helmuth. "Die Rechtsstellung des Präsidenten der Republik in der Verfassungsurkunde und in der politischen Wirklichkeit". In *Die Burg. Einflussreiche politische Kräfte um Masaryk und Beneš, vol II.* Oldenbourg: München, Wien, 1974.

Slováci a ľudovodemokratický režim. Bratislava: Literárne informačné centrum, 2016.

Šrobár, Vavro. "Československá otázka a 'hlasisti' (k 60. Narodeninám dra. P. Blahu). *Prúdy XI*, no. 5 (1927): 267-276.

Šrobár, Vavro. *Osvobodené Slovensko. Pamäti z rokov 1918–1920*. Praha: Náklad Gustav Dubského, 1922.

Štefánek, Anton. *Masaryk a Slovensko*. Praha: Náklad spisovatelový, 1931.

Štefanský, Michal a Slavomír Michálek. *Míľniky studenej vojny a ich vplyvy na Československo (od Trumanovej doktríny po Vietnam)*. Bratislava: Veda, 2015.

Strapcová, Katarína. "Bratislavská mládež kontra *Golem*". In *Storočie škandálov. Aféry v moderných dejinách Slovenska*. Bratislava: Spoločnosť Pro Historia, 2008.

Sugar, Peter F., Péter Hanák and Tibor Frank, eds. *A History of Hungary*. Bloomington: Indiana University Press, 1994.

Sum, Antonín. *Osudný krok Jana Masaryka*. Praha: Nadace Janua, Masarykovo demokratické hnutí, 1996.

Taubman, William. *Krushchev. The Man and his Era*. New York: Norton, 2003.

Teich, Mikuláš, Dušan Kováč and Martin D. Brown, eds. *Slovakia in History*. Cambridge: Cambridge University Press, 2011.

Truhlar, Dalibor. *Thomas G. Masaryk. Philosophie der Demokratie*. Frankfurt a. Main: Peter Lang, 1994.

Urban, Zdeněk. "K Masarykovu vztahu ke Slovensku před první světovou válkou". In *Masaryk a Slovensko (soubor statí)*. Praha: Masarykova společnost a Ústav T. G. Masaryka, 1992.

Ulč, Ota, *Komunistická justice a třídní boj*. Praha: Stilus Press, 2016.

Vaksberg, Arkady. *Stalin's Prosecutor. The Life of Andrei Vyshinsky*. New York: Grove Weidenfeld, 1990.

Vévoda, Rudolf. "Sedm našich kamarádů. Ke konfliktu mezi levicovými intelektuály v dobe bolševizace KSČ". In *Český a slovenský komunismus (1921–2011)*. Praha: Ústav pro studium totalitních režimů, 2012.

Viest, Rudolf M. *General Viest's notebooks. Call to arms came in 1938*. Brainigsville, PA: JMV, 2009.

Vladimír Clementis o sebe a o Slovensku. Topoľčany: Edícia osobnosti ľavice, primoprint, 1998.

Vladimír Clementis. 1902–1952. Zborník príspevkov z konferencie 28. 5. 2002 v Bratislave. Bratislava: Ministerstvo zahraničných vecí Slovenskej republiky, Slovenský inštitút medzinárodných štúdií, 2002.

Vodička, Karel. "Wie der Koalitionsbeschluss zur Auflösung der ČSFR zustande kam". *Osteuropa 45*, no. 2 (1994): 175-186.

Williams, Kieran. *The Prague Spring and its Aftermath. Czechoslovak Politics 1968–1970*. Cambridge: Cambridge University Press, 1997.

Winters, Stanley B., ed. *T. G. Masaryk (1850–1937). Thinker and Politician*. Basingstoke: MacMillan, SSEES, University of London, 1989.

Zavacká, Marína. "Whispered rumor as a kind of independent political news service in Slovakia in 1953: People and state reacting on the death of J. V. Stalin and Klement Gottwald". In *Slovak Contributions to 19th International Congress of Historical Sciences.* Bratislava: Veda, 2000.

Zemko, Milan. "Prúdisti v čase, ktorý trhol oponou". In *Kapitoly z histórie stredoeurópskeho priestoru v 19. a 20. Storočí. Pocta k 70-ročnému jubileu Dušana Kováča*. Bratislava: HÚ SAV, 2012.

Zpráva súdruha Václava Kopeckého a Štefana Bašťovanského na zasadaní ústredného výboru Kommunistickej Strany Československa dňa 21. Februara 1951. Bratislava: kultúrno-propagačné oddelenie sekretariátu ÚV KSS, no date mentioned, most probably 1951.

Texts and broadcasts by Clementis

Clementis, Vladimír a Lída Clementisová. *Daleko od Teba*. Bratislava: Tatran, 1972.

Clementis, Vladimír a Lída Clementisová. *Listy z Väzenia*. Bratislava: Tatran: 1968.

Clementis, Vladimír, Dr. *Odkazy z Londýna*. Bratislava: Nakladateľstvo Obroda, 1947.

Clementis, Vladimír. "Agrarizmus ako nova 'ideológia'". *DAV I* (1924): 34-39. In *Vzduch našich čias. Články, state, prejavy, polemiky 1922–1934, vol I*. Bratislava: Vydavateľstvo politickej literatúry, 1967.

Clementis, Vladimír. "Ano, ano – nie, nie!" *Slovenské zvesti III*, no. 182, 18 September 1938, 3. In *Vzduch našich čias. Články, state, prejavy, polemiky 1922–1934, vol II*. Bratislava: Vydavateľstvo politickej literatúry, 1967.

Clementis, Vladimír. "Atentát na Hitlera". In *Odkazy z Londýna*. Bratislava: Obroda, 1947.

Clementis, Vladimír. "Autonómia?" *Svět v obrazech*, 20 March 1938, no. 10, 4-5. In *Vzduch našich čias. Články, state, prejavy, polemiky 1922–1934, vol II*. Bratislava: Vydavateľstvo politickej literatúry, 1967.

Clementis, Vladimír. "Banská Bystrica – zase slobodná!". In *Odkazy z Londýna*. Bratislava: Obroda, 1947.

Clementis, Vladimír. "Československí robotníci v Nemecku". In *Odkazy z Londýna*. Bratislava: Obroda, 1947.

Clementis, Vladimír. "Čierne Turice košutské". *DAV IV*, no. 5-6 (1931): 4-9.

Clementis, Vladimír. "Hitler, Hlinka – jedna linka!" In *Odkazy z Londýna*. Bratislava: Obroda, 1947.

Clementis, Vladimír. "K národnostnej otázke". *DAV I*, no. 1 (1924): 2-4.

Clementis, Vladimír. "Kapitoly o nás". *Mladé Slovensko V*, no. 3 (1923): 66-69. In *Vzduch našich čias. Články, state, prejavy, polemiky 1922-1934, vol I.* Bratislava: Vydavateľstvo politickej literatúry, 1967.

Clementis, Vladimír. "Nad rovom Vančuru". In *Odkazy z Londýna.* Bratislava: Obroda, 1947.

Clementis, Vladimír. "O veciach budúcich". In *Odkazy z Londýna.* Bratislava: Obroda, 1947.

Clementis, Vladimír. "Potemkinove dediny zo železobetonu". *DAV IV*, no. 2 (1931): 10-11.

Clementis, Vladimír. "Prejav v poslaneckej snemovni 29. Apríla 1936". In *Vzduch našich čias. Články, state, prejavy, polemiky 1922-1934, vol II.* Bratislava: Vydavateľstvo politickej literatúry, 1967.

Clementis, Vladimír. "SLOVÁK sa diva na SSSR". *DAV 8*, no. 1 (1935): 8-11.

Clementis, Vladimír. "Slovenské národné povstanie!" In *Odkazy z Londýna.* Bratislava: Obroda, 1947.

Clementis, Vladimír. "Slovenské ženy". In *Odkazy z Londýna.* Bratislava: Obroda, 1947.

Clementis, Vladimír. "Slovenskí robotníci v Nemecku". In *Odkazy z Londýna.* Bratislava: Obroda, 1947.

Clementis, Vladimír. "Slovensko vypovedalo vojnu Amerike". In *Odkazy z Londýna.* Bratislava: Obroda, 1947.

Clementis, Vladimír. "Slovenský ľud a odkaz T. G. Masaryka". In *Vzduch našich čias. Články, state, prejavy, polemiky 1922-1934, vol II.* Bratislava: Vydavateľstvo politickej literatúry, 1967.

Clementis, Vladimír. "Tanier boršču a pohár piva". *DAV IV*, no. 3 (1931): 12-13.

Clementis, Vladimír. "V druhom roku piatiletky". *DAV IV*, no. 1 (1931): 4-5.

Clementis, Vladimír. "Volebná porážka komunistov". *DAV III*, no. 1 (1929): 6-7. In *Vzduch našich čias. Články, state, prejavy, polemiky 1922–1934, vol I.* Bratislava: Vydavateľstvo politickej literatúry, 1967.

Clementis, Vladimír. "Vyhnať židov do Palestíny a Birobidžanu? Lex Sidor. Jeho smiešna demagogia tam, kde je 'vážne' mienený". *DAV 10*, no. 4 (1937): 3-5.

Clementis, Vladimír. "Vysťahovanie Čechov zo Slovenska". In *Odkazy z Londýna*. Bratislava: Obroda, 1947.

Clementis, Vladimír. *Naša zahraničná politika*. Praha: Orbis, 1947.

Clementis, Vladimír. *Nedokončená kronika*. Bratislava: Slovenské vydavateľstvo krásnej literatúry, 1964.

Clementis, Vladimír. *Vzduch našich čias. Články. State, prejavy, polemiky vol I 1922–1934, vol II, 1934–1938.* Bratislava: Vydavateľstvo politickej literatúry, 1967.

Statement made by Dr. Vl. Clementis before the Foreign Affairs Committee of the Constituent National Assembly on December 2, 1947 on the subject of Germany. Praha: Orbis, 1947.

Archival sources

"AGREEMENT between Czechoslovakia and Hungary concerning Exchange of Population". AMZV, GS-A 1945–1954, carton no. 164, 11 pages, type-written.

"IZRAEL. REAKCE NA PROCES SE SLÁNSKÝM A SPOL. /Dokumentační přehled od 21. XI. – 7. XII.52/". AMZV, GS-A 1945-1954, carton 155, 14 pages, typewritten, classified *Tajné*.

"Letter of Lída Clementisová to Dr Miloš Ruppeldt". SNA OF VC, sent from Prague to Bratislava, 20 August 1963, 2 pages, typewritten.

"Návrh na úpravu vzájemních vztahů mezi ČSR a Izraelem", 5 July 1954. AMZV, GS-A 1945-1954, carton 155, 35 pages, typewritten, classified *Tajné*.

"Prednaška pána ministra k zamestnancom MZV u príležitosti výročia úmrtia V. I. Lenina". AMZV, GS-A 1945-1954, carton 67, 5 pages, typewritten.

"Prejav štátneho tajomníka Dr. Vl. Clementisa pri smútočnom shromáždení zamestnancov ministerstva zahraničných vecí dňa 11. Marca 1948". AMZV, GS-A 1945-1954, carton 67, 2 pages, typewritten.

"Řeč min. dr. Clementise u Gen. Shromáždění", 29. Září 1949". AMZV, GS-A 1945-1954, carton 78, 46 pages, English, typewritten.

"Řeč st. taj. Clementise v Maďarské komisi dne 20. Září 1946". AMZV, GS-A 1945-1954, carton no. 65, 23 pages, English, typewritten.

"SPEECH of Mr. ALADÁR SZEGEDY-MASZÁK, Envoy Extraordinary and Minister Plenipotentiary, Representative of the Hungarian Delegation in the Territorial and Political Commission for Hungary, September 18th, 1946". AMZV, GS-A 1945–1954, carton no. 164, 16 pages, typewritten.

"Statement by Secretary of State Dr VLADIMÍR CLEMENTIS, delivered in the Foreign Affairs Committee of the Constituent National Assembly on 31 October, 1946". SNA, OF VC, carton aj 14, 21 pages, English, typewritten.

"Zápis ze schůze pol. Sekretáriatu ÚV-KSČ k procesu s protistátním centrem, dne 17. listopadu 1952". AMVZ GS-A 1945-1954, carton 96, 5 pages, typewritten, addressed to Široký, 18 November 1952, classified *Príšně tajné* (top secret).

"Zpráva štátného tajomníka v MNO o inšpekčnej ceste ministra NO a štát. tajomníka po južnom pohraničí Slovenska". AMZV, GS-A 1945-1954, carton no. 164, 6 pages, typewritten.

ABS USTRČR, Fond 319, sign. 319-34-13, confirmation of Lída Clementisová, signed by her and two witnesses on 23 April 1957, 1 page, typewritten.

ABS USTRČR, Fond 319, sign. 319-34-13, letter from Lída Clementisová to Karol Bacílek, 7 December 1952, hand-written, 3 pages.

ABS USTRČR, Fond 319, sign. 319-34-13, letter from Lída Clementisová to Dr. Bartušek, general prosecutor, 13 February 1957, hand-written, 4 pages.

ABS USTRČR, Fond 319, sign. 319-34-13, letter from the Ministry of Higher Education to the Ministry of National Security, 1 page, typewritten, classified *Tajne* (secret).

ABS USTRČR, MNB 2_1 Z_1480 podsvazek 43.

ABS USTRČR, MNB 2_1 Z_1480 podsvazek 44.

ABS USTRČR, MNB 2_1 Z_1480_podsvazek 65.

ABS USTRČR, MNB 2_1_35.

ABS USTRČR, MNB 2_10.

ABS USTRČR, MNB 2_11.

ABS USTRČR, MNB 2_8.

ABS USTRČR, MNB 2_9.

ABS USTRČR, YSGŠ, sign. a. č. 9479 Vlado Clementis.

Andrei Ia. Vyšinskii's telegramme. AMZV, GS-A 1945-1954, carton 78, 1 page, telegramme sent by Western Union on 28 October 1949, in Russian.

Clementis, Vladimír. "Pozdravný telegram s. V. Širokým na zasedání ÚV KSS – 11. XI. 49". AMZV, GS-A 1945-1954, carton 78, 1 page.

Clementis, Vladimír. "Přednáška v klube právnikov na tému: Spojené národy a niektoré z ich právnych problémov". SNA, OF VC, carton aj 21, 14 pages, typewritten.

Clementis, Vladimír. "Prejav na IX. sjazde KSČ z 27. Mája 1949". SNA OF VC, carton a.j. 56, 11 pages, typewritten.

Clementis, Vladimír. "Prejav o medzinárodnej situácii z 8. Júna 1945". SNA, OF VC, carton aj 2, 34 pages, typewritten.

Clementis, Vladimír. "Prejav v rozhlase z 20. Marca 1948 o Janovi Masarykovi / interview/". AMZV, GS-A 1945-1954, carton 65, 6 pages, typewritten.

Clementis, Vladimír. Untitled speech at the UN on 16 September 1946. AMZV, GS-A 1945–1954, carton no. 164, 13 pages, typewritten.

Masaryk, Jan. Untitled speech at the UN. AMZV, GS-A 1945-1954, carton no. 164, 8 pages, English, typewritten.

Telegramme from Slánský to Clementis, 15 September 1950. SNA OF VC, carton a. 9., 97, 1 page, typewritten.

The Daily Telegraph, 11. VII. 1947, SNA, OF VC, carton aj 1.

Internet sources

Almog, Shmuel. "What's in a hyphen?" on http://sicsa.huji.ac.il/hyphen.html.

Arendt, Hannah on http://plato.stanford.edu/entries/arendt/#AreTheJud.

Armistice treaty with Hungary on http://avalon.law.yale.edu/wwii/hunga01.asp.

Bierut, Bolesław on http://www.president.pl/en/president/polish-presidents/boleslaw-bierut/.

Birobidžan on http://www.jewishvirtuallibrary.org/jsource/judaica/ejud_0002_0003_0_03013.htmland.

Blunt, Anthony on http://www.telegraph.co.uk/news/uknews/5889879/Anthony-Blunt-confessions-of-spy-who-passed-secrets-to-Russia-during-the-war.html.

Blunt, Anthony: Confessions of spy who passed secrets to Russia during the war on http://www.telegraph.co.uk/news/uknews/5889879/Anthony-Blunt-confessions-of-spy-who-passed-secrets-to-Russia-during-the-war.html.

Café Štefanka on: http://www.cafestefanka.sk.

Cairncross, John on http://www.independent.co.uk/news/people/obituaries-john-cairncross-1576877.html;

Cambridge spies on http://www.bbc.com/news/uk-england-cambridgeshire-28143770.

Catch-22 on http://www.merriam-webster.com/dictionary/catch–22.

Chmelar, Eduard on http://www.pluska.sk/plus7dni/rozhovor/otec-naroda.html.

Cicero, Marcus Tullius, *De Oratore*, II, 36; https://archive.org/stream/cicerodeoratore01ciceuoft/cicerodeoratore01ciceuoft_djvu.txt.

Cicero's *Oratory and Orators* by J. S. Watson. New York: Harper & Brothers, 1860. On http://archive.org/stream/ciceroonoratoryo00cice#page/92/mode/2up.

Cold War International History Project on https://www.wilsoncenter.org/program/cold-war-international-history-project.

Comintern meetings on http://www.marxisthistory.org/subject/usa/eam/comintern.html.

ČT documentary on Jan Masaryk's death on http://www.ceskatelevize.cz/porady/10354181410-krok-do-prazdna-jana-masaryka-aneb-dokonaly-zlocin/.

Czech criminologists on Jan Masaryk's death on http://pravyprostor.cz/smrt-jana-masaryka-ocima-kriminalisty-evidentni-vrazda/.

Czechoslovak radio broadcasts during WWII on http://www.radio.cz/en/section/one-on-one/london-calling-researcher-erica-harrison-on-fascinating-history-of-czechoslovak-exile-governments-wartime-bbc-broadcasts.

Czechoslovak Socialist Academy on http://www.cojeco.cz/index.php?detail=1&id_desc=88652&title=Socialistick%E1%20akademie&s_lang=2.

David-Fox, Michael. "The Myth of the Soviet Potemkin village". On http://www.histoire.ens.fr/IMG/file/Coeure/David-Fox%20Potemkin%20villages.pdf.

Goethe's *The Sorcerer's Apprentice* on germanstories.vcu.edu/goethe/zauber_dual.html.

Hácha, Emil on http://ww2db.com/person_bio.php?person_id=217.

Herzl, Theodor on http://www.jewishvirtuallibrary.org/jsource/biography/Herzl.html.

Heydrich's killing on http://www.bbc.com/news/world-europe-18183099.

Holec, Roman. "The Great Depression of 1929–1933 from the point of view of Czechoslovak financial experts and economists". On http://research.uni-leipzig.de/~eniugh/congress/fileadmin/eniugh2011/papers/Roman_Holec_TheGreatDepressionFromthePointofViewofCzechoslovak_2014-09-01.pdf.

Holodomor on http://www.ncas.rutgers.edu/center-study-genocide-conflict-resolution-and-human-rights/ukrainian-famine.

Kubovi's report to the Knesset on http://www.jta.org/1952/12/04/archive/israel-cabinet-holds-two-sessions-on-prague-trial-hears-envoy.

Lidice and Ležaky on http://www.lidice-memorial.cz/en/.

Lukes, Igor. *Rudolf Slansky. His Trial and Trials. Cold War International History Project Working Paper no. 50* (Washington, D.C.: Woodrow Wilson Center, 2008), on https://www.wilsoncenter.org/publication/rudolf-slansky-his-trials-and-trial.

Mandel, Ernest on http://www.ernestmandel.org.

Marshall Plan on http://marshallfoundation.org/marshall/the-marshall-plan/.

Masaryk Institute and the Archive of the Academy of Sciences of the Czech Republic on http://www.mua.cas.cz/index.php/en/.

Ogoniok on http://www.pressreader.com/russia/ogonyok.

Operation Anthropoid on http://www.holocaustresearchproject.org/nazioccupation/heydrichkilling.html.

Oren, Mordechai and Israel Shimon Orenstein on http://www.jta.org/1953/11/03/archive/oren-sentenced-in-prague-to-15-years-orenstein-gets-life-term.

Orwell, George. *Ninety-Eighty-Four* on http://orwell.ru/library/novels/1984/english/en_app.

Perović, Jeronim. "The Tito-Stalin Split: A Reassessment in Light of New Evidence". *Journal of Cold War Studies 9*, no. 2 (2007): 32-63. On http://www.zora.uzh.ch/62735/1/Perovic_Tito.pdf.

Potsdam Conference on http://avalon.law.yale.edu/20th_century/decade17.asp.

POW camps in Great Britain on http://www.theguardian.com/news/datablog/2010/nov/08/prisoner-of-war-camps-uk#data.

Šišjaková, Jana. "Rodina vo vojne", on http://www.forumhistoriae.sk/FH1_2009/texty_1_2009/sisjakova.pdf;

Šišjaková, Jana. "Židovská rodina v konfrontácii s povojnovou situáciou a antisemitizmom na Slovensku (1945-1946)". On http://forumhistoriae.sk/documents/10180/39170/sisjakova.pdf.

Soviet-Czechoslovak Treaty of Alliance on http://www.jstor.org/stable/2213972?seq=1#page_scan_tab_contents.

Stade Roland Garros on http://edition.cnn.com/2011/SPORT/tennis/06/03/tennis.roland.garros.war.camp/.

Streicher, Julius on: https://www.jewishvirtuallibrary.org/jsource/Holocaust/Streicher.html.

Sulzberger, Cyrus Leo on http://www.nytimes.com/1993/09/21/obituaries/c-l-sulzberger-columnist-dies-at-80.html?pagewanted=all.

Svoboda, Ludvík on http://www.hrad.cz/en/president-of-the-cr/former-presidents/ludvik-svoboda.

The Blitz on http://www.bbc.co.uk/history/events/the_blitz.

The case of Jan Masaryk's death on http://www.radio.cz/en/section/curraffrs/police-close-case-on-1948-death-of-jan-masaryk-murder-not-suicide

The fifth British spy on http://www.bbc.com/news/uk-england-cambridgeshire-28143770.

The YIVO Encyclopedia of Jews in Europe on http://www.yivoencyclopedia.org.

Tzvi Ben-tzur. "The Czechoslovak Arms Deals during the War of Independence". On http://www.palyam.org/English/ArmsShips/Czechoslovakia-en.

UN on http://www.un.org/en/index.html.

UN Security Council on http://www.un.org/en/sc/members/elected.asp.

Vančura, Vladislav on http://www.radio.cz/en/section/czechs/vladislav-vancura.

Zídek, Petr on http://www.lidovky.cz/pohnute-osudy-jana-masaryka-vysvobodila-az-smrt-ale-jak-to-s-ni-bylo-11m-/lide.aspx?c=A150924_214311_lide_ELE

Films

Anthropoid (2016) on http://www.imdb.com/title/tt4190530/.

Das Leben der Anderen (The Lives of Others) (2006) on http://www.imdb.com/title/tt0405094/.

L'aveu (The Confession) (1970) on http://www.imdb.com/title/tt0065439/.

No place to go (Die Unberührbare) (2000) on http://www.imdb.com/title/tt0235841/.

Obchod na korze (The Shop on Main Street) (1965) on http://www.imdb.com/title/tt0059527/.

Operation Daybreak (1975) on http://www.imdb.com/title/tt0075019/?ref_=nm_flmg_dr_10.

Smrť ministra (The Death of a Minister) (2009) on http://www.noviny.sk/c/slovensko/vcera-odpremierovali-slovensky-film-smrt-ministra.

Triumph des Willens (Triumph of the Will) (1935) on http://www.imdb.com/title/tt0025913/.

Ucho (The Ear) (1970) on http://www.imdb.com/title/tt0066498/.

Index

A

agitprop 77
Agrarian Party 59, 60, 61, 62
alcoholism 77, 79
Allied Control Commission 220, 238
Allied landing in Normandy 173, 180, 336
antisemitism 29, 30, 31, 32, 106, 107, 108, 109, 111, 115, 135, 286
applied historical materialism 101
architecture 71
Arendt, Hannah XVI, 30, 316, 317
Aron, Raymond XVIII, 314
Avriel, Ehud 264, 265, 296

B

Bacílek, Karol 298, 300, 302, 304
Balkan federation 212
Banská Bystrica 4, 119, 131, 182, 186, 187, 336
Bašťovanský, Štefan 283, 289
Bauer, Otto 95
BBC 4, 8, 131, 150, 155, 329, 335
Beck, Józef 98
Belarus 9, 75
Beneš, Edvard XIII, 3, 4, 6, 17, 21, 22, 28, 97, 112, 117, 125, 129, 131, 134, 135, 136, 145, 147, 149, 155, 174, 184, 186, 187, 208, 209, 228, 246, 254, 255, 264, 266, 280, 285, 295, 296, 332, 333, 336, 337, 338, 340
Ben-Gurion, David 262, 296, 340
Berlin, Isaiah 15, 321
Bidlo, František 87
Biebl, Konstantín 96
Big Four 221, 238

Birobidžan 106, 109, 110
Blaho, Pavol 45, 48
Bohdan Pavlů 49
bourgeois idea 58, 59
Brik, Lilia 78
Brik, Osip Maksimovič 78, 79

C

call to arms 104
Cambridge University 309
Camus, Albert XIX
Castro, Fidel XXX
catch-22 situation 255
Catholic clergy 81, 117, 315
Čatloš, Ferdinand 157
Čechoslovák 148
Černova 90
Charter 77 47
China 16, 274, 275, 276
Christmas Agreement 206
Churchill, Winston 147, 230, 234, 312, 336
Cold War XI, XII, 8, 9, 16, 205, 206, 211, 225, 236, 260, 262, 263, 264, 309, 310, 313
Cold War International History Project 16, 260
Cominform 211, 212, 214, 339, 340
Comintern 53, 54, 56, 64, 95, 96, 105, 119, 121, 135, 312
conspiracy 2, 111, 267, 269, 286, 289, 291, 341, 342, 343
conspiracy theories 111
Czechoslovak arms deals 262
Czechoslovak exile army 136, 334
Czechoslovak Refugee Committee 140

Czechoslovak-Hungarian Treaty on Friendship, Co-operation and Mutual Assistance 206
Czechoslovakism 13, 16, 17, 20, 23, 25, 27, 29, 55, 116, 166, 327
Czernín Palace 197, 250, 258, 259, 279, 282, 340

D

DAV XVII, XXI, XXIII, XXVI, 12, 46, 48, 51, 52, 53, 54, 56, 57, 60, 66, 69, 80, 84, 86, 87, 88, 89, 90, 91, 93, 106, 114, 151, 152, 192, 271, 280, 294, 327, 329, 330, 331, 332
de Beauvoir, Simone XXIX
de-Austrianization 60
defenestration 253
de-Magyarization 60
Dérer, Ivan 67, 68
Detvan 18, 46, 47, 48, 51, 68, 330
divide et impera 174
Dollfuss, Engelbert 164
Dubček, Alexander 5, 7, 304, 305, 320, 326, 344
Ďurčanský, Ferdinand 164

E

Ehrenburg, Ilia XIX, 69, 76, 137, 331
Eizenštein, Sergei XXII
Esterházy, János 163
exile *odboj* 145
expulsion (*odsun*) 208

F

Fascism XVI, XXVII, 32, 37, 80, 85, 98, 100, 105, 114, 117, 119, 121, 122, 165, 166, 249, 312
Fierlinger, Zdeněk 251
First Republic XXI, XXIII, 2, 13, 14, 23, 28, 32, 48, 93, 99, 154, 165, 207, 246, 249, 264, 280, 284, 320

Five-Year Plan 69, 71, 72, 76, 83, 85, 86
Fučík, Julius 87

G

Gabčik, Jozef 159, 336
Garrigue, Charlotte 19
Gašpar, Tido Jozef XXIV, 160, 162
German minority 19, 245
German-Slovak *Schutzvertrag* 152, 169
Gestapo 117, 159, 171, 275
Gide, André XIX, XXVI, XXVII
Glaeser, Ernst 73, 79
Golem 102, 164, 332
Golian, Ján 182
Gorkii, Maksim 76, 90
Gottwald, Klement XXI, 4, 7, 52, 57, 87, 95, 98, 129, 131, 135, 149, 186, 205, 209, 213, 214, 215, 223, 225, 233, 237, 251, 252, 253, 254, 259, 270, 272, 274, 276, 277, 279, 280, 282, 285, 286, 293, 300, 312, 318, 319, 320, 331, 336, 337, 338, 339, 340, 341, 343
GPU 75
Great Depression 84
Great Powers 217, 230, 234, 235, 245
Greek civil war 212
Gruzdev, Ilia 76
Gyöngyössi, János 243, 250

H

Hajdu, Vavro 1, 2
Havel, Václav 3, 9
Hegelian dialectic 50
Heidegger, Martin 47
Heller, Joseph 255
Hemingway, Ernest 38
Henlein, Konrad 27, 97, 123, 126, 127, 128, 163, 249
Herzl, Theodor 33

Heydrich, Reinhard 100, 159, 160, 161, 336
historic rights of the lands of the Bohemian Crown 18
Hlas (*The Voice*) 24
Hlinka, Andrej XXV, 13, 26, 27, 52, 60, 61, 68, 106, 117, 118, 122, 123, 124, 128, 156, 162, 163, 164, 165, 166, 167, 247, 294, 333
Hodža, Michal Miloslav 17, 60, 61, 62, 63, 64, 68, 134, 135, 333
Hodža, Milan 17, 21, 60, 61, 62, 63, 64, 68, 134, 135, 333
Hoffmeister, Adolf 276, 277
Holdoš, Ladislav 149, 291, 343
Hollý, Ján 45
Horáková, Milada 211, 298, 342
Horthy, Míklos 98, 117, 119, 157, 250
HSĽS 27, 28, 32, 52, 61, 66, 67, 79, 80, 81, 93, 99, 100, 101, 102, 105, 106, 118, 122, 123, 124, 126, 153, 162, 163, 164, 165, 166, 332, 333
Hungarian Iron Cross 243
Hungarian minority 19, 242, 246, 249
Hurban, Jozef Miloslav 17, 43, 94
Hus, Jan 54
Husák, Gustáv 10, 29, 114, 129, 131, 149, 195, 215, 273, 279, 280, 281, 283, 284, 286, 287, 291, 295, 304, 306, 317, 320, 323, 333, 339, 342, 343
Husserl, Edmund 47

I

IMRO 65
interbrigadisty 134, 136, 145

J

Janošík 89, 90
Jewish Agency 263, 265

K

Karmasin, Franz 163, 164
Keppler, Wilhelm 164
Kershaw, Ian 14, 123
Kisch, Egon Erwin 73
Klíma, Ivan XXVIII, XXX
Klofáč, Václav 21
Knesset 264, 266
Koestler, Arthur XVIII, XIX
Köhler, Bruno 135, 215
Kolder and Barnabite commissions 303, 304
Komsomoltsi 77
Kopecký, Václav XXI, 283, 289
Košice Agreement 208, 209, 215, 216, 217, 218, 223, 336, 337
Kosincev, Grigorii M. 76
Košuty 84, 85, 86, 87, 88, 91, 93, 94, 154, 332
Kovály, Heda Margolius 1, 299
Kramář, Karel 21, 60, 100, 112
KSČ XX, XXV, 1, 3, 4, 5, 6, 7, 12, 13, 28, 29, 38, 51, 52, 53, 55, 58, 61, 66, 67, 68, 83, 84, 85, 86, 94, 95, 97, 98, 99, 103, 104, 105, 114, 118, 119, 121, 126, 131, 133, 134, 135, 146, 149, 150, 185, 205, 207, 208, 209, 210, 228, 250, 251, 253, 261, 272, 279, 281, 284, 285, 298, 304, 305, 317, 318, 320, 327, 328, 330, 331, 332, 340, 341, 343, 344
Kubiš, Jan 159, 336
Kultúrný život (*Cultural Life*) 304
Kun, Béla 92

L

language law of 1868 40
League of Nations 230
Leninism XI, XIX, 1, 5, 6, 7, 9, 15, 29, 37, 38, 51, 52, 53, 59, 60, 61, 69, 75, 84, 116, 135, 212, 233, 271, 273, 284, 285, 293, 309, 310, 311, 312, 315, 316, 317, 320, 323, 325, 326, 327

letter of the twelve 95, 96
Lex Apponyi of 1907 44
Ležaky 160, 336
Liberalism 13, 312
Lidice 160, 336
Lidové Noviny 97
Liptovský Svätý Mikuláš 94
Löbl, Evžen (Eugen) 2, 299
London, Artur 1, 2

M

Machiavelli XX, 35, 113
Magyarization 31, 40, 42, 44
Maiakovskii, Vladimír XXII
Maiakovskii, Vladimír Vladimírovič XXII, 78
Maierchold, Viacheslav XXII
Major, Štefan 88, 86, 87, 89, 90, 91, 92, 93, 94, 332
manifesto of the seven 95
Maoism XXX
Marr, Wilhelm 31
Marshall Plan 235, 236, 237, 238, 239, 241, 254, 263, 339
Marshall, George C. 174, 186, 187, 212, 235, 236, 237, 238, 239, 241, 254, 263, 339
Martin 8, 40, 43, 116, 329
Martin circle 116
Martin Declaration 21
Marx, Karl XVI, XVIII, XX, 7, 15, 38, 59, 122, 149, 271, 326
Marxism XI, XVIII, XXXI, 1, 5, 6, 7, 9, 15, 29, 37, 38, 51, 52, 53, 59, 60, 61, 64, 69, 75, 84, 116, 122, 135, 212, 214, 233, 271, 273, 284, 285, 293, 309, 310, 311, 312, 315, 316, 317, 320, 323, 325, 326, 327
Masaryk, Jan XVI, 3, 4, 17, 18, 19, 20, 21, 22, 23, 24, 27, 38, 44, 46, 54, 55, 60, 85, 91, 103, 111, 112, 113, 114, 115, 116, 117, 118, 121, 122, 129, 155, 156, 159, 166, 178, 206, 207, 209, 221, 232, 237, 243, 246, 250,

251, 252, 253, 254, 255, 256, 257, 258, 259, 264, 265, 266, 296, 311, 332, 339, 340
Masaryk, Tomáš G. 3, 111
McCarthy, Joseph M. 323
Meir, Golda 269
Miłosz, Czesław 313
Mladé Slovensko 45, 48
Molotov-Ribbentrop Pact 5, 146
Montand, Yves 1
Moravec, Emanuel 100, 117, 161
Moscow trials XXVIII, 35
Munich Agreement 3, 4, 27, 122, 123, 126, 127, 147, 157, 242, 285
Murgaš, Karol 163

N

national chauvinism 42, 58
National Front 13, 186, 208, 209, 237, 253, 273, 284, 327, 337
National-Socialism 37
natural law 17, 18
Nejedlý, Zdenek 55, 114, 228
NEP 74
Neumann, Stanislav Kostka 95
New York Times 277, 319
Nezval, Vítezslav XVIII, XXII, 96
Nietzsche, Friedrich XVIII, 43, 59
Nitra 86, 162
NKVD 1, 32, 207, 251, 252, 254, 286, 288, 290, 323
Novomeský, Laco XV, XVIII, XXI, 10, 39, 51, 86, 96, 149, 190, 191, 192, 215, 271, 279, 280, 281, 283, 284, 287, 295, 304, 305, 317, 320, 323, 342, 343, 344
Novotný, Antonín 7, 286, 298, 304, 343
NSDAP 37, 106, 121, 136

O

Ogoniok 78
Okáli, Daniel 48, 51

Operation Anthropoid 159
Orwell, George XVIII, 38, 56
Osuský, Štefan 134, 135, 136

P

Palestine 30, 33, 106, 108, 109, 260, 261, 262, 263, 338
Paris Peace Conference 231, 232, 244, 249, 320
partition of Germany 230
Pasternak, Boris XXII
Peroutka, Ferdinand 20, 85, 254, 322
Piešťany 163, 164, 165
Pittsburgh Agreement 18, 21, 22
plan of 14 points 17
Plato 23
pogrom 102, 163, 261
Prague centralism 28
Preiss, Jaroslav 100
Prúdy (*Currents*) 24

R

Rádl, Emanuel 47
Rajk, László XI, 35, 270, 273, 296, 341
Rákosi, Mátyás 273, 274
Rašín, Alois 21
Realism 13, 24
Realpolitik XII, 54, 212
Red Army 73, 74, 99, 100, 131, 157, 160, 172, 173, 174, 175, 176, 177, 179, 180, 182, 186, 213, 222, 236, 242, 316, 337
Revúca, Veľká 43
Ripka, Hubert 134
Rolland, Romain 90
Roosevelt, Franklin D. 3, 156, 230, 234, 250, 335, 336
Rousseau, Jean-Jacques 17, 23
Rovný s rovným 125
Rozmluvy 225

S

Šalda, František X. XXVI
San Francisco 216, 221, 337
Sartre, Jean-Paul XVIII, XXIX, 313, 314
Sasinek, František 45
Seifert, Jaroslav XVIII, 95
Seton Watson, Robert 91, 246
Seyss-Inquart, Arthur 164
Sidor, Karol 80, 83, 101, 102, 103, 106, 109, 110, 127, 128, 164
Signoret, Simone 1
Sino-Soviet Treaty of Friendship and Alliance 274
Siracký, Andrej 48, 51
Široký, Viliam 2, 135, 149, 198, 267, 273, 276, 278, 279, 280, 281, 286, 298, 312, 318, 341, 342, 343
Slánský, Rudolf XII, XXI, 2, 6, 7, 10, 33, 129, 205, 211, 259, 260, 266, 267, 268, 269, 270, 278, 281, 286, 287, 289, 291, 293, 294, 295, 296, 298, 299, 301, 305, 312, 318, 325, 336, 343
Slavík, Juraj 87, 89
Slovák 80, 81, 82, 83, 164
Slovak autonomism 28
Slovak bourgeois nationalism XXIII, 10, 149, 207, 283, 342, 344
Slovak literature 43, 47, 151
Slovak National Council 6, 21, 184, 186, 200, 207, 210, 215, 218, 329, 336
Slovak National Uprising 4, 131, 181, 186, 187, 283, 336
Slovak Robin Hood 84, 89
Slovak Social Democratic Party 42
Socialist Academy 228, 231
Soukup, František 21
Soviet Communist Party 6, 52, 57, 96, 121, 271
Spanish Civil War XI, 38, 310, 312
Spíš 43
Spring of Prague 29

Šrobár, Vavro 21, 22, 24, 48, 60, 68, 99, 115, 329
Stade Roland Garros 136, 334
Stalingrad 72, 151, 159, 170, 171, 174
Stamboliiskii, Aleksandar 65
status quo ante Munich 155
Štefánek, Anton 64, 115
Štefánik, Milan Rastislav 17, 21
Stránský, Jaroslav 97
Štúr, Ludovít 17, 101, 102, 181, 200
Sudetenland 28, 333
Sulzberger, Cyrus Leo 277
Švehla, Antonín 21, 64
Švejk 74
Šverma, Jan XXI, 135, 136
Svoboda, Ludvík 172, 242
system of collective security 228
Szegedy-Maszák, Aladár 244, 245, 246, 247, 248, 249

T

Tatlin, Vladimír XXII
Teige, Karel XVIII, XXII, XXVI, 96
Tel Aviv 266, 267, 268
the Blitz 140
Tigrid, Pavel 225, 322
Tiso, Jozef 3, 27, 110, 147, 151, 152, 153, 154, 155, 158, 160, 161, 162, 163, 164, 166, 167, 168, 169, 171, 173, 175, 177, 178, 180, 181, 182, 183, 185, 186, 283, 284, 333, 334, 336
Tito, Josip Broz 195, 203, 211, 212, 213, 214, 269, 270, 287
Titoism 2, 213, 270, 286, 288, 341, 343
Trianon 20, 22, 98
Tuka, Vojtěch 92, 93, 158, 161, 162, 163, 165, 166, 168, 171, 182, 183, 294

U

Ukrainian famine 79
UN Security Council 206, 231, 236, 252, 275, 341
unification of legislation 99
UNO XX
Urban, Milo XXIV, 160, 161, 162
USA XX, 3, 7, 14, 16, 18, 20, 22, 29, 37, 134, 147, 158, 219, 220, 222, 223, 224, 225, 226, 227, 231, 232, 235, 236, 237, 238, 253, 263, 264, 270, 277, 296, 322, 328, 330, 337

V

Václav Klaus 8
Vančura, Vladislav 159, 161
Varga, Eugen 64
Velvet Divorce 8
Velvet Revolution 8
Versailles 22, 219
victorious February 6, 99, 251, 320
Vienna Arbitration 27
Viest, Rudolf 4, 182
Vyšinskii, Andrei Ia. 218, 271, 274, 275, 277, 278, 319

W

Weiskopf, Franz Carl 73
Weizmann, Chaim 269
Western Capitalist Imperialism XII, 2, 33
Western intellectuals XVI, 311
World Jewish Congress 267

Z

Zenkl, Peter 209
Žilina Agreement 27, 28, 123, 165
Zionism 2, 30, 32, 33, 106, 108, 109, 264, 286, 296, 343
Zorin, Valerian A. 218, 219, 221

***ibidem**.eu*